EAST ASIAN SOCIAL SCIENCE MONOGRAPHS

BRITISH INDUSTRIAL INVESTMENT IN MALAYSIA 1963–1971

BRITISH INDUSTRIAL INVESTMENT IN MALAYSIA 1963–1971

JUNID SAHAM

KUALA LUMPUR
OXFORD UNIVERSITY PRESS
OXFORD NEW YORK MELBOURNE
1980

Oxford University Press
OXFORD LONDON GLASGOW
NEW YORK TORONTO MELBOURNE WELLINGTON
KUALA LUMPUR SINGAPORE HONG KONG TOKYO
DELHI BOMBAY CALCUTTA MADRAS KARACHI
NAIROBI DAR ES SALAAM CAPE TOWN

ISBN 0 19 580418 X (*boards*)
ISBN 0 19 580489 9 (*limp*)

Printed in Singapore by Kyodo-Shing Loong Printing Industries Pte. Ltd.
Published by Oxford University Press, 3, Jalan 13/3,
Petaling Jaya, Selangor, Malaysia

To Oi Lin, Adam, and Adilah

Preface

I feel that I should perhaps try to justify this book which deals with a number of important issues relating to British capital in Malaysian manufacturing in the 1960s. I can only do so by saying that this book is a modest attempt at an empirical inquiry into the affairs of British manufacturing companies in the early stages of Malaysia's industrial development. I intend neither to blame nor praise British manufacturing enterprises in the country. Rather I have tried to gather as much information about them, and analyse the facts as objectively as possible.

No special reason is given for the period chosen 1963–1971, except that the period coincided with the years following the formation of Malaysia and a period marking the beginning of intensified development of the country's manufacturing sector. Much of the data may appear static, but I hope other more enterprising writers may perhaps wish to continue the path of this preliminary study, and embark on a more sophisticated and up-to-date analysis of British enterprises in the country.

When this study was first conceived during my days as a graduate student in the United Kingdom during 1972 to 1974, there was a real dearth of data pertaining to British companies and industrial capital in Malaysia. It was necessary to supplement the inadequate published and official data by field studies, mainly in London, namely by talking to various company representatives, and officials of the Malaysia–Singapore Commercial Association Incorporated; the Department of Trade and Industry; the Bank of England; Confederation of British Industry; the Overseas Development Administration; the Rubber Growers' Association; the Malayan Chamber of Mines and the Federation of Commonwealth Chambers of Commerce. The company representatives interviewed provided much of the information used in this study. Their requests for anonymity prevent me from listing their names and those of their companies.

The general issues dealt with in this study concern the nature and consequences of British companies in Malaysian manufacturing. By examining these issues, this present study covers a number of problems of current concern and interest to the general reader and students of foreign investment in developing countries. So far as is known, this is the first empirical study inquiring into the affairs of British manufacturing enterprises since the formation of Malaysia.

I have written with the general reader in mind, and hope that the book will be useful to a number of those who are keen to know the role of private foreign investment in Malaysian industries. I realize that different parts of the subject matter of the study vary in difficulty. Some of the things I want to say about British investment, although important, come so dangerously near to being self-evident as to sound banal, while on the other hand, the treatment of particular aspects ideally calls for more sophisticated analysis. I have tried to avoid the esoteric approach. In attempting to analyse information as well as present complex ideas and theories in a reasonably succinct and straightforward way I have certainly over-simplified some; but I hope that the specialist accountant, economist, investment analyst, or whoever he may be, will be tolerant of my approach. If readers are stimulated to be interested in carrying out further studies into foreign investments continuing the trend started in Chapter 9 of this book, I will have achieved my main objective.

A number of people have been very helpful in the course of my research into the information contained in this book. In particular, Mr. O. S. Hiner and Dr. R. M. Lawson of the University of Hull, England, guided me in the original research into this study. Mr. B. K. Parkinson, an Economist of the Asian Development Bank in Manila, helped me a great deal with his comments at the early stages of the research. Together they saved me from falling into a number of pits and their help is gratefully acknowledged.

The field work for this study in the United Kingdom in the years 1972–4, would not have been possible without the help of the following people who introduced me personally to individual company representatives: Mr. W. C. S. Corry of the Malaysia–Singapore Commercial Association Inc., Mr. H. E. Nichols of the Federation of Commonwealth Chambers of Commerce, Mr. G. W. Rothery and Mr. R. A. Arthur of the Commonwealth Development Finance Co. Ltd., Mr. J. Wilson of the Chartered Bank, London, Mr. Rahim Aki of the Malaysian Trade Commission, London, Mr. C. McErlane of the Department of Trade and Industry, Mr. G. O. Randle of the Bank of England, Mr. W. G. G. Kellett of the Rubber Growers' Association, Mr. A. D. Dawson of the Malayan Chamber of Mines, Sir Michael Walker of the Overseas Development Administration, Mr. R. E. Marsh of the Confederation of British Industry, and

Mr. D. B. Johns of the Crown Agents. To all these people I express my thanks and appreciation. I am also very grateful to the various company representatives who gave me their valuable time to discuss matters pertaining to the subject of this study.

I am thankful to Miss Maria Law for diligently typing the original manuscript from my illegible handwriting. I wrote this book in my spare time amidst pressures of work, and my greatest debt is to my own family, especially Oi Lin whose support and encouragement have kept me going. The shortcomings as well as errors of commission and omission of this book must remain my own.

Kuala Lumpur
December 1978

JUNID SAHAM

Contents

Tables

Figures

Figures

Introduction

THIS book studies the role of British industrial firms in the Malaysian economy from 1963, when Malaysia was formed, to the first quarter of 1972. During these years the government began in earnest to attract foreign investors into the manufacturing sector, thereby bringing about intensive involvement of British and other foreign industrial capital as well as significant changes in the Malaysian economy.

The general issues relating to British capital in Malaysian manufacturing are dealt with in the various chapters of the book. How did British companies become involved in manufacturing? What are their views on the prospects of manufacturing? How much capital have they invested in Malaysian industries? How did they respond to the government incentives, requests, and the general industrialization programme? What impact have they had on the industrial structure and efficiency? How profitable are they? What role do the British-based multinational enterprises play in the economy? And, what are the effects of British industrial companies on the economic goals and policy of Malaysia? By examining these issues, this present inquiry covers a number of problems of current concern in analysing various aspects of international investments.[1]

Intrinsically important in the study is the role of the agency houses in promoting British industrial investment, the behaviour of British companies in the economy, and the attitude of executives towards investment in the economy. The performance of the manufacturing companies is assessed by examining their profitability.

The role of the multinational enterprises is studied because they are important as instruments of international movement of capital.[2] Most of the studies made hitherto on multinational enterprises are about U.S.-based enterprises; the present study on British-based multinational enterprises provides an analysis of the nature and consequences of multinational enterprises in a developing country like Malaysia.

Although a number of studies are available which evaluate the impact of British overseas investments in the U.K.[3] there has never been any evaluation of the effect of British investments on the Malaysian economy, in particular in the manufacturing sector. By examining the role of British manufacturing companies in Malaysia, this inquiry provides a case study of private foreign industrial investment in a country that is trying to industrialize under a free-enterprise system.

The field work for the study was undertaken in Britain because the information was obtained primarily from the head offices of the investing companies[4] where the decisions to invest in Malaysian industry were first conceived. Strategic planning and control, and in some cases operational decisions too, concerning the overseas subsidiaries were made at the head offices in Britain.

CONCEPTS OF INDUSTRIAL INVESTMENT

In much of the development literature, the term 'industrialization' denotes at least three elements associated with the development processes, i.e., the growth of manufacturing which often, but not invariably, accompanies certain stages of material advance; the modernizing of attitudes, institutions, and economic processes; and the subsidization of manufacturing by governments.[5] These elements, in the Malaysian context, are often present simultaneously, but they are quite distinct. The most frequent use of the term 'industrialization' is interpreted here as manufacturing, while 'industry' and 'manufacturing' are used interchangeably.

The term 'manufacturing', unless otherwise stated, here bears the same meaning as that defined by the United Nations International Standard Industrial Classification of All Economic Activities (ISIC), 1958, i.e., the mechanical or chemical transformation of inorganic or organic substances into new products, the assembly of component parts of manufactured products—except in cases where the activity is appropriately described as construction and the repair of parts or the whole of manufactured products.[6]

As used in the text, British 'direct investment in manufacturing' means manufacturing investments in which the controlling and managing interests are held by British nationals. The term 'control-managing interests' refers to the power to decide how the investing companies should allocate their resources, exercise control over the strategic plans of the companies, and select the top executives. The words 'companies', 'firms', 'enterprises', 'concerns', and 'businesses' are used interchangeably for the sake of variety.

A company is controlled by British interests when at least 12.5 per cent of the company's equity is in British hands. Some of the companies consulted for this study are 100 per cent British-owned. Many are managed by locally recruited executives, who no doubt exercise some measure of managerial planning and control, but the strategic planning and control remains with the head offices in Britain.[7]

GATHERING DATA

In the initial stage of the survey some time was spent discussing British investment in Malaysia with representatives of the Economics and Statistics Division of the Department of Trade and Industry (DTI), and the Bank of England. The DTI representatives provided invaluable quantitative estimates of British direct investments in the country. The representative of the Bank of England provided qualitative information on British capital overseas. At both the DTI and the Bank of England, permission was given to read their collections of books and pamphlets on inflows and outflows of British capital. The aggregate data thus obtained form a substantial basis of this study.

Additional aggregate data were obtained from Malaysian and British government publications, annual reports of companies, and information gathered from the Stock Exchanges of Malaysia and Singapore. It was clear that specific data on company operations and qualitative information on British subsidiary companies were also essential and for this the companies themselves were considered to be the best sources of information.

Initial contacts with companies were made through the Secretary to the Malaysia–Singapore Commercial Association Inc. (MSCA); the Secretary to the Federation of Commonwealth Chambers of Commerce (FCCC); the Assistant Director, Overseas, of the Confederation of British Industry (CBI); a representative of the Overseas Development Administration (ODA); a representative of the Commonwealth Development Finance Corporation (CDFC); and the Trade Commissioner for Malaysia in the United Kingdom. I also approached the (1972) High Commissioner for Malaysia in the United Kingdom, who in private life was on the board of directors of several British companies, and whose law firm in Kuala Lumpur served as the legal adviser to many other foreign companies.

The MSCA and the FCCC provided the full list of their members with direct investment in Malaysia. The Secretary to the British Malaysian Industry and Trade Association (BMITA) in Kuala Lumpur also provided a list of members, many of whom are British manufacturing companies in Malaysia. Altogether, at the beginning of the field work in March 1972, there were approximately 210 British companies with subsidiaries in Malaysia, but not all had production facilities. The companies selected for interviews were those engaged in manufacturing as defined earlier.

Altogether 103 companies (selected from the MSCA, the FCCC and the BMITA lists) represented by fifty-seven people—hereafter referred to as 'companies', 'firms', 'firm representatives', 'interviewees', 'executives', or 'informants'—were interviewed.

PROBLEMS AND DIFFICULTIES IN DATA COLLECTION

Problems arose in data collection because many firms interviewed did not publish separate reports and accounts of their businesses in Malaysia for the period covered by the present study, but provided consolidated reports and accounts for their enterprises as a whole, which did not actually give sufficient specific data about the Malaysian subsidiaries. Most lacking were detailed statistical data (e.g. cost of input, time series on output, sales, share of the market, number of employees by job categories, inter-industry purchases, structure of funds employed, and so on), which many executives claimed could not be produced easily in detail. In such cases, reliance had to be placed on whatever information the interviewees gave.

Some interviewees claimed to have no records of their initial involvement in Malaysian manufacturing, since in addition they had business interests in agriculture, mining, and trade, in which the manufacturing aspects of their enterprises were so much intertwined. Some interviewees claimed to have no memory of the data sought. Many executives were not prepared to divulge much of the statistical information required, because they claimed that the competitive nature of their Malaysian operations prevented them from releasing information considered confidential. Very little information could be obtained on take-overs, mergers, and initial sources of capital of the investing concerns.

Many of those companies which gave some information on output, sales, profitability, breakdown of costs of inputs, employment, sources of capital, and export performance were reluctant to give exact figures. Such information was generally only approximations. However, when cross-checked with other firms and other informants (e.g. Malaysian businessmen interviewed), it appeared to be reasonably accurate.

SCOPE OF STUDY

The field work for this study was completed in November 1973. The statistical limitations have affected the scope of the study, a great deal of which is devoted to examining the qualitative information derived from the executives interviewed.

The role of the agency houses in promoting British industrial investment, although quite complex, is presented in a manner which simplifies the relationship of the agents and the manufacturing companies. Since most agency houses have interests in virtually every branch of the Malaysian economy, the description of their activities in this study is limited only to their associations with manufacturing companies.

The motivation to invest, in many of the companies interviewed, was primarily linked to their market. Brief mention is made of the nature of the market confronting British companies based on the executives' perception of their market and whatever company market data they have.

The structure and organizational characteristics of the investing companies are described on the basis of their forms during the period covered by the study. These characteristics are rendered imperfect not only by limited statistical information, but also by changing circumstances confronting the companies.

There is a chapter on profitability of British industrial investment, which is an attempt to measure the performance of the companies interviewed. Finally, the chapter on the evaluation of the impact of industrial firms on the economy takes a broader approach in assessing the benefits and costs generated from the investments.

The picture presented here is largely the retrospective vision derived during the period of research. The picture of British industrial investment presented here marks an important watershed in the history of British capital in the *laissez-faire* days of foreign investment in the country and the more regulated conditions of the post-1970s.

1. See for example R. Vernon, *The Economic and Political Consequences of Multinational Enterprise: An Anthology*, Harvard, Graduate School of Business Administration, 1972; J. H. Dunning, ed., *International Investment, Selected Readings*, Penguin, 1972; and Department of Economics, University of Reading, 'Research on International Investment and Business Studies' (mimeo.), 1974.

2. See J. H. Dunning, ed., *The Multinational Enterprise*, George Allen and Unwin, 1971, Chapter 1. See also U.N. Department of Economic and Social Affairs, *Multinational Corporations in World Development* (ST/ECA/190), New York, U.N., 1973; and

D. Wallace Jr. and H. Ruoff-Koch, eds., *International Control of Investment,* Praeger, 1974.

3. See for example W. B. Reddaway, S. J. Potter, and C. T. Taylor, *Effects of U.K. Direct Investment Overseas*, Cambridge University Press, 1967 (Interim Report) and 1968 (Final Report); and J. H. Dunning, *Studies in International Investment*, George Allen and Unwin, 1970, and the references therein.

4. Originally I approached the Secretary of the British Malaysian Industry and Trade Association in Kuala Lumpur asking him whether it was possible to conduct the study in Malaysia. He recommended that the kind of study I had in mind was best conducted in Britain where vital information about British overseas companies is best obtained.

5. See discussions on the concepts of industrialization in the context of development in H. G. Johnson, *Economic Policies Towards Less Developed Countries*, George Allen and Unwin, 1967, pp. 45–8; P. T. Bauer, *Dissent on Development, Studies and Debate in Development Economics*, Weidenfeld and Nicolson, 1971, *passim*; and P. T. Bauer and B. S. Yamey, 'Industrialization and Development: The Nigerian Experience', *The Economic History Review*, n.s. Vol. 25 (4), November 1972, p. 684.

6. U.N., *Statistical Papers, Series M, No. 4*, Rev. I, New York, U.N., 1958

7. Over the years there has been a loosening of control of the subsidiaries from the head offices.

1 Background: The Malaysian Economy

THE CHANGING ECONOMY

THE extension of British colonization and its rule of law in late nineteenth-century Malaya effected a stable form of government under which the economy developed into one that specialized in the production of raw materials, notably rubber, tin, and spices for the world market.[1] European capital, particularly British, entered at a substantial rate through private enterprises in the early twentieth century.[2] At first British economic interest was concentrated in commerce, then later in agriculture and mining.[3] In general, private foreign investment in manufacturing was insignificant until the late 1950s when a small number of British companies became engaged in local manufacturing.

THE ECONOMY IN THE 1950s

Economic activity in the 1950s was seen to function at three levels: the peasant economy of rice cultivation, fishing, and mixed farming; the free trade economy that revolved around the entrepôt trade of Penang and Singapore; and the economy associated with the production of rubber and tin.

The free trade economy of the ports was very prosperous. According to Silcock[4] the 'system of management' in the free trade economy was largely responsible in assisting the development of foreign interest in the rubber and tin industries. The system of management he referred to concerned the agency houses which still continue to be the promoters of British economic interests in Malaysia today.

The small number of British companies known to be engaged in manufacturing was associated with processing rubber, smelting tin, manufacturing cement, food, beverage, tobacco, and those in light engineering works subsidiary to the plantations, mines, and ports.[5] There was no means of knowing the magnitude of capital involved, as companies were secretive and no research had been made into the question of estimating capital.

In 1955, the International Bank for Reconstruction and Development Mission Report recommended that industrialization in the country should follow 'the pattern of individually small advances over a wide range of industries catering chiefly to the domestic and nearby market'.[6] The recommendations of the IBRD were incorporated in a White Paper (No. 30), tabled in parliament in 1957. Following these recommendations, the government set up an industrial development division within the Ministry of Commerce and Industry, charged with the responsibility of administering industrial development in Malaysia. The IBRD policy recommendations also formed the basis of the *Pioneer Industries (Relief From Income Tax) Ordinance, 1958,* which was the basic instrument of industrial promotion in the late 1950s.

THE ECONOMY IN THE 1960s

In 1963, another IBRD Mission[7] came up with recommendations on administrative arrangements for co-ordinating and integrating development planning, including industrial development in Malaysia. The Rueff Report (1963) subsequently became the foundation of the present industrialization programme. The *Pioneer Industries Ordinance, 1958* was modified into the *Pioneer Industries (Variation) Act, 1965*, then later into the *Investment Incentives Act, 1968* which became the document guiding industrial development in the 1960s. The Act and its main amendments are contained in the *Investment Incentives (Amendment) Act, 1971* which is (at the time of writing) currently in operation.

The Rueff Report remarked that although the economic progress of Malaysia in the preceding decade had been 'impressive', the potential for enhancing economic growth lay in diversifying the economy, especially through a rapid expansion in manufacturing. The government should continue to maintain the free market mechanism as the basic guide to decision-making by entrepreneurs. Administrative devices such as quotas and controls should not be adopted to promote or regulate industrial development. A Tariff Board should be set up to advise the government on levels of tariffs, which should be periodically reviewed to ensure judicious use of tariffs to protect the domestic market. The government should create free trade zones and provide in these zones, storage facilities where investors could, for a small fee, store goods destined for re-export, untaxed. In sum, the Rueff Report policy recommendations represented what the authors considered as concrete steps which should be taken in the field of economic policy to effect such economic co-ordination in the various states of Malaysia to produce the maximum advantage to the country.[8]

The government followed the Rueff Report recommendations faithfully. Throughout the 1960s and early 1970s the economy developed under free enterprise in which the official policy encouraged private foreign investment[9] and the role of government was, as suggested by the Report, limited to 'the preservation, or even the further improvement, of a favourable investment climate'.[10]

The economy achieved a moderate rate of growth in the 1960s, when the annual rate of growth of the gross national product (GNP) was 6 per cent. Between 1965 and 1970, the annual growth rates in gross investment, private investment, and public investment were 6.4 per cent, 9.6 per cent, and 1.9 per cent[11] respectively, while the population grew at a rate just below 3 per cent per annum.

Per capita GNP, at 1965 prices, grew at a rate of 2.8 per cent per annum. Per capita real income grew at 2.2 per cent, while per capita consumption grew at 1.5 per cent per annum (Table 1.1).

TABLE 1.1

SELECTED INDICATORS OF ECONOMIC PERFORMANCE IN MALAYSIA

Indicator	*Period and Annual Rate of Growth*	*(% p.a.)*	*Amount 1970 ($ million)*	*Amount 1972 ($ million)*
Gross national product (at current prices)	1960–1970*	5.7	9,775	10,634
	1965–1970	6.0^{+}		
	1967–1972	6.0	11,629	12,906
Real gross national income ‡	1965–1970	5.3	11,190	. . .
Per capita GNP	1965–1970	2.8	1,054	1,123
Per capita real income	1965–1970	2.2	1,022	. . .
Per capita consumption	1965–1970	1.5	805	. . .
Total consumption expenditure	1965–1970	6.2	9,496	10,771
Total investment expenditure	1965–1970	6.4	1,928	2,227
Gross national savings	1965–1970	6.9	2,145	2,033
Exports (f.o.b.)	1960–1970*	3.8	4,691	4,568
	1965–1970	6.3	5,666	5,470
	1967–1972	5.3		
Imports (c.i.f.)	1960–1970*	5.1	4,341	5,080
	1965–1970	4.9	4,340$^{\phi}$	5,920
	1967–1972	9.2		

(*Continued*)

TABLE 1.1 (*Continued*)

Gross Domestic Product by Industrial Origin (at factor cost and in current prices)

Indicator	*Period and Annual Rate of Growth*	*(% p.a.)*	*Amount 1970 ($ million)*	*1972 ($ million)*
Agriculture (z)	1960–1970*	1.5	2,150	
	1965–1970	5.9	2,439	2,375
	1967–1972	3.0		
Mining and quarrying	1960–1970*	6.2	548	...
	1965–1970	1.1	580	615
	1967–1972	4.8		
Manufacturing	1960–1970*	11.4	1,254	...
	1965–1970	9.9	1,354	1,471
	1967–1972	11.9		
Construction	1960–1970*	6.9	290	...
	1965–1970	4.1	329	470
	1967–1972	6.5		
Electricity, water, and sanitary services	1960–1970*	12.1	233	...
	1965–1970	8.1	254	295
	1967–1972	7.7		
Other services (g)	1960–1970*	6.1	3,624	...
	1965–1970	5.7	4,283	4,875
	1967–1972	6.0		
Consumer price index (1967 = 100)	1960–1970	0.9	100.6	104.8
	1967–1972	0.9		
Money supply (w)	1960–1970	6.8	£2,071 m	£2,243 m⊕
	1967–1972	8.6		
Population	1960–1970	2.9	10.8 m	11.4 m
	1967–1972	2.9		

Source: Derived from data in the *Second Malaysia Plan, 1971–75*; *The Treasury Economic Report 1972–1973*; and *Bank Negara Quarterly Economic Bulletin, March 1973.*

Notes: * Data refer to West Malaysia only.

\+ At 1965 prices.

p Provisional.

/ Real purchasing power of national product after adjustment for price changes.

ϕ Revised figure taking into consideration purchases of ships by the Malaysian International Shipping Corporation (MISC).

⊕ As at July 1972.

(z) Excluding forestry and fishing.

(g) Including transport, communication, trade, banking, insurance, public administration, and dwellings.

(w) Currency in circulation (outside banking system and the Treasury) plus demand deposits of private sector including local governments and statutory authorities.

... Not available separately.

Savings constituted 17.8 per cent of GNP, while investment made up 15.8 per cent of GNP for the years 1966–70.[12] The surplus of savings over investment in the private sector enabled the government to maintain a high level of domestic borrowing,[13] but it did not prevent a financing problem from arising in the public sector so that reliance had to be placed on foreign sources of financing for development.[14] Merchandise exports grew at the rate of 6.3 per cent per annum and imports grew at 4.9 per cent per annum. In brief, the economy achieved moderate growth in the late 1960s.

THE EXPANDING INDUSTRIAL SECTOR

Two important points concerning the whole economy and the manufacturing sector are contained in Table 1.1. The first point is that the moderate growth of the economy has been achieved without severe inflation, as suggested by the low growth of consumer price index.[15] Money supply, which grew at 6.8 per cent in the period 1960–70 has been closely in line with the growth in GNP of about 6 per cent per annum. The second point is that the economic sector with the fastest growth in the 1960s was the manufacturing sector. Also the manufacturing sector, compared to all other underdeveloped countries,[16] developed with very little protection, and in some cases, none.[17]

By 1972 manufacturing was a growth leader in the Malaysian economy[18] and in 1973 the expansion of output, employment, and exports of the manufacturing sector exceeded the targets envisaged in the Second Malaysia Plan.[19]

The prominent role expected of the manufacturing sector is illustrated by Table 1.2.

It is envisaged that by 1985 the output of manufacturing activities will exceed that of agriculture. At the same time, employment in the industrial sector will be about one-half the number employed in agriculture.

It is clear that from the 1970s onwards, the structure of the Malaysian economy will be significantly different from what Professor Silcock and the World Bank observed in the mid-1950s. As noted earlier, prior to the 1960s most private foreign firms were engaged in the production of rubber, or other commercial crops, and in tin mining. Private foreign investment has since then continued to expand in the economy, particularly in the industrial sector, under the government policy of pursuing development according to the principle of free enterprise.[20] In the early 1960s private foreign investments were found mainly in light manufac-

TABLE 1.2
MALAYSIA, EMPLOYMENT AND OUTPUT IN MANUFACTURING, 1960–1990

Year	*Employment*		*Gross Domestic Product*	
	Number ('000)	*Percentage of Manufacturing Employment in Total*	*Amount (in Constant 1970 Prices) $ million*	*Percentage of Manufacturing Output to Total Output*
1960	243	7.3	453*	9.0
1965=	217=	8.4	682*	10.4
1970	318	9.6	1,354	13.6
1975	479	12.2	2,609	18.0
1980	716	15.4	4,765	23.3
1985	1,000	18.5	8,212	28.9
1990	1,342	21.7	13,835	35.2

Sources: Data for 1960 derived from the *Rueff Report, 1963.*
Source of data for 1965, *First Malaysia Plan, 1966–1970;* for other years the source of data is the *Mid-Term Review of the Second Malaysia Plan, 1971–1975.*

Note: According to the *Mid-Term Review* (p. 69), in the period 1971–1990, manufacturing output will grow at 12.3 per cent per annum. In the same period, employment in manufacturing is expected to grow at 7.5 per cent per annum, and agricultural employment is expected to grow at about 1.3 per cent per annum.
* Amounts at current prices.
= Data refer to West Malaysia only.

turing and in the processing of primary products. A few foreign firms invested in either petroleum, chemicals, iron and steel, general machinery, or consumer goods. The Asian Development Bank (ADB) observed that the contribution of new private foreign investment had been greatest in modernizing industrial development. Private foreign investment has been responsible for creating import substitution industries, increasing industrial output, and expanding exports of manufactured goods.[21]

THE BRITISH STAKE IN MALAYSIAN INDUSTRY

Among all the private foreign investors in the Malaysian industrial sector in the 1960s, the British were the largest and most important.[22]

Nineteen per cent of the gross value of sales of manufacturing establishments covered by the census in 1968 belonged to British concerns. Of the total manufacturing value added of $874 million for establishments surveyed in that year, 21 per cent or $181 million originated from British-owned manufacturing establishments. In the same year, British manufacturing establishments accounts for about 9,200 full-time (about 8 per cent of total) employees in the Malaysian manufacturing sector.

In 1970, empirical investigation estimated that almost 45 per cent of total foreign investment in Malaysia belonged to companies and individuals resident in Britain.[23] In absolute terms, the book value of direct British investment, excluding oil, insurance, and banking, was about £185 million,[24] or approximately M$1,360 million.

Industrial and trading investments made up just over one-quarter of this amount. In 1972, according to a government estimate,[25] British capital excluding capital belonging to British nationals resident abroad, constituted the second largest amount after Singaporean capital in government-approved ('pioneer') companies. In the same year, the third, fourth, fifth, and sixth largest investment in government-approved companies came, respectively, from the United States, Japan, Hong Kong, and the West Indian Islands. It seems clear that Britain has a comparatively large direct investment in manufacturing companies in Malaysia.

With such a predominant position it is essential to understand the role of British investment in the development of the country. This study attempts to inquire into the nature and consequence of British capital investment in the manufacturing industry in Malaysia.

1. See Lim Chong Yah, *Economic Development of Modern Malaya*, Kuala Lumpur, Oxford University Press, 1967.

2. See G. C. Allen and A. G. Donnithorne, *Western Enterprise in Indonesia and Malaya*, George Allen and Unwin, 1962.

3. See also Yip Yat Hoong, *The Development of the Tin Mining Industry*, Kuala Lumpur, University of Malaya Press, 1969; J. H. Drabble, 'Investment in the Rubber Industry in Malaya, *c.* 1900–1922', *Journal of South East Asian Studies*, Vol. 3/(2), September 1972; and D. Lim, *Economic Growth and Development in West Malaysia*, Kuala Lumpur, Oxford University Press, 1973.

4. T. H. Silcock, *The Economy of Malaya: An Essay in Political Economy of Development*, Singapore, Eastern Universities Press, 1954 (reprinted 1968).

5. Allen and Donnithorne, op. cit., p. 158 et seq., p. 261, and *passim*.

6. The International Bank for Reconstruction and Development, *The Economic Development of Malaya*, Baltimore, Johns Hopkins Press, 1955, commonly referred to as IBRD 1955 Report.

7. The International Bank for Reconstruction and Development, *Report on the Economic Aspects of Malaysia*, Kuala Lumpur, Government Press, 1963, hereafter referred to as the *Rueff Report, 1963*.

8. *Rueff Report, 1963*, pp. 5, 9, 38, 41, 56, 57, 86–7 and 92–3.

9. See the Asian Development Bank, *Southeast Asia's Economy in the 1970s*, Longman, 1971, p. 388. Throughout this study this work is referred to as the ADB (1971) Report. The author of the overall report is Professor H. Myint.

10. *Rueff Report, 1963*, p. 37. According to an UNCTAD finding (see UNCTAD paper TD/B/C.3(VI)/Misc.I, Geneva, 1973, p. 66) the policy of the Malaysian government towards private foreign investment is one of surveillance rather than control.

11. See *Second Malaysia Plan, 1971–75*, p. 26 (at current prices).

12. *Second Malaysia Plan, 1971–75*, p. 32.

13. Loc. cit., p. 35.

14. ibid.

15. According to the *U.N. Economic Survey for Asia and the Far East, 1972* (p. 73), in contrast to the annual compound rate of growth of consumer price index (1960 = 100) of 1 per cent for Malaysia in the period 1960/8, the rates of growth of prices for the other countries in South-East Asia exceeded that of Malaysia. For instance the consumer price index in Thailand for the same period grew at 2.2 per cent; in the Philippines, 4.9 per cent, and in Indonesia, 185.7 per cent. In the 1960s there is little doubt that economic growth in Malaysia was achieved with little inflation. See details in the *Economic Survey for Asia and Far East, 1972*, Bangkok, United Nations, 1973, p. 73. See also D. J. Blake, 'Inflation in Malaysia: Its Nature and Extent', *United Malayan Banking Corporation Economic Review*, Vol. X(1), 1974, pp. 43–5.

16. B. Balassa, *et al.*, *The Structure of Protection in Developing Countries*, Baltimore, Johns Hopkins University Press, 1971, p. 205 et seq. See also Chapter 9, Table 9.14 of this study.

17. *Economic Bulletin for Asia and the Far East*, Vol. 23 (3), December 1972, p. 27.

18. *The Treasury Economic Reports, 1972–3*, Kuala Lumpur, 1972, p. 30.

19. See *Mid-Term Review of the Second Malaysia Plan, 1971–75*, Kuala Lumpur, Government Press, 1973, pp. 141–2.

20. The principle of free enterprise is very closely adhered to by the government. See text of speech, 'Why Malaysia wants Foreign Investors' by Tengku Razaleigh Hamzah, in *Straits Times*, 21 November 1972, p. 7. See also government investment promotion advertisement in *Fortune*, Vol. 89(5), May 1974. See J. M. Gullick, *Malaysia*, Ernest Benn Ltd., 1969, p. 225 for criticism of this principle of free enterprise for Malaysia.

21. *ADB Reports* (1971), pp. 389–90.

22. *Census of Manufacturing Industries, 1968*, Kuala Lumpur, Department of Statistics, 1970, p. 38.

23. Information privately gathered from the Confederation of British Industry in 1972. The proportion of British overseas investments in Malaysia is greater than the 45 per cent estimated here, if amounts of British capital controlled and managed from Singapore, Hong Kong, Australia, and the tax haven territories are included. Unofficially, the CBI estimated that in 1970 nearly 65 per cent of the total foreign capital in Malaysia belonged to British interests.

24. All values in £ sterling are estimates of the Economics and Statistics Division of the Department of Trade and Industry, privately communicated to the writer. The M$ refers to Malaysian dollars which hereafter will be simply noted as $. Conversion rates were as follows: 1963–7, £1 = $8.57; 1968–70, £1 = $7.35, and thereafter, the rates varied from $5.50 to $6.50 per £1.

25. Of the $403 million share capital in the government-approved industrial companies, 28.5 per cent came from Singapore, 21 per cent from U.K., 15 per cent from U.S.A., 11.7 per cent from Japan, 9.4 per cent from Hong Kong, 7 per cent from the West Indies and the rest from other countries. See *Malaysian Industrial Digest*, Vol. 6(1), First Quarter, 1973.

2 Malaysia's Share of U.K. Investment

BRITISH CAPITAL IN MALAYSIA IN PERSPECTIVE

PRIOR to 1921 the principal beneficiaries of British overseas investments had been the Americas and the White Commonwealth.[1] British investments in the states of Malaysia had never been given important consideration by any of the well-known writers[2] apart from references to rubber and tin.

Two main reasons may be advanced to account for this apparent lack of interest in U.K. direct investment in Malaysia. Firstly, the amount of British capital in the states of Malaysia before 1930 was very small—less than 1 per cent of total British overseas investment at that time. By way of contrast, as can be seen from Table 2.1 below, the Americas, Europe, and the White Commonwealth together absorbed more than 80 per cent of total British overseas investment at this time.

British capital in British Malaya and Borneo amounted to £33.1 million which represented 0.9 per cent of the total investment overseas by the U.K. in 1913.

Secondly, the British government was not interested in the Malay states in the early days of British contacts.[3] During the eighteenth and nineteenth centuries, British interest there was confined to trade only, particularly trade with China using the Straits Settlements as the Far East trading outposts.[4]

As British settlements developed in these trading outposts, many private traders made their headquarters in the Straits Settlements, particularly in Singapore. From these trading outposts the traders developed a permanent trading network throughout the Malay Archipelago, independent of the China trade.

The Straits traders, as these Far Eastern merchants were referred to, commanded an influential Parliamentary lobby in London, supported by the rising English manufacturing interests in the early 1890s for whom the Malay Archipelago was to become an important market. The Straits traders, many of whom were the

TABLE 2.1
ESTIMATED BRITISH OVERSEAS INVESTMENTS IN SELECTED COUNTRIES, 1913

Countries	*Amount (£ Mil.)*	*Per Cent*
United States of America	754.6	20.0
Latin American countries	756.6	20.1
Canada and Newfoundland	514.9	13.7
Australia and New Zealand	416.4	11.1
South Africa	370.2	9.8
Other European countries	218.6	5.8
Sub-total	3,031.3	80.5
India and Ceylon	378.8	10.0
West Africa	37.3	1.0
Other foreign countries	253.5	6.8
Other British colonies	29.3	0.8
British Malaya and Borneo	33.1	0.9
Sub-total	732.0	19.5
Total Overseas Investment	3,763.3	100.0

Source: Royal Institute of International Affairs, *The Problem of International Investment, 1937*, Frank Cass Ltd., 1965 (originally published by Oxford University Press, 1937).

Note: Amount refers to book values of investments.

forerunners of the 'agency house' merchants (whose role in the growth of British industrial investment in Malaysia was vital) were tough, hard-headed businessmen, determined to succeed by pushing forward their firms' affairs and resolved to seek gain in every way they knew.[5]

Through the lobbyists at Westminster and the powerful manufacturing concerns of the Midlands, the traders persuaded Britain to intervene in their support in the area now constituting the states of Malaysia.

The 1870s marked the beginning of British political support for their trading nationals in British Malaya. But, even after Britain acquired judicial and administrative supremacy in British Malaya, she had few interests outside the Straits Settlements. The Malay territories were governed by a type of 'agency system' whereby the British government's chief agent in the Far East, Sir Andrew Clarke, aimed only at securing sufficient stability in the area, and sufficient control over the native rulers to prevent other powers from intervening in the lucrative trade of the Malay Archipelago.[6]

It was trade and not direct investment that was the main preoccupation of British businessmen at the time.

COMMERCE AND THE BEGINNING OF DIRECT INVESTMENT

The commercial role of the Straits Settlements of which Singapore was the most important was that of a 'gigantic funnel and sorting house combined'.[7] Manufactured goods from England, and opium and piece-goods from the Middle East and India were distributed throughout South-East Asia; the produce of that area (generally known as Straits produce)[8] was collected and redirected to India, China, and Europe.

A large amount of goods sent from China to Europe were transshipped at Singapore, an arrangement made necessary by the East India Company's rule that debarred English private traders from shipping goods direct from China to Europe, and vice versa.[9]

Until the early 1900s, British interest in the states of Malaysia was confined to trade and commerce. British industrial investments did not develop as quickly in this country as they did in the White Commonwealth countries.[10] British traders did not venture into manufacturing because their trading and commercial activities (and later rubber and tin mining) were more profitable.

Singapore grew into a city-state as a result of the British Far East trade. Any industrial investments which followed trade in the early 1900s took place in Singapore,[11] thus providing the island with its industrial base. Apart from British investments in the plantations and mines, the states of Malaysia received only the spill-over of the largely Singapore-based distributive trade. Even in the present 1970s most of the large British trading firms have their headquarters in Singapore from where they service their South-East Asian operations, although an increasing number of British industrial companies in the mid-1970s are also based in Malaysia.

Many British firms operating in Malaysia have their holding companies in Singapore partly for historical reasons, and partly because of the availability of international communications as well as the financial and commercial network available there.[12] Until May 1973, no necessary complication arose as a result of companies having their regional headquarters in Singapore, since the currencies of Malaysia and Singapore were freely interchangeable at par.

The organized development of tin, and later rubber, industries, the two main foundations of the modern Malaysian economy, in the early years of the twentieth century,[13] marked the beginning of a more substantial stake of British capital in the Malaysian economy. By the end of the 1930s, according to Callis[14] Britain became the largest single foreign investor in the country, accounting for over 70 per cent of all foreign capital in the country.

The £33.1 million invested in the country in 1913 (Table 2.1) increased to £108 million by 1930,[15] an increase of over 226 per cent.

THE DIMENSIONS AND DISTRIBUTION OF BRITISH FOREIGN INVESTMENT

The estimated £108 million British capital in Malaya in 1930 included about £4 million of government securities representing British holdings of the then Dutch East Indies government. Table 2.2 shows that the British capital investment in Malaya in 1930 represented about 3.2 per cent of her total overseas investments in that year.

In 1930, almost 93 per cent of British capital in Malaya was in plantations and mines; the remaining 7 per cent being in government bonds and public utilities. Such a distribution contrasted with the general pattern of British overseas investments, two-thirds of which according to Table 2.2 were in foreign government and municipal bonds, public utilities, and railways.

This situation was a reflection of the wealth of British Malaya whose government at that time found it unnecessary to borrow from Britain, or from anywhere else. Much of the finance of public utilities and government undertakings was locally raised, mainly from revenues. Indeed, British Malaya, unlike most other countries in the inter-war years, was not a borrowing country; she was a net financial contributor to Great Britain during that period.[16]

By comparison with aggregate British investment in temperate countries, British capital investment in Malaya was insignificant. As shown in Table 2.3 British overseas investments in Malaysia in the period 1958–68 made up a little over 3 per cent of the total U.K. direct capital stake abroad.

The bulk of the U.K. overseas investments (64 per cent in 1958, and 67 per cent in 1968) had hitherto been located in those countries which may be considered to have well passed the 'take-off' stage, namely the White Commonwealth, America, and Europe. Table 2.3 also shows that British investments in the European Economic Community as well as in the other European countries grew rapidly during the 1958–68 decade.

During the period 1958–64 the bulk of the flow of private

TABLE 2.2

ESTIMATED DISTRIBUTION OF BRITISH OVERSEAS INVESTMENTS IN SELECTED COUNTRIES, 1930

Countries	*Proportion of Investment in:*		*Total Investment in Each Country*	
	Govt. Bonds (%)	*Other Investments* (%)	(£ *Mil.*)	(%)
United States of America	...	100.0	200	5.9
Latin American countries	89.6	10.4	694	20.5
Canada and Newfoundland	76.7	23.3	446	13.2
Australia and New Zealand	89.6	10.4	617	18.2
South Africa	62.9	37.1	224	6.6
Other European countries	68.6	31.4	245	7.2
India and Ceylon	79.3	20.7	458	13.5
Other foreign countries	59.4	40.6	260	7.7
Other British colonies	72.4	27.6	134	4.0
Malaya	7.4	92.6	108	3.2
Total	70.9	29.1		100.0
(Total British Overseas Investment)	£2,400 mil.	£986 mil.	£3,386 mil.	

Source: Data based on Royal Institute of International Affairs, *The Problem of International Investment, 1937*, Frank Cass Ltd., 1965, p. 143, and *passim*.

Notes: Investment in government bonds includes investment in public utilities and railways. Other investment represents direct investments in mining, plantations, and manufacturing affiliates.

... = Not available separately.

The total of £3,386 million estimate represents about 85 per cent of all long-term capital invested by Britain in 1930.

capital from the U.K. went to the developed countries where prospects for investment had improved.[17] Such considerable changes in the structure of U.K. investments reflected that if direct investments were to play a part in promoting economic development of

TABLE 2.3

BRITISH OVERSEAS INVESTMENTS, 1958–1968

	Book Values of Net Assets Attributable to British Concerns at Year Ends (£ million)			*Increase in Amounts between 1958–68*
Country/Area	*1958* (%)	*1963* (%)	*1968* (%)	(%)
Australia	325.1 (12.8)	573.0 (15.8)	966.4 (17.3)	(197.2)
Canada	258.4 (10.2)	500.0 (13.7)	686.9 (12.3)	(165.8)
New Zealand	79.6 (3.2)	113.8 (3.1)	139.7 (2.5)	(75.5)
South Africa	201.5 (7.9)	319.4 (8.8)	585.6 (10.5)	(190.6)
The E.E.C.	145.2 (5.7)	315.5 (8.7)	628.9 (11.3)	(433.1)
Other European Countries	65.8 (2.6)	97.2 (2.7)	152.7 (2.7)	(132.1)
The U.S.A.	540.5 (21.3)	321.1 (8.8)	600.0 (10.7)	(11.0)
Latin America	105.0 (4.1)	183.5 (5.0)	233.4 (4.2)	(122.3)
India	187.8 (7.8)	274.8 (7.6)	277.2 (5.0)	(89.4)
Malaysia	94.0 (3.7)	131.7 (3.6)	172.6 (3.1)	(83.6)
All Other Countries	533.8 (21.0)	805.0 (22.1)	114.9 (20.4)	(73.4)
Total	2,536.7 (100)	3,635.0 (100)	5,585.3 (100)	(120.2)

Source: *Board of Trade Journals*, 14 September 1963, 7 August 1964, 23 September 1970; and Central Office of Information, *Britain's International Investment Position* (Pamphlet No. 98), HMSO, 1970.

Note: Percentages in brackets do not exactly add up to 100 because of rounding off.

the less developed countries (LDCs)[18] it would be essential to have a reasonable climate for such investment.[19]

Table 2.4 summarizes the position of world overseas direct investment of the U.K. and the countries belonging to the Development Assistance Committee of the Organisation for Economic Cooperation and Development (DAC/OECD) in 1966. It can be seen that U.K. overseas direct investment of US$16,002 million constituted about 18 per cent of the accumulated world overseas direct investments made by the DAC/OECD countries in 1966 totalling US$89,583 million (columns *3*, *5*, and *viii*). Of the total world overseas direct investments by these countries, about 33 per cent was held in the LDCs (column *ix*), whereas the U.K. had about 39 per cent of her total overseas direct investment in the LDCs (column *v*). The total U.K. foreign investment in the LDCs then constituted 21 per cent of the total overseas direct investment of the DAC/OECD countries in the LDCs (column *vi*); con-

TABLE 2.4
ESTIMATED DIRECT OVERSEAS INVESTMENTS BY U.K. IN MALAYSIA, AND BY THE DAC/OECD COUNTRIES IN THE WORLD, 1966
(in US$ million)

	Investments by													
	U.K. in			*DAC/OECD in*										
	(1)	*(2)*	*(3)*	*(4)*	*(5)*	*(i)*	*(ii)*	*(iii)*	*(iv)*	*(v)*	*(vi)*	*(vii)*	*(viii)*	*(ix)*
Investment Category	*Malaysia*	*The LDCs*	*The World*	*The LDCs*	*The World*	*(1) as % of (2)*	*(1) as % of (3)*	*(1) as % of (4)*	*(1) as % of (5)*	*(2) as % of (3)*	*(2) as % of (4)*	*(2) as % of (5)*	*(3) as % of (5)*	*(4) as % of (5)*
A	...	2,167	4,200	11,892	25,942	–	–	–	–	52	18	8.4	16.2	45.8
B	27.2	298	759	2,801	5,923	9.1	3.6	1.0	0.5	39	11	5.0	12.8	42.3
C	51.9	1,471	6,028	8,047	36,246	3.5	0.9	0.6	0.1	24	18	4.1	16.6	22.2
D	299.2	2,255	5,015	7,230	21,472	13.3	5.9	4.1	1.4	45	31	10.5	23.4	33.7
Total	378.3	6,184	16,002	29,970	89,583	6.1	2.4	1.3	0.4	39	21	6.9	17.9	32.7

Source: Data taken from *The Flow of Financial Resources to Developing Countries*, Paris, OECD, 1973; and data for U.K. investments obtained from Economics and Statistics Division of the Department of Trade and Industry.

Notes: A Investment in petroleum
B Investment in mining and smelting
C Investment in manufacturing
D Investment in agriculture and other activities
... Not available separately

DAC/OECD countries are Australia, Austria, Belgium, Canada, Denmark, France, W. Germany, Italy, Japan, Holland, Norway, Portugal, Sweden, Switzerland, United Kingdom, and the United States. For a list of the LDCs see *Development Co-operation, 1973 Review*, Paris, OECD, 1973, pp. 216–17.

stituting approximately 7 per cent of all the world's overseas foreign investments of the DAC/OECD countries (column *vii*).

Of the total U.K. foreign investment in the LDCs of US$6,184 million, about 6 per cent (US$378.3 million) was held in Malaysia (column *i*). This however represented only about 2.4 per cent of the world total of U.K. overseas direct investment in 1966 (column *ii*), and about 1.3 per cent of the total overseas direct investments of the DAC/OECD countries in the LDCs (column *iii*). In terms of the world's direct overseas investments of the DAC/OECD countries in 1966, as illustrated by column *iv* of Table 2.4, the British capital stake in Malaysia was extremely small—a mere 0.4 per cent.

Table 2.4 also shows some interesting patterns of the industrial distributions of overseas direct investments. Manufacturing investment, for instance, predominated in the developed countries—a point also made by R. S. May.[20] In all the LDCs, private foreign investments in agriculture, mining, and petroleum taken together were relatively more important than investment in manufacturing (columns *2* and *4*). In general, a little over one-quarter of all overseas direct investments in the LDCs was in manufacturing, while more than 70 per cent of foreign investments in LDCs in 1966 was in agriculture and extractive industries, mainly mining and petroleum.

Of the U.K. capital stake in Malaysia (column *i*) the largest amount in 1966 was, and still is, in agriculture, with manufacturing next in importance, representing almost 14 per cent of total U.K. overseas investment there. The British manufacturing interest in the country, however, formed less than 1 per cent of the U.K. total overseas investment in manufacturing (column *ii*), and by comparison with the world total of manufacturing investments of the DAC/OECD countries it was even smaller—0.1 per cent—(column *iv*). The point is obvious: in world perspective British manufacturing investment in Malaysia appears unimportant. But global aggregate data tend to camouflage the real picture of British industrial capital in Malaysia, since they do not show the dominant place of U.K. manufacturing interests; see Chapter 1, 'The British Stake in Malaysian Industry'.[21]

The broad pattern of British overseas investment by industry and area at the beginning of 1966 is summarized in Table 2.5. What is important is that the manufacturing aspect of British overseas investments was found largely in the developed countries, namely Australia, Canada, the E.E.C. countries, South Africa, and the United States. Also, investments were more diversified in the richer Commonwealth countries of Australia and Canada than in the less developed Commonwealth countries. In Australia, significant British foreign investments were in agriculture, mining and smelting, construction, engineering, manufacturing, and shipping; and in Canada, mining and smelting, construction, engineering, manufacturing, and distribution. South Africa too was an important host to significant British capital engaged in construction, engineering, manufacturing, and shipping industries.

In general, manufacturing and engineering investments which together accounted for about 57 per cent of all overseas investments shown in Table 2.5 were of little importance in the less developed countries. India was an exception with about £15 million of British overseas investments in engineering and manufactur-

TABLE 2.5

LOCATION BY AREA/COUNTRY, AND BY INDUSTRIAL CATEGORY OF SIGNIFICANT U.K. OVERSEAS INVESTMENTS AT YEAR END, 1965

I. *Agriculture*	£365 m.	II. *Mining*	£271 m.
	£ mil.		£ mil.
Malaysia	96	Canada	88
India	79	Australia	77
Australia	48	Commonwealth Africa	59
Ceylon	37	U.S.A.	54[φ]
III. *Engineering**	**£394 m.**	**IV. *Manufacturing***	**£1,709 m.**
	£ mil.		£ mil.
Australia	206	Australia	272
India	151[@]	W. Europe (non-E.E.C.)	246
Canada	81	U.S.A.	243
South Africa	60	Canada	224
New Zealand	58[@]	South Africa	215
		The E.E.C.	190
V. *Construction*	**£50 m.**	**VI. *Transport***	**£139 m.**
	£ mil.		£ mil.
Australia	8	Canada	33
Nigeria	8	Portugal	17
South Africa	6	Commonwealth W. Indies	15
Canada	6	Latin America	23
VII. *Distribution*	**£671 m.**	**VIII. *Shipping***	**£85 m.**
	£ mil.		£ mil.
The E.E.C.	113	Commonwealth W. Indies	27
Commonwealth Africa	80	New Zealand	22
W. Europe (non-E.E.C.)	171	Australia	14

Source: *Board of Trade Journal*, 21 June 1968 (Table 4).

Note: The criterion of significance is taken as at least 10 per cent of the total amount of each of the industrial categories. The figures in the boxes indicate the estimated book values of assets attributable to the investments.

@ Including manufacturing.

φ Including agriculture.

* Electrical, mechanical and marine engineering, including vehicle and shipbuilding.

ing in 1966. In the same year in Malaysia the significant overseas investment by the U.K. was in agricultural investment, amounting to about £96 million. This situation hid the actual investment position of Britain in the Malaysian economy, giving the impression that other avenues of capital investment apart from agriculture were unimportant. In fact, Britain has been the most important single foreign investor in the country, and the capital invested includes investment in manufacturing as well as other non-agricultural activities.

THE SIZE AND COMPONENT OF BRITISH CAPITAL IN MALAYSIA

In 1930, as noted in Table 2.2, the amount of British capital in Malaya was estimated to be around £108 million. According to Callis[22] there was a reduction of 17 per cent of foreign investments in Malaya during the period 1930–7.[23] There seemed to be no reliable estimate of British capital in the states of Malaysia between the years 1930 and 1960.

According to information gathered from the Bank of England, the amounts of the nominal capital of British companies varied from £67 million in 1938 to £69 million in 1957, thus suggesting a decline of about 13 per cent in the level of British investment between 1930 and 1957. In the absence of other indicators, Table 2.6 below has been computed to show a rough outline of British capital in Malaysia. It suggests no dramatic changes in the amounts of British investment from 1930 to 1960.

TABLE 2.6
ESTIMATED LEVELS OF BRITISH CAPITAL IN MALAYSIA, 1930–1960

Year	*Amounts (£ mil.)*	*Year*	*Amounts (£ mil.)*
1930	108.0$^{\phi}$	1955	71.0*
1938	67.0*	1957	69.0*
1948	64.0*	1958	94.0$^{\phi}$
1950	69.0*	1960	110.5$^{\phi}$

Sources: Data derived from the DTI and the Bank of England.
Notes: ϕ Amount referring to book values of net assets attributable to British interest.
* Amount indicating the nominal capital value of British capital invested in the country.

In terms of book values of net assets belonging to British investors in Malaysia, the amount in 1960 was only about 2.3 per cent higher than in 1930. At least three events helped to account for the relative stagnation of British capital in the country during the 1930–60 period; the depression of the 1930s, the period of Japanese occupation of the country from 1941 to 1946, and the period 1947 to 1960 characterized by disruptive political and terrorist activities which did not encourage British investment.

In fact, British capital in the country, according to the estimated book values provided by the Economics and Statistics Division of the Department of Trade and Industry (DTI) shown in Table 2.7 below, between 1960 and 1971 increased annually at erratic rates. In broad terms, the £110.5 million invested in 1960 increased to £195.9 million in 1971, showing an increase of about 77.3 per cent during the period 1960 to 1971.

TABLE 2.7
ESTIMATED BOOK VALUES OF BRITISH INVESTMENTS IN MALAYSIA, 1960–1971

	(1) Total Amount		*(2) Amount Attributable to Manufacturing*		*(3) (2) as Per Cent of (1)*
Year	*(£ mil.)*	*($ mil.)*	*(£ mil.)*	*($ mil.)*	
1960	110.5	946.9	...	...	...
1961	119.3	1,022.4	...	...	...
1962	126.7	1,085.8	...	...	...
1963	131.7	1,128.7	15.5	132.8	11.8
1964	138.4	1,186.1	17.4	149.1	12.6
1965	144.0	1,234.1	19.9	170.5	13.8
1966	144.4	1,237.5	19.8	169.7	13.7
1967	174.5	1,495.5	22.9	196.3	13.1
1968	172.6	1,268.6	21.6	158.8	12.5
1969	172.6	1,268.6	21.6	158.8	12.5
1970	182.8	1,343.6	19.2	141.1	10.5
1971	195.9	1,439.8	22.5	165.4	11.5

Source: Data derived from DTI.
Notes: Not available separately.
Total amount invested excludes investments in banking, insurance and oil, estimated to be around £200 million in 1972. $ refers to Malaysian dollar.

A number of political events in the 1960s created uncertainties in the minds of foreign investors about the future economic stability of the country. Malaya, which became politically independent from the British in 1957, joined together with Sabah, Sarawak, and Singapore to form Malaysia in 1963. In 1965, Singapore became a separate political entity. From 1963 to 1966 Malaysia's neighbour, Indonesia, maintained a political 'confrontation' policy (of 'crush neo-colonial British interest in Malaysia') towards Malaysia. The pound sterling was devalued in 1967 and there was much talk and plan of the British withdrawal from military bases 'East of Suez'. In 1969, there were civil disturbances in Kuala Lumpur and in other major towns of the country.

Political events alone did not fully explain the sluggish inflows of new British capital into the country. The generally depressed prices for Malaysia's exports of rubber and tin—brought about by competition from synthetic substitutes and the generally low income elasticity of demand for these export items—the restricted opening of new land for plantations and mining[24] as well as the gradual depletion of ore reserves all combined to halt any substantial new British investments in rubber and tin, the traditional spheres of British direct investment in the country. There was however an increase in acreage of oil palm cultivation, but in the 1960s this was partly due to the conversion of rubber lands to palm oil cultivation.[25] In the late 1960s, there was a general decline of private investment in perennial crops,[26] while the level of mining output during the same period declined owing to gradual exhaustion of ore deposits.[27] Restrictions on capital outflow from the U.K. brought about by the disequilibrium in her balance of payments, together with the preoccupation of a large number of British businessmen in the late 1960s with the investment prospects of the E.E.C. were contributory factors that discouraged large outflows of capital from the U.K. into Malaysia.

As illustrated in Table 2.7, British investment in manufacturing increased from £132.8 million in 1963 to £165.4 million in 1971 indicating an increase of 24.5 per cent for the period. A general remark about the book values used in the Table is appropriate so that the figures may be interpreted accurately. The use of book values or balance sheet figures of investing companies' net assets, i.e. fixed assets less accumulated depreciations, plus current assets less current liabilities, may lead to an understatement of the total value of British capital overseas. It is also possible that the diversity of accounting practices may also render balance sheet figures inaccurate and incomparable. Price changes can also affect the 'true and fair' nature of balance sheet figures.[28] The balance sheet values of fixed assets acquired some years ago are, unless there has been a recent revaluation, likely to be appreciably lower than current market or replacement values. In individual cases, as in companies that acquired lands, buildings, and expensive equipment, fixed assets shown in balance sheets may be quite unrealistic since they recorded the costs of initial investments made at various past dates. Some companies do revalue their assets periodically and adjust the values shown in their books accordingly.

In presenting the magnitude of British investments in Malaysia the use of market values would have been more realistic,[29] but it is not always possible to calculate these accurately. This is because market values are significantly influenced by expectations about the future earnings to which the assets give rise, and may fluctuate widely in the short period in response to changes in those expectations. Furthermore, technical change may lead to obsolescence, and cause particular assets to lose a significant proportion of their value. Book values are used here because they are the only values available from private and official sources.

The use of book values shows approximate but revealing trends in direct British investment in Malaysia. It is important to remember that the market or replacement values of British capital invested in Malaysian industries were larger than those shown in the book values. The official statistics on foreign investments in Malaysian industries tended to understate the British interest there, since a considerable proportion of capital classified as coming from Canada, Hong Kong, India, Singapore, and the 'tax haven territories' in fact belonged to British nationals.[30] An equally relevant note is the presence of goodwill—in the accounting sense—in those British companies that have been established in Malaysia over the years. The market values of these companies as going concerns were very much higher than net asset values suggested by the balance sheet figures. Therefore, it is probably more appropriate to consider the actual British capital stake in Malaysia as being very much more than the figures shown in the estimates in Table 2.7.

Table 2.8 supports the point established earlier about the predominant involvement of British foreign investment in the agricultural and mining sectors of the Malaysian economy. Agriculture and mining accounted for 93 per cent of British capital in the country in 1930; and in 1936 investment in primary activities accounted for almost the same proportion. In the second half of the 1960s, the absolute amounts invested in agriculture and min-

TABLE 2.8
THE COMPONENTS OF BRITISH DIRECT INVESTMENTS IN MALAYSIA, 1930–1970

	1930		*1936*		*1965*		*1968*		*1970*	
	(£ *mil.*)	(%)	(£ *mil.*)	(%)	(£ *mil.*)	(%)	(£ *mil.*)	(%)	(£ *mil.*)	(%)
1. Agriculture	92	(85.2)	94.1	(80.5)	95.6	(66.4)	109.4	(63.4)	112.5	(61.6)
2. Mining	8	(7.4)	13.1	(11.2)	10.4	(7.2)	16.5	(9.6)	15.6	(8.5)
3. Distribution	...	...			15.0	(10.4)	21.6	(12.5)	27.8	(15.2)
4. Manufacturing	...	...			19.8	(13.8)	21.6	(12.5)	19.2	(10.5)
5. Other Activities	8	(7.4)	9.7	(8.3)	3.2	(2.2)	3.5	(2.0)	7.7	(4.2)
Total	108	(100)	116.9	(100)	144.0	(100)	172.6	(100)	182.8	(100)

Source: Data derived from field work and sources noted in Tables 2.2–2.7 above.

Notes: Investment figures do not include capital invested in banking, insurance, and oil.
... Amount not available separately, and included in item 5.

ing increased slightly from £106 million in 1965 to £128.1 million in 1970. The proportion of British capital in the two sectors remained at about 70–74 per cent of all capital invested by the U.K. in the country in the late 1960s.

The point of immediate interest to the present study, as highlighted by Tables 2.7 and 2.8, is that British investment in manufacturing in the country in the 1960s became relatively more important, and had very important consequences on the economy, although the available literature on foreign investment in the country has not made any systematic attempt at delineating the nature and consequences of British industrial capital in the country.

1. This assertion is based on E. A. G. Robinson, *Fifty Years of Commonwealth Economic Development*, Cambridge University Press, 1972. The term 'White Commonwealth' used by Professor Robinson in a technical sense, refers to Australia, Canada, New Zealand, Rhodesia, and South Africa.

2. See, for example, Sir George Paish, 'Great Britain's Capital Investment in Other Lands', *Journal of the Royal Statistical Society*, Vol. 72, 1909, pp. 456–80, and discussion on the paper in the same source, pp. 481–95; C. K. Hobson, *The Export of Capital*, Constable, 1914, reissued in 1963 with a Preface by Sir Roy Harrod; L. H. Jenks, *The Migration of British Capital to 1875*, Jonathan Cape, 1927 (rev. ed. 1938); H. Fei, *Europe: The World's Banker, 1870–1914*, Yale University Press, 1954; A. K. Cairncross, *Home and Foreign Investments 1870–1913*, Cambridge University Press, 1953, and A. H. Imlah, *Economic Elements in the Pax Britannica*, Harvard University Press, 1958. Even recent studies such as the one by W. E. Reddaway *et al.*, *Effects of U.K. Direct Investment Overseas*, Cambridge University Press, 1967 and 1968, and the various studies on foreign investment by Professor Dunning cited elsewhere in this study make little reference to other avenues of British capital in Malaysia apart from rubber and tin investments.

3. This statement is based on an authoritative study on the early involvement of Britain in Malaya by C. D. Cowan, 'The Origins of British Political Control in Malaya, 1867–1878', University of London, Ph.D. thesis, 1955.

4. See C. D. Cowan, *Nineteenth Century Malaya*, Oxford University Press, 1961. See also E. Thio's essay in *Papers in Malayan History*, University of Singapore, 1962, particularly the references cited therein on page 121; and K. G. Tregonning, *A History of Modern Malaya*, Eastern Universities Press, 1964, as well as Gullick, *Malaysia*, Ernest Benn Ltd., 1969.

5. This statement is taken from S. Cunyngham-Brown, *The Traders*, Guthrie & Co. Ltd., 1971, a book which gives an excellent account of the part played by the Straits traders in British Malaya.

6. See C. D. Cowan, *Nineteenth Century Malaya*, Chapter V, for a fuller account of the governing system and the reasons for governing the area.

7. For details see C. D. Cowan, ed., 'Early Penang and the Rise of Singapore', *Journal of the Royal Asiatic Society Malayan Branch*, Vol. 14, Part 3, 1936; and J. Cameron, *Our Tropical Possessions in Malayan India: Singapore, Penang, Province Wellesley, Malacca*, London, 1865.

8. The term covers all products of the Malay Archipelago. See details in *The Entrepot Trade of Singapore*, DTI BMA (M) Singapore, 1945.

9. The East India Company had paramount power in Malaya in the nineteenth century, and as such they controlled much of the commerce of the area. Their investment interest in the area, however, remained peripheral for a long time. See C. D. Cowan, *Nineteenth Century Malaya*, pp. 17–20, and *passim*. See also H. B. Morse, *Chronicles of the East India Company Trading to China*, Vol. 11, London, 1926.

10. Manufacturing came naturally to the White Commonwealth in the sense that technically and culturally the White Commonwealth shares the same tradition as Britain. See E. A. G. Robinson, op. cit., p. 5 and *passim*.

11. Allen and Donnithorne, *Western Enterprise in Indonesia and Malaya*, pp. 236 and 263.

12. Many other factors, e.g. the growth of shipping and the growth of activities and institutions ancillary to international trade, also helped in contributing to the development of Singapore as a commercial centre in South-East Asia. See for example G. Bogaars, 'The Effect of the Opening of the Suez Canal on the Trade and Development of Singapore', *Journal of the Royal Asiatic Society Malayan Branch*, Vol. 28, March 1955, pp. 99–143; and S. Y. Lee, 'The Asian Dollar Market in Singapore', *Malayan Economic Review*, Vol. 16(1), April 1971, pp. 46–56.

13. See Allen and Donnithorne, op. cit., and the references cited *passim* in the Introduction to this study.

14. H. G. Callis, *Foreign Capital in South-East Asia* (mimeo.), New York, Institute of Pacific Relations, 1942, p. 52. Callis wrote: 'The British stake is, in fact, preponderant in every line of economic activity which is of importance to the economy of British Malaya, in agriculture . . . mining . . . trade and banking . . . and industry.'

15. Royal Institute of International Affairs, *The Problems of International Investment*, p. 142. See also Table 2.2.

16. The vitality of British Malaya to the British Empire is noted in M. Greenberg, 'Malaya—Britain's Dollar Arsenal', *Amerasia*, Vol. 5, June 1941, pp. 144–51. See also D. J. Li, *British Malaya: An Economic Analysis*, New York, American Press, 1955, pp. 34–5, and *passim*. Even during the period presently studied, Malaysia is a net financial contributor to the U.K. in the sense that more funds flow from Malaysia to the U.K. than vice versa; see Chapter 9.

17. R. S. May, 'Direct Investment in Less Developed Countries: British Investment 1958–65', *Journal of Development Studies*, Vol. (3), April 1968, pp. 386–423.

18. In the literature of development economics 'less developed', 'underdeveloped', and 'developing' are adjectives interchangeably used to describe the poor countries of Africa, Asia, and Latin America. Sometimes these countries are also referred to as the 'Third World'; see D. Seers and L. Joy, eds., *Development in a Divided World*, Pelican, 1971, p. 9. Throughout this study 'less-developed' and 'underdeveloped' are used interchangeably, for the sake of variety, to describe countries with low per capita income.

19. May, 'Direct Investment in Less Developed Countries', pp. 421–2.

20. May, ibid. May also observed significant increases in new manufacturing investments in the LDCs during the period covered by his study.

21. The position of British manufacturing companies in Malaysia is further discussed in Chapters 5, 6, and 7 where it will be seen that these companies occupy a very prominent place in the country's manufacturing sector.

22. Callis, *Foreign Capital in South-East Asia*, p. 56.

23. Callis did not give any reason for the decline in the level of foreign investment, but it is reasonable to argue that the reduction in foreign investment was associated with the depression of the 1930s and the imposition of international restriction schemes on the rubber industry (see discussion in Lim Chong Yah, *Economic Development of Modern Malaya*, Chapter 3, especially pp. 78-83). A certain amount of capital outflow also took place in the mining industry when it was hit by the depression and the tin-control schemes of the 1930s.

24. Land development for agriculture is mostly carried out by government organizations rather than private investors; see *Second Malaysia Plan, 1971–75*, pp. 124–7. Exhaustion of ore deposits and the imposition of quotas under the International Tin Agreement limited the expansion of tin mining in the late 1960s; see *Mid-Term Review of the First Malaysia Plan, 1966–70*, p. 21. Exploitation of tin deposits in offshore areas may be an opening for new investment in mining; see *Second Malaysia Plan, 1971–75*, p. 172.

25. *Second Malaysia Plan, 1971–75*, p. 123.

26. ibid., p. 84.

27. ibid., pp. 171–2.

28. See 'How Inflation Warps Accounts', *The Economist*, 16 January 1971. In the Malaysian case, the balance sheets of companies are not too distorted since domestic prices in the country in the 1960s were quite stable. See also Chapter 1, footnote 15.

29. Alternatively, the insurance values of the assets including inventory may be used; but not many of the companies consulted in this study could furnish certified insurance values of their investments in Malaysia.

30. Information derived from Confederation of British Industry, during field work.

3 The Malaysian Climate for Investment in Manufacturing

INTRODUCTION

WRITERS on foreign investment[1] recognize that the investment climate of the host country is determined by a number of factors, e.g. the host government's policy towards economic development, the profit motive, repatriation of capital and profits by foreigners, the maintenance of currency stability, the restrictions imposed on foreign investment, the maintenance of political stability, and the use of tariffs to protect newly established industries. To a lesser extent, the availability of skilled labour and raw materials necessary for industries is an integral part of the favourable investment climate: but the crucial element in attracting private foreign investment is the attitude of the government of the host country towards private foreign investment as a whole.

The discussion and the relevant data pertaining to Malaysia in the 1960s mainly concern West Malaysia. It will probably not lead to any serious distortion or misconception to take the general picture portrayed here as that of Malaysia as a whole because British investment is mainly located in West Malaysia. Private foreign investment in manufacturing in East Malaysia is minor, and is highly concentrated in primary processing and packaging activities. Furthermore, the territories now forming East Malaysia were British colonies before the formation of Malaysia in 1963.

In Malaya, where the *laissez-faire* doctrine prevailed as in other British colonies, the government document, *Draft Development Plan, 1951,* stated that it was no part of government policy to undertake the direction of the flow of trade. The aim was rather to obtain a clear field for the skill and enterprise of the private trader. Government intervention was limited to the prevention of dumping of cheap goods into the country from hard currency sources (non-sterling areas) whenever the pound sterling came under pressure.[2]

TABLE 3.1
FINANCING PRIVATE INVESTMENT IN MALAYSIA,
1970–1975
($ million)

Private investment target	1970	$1,236	
	1975	$1,881	
Cumulative target	1970–5	$7,843	
Average annual growth rate of private investment envisaged			8.8%
Planned financing of target			
Transfers and loans from public sector		$ 742	9.4%
Private foreign financing		$1,150	14.7%
Reinvestments*		$4,000	51.0%
Private equity and loans		$1,951	24.9%
Total source of finance		$7,843	100.0%

Source: Data derived from *Second Malaysia Plan, 1971–1975*, pp. 87 and 92.
Note: * Mainly depreciation and retained earnings of private foreign companies.

ATTITUDE TOWARDS PRIVATE FOREIGN INVESTMENT

Malaysia, unlike some other underdeveloped countries, welcomes foreign investment not only for its anticipated contribution to the growth of the national income and employment, but also for introducing modern industrial technology.[3] Foreign capital is treated on the same basis as local capital with an added guarantee given to the former against expropriation.[4]

The government desire for private foreign capital in the country is indicated by the fact that more than half of the finance for private investment in the Second Plan period is expected to come from foreign sources.

About 64 per cent, or $5,150 out of a total of $7,843 million of the finances for the private sector in the period 1970 to 1975 (as shown in Table 3.1) was anticipated to come from foreigners including expected reinvestments in the existing private foreign companies.

The bulk of private foreign investment is expected to enter the manufacturing sector, although the government generally does not exert strict control over the direction in which private investment moves.[5] Some foreign private capital may find its way into other sectors, notably commerce, but the government's main objective in attracting the foreign investor is to persuade him to enter into manufacturing, which is regarded as a strategic sector in the economic plans.[6]

Table 3.2 below shows the position of foreign capital in the country's economy in 1968. Of the book values of company fixed assets in the country, 56.5 per cent or $2,115 million belonged to foreigners. More important than the total figure for all industries is the extent of control by foreigners in the individual industries. In

TABLE 3.2

FOREIGN OWNERSHIP OF COMPANY FIXED ASSETS, 1968

($ million)

Economic Sector	*Foreign Controlled*	*Locally Controlled*	*Company Fixed Assets, Total*
1. Rubber	778 (74.7)	265 (25.3)	1,043 (27.9) (100.0)
2. Other agriculture	124 (53.7)	107 (46.3)	231 (6.2) (100.0)
3. Tin mining	184 (60.7)	119 (39.3)	303 (8.1) (100.0)
4. Other mining	125 (84.4)	23 (15.6)	148 (3.9) (100.0)
5. Manufacturing	473 (49.2)	489 (50.8)	962 (25.7) (100.0)
6. Construction	13 (28.9)	32 (71.1)	45 (1.2) (100.0)
7. Wholesale trade	230 (65.7)	120 (34.3)	350 (9.4) (100.0)
8. Retail trade	21 (31.8)	45 (68.2)	66 (1.8) (100.0)
9. Other industry	167 (28.0)	428 (72.0)	495 (15.9) (100.0)
10. Total assets	2,115 (56.5)	1,628 (43.5)	3,743 (100.0) (100.0)

Source: Data based on Department of Statistics, *Report on the Financial Survey of Limited Companies*, Kuala Lumpur, *c.* 1970.

Notes: Figures in brackets are percentages. The amounts refer to book values of net fixed assets of companies with limited liabilities covered by the survey.

As already explained, the book values tend to understate the real magnitude of the assets. The survey on which the data was based had a 96 per cent coverage of all companies in the year of the survey.

the rubber industry, foreign companies own about 75 per cent of the fixed assets, and they also control 67 per cent of wholesale trade, 85 per cent of mining, and 49 per cent of manufacturing. Even in the retail trade, more than 30 per cent of the assets was foreign-owned. There was hardly any branch of the economy in which foreign investment was not present.

It is vital to note that the amounts of foreign ownership shown in Table 3.2 are understated because book values do not reflect the market values and, more important, the fact that data in the Table exclude banks, insurance companies, nominee companies, shipping and airline companies, as well as non-profit making organizations (e.g. churches), all of which have substantial assets, a large proportion of which belong to foreigners.[7]

In spite of the predominant foreign ownership of capital in the country, the government does not feel it necessary to curb further inflows of new foreign investments. On the contrary, it feels that in the absence of aid the flow of private foreign capital should increase[8] since without such capital inflows there would be gaps in financing economic plans. With two exceptions[9] there has been no expression of extreme nationalistic sentiment against the presence of foreign investment. This contrasts favourably with attitudes in less developed countries, or even newly developed countries such as Australia and Canada.[10] In principle the government is eager to promote foreign capital that will form 'joint-ventures' with local interest.[11] In practice, all forms of foreign ownership including 100 per cent ownership are allowed.[12] Foreign-owned companies, once established in the country, have the same rights, privileges, duties and obligations as similar domestically-owned companies.

THE GOVERNMENT AND THE MANUFACTURING SECTOR

The Malaysian government is now explicit in its policy towards the manufacturing sector. Until recently it had never played a role in the industrial expansion of the country[13] and even today the responsibility for manufacturing operation is left to the private sector.[14] Its role is confined to maintaining a favourable investment climate and to providing industrial estates, transport, power, and communication facilities, and inducements to invest (in the form of tax concessions and other privileges embodied in the Investment Incentives Act 1968 as amended).

The government has entrusted the whole implementation of the programme to encouraging the inflow of foreign capital to industry to the Federal Industrial Development Authority (FIDA), a statutory body [now renamed MIDA, Malaysian Industrial Development Authority] which provides services especially geared to the needs of the investors. Working in close co-operation with FIDA, is the Capital Investment Committee (CIC), a body headed by a government Minister whose main function is to review industrial development in the country. Representative of manufacturers, industrialists, and people in commerce form an advisory body known as the Private Sector Advisory Panel (PSAP) which advises the CIC. This arrangement enables the government to keep in touch with the views of the private sector on matters relating to industrial development.

The government adopts direct and indirect measures to promote manufacturing. Among the indirect measures are the provision of physical facilities, guarantees against uncompensated nationalization, and the upholding of guarantees for freedom of capital and profit repatriation by the private foreign investor. Other indirect measures are to adopt policies towards maintaining a favourable investment climate, namely (a) that of encouraging a healthy and responsible trade unionism by arranging for labour legislation and statutory requirements such that they allow for free negotiations and wage bargaining; (b) its policy of exercising conservative fiscal and monetary policies in order to convince investors that the government is a prudent spender of scarce resources; (c) its policy of maintaining currency stability and a large external reserve balance to convince foreigners of its capability to meet its international financial obligations; and (d) its acceptance of obligations set out in Article VIII of the International Monetary Fund Agreement, thus enhancing the international standing of the Malaysian dollar. Under the obligations laid out in Article VIII, the country may not, without prior approval of the IMF, impose restrictions on payment or transfers for international transactions, or engage in discriminatory currency arrangements, or adopt multiple exchange rates.

The direct measures adopted by the government to promote manufacturing may be classified into (i) support activities (ii) fiscal incentives, and (iii) direct involvement. The support activities undertaken by the government cover a wide field. Direct support includes:

(a) The offer of medium- and long-term loans from the government-sponsored, but privately managed, agency, the Malaysian Industrial Development Finance Ltd. (MIDFL). The MIDFL is only one of the numerous other sources of industrial finance in the private sector. There are at least forty commercial banks in the country in addition to the various merchant banking organizations that have developed in the late 1960s. Also, there is a well-developed local share market with adequate facilities for underwriting new issues. There is no real shortage of local capital[15] and industrial shares are often over-subscribed–in certain cases over-subscribed twenty times.[16] The presence of local capital has led to a situation whereby foreign companies raise most of the funds they require from local sources.

(b) The offer of easy credit terms for standard factory buildings on industrial sites from the MIDFL's subsidiary, the Malaysian Industrial Estates Ltd. (MIEL).

(c) The provision of industrial estate locations from the various States Economic Development Corporations (SEDCs).

(d) The provision of various technical and research facilities by government-sponsored bodies such as the National Productivity Centre (NPC), the Standards Institute of Malaysia (SIM), the National Institute for Scientific and Industrial Research (NISIR) (SIM and NISIR have been combined and is now called SIRIM–Scientific and Industrial Institute of Malaysia), and the Malaysian Industrial Development Consultancy Ltd. (MIDCL).

(e) Perhaps the most important of all the direct supports is the compulsory patronage by the various government departments of approved domestically manufactured goods.

The fiscal incentives extended by the Malaysian government for the purpose of promoting industrial investment include tariff protection, import duty relief, accelerated depreciation allowances on machines and other fixed assets, payroll-tax relief, and 'pioneer status'[17] income-tax holidays.

Government-initiated incentives are embodied in the *Investment Incentives Act, 1968* and the *Investment Incentives (Amendment) Act, 1971*. Many of the provisions of the latter Act are designed to encourage the growth of manufacturing for exports, while the former Act provides incentives applicable to all industries in general.

Tariff protection for local industries is also given by the government, but in the 1960s the level of protection given was low by standards prevailing in most underdeveloped countries.[18] This is partly because the country has not suffered any balance of payments difficulties, and more important perhaps also because the government in granting tariffs to protect industries has frequently expressed its anxiety about over-protection,[19] believing that protection in principle is designed to be a temporary expedient only.

It is certainly not the intention of the government to support indefinitely firms which have little or no prospect of becoming viable in the absence of foreign competition. The purpose of tariff protection for industries in the Malaysian context is to help firms to surmount those initial obstacles which frequently beset nascent industrial ventures in the early years of their establishment.[20]

The government has also enacted an ordinance allowing for the establishment of free trade zones (FTZ) as recommended in the Rueff Report. Among the salient provisions of the FTZ ordinance are: (a) goods of any description, except those which are specifically prohibited by law, can be brought into an area designated as FTZ without payment of any customs duty or excise duty, and dutiable goods can be used in the FTZ with the permission of the Superintendent of Customs and Excise; (b) goods can be sold (but not to retail trade), stored, exhibited, broken up, repacked, assembled, cleaned, mixed, or otherwise manipulated or manufactured in the FTZ; (c) goods in the FTZ can be removed for export or sent into another FTZ either in the original package or in the manufactured forms; and (d) for the purposes of the Customs Act 1967, a free trade zone shall be deemed to be a place outside Malaysia, although of course physically it is in the country, and in certain cases the FTZ are located in centres of population concentration.[21]

As for the direct participation of the government in manufacturing referred to above, this is done through its agencies such as MARA, the Majlis Amanah Rakyat (Council for Indigenous Peoples), and PERNAS, the Perbadanan Nasional (National Corporation), with the expressed intention that such participation is only temporary. Ventures started with government participation will be turned over to private ownership and management as soon as they are viable,[22] and the few examples of such ventures (e.g. the batik-making industry and the boat-building yard on the East Coast) are in fact managed by private persons with the government providing part of the capital and some technical supervision. Government direct participation in manufacturing is not intended to usurp the role of the private investor.

REGULATIONS

Few regulations are imposed by the government on the manufacturing sector. For instance there is no specific legislation for licensing in industry. A foreign company may either be operated as a branch of a foreign incorporated company in the country, or established as a locally incorporated entity by itself or in joint-venture with local partners.[23] Within one month of its establishing a place of business in the country, a company must register with the Registrar of Companies as stipulated under the provisions of the Company's Act 1965. This Act legislates for the incorporation of limited liability companies and provides certain legal requirements to protect shareholders. Since the mid-1960s companies wishing to set up manufacturing facilities are required to apply for approval from the Ministry of Commerce, even though they may be registered with the Registrar of Companies.

As a general rule, companies which manufacture for the domestic market are required to have at least one-half of their equity capital in the hands of local people, but in practice the ratio of foreign to local equity participation is often left to the investing company. Companies manufacturing specifically for the export market frequently control 100 per cent of their equity as they are permitted to do. There is at present no specific control over the structure of capital of the investing companies so that many companies can in fact devise their own system of capital gearing or leverage.

In return for incentives given by virtue of the Investment Incentives Acts the foreign investor must meet three broad requirements. Firstly, companies are expected to offer an increasing proportion of their equity holdings to local people. Secondly, companies are required to increase the number of local people employed among the chief executive ranks,[24] and finally companies are required to use an increasing proportion of locally-available factor inputs. In addition, the companies are also encouraged to export their manufactured products.[25] In essence, the Malaysian industrialization policy is flexible and, as will be indicated later, the flexibility is an attractive feature of the industrialization programme.

POLITICAL STABILITY

A most important function that the government tries to perform in creating a favourable investment climate is the maintenance of political stability. The government is run by a well-established Civil Service, and there seems little danger of a radical policy reversing the trend of events.

The general investment climate may be summarized as in Table 3.3.

TABLE 3.3
GENERAL OUTLINE OF THE INVESTMENT CLIMATE IN MALAYSIA

		Remarks
I.	*General Government Policy*	
a)	Policy towards private enterprise	Favourable attitude towards private enterprise.
b)	Policy towards foreign investment	Private foreign investment is welcome.
c)	Regulations on foreign investment	No specific restriction; no separate law for foreigners. Local and foreign companies subjected to the same law.
d)	Commitment to economic development	Government is intent on developing the country as evidenced by the existence of the economic plans.
II.	*Industrialization Policy*	
a)	Role of government	Limited to provision of incentives and economic infrastructure. Limited direct participation.
b)	Instruments of industrialization	Well-defined institutions, e.g. FIDA, CIC, PSAP, MIDFL, and MIEL designed to assist industrial programme.
c)	Industrial incentives	Tax holidays up to ten years, and other concessions, enumerated in the Investment Incentives Acts.
III.	*Other Economic Policy*	
a)	Internal economic policy	The government is committed to maintaining monetary and fiscal stability.
b)	Policy towards capital repatriation	Very liberal foreign exchange policy. High levels of external reserves. Subscribes to IMF Article VIII.
c)	Policy towards protection	When necessary, protection is given to investors.

IV. *Other Factors*

Domestic capital is available. Domestic credit system and management are well developed. Underwriting and related facilities for company formation are also available.

The government is conscious of the need to maintain a stable political environment, and is so far successful.

HOW BRITISH INVESTORS EVALUATE THE INVESTMENT CLIMATE

Table 3.4 below reflects the views of companies consulted in the course of the present study. One hundred and three companies were asked to evaluate the various aspects of the economic environment outlined in the previous section according to whether

TABLE 3.4

HOW BRITISH COMPANIES REGARD THE VARIOUS ASPECTS OF THE ECONOMIC ENVIRONMENT FOR THE PRIVATE FOREIGN INVESTOR IN MALAYSIA

(by per cent)

Aspects of the Economic Environment as Outlined in the Previous Section	*'Important'*	*Regarded as 'Moderately Important'*	*'Not Important'*	
No restriction or discrimination imposed on the private foreign investor	100.0	–	–	(N=103)
Freedom to remit capital and profits from the country	100.0	–	–	(N=103)
Internal economic stability	99.0	1.0	–	(N=103)
International currency stability	99.0	1.0	–	(N=103)
Government commitment to achieving economic growth	95.9	4.1	–	(N= 97)
Government provision of economic infrastructure	94.7	1.5	3.8	(N=103)
Availability of local capital	78.4	17.6	4.0	(N=102)
Political stability	69.9	30.1	–	(N= 93)
Willingness of government to grant tariff protection	62.4	35.6	2.0	(N=101)
Tax concessions	52.4	45.6	2.0	(N=103)

Source: Interviews.

they thought the factors were 'important', 'moderately important', or 'not important', in encouraging the growth of foreign investment in the light of their experience in the country.

All companies regarded freedom from restrictions on their activities and the freedom to remit capital and profits as important aspects of the economic environment. Nearly all considered internal economic stability and international currency stability to be important, although they realized that it is difficult to achieve stability in the process of development. It is a great achievement that Malaysia has been able to experience considerable economic growth without inflation or changes in the external value of its currency. The lack of inflation in the 1960s was related to the conservative internal fiscal and monetary policies of the country.[26]

The lack of restriction on the external remittances of funds from the country was supported by the maintenance of relatively large external reserves,[27] supported by high earnings from the primary exports of rubber, tin, palm oil and timber,[28] and recently petroleum.[29]

Ninety-six per cent of companies regarded the government's commitment to achieving economic growth as important,[30] though to 4 per cent it was only of moderate importance, since their activities in other parts of the world were more important to them than those in Malaysia. To 95 per cent of the companies, the provision of infrastructure by the government was important, though 3.8 per cent of companies interviewed did not consider it so since they had initially provided their own power, water, transport, and communication facilities.

The availability of capital locally was regarded as either important or moderately important by the majority of British firms. Four per cent did not consider this factor important since they relied on their own resources.

Political stability was regarded as either important or moderately important by the great majority of the interviewees. Some companies did not feel the politics of the country was of material consideration. These companies have investments in other parts of the world where they have learnt to cope with situations involving political instability. They were not very impressed by the system of checks and balances characteristic of democratically elected governments. Some even stated that their companies were more attracted to countries with 'benevolent dictatorship, which were not anti-business and not against profits' than to those democratic countries where the leaders begrudge the profit motive and private enterprise. Generally the businessmen indicated that so long as there was no civil disturbance in the country, the political inclination of the government was of little relevance to them, provided the government was not against foreign investment.

About 52 per cent thought tax concessions given by the government were important, while nearly 46 per cent thought them of moderate importance. Two per cent did not view concessions as of any importance to the foreign investors.

Since tax and other concessions had been commented upon by the interviewees, and have policy implication they merit further comment.

GOVERNMENT CONCESSIONS AND BRITISH INVESTMENT

The tax relief offered in Malaysia has, according to the many firms interviewed, no real merit as a special investment attraction, since all other countries in South-East Asia have almost identical investment incentives.[31] At best, tax concessions were considered an additional attraction only after the initial decision to invest had been made. The firms did not find the structure of company taxation in the country unduly burdensome and as a matter of principle they did not regard paying company taxation as objectionable. Whatever gains a company gets out of the tax relief arrangement benefits the U.K. Inland Revenue. This arose because since 1965 the British corporation tax system under which overseas companies operate instructs companies to pay to the U.K. Inland Revenue Authorities the difference between the amounts of tax paid abroad and that which under British tax would have to be paid in Britain.[32] Thus whatever tax benefit the host country conferred on the investing company went to the British government, in which case the investing company did not gain directly from Malaysian tax concessions, and the Malaysian Inland Revenue seemed to be the real loser.[33]

One does not actually know whether in general tax concessions given to foreign investors other than British companies had the same net effects. If the tax concessions have had a similar effect, then from the point of policy making, a case can be made for scaling down the tax relief system offered to foreign investors.

Companies interviewed believed that of all the tax concessions given by the government, the Investment Tax Credit scheme was the most attractive. In substance the scheme was an allowance in respect of capital expenditure incurred, calculated at a rate individually decided by the Minister of Finance of not less than 25 per cent.[34] Whereas a company which did not expect to become profitable for the initial years of its operation would get little benefit from the tax relief mentioned earlier, it might find the proviso of the carry-forward of operating loss proviso of the Tax Credit scheme attractive.[35] In effect the scheme represented a partial tax relief.[36]

In both the tax relief and the tax credit schemes the keynote of their operations was the removal of income tax liabilities that would otherwise accrue. Exemption from income tax was of less importance to companies partly because in the formative years it was likely that they had operating losses. As far as those companies consulted were concerned, the tax concessions were merely considered as a signalling mechanism to show that the country welcomed the foreign investor. As an instrument for attracting investors, it would appear that the tax concessions were an inefficient, non-selective, and costly device.

The reactions of the British investor to other concessions such as government patronage of locally-manufactured products, and export incentives as embodied in the Incentive Act were varied, though companies welcomed any measure that attempted to increase their profits.

Government patronage was considered beneficial, but some interviewees felt that they should not rely on the government alone. To the majority of the companies government custom had not been significant, though to others, because of the nature of their products, the government was a major customer.

Of the major export incentives, the concession in the form of deductions[37] from taxable profits in respect of expenses incurred for the promotion of exports seemed very attractive. The deduction represented to the companies as additional expense deductions over and above those already provided for under the *Income Tax Act, 1967*. The net effect was double deduction of expense, which in turn had the effect of subsidizing the export promotion activities of the companies. Such subsidizing effects represented additional benefits to those firms which had international marketing networks.

The accelerated depreciation allowances prescribed in the Incentive Act 1968 were useful, but as far as the British companies were concerned the scheme was not new.[38]

Essentially the accelerated depreciation allowances had the effect of allowing more than 90 per cent of capital expenditure of companies benefiting from the scheme to be written off in five years.[39] This compared favourably with the normal depreciation allowances which permit capital expenditure to be written off in about twenty years. To the companies having such an incentive, the accelerated depreciation allowed them to postpone some tax liabilities into the future. They therefore benefited from the compound interest on the postponement. The net consequences were twofold: firstly, the liquid resources of these companies were increased, and secondly, the riskiness of their investments was reduced. On both counts, the profitability of the companies was enhanced. From the host government's point of view, taxation was not entirely forgone; it was merely postponed to a future date when the incentive was removed and when the companies concerned had assumed a normal trading position. There is therefore much to be said for the accelerated depreciation allowance as a less wasteful form of investment incentive.

The other major export incentive was the export allowance scheme which in principle worked in the same manner as the deductions allowed in respect of the expenses incurred for export promotion mentioned earlier.[40] Companies found the scheme attractive, except for the rigid and complicated strictures governing the granting of it.

In general, companies found concessions useful in contributing towards their profits. They preferred receiving incentives that had the net effect of subsidizing their operations to those that merely granted them tax concessions. The former permitted them to increase their liquidity. The latter, under the prevailing U.K. tax structure, had the tendency of ultimately channelling whatever gains derived from the tax concessions to the British Inland Revenue. The policy implication is obvious. It would be sensible to concentrate on those investment incentives that give benefits to the foreign investor and which incur least cost to the government.

SOME POSSIBLE DETERRENTS TO INVESTMENT

British investors look with some trepidation at some of the measures adopted by the government in its bid to carry out the so-called 'strategy for restructuring' the economy[41] envisaged in the economic plans. There were extensive comments on three specific issues which may be construed as departures from the policy of government non-interference in the private sector: (a) competition from PERNAS, the National Corporation, (b) government request to employ more Malays, and (c) government insistence on more Malay equity participation. Although these departures are a recent (since 1971) phenomenon, the feeling exists among many companies that such deviations of policy may inhibit future investment in the private sector. Even so, company representatives did not completely disagree with the underlying motives of the government in making such incursions into the private sector.

Table 3.5 outlines the general views of the companies on some of the deterrents to private foreign investment.

The first issue widely commented upon was the establishment of PERNAS, the National Corporation, in 1969.[42] Sime Darby Holdings Ltd. was quick to come to terms with PERNAS by forming a joint-venture trading and distributing firm, Pernas-Sime Darby Sendirian Berhad, in 1971.[43] Many companies with substantial government contracts were afraid that the government would instead place its orders with PERNAS or its affiliates. Established British companies which manufactured tyres and rubber products were angered by the establishment of the PERNAS joint-venture company, Goodyear Malaysia Berhad, involving a company new to Malaysia, to manufacture tyres and rubber products.

Similarly the establishment of other PERNAS concerns such as Pernas-Plessey Electronics Berhad and others caused concern among the better established British companies in the country. Other plans of PERNAS to enter into the mining, hotel, oil exploration, and manufacturing industries were mentioned as examples of government-sponsored encroachments into fields which companies felt should be left to private enterprise.

British companies feared that PERNAS, being government-sponsored, might be given unfair advantage over existing foreign companies of long standing. Although unable to give specific evidence of favouritism shown to PERNAS, they were worried that PERNAS or its affiliates might eventually destroy the competitiveness of the Malaysian market. Hence, 72 per cent of company representatives regarded state competition through PERNAS as an important deterrent, while 27 per cent thought it was of moderate importance. A small percentage, 5.8 per cent of interviewees, considered state competition through PERNAS unimportant because they were confident of their efficiency and they were independent of government patronage. Moreover, they believed PERNAS, like other commercial undertakings organized by the state, would make slow progress and have little impact on the private sector.

The second issue viewed with trepidation by about 70 per cent of the company representatives was the government request to foreign companies to employ more Malays. While all firms agreed with the previous Malaysian government policy of 'polite persua-

TABLE 3.5
THE VIEWS OF COMPANIES ON SOME DETERRENTS TO PRIVATE FOREIGN INVESTMENT
(by per cent)

Factors	*Regarded as being* 'Important'	'Moderately Important'	'Not Important'	
State competition through PERNAS, the National Corporation	72.3	26.7	5.8	(N=103)
Government insistence on having more Malay people employed by the private sector	69.9	18.4	11.7	(N=103)
Government insistence on having Malay equity participation in manufacturing	67.9	26.2	5.8	(N=103)
Relative smallness of the local market	67.1	12.6	20.4	(N=103)
Slowness of government bureaucracy	58.2	30.1	11.7	(N=103)
Government 'Malaysianization' policy	57.2	39.6	3.3	(N= 91)
Unnecesary government interference in the private sector	6.2	57.8	35.9	(N= 64)
Competition from too many investors in the same product/industry	5.3	48.4	48.4	(N= 95)
High cost of labour relative to level in other countries in the region	16.3	32.7	51.0	(N= 49)
Degree of corruption within the government departments	—	28.6	1.4	(N= 98)

Source: As in Table 3.4.
Note: Percentages are rounded off.

sion', many would resent a government directive on this issue. So far, no government directive has been issued on the question of employment of Malays.[44]

In practice British firms tended to employ more non-Malays, particularly Chinese. Also many clients of British firms were smaller Chinese-owned firms, and many products of British companies, e.g. machine parts, steel products, building materials, chemicals, and other semi-processed industrial materials, were inputs for Chinese-owned factories. It would thus seem sensible, from the British companies' point of view, to employ Chinese to sell manufactured products to other Chinese. Since industries were located in the urban areas where the majority of the population were Chinese, it seemed natural that more Chinese than Malays would be employed in industry.

To 18.4 per cent of the companies, the question of Malay employment in British companies was regarded as a deterrent of moderate importance. As and when a larger number of Malays became qualified, this group of companies believed that there could be no reason why Malays could not be employed at the executive level in industries. The 11.7 per cent of the company informants who did not regard the question as an important deterrent said that they already had in their Malaysian subsidiaries a number of Malays at the executive and technical levels.

The third main issue extensively commented upon related to the previous issue: the matter of government's insistence on having Malay equity participation in manufacturing. Companies believed it was inappropriate for them in principle to discriminate the share allotments of their equities on a racial criterion. Most of the large British companies were publicly owned with shares quoted on the local stock exchange. There was nothing to prevent anyone from acquiring shares in these companies in the local stock market. The real reason why not many Malays, compared to other races,[45] owned shares in British companies, was that few Malays could afford to buy them.

It seemed apparent that the government's insistence on Malay equity participation was an ill-conceived policy. Some Malays, according to the interviewees, were not bona fide providers of the funds for company shares applications.[46] Hence in certain cases even where there were share allotments to Malays it was not at all certain that the Malays would be the beneficiary of such special allotments. It would appear that the stipulation in the *Second Malaysia Plan, 1971–75* that 30 per cent of all industrial and commercial equities should be in the hands of the Malay population[47] was not wise because companies viewed it as a deterrent to the foreign investor,[48] and an unnecessary interference in the workings of the free market.

The relative smallness of the local market was regarded as either an important or a moderately important deterrent to foreign investment by the majority of the informants. The local market was considered not large enough to allow full advantage to be taken of economies of scale or major technological innovation, and thus companies found limited scope to further reinvestments. About 20 per cent of the representatives did not think the market an important deterrent because the nature of their products allowed them to scale their production capacities according to market requirements. Even though the market was thought to be a deterrent by the companies, they nevertheless found that it was a growing one. The influx of new companies, mainly non-British, in the early 1970s provided some indication that the local market had not deterred other manufacturers from coming into the country to set up production facilities.[49]

Companies' representatives found that a wide gap existed between what the official investment promotion literature promised and what happened in practice. This they believed was largely due to the slowness of the government bureaucracy—a factor considered by about 88 per cent of the informants to be important or moderately important in deterring investors.

On the other hand, several company representatives who personally knew many top government officials were less critical of the slowness of the government machinery. They found that government departments were no slower than those in other underdeveloped countries where they had investments. It would seem that the 'old-boy network' cultivated between British executives and Malaysian civil servants was one reason why British investors have been able to get on well in the country. From the point of view of national economic development it is certainly not in the interest of Malaysia if foreign investment depends not on what the investor can offer but on whom he happened to know in the country.

Very few firms found the government Malaysianization policy unreasonable. However, 57.2 per cent of the interviewees regarded it as an important deterrent, and 39.6 per cent regarded it as a moderately important deterrent to foreign investment. Only 3.3 per cent of representatives regarded the issue as unimportant in deterring foreign investment. Invariably the foreign investors preferred to have their own nationals occupying senior jobs in their overseas organization.

High labour costs, relative to those in other countries in the region, were according to some respondents (49 per cent, or twenty-four companies as indicated in Table 3.5) either an important or moderately important deterrent to private foreign investment. To 51 per cent the question of labour costs was not regarded as an important deterrent to investment. In the 1960s many Malaysian skilled workers, e.g. fitters, turners, electricians, welders, and mechanics, who were relatively more expensive to employ compared to similar workers in Thailand, Taiwan, or Indonesia, emigrated to Singapore where wages were even higher than in Malaysia. The net result was a general shortage of skilled workers which in turn tended to raise wages for skilled workers in the country. The situation incurred firms' costs in training new entrants to the field, and in many cases expatriate technicians had to be brought into the country not only to run the plants, but also to train local workers.[50]

THE MANUFACTURING SECTOR

In spite of the higher national income of Malaysia in relation to the developing ECAFE (now ESCAP) countries, her manufacturing activities have been relatively smaller than those prevailing in most neighbouring countries. (See Table 3.6.)

The need for structural changes in the economy by greater development in the manufacturing sector[51] was realized, based on a number of considerations. Firstly, there was little prospect of increasing the export proceeds from the primary sector owing to the expected decline in the price of natural rubber, and the apparent uncertain prospects of increased income from palm oil, tin, and iron ore in spite of increases in the volumes exported. It was argued that import substitution was an essential part of growth strategy in the economic plan[52] and the best prospects for import substitution were to be found in the industrial sector.[53]

Secondly, the relatively high rate of unemployment among the younger age groups in the large towns[54] and the generally high level of unemployment in the country, conservatively estimated at around 6–8 per cent of the total labour force,[55] emphasized the need for additional employment opportunities which might be found in industries.[56] Thirdly, the growth of manufacturing was considered a means of long-run diversification in the economy, decreasing the dependence on a few primary export commodities.[57] Fourthly, it was recognized that the attainment of the long-range investment and growth targets would mean increased import requirements of capital goods and intermediate industrial materials. To avoid a foreign exchange gap, it seemed necessary to undertake the local manufacture of certain final consumer goods which had previously been imported. Fifthly, industry was ex-

TABLE 3.6

SELECTED ECAFE COUNTRIES: SECTORAL ORIGIN OF GROSS DOMESTIC PRODUCT AND PER CAPITA GNP

Country and Year	*Agriculture, Forestry and Fishing*	*Mining, Quarrying*	*Manufacturing*	*Construction*	*Electricity, Water, Sanitation*	*Transport and Communications*	*Wholesale and Retail Trade*	*Others@*	*Per Capita GNP (1967) in US$*
				(as % of GNP)					
Malaysia									
1955	46.5	5.5	5.3	+	4.0	+	9.6	29.2)	
1960	37.8	5.9	8.7	3.0	1.3	3.6	15.5	24.1)	314
1968	32.3	8.4	12.3	4.0	2.5	4.0	14.2	22.4)	
Philippines									
1950	39.4	0.8	12.3	6.6	0.6	3.0	13.0	24.4)	
1960	31.5	1.1	18.6	3.4	0.9	4.0	15.0	28.0)	278
1968	35.4	1.7	17.4	3.3	0.6	3.5	10.6	27.5)	
Thailand									
1951	50.1	1.9	10.3	2.9	0.1	3.1	18.0	13.6)	
1960	39.8	1.0	12.5	4.6	0.4	7.5	15.1	19.1)	155
1968	31.5	1.8	15.0	7.0	1.1	6.2	17.3	20.2)	
Taiwan									
1951	34.6	1.3	13.5	4.1	1.3	4.6	13.8	27.0)	
1960	31.4	2.3	17.3	4.2	1.8	5.0	14.2	24.4)	274
1968	23.0	1.7	22.8	4.7	2.1	6.2	13.4	25.4)	
Indonesia									
1958	52.5	0.8	13.1	2.1	. . .	3.8	10.6	16.5)	
1960	53.9	3.7	8.4	2.0	. . .	3.7	14.3	13.7)	104
1968	51.7	3.8	8.9	2.1	. . .	2.0	17.9	13.6)	

Source: Compiled from data in various issues of the *U.N. Economic Bulletin for Asia and the Far East.*

Note: @ Banking, Insurance, Real Estate, Dwellings, Public Administration, and Services.

\+ Not available separately, but included in another sector.

. . . Negligible.

pected to contribute to the growth of output, the expansion of exports, and increase of employment,[58] and finally it seemed probable that by the mid-1980s certain natural resources in the nature of underdeveloped land and forest reserves, would have been largely exploited. A case can be made for establishing a sound industrial base well in advance of this likely decline in the range of opportunities for profitable investments in the primary sector. The country's planners also hoped to rectify the regional lop-sided development in the country by persuading industrialists to set up manufacturing in the less developed areas of the country.[59]

TRENDS IN THE MANUFACTURING SECTOR

The industrial sector exhibits diverse characteristics in the degree of specialization, division of labour, and technology of the manufacturing establishments. This diversity is evident from the simple family concern of 'batik' manufacturing in Kelantan, or the backyard 'soy-sauce' factory in Pudu or Puchong, to the sophisticated manufacture of road tankers and electromagnetic ore separators from copper, steel, and alloys at Harper Gilfillan's engineering works near Kuala Lumpur. A certain amount of 'dualism' exists in the manufacturing sector where the indigenous manufacturers tend to be found in the technologically simple manufacturing branches, and foreign-owned concerns in the sophisticated and capital-intensive industries.

The planners have classified Malaysian manufacturing into three categories:[60] (a) the processing of agricultural products in factories off-estates, e.g. rubber milling, latex processing, copra and palm oil milling, and tea processing; (b) the manufacture of consumer and intermediate goods with the use of local and imported raw materials, e.g. the processing and manufacture of food, beverage, and tobacco products, textiles, footwear, furniture and fixtures, paper and paper products, printing, publishing and allied activities, leather and leather products, rubber products, chemicals and chemical products, petroleum products, and non-metallic mineral products; and (c) overlapping with (b) above, are those industries which produce capital goods, as well as intermediate and consumer goods.

In the 1960s industries with the highest value added were the industries processing food, rubber, wood, and chemical products utilizing the products of the country's most important primary activities, namely agriculture, fishing, forestry, and mining. Manufacturing activities with the smallest value added were leather, textile, footwear, and paper and paper products. The low level development of these activities seemed to have been in part due to the scarcity of local supplies of the requisite raw materials, and in part due to the unprotected nature of the local market *vis-à-vis* other cheaper sources of goods such as India and Hong Kong. Manufacturing activities that contributed a medium amount to value added were tobacco manufacturing, non-metallic mineral product manufacturing, and the manufacture of metal products, machinery, and transport equipment. Most manufacturing activities were the result of the backward and forward linkages[61] of the dominant primary industry. There was also an element of natural protection as in the case of products (e.g. cement and beer) with high bulk-value ratios, and those products that may be regarded as 'perishables', such as certain types of food and newspapers, which therefore must be manufactured locally. In other industries such as tobacco and tobacco products, local manufacturing activities were aided by protective tariffs. The dominant factor encouraging the development of industry has been the growth of the domestic market brought about by the growth of per capita income,[62] though more recently, the growth of the export market has provided increasing impetus.

Table 3.7 summarizes the industrial trends in the 1960s. The largest contributors to manufacturing growth were the manufacture of chemicals and petroleum products (17.2 per cent), food (16.6 per cent), wood products (10 per cent), and non-metallic mineral products (7.6 per cent). Processing of agricultural products off-estates, processing of rubber, and manufacture of tobacco products each contributed to about 6 per cent of sectoral growth of manufactures from 1963 to 1968.

Employment grew fastest in those manufacturing activities which expanded rapidly between 1963 and 1968. For example, employment growth was 34.7 per cent in the basic metal industries where value added expanded by 42.6 per cent. Similarly employment growths were 28.5 per cent, 26.5 per cent, and 17.6 per cent respectively in the industries manufacturing electrical machinery, textiles, and transport equipment.

On the other hand, employment grew least in those industries where value added increased least; e.g. furniture making and processing of agricultural products off-estates with respective increases of 5.2 per cent and 9.4 per cent, and had respectively 3.1 and 2.8 per cents growths of employment. Manufacturing of beverages and tobacco which expanded at moderately high rates of

TABLE 3.7

WEST MALAYSIA, VALUE ADDED AND EMPLOYMENT IN MANUFACTURING, 1963–1968

Industry and Code	*Value Added in $ mil. Current Price*				*Employment ('000)*		
	1963	*1968*	*Growth: 1963–8 (%)*	*Contribution to Growth (%)*	*1963*	*1968*	*Average Annual Growth (%)*
Off-estates processing	49	77	9.4	6.2	9.4	10.7	2.8
30. Food	65	140	16.7	16.6	13.8	18.9	6.5
31. Beverage	13	36	22.6	5.1	2.2	2.3	0.1
32. Tobacco	28	57	15.1	6.3	3.9	4.1	0.1
33. Textiles	4	20	43.9	3.4	1.4	5.1	26.5
34. Footwear	4	8	14.0	0.8	1.2	3.5	23.9
35. Wood products	49	94	13.9	10.0	12.0	19.5	10.2
36. Furniture	8	10	5.2	5.2	0.5	2.4	3.1
37. Paper	3	6	14.9	0.7	0.6	1.4	18.4
38. Printing	29	53	12.4	5.1	6.9	9.6	6.8
39. Leather	1	1	—	—	0.2	0.3	8.4
40. Rubber products	23	51	17.2	6.2	6.7	8.4	4.6
41. Chemicals) 42. Petroleum)	42	120	23.4	17.2	4.1	6.1	8.3
43. Non-metallic mineral products	28	62	17.5	7.6	5.0	7.2	12.7
44. Basic metals	4	21	42.6	3.9	0.7	3.1	34.7
45. Metal products	23	39	11.4	3.6	5.4	8.0	9.3
46. Machinery	15	25	11.4	2.3	4.1	6.0	7.9
47. Electrical machinery	5	21	34.6	3.5	0.6	2.1	28.5
48. Transport equipment	6	19	25.5	2.8	1.6	3.6	17.6
49. Miscellaneous	23	14	10.7	–2.0	1.7	2.8	10.5
Total	420	824	15.5	100.0	84.2	125.5	8.3

Source: *Census of Manufacturing Industries*, 1963 and 1968.

value added (22.6 per cent and 15.1 per cent), each accounted for only 0.1 per cent of the increase in manufacturing employment. This is explained by the comparatively capital intensive nature of these two types of manufacturing in the country.

In the 1963–8 period manufacturing output in aggregate grew at 15.5 per cent, while manufacturing employment grew at 8.3 per cent. According to official calculation, manufacturing value added rose at 9.9 per cent annually during 1960–5, and at 10.4 per cent during 1966–70.[63] Exports of manufactured goods, though small, grew steadily at an average of 14.2 per cent annually in the 1960s.[64]

As summarized in Table 3.8 below, compared to the primary sector, the manufacturing sector was a major growth leader, with its growth rate of about twice that of the GDP for the decade preceding 1970, and in the early 1970s the manufacturing sector is a growth leader in the economy.[65]

Manufacturing activities that expanded in the early 1970s were textile and clothing, footwear, wood products (sawn timber, plywood, and veneer) chemical products (mainly plastics), non-metallic mineral products (mainly cement), basic metal industries, and electrical machinery and appliances (particularly electronic goods).[66] Compared to these, the manufacture of food, beverage, and tobacco products were less significant in terms of growth. Employment in the manufacturing sector during the 1970–3 period grew at an average rate of 9.5 per cent per annum,[67] which was 2.5 per cent higher than the 7 per cent growth rate envisaged in the Second Malaysia Plan. At the same time, exports of manufactured products grew at nearly double the rate of increase in total exports of 10 per cent per annum from 1970 to 1973.[68]

TABLE 3.8
MALAYSIA, GROWTH RATES OF OUTPUT IN THE VARIOUS SECTORS OF THE ECONOMY
(per cent per annum)

Sector	*1960–1970*	*1967–1972*	*1971–1973*
1. Agriculture (including rubber replanting)	1.5	3.0)	10.2
2. Forestry and fishing	8.3	6.7)	
3. Mining and quarrying	6.2	4.8	7.1
4. Manufacturing	11.4	11.9	16.1
5. Construction	6.9	6.5	16.1
6. Electricity and water	12.1	7.7	10.5
7. Other services	6.1	6.0	12.4
Gross domestic product (at factor cost)	5.5	6.1	8.9

Source: *Economic Report*, Kuala Lumpur, The Treasury, December 1972, pp. 58–9, and *Mid-Term Review of the Second Malaysia Plan, 1971–1975*, p. 40.

TABLE 3.9
ESTIMATED VALUES OF IMPORTED AND LOCALLY MANUFACTURED GOODS, 1961–1971

	Amounts in $ million at current prices									
	1961	(%)	*1963*	(%)	*1966*	(%)	*1970*	(%)	*1971*	(%)
Semi-manufactured goods	473)		546)		605)		771)		768)	
Machinery and equipment	458)	*71.7*	613)	*71.7*	800)	*67.2*	1,197)	*61.6*	1,344)	*61.1*
Miscellaneous manufactures	161)		187)		189)		204)		198)	
Locally manufactured goods	444	*28.3*	547	*28.3*	779	*32.8*	1,354	*38.4*	1,471	*38.9*
Total	1,536	(*100*)	1,893	(*100*)	2,376	(*100*)	3,546	(*100*)	3,781	(*100*)

Source: Calculated from data in Department of Statistics, *Monthly Bulletin of External Trade*, Kuala Lumpur (various issues); and *Annual Bulletin of Statistics*, Kuala Lumpur (various years).

The manufacturing that developed in the 1960s was a mixture of import-substituting industries and those that catered for both domestic and export markets.[69] As a proportion of the total domestic market of manufactured goods, the manufacturing output of the industrial sector has increased over the years. Table 3.9 shows that more than 70 per cent of the aggregate domestic demand for manufactures was met by imports in the early 1960s.

In 1970, more than 60 per cent of the domestic market for manufactures was supplied by imports. The scope for expanding local manufacturing was great, since the existing local manufacturing supplied only about 39 per cent of the estimated demand for manufactures.

The trends in the manufacturing sector in the late 1960s and the early 1970s can be summarized as in Table 3.10.

On the evidence of growth in industrial output, employment, and exports, the manufacturing sector which mainly began in the early 1960s expanded at considerable annual rates. The planners anticipated that Malaysia would join the league of 'semi-industrialized' countries in the 1980s.[70]

SIZE OF MANUFACTURING ESTABLISHMENTS

In terms of employment the average size of manufacturing establishments in the country was (and still is) quite small. In the

TABLE 3.10

MANUFACTURING OUTPUT, EMPLOYMENT AND EXPORTS IN MALAYSIA

Year	*Value Added ($ million at current prices)*	*Employment ('000)*	*Gross Value of Manufactured Exports ($ million at current prices)*
1965	682	217	282
1968	941	246	362
1970	1,354	318	924
1973	2,116	418	1,550
1975*	2,660	479	1,708
Average Annual Growth Rate (%):			
1966–1970	10.4	4.5	12.8
1971–1973	12.5	9.5	18.8
1974–1975*	12.1	7.0	5.0

Source: *Second Malaysia Plan, 1971–1975,* p. 148, and *passim*; and *Mid-Term Review of the Second Malaysia Plan, 1971–1975,* Chapter VIII.

Note: * Revised target of the Second Malaysia Plan.

1960s, the average number of full-time employment was about ten workers per establishment. In 1963 for instance (see Table 3.11), industrial establishments employing ten full-time workers each accounted for 82 per cent of total manufacturing establishments. However, they contributed only about 14 per cent of total manufacturing output. On the other hand, establishments employing between eleven and 199 workers each accounted for about 18 per cent of total establishments, but they contributed just over 60 per cent of sales and nearly 62 per cent of value added. In the same year, industrial establishments with over 200 workers each constituted 0.5 per cent of the total number of establishments, although they contributed to 27.4 per cent sale and 24.2 per cent manufacturing value added. The situation in 1968 was not radically altered.

Seventy-eight point two per cent of industrial establishments which employed ten or fewer workers contributed 8.3 per cent of sales, and 7.9 per cent of industrial value added. Those establishments employing eleven to 999 workers each accounted for 20.7 per cent of the total number of establishments, 56.4 per cent of sales, and 53 per cent value added in the same year. The firms

TABLE 3.11

WEST MALAYSIA, SIZE GROUPS OF INDUSTRIAL ESTABLISHMENTS BY EMPLOYMENT, TURNOVER, AND VALUE ADDED, 1963 AND 1968

Year	*Distribution of*	*Employment Size Group (Full-time Employees)*			
		1–10	*11–199*	*Over 200*	*Total*
1963	No. of establishments	7,328	1,578	40	8,856
	(per cent)	(81.7)	(17.8)	(0.5)	(100)
	Gross value of sales ($ mil.)	207	1,020	462	1,689
	(per cent)	(12.3)	(60.3)	(27.4)	(100)
	Value added ($ mil.)	59	259	102	420
	(per cent)	(14.1)	(61.7)	(24.2)	(100)
1968	No. of establishments	7,041	1,873	97	9,011
	(per cent)	(78.2)	(20.7)	(1.1)	(100)
	Gross value of sales ($ mil.)	256	1,738	1,085	3,079
	(per cent)	(8.3)	(56.4)	(35.3)	(100)
	Value added ($ mil.)	69	463	342	874
	(per cent)	(7.9)	(53.0)	(39.1)	(100)

Source: *Census of Manufacturing Industries in the States of Malaya, 1963*, and *Census of Manufacturing Industries, West Malaysia, 1968.*

TABLE 3.12

WEST MALAYSIA, NUMBER OF INDUSTRIAL ESTABLISHMENTS BY SALES SIZE GROUP, VALUE ADDED AND GROSS SALES, 1963 AND 1968

Year	*Distribution of*	*Gross Sales Size Group*			
		Below $999	*$100,000– $999,999*	*Over $ 1 mil.*	*Total*
1963	No. of establishments	7,202	1,384	270	8,856
	(per cent)	(81.4)	(15.6)	(3.0)	(100)
	Value added ($ mil.)	55.6	129.7	235.0	420.3
	(per cent)	(13.3)	(30.8)	(55.9)	(100)
	Gross sales ($ mil.)	77.2	457.7	1,154.5	1,689.4
	(per cent)	(8.3)	(23.4)	(68.3)	(100)
1968	No. of establishments	6,839	1,722	452	9,013
	(per cent)	(75.9)	(19.1)	(5.0)	(100)
	Value added ($ mil.)	50.2	180.2	634.4	873.8
	(per cent)	(6.1)	(20.2)	(73.7)	(100)
	Gross sales ($ mil.)	140.4	541.1	(2,397)	3,087.5
	(per cent)	(4.6)	(17.6)	(17.8)	(100)

Source: As for Table 3.11.

employing over 200 workers constituted 1.1 per cent of total establishments, 35.3 per cent sales, and 39.1 per cent value added in manufacturing in 1968. Clearly, manufacturing establishments in the country were predominantly small, with a few large ones dominating the industrial scene. Table 3.11 shows that large establishments with over $1 million sales, though few in number, accounted for large proportions of value added, 55.9 per cent and 73.7 per cent respectively, and large proportions of sales, 68.3 per cent and 77.8 per cent for 1963 and 1968 respectively.

Small establishments each with sales below $100,000, though numerous, accounted for 13.3 per cent and 6.1 per cent value added of industry, while also accounting for 8.3 per cent and 4.6 per cent of sales in the two respective years of 1963 and 1968. Medium-sized establishments with sales between $100,000 and $999,999 each constituted 15.6 per cent of the total number of establishments in 1963, and 19.1 per cent in 1968. In terms of value added the group was responsible for 30.8 per cent and 20.2 per cent respectively in 1963 and 1968. In the same two years, the group contributed to 23.4 per cent and 17.6 per cent of gross manufacturing sales.

The general picture of the Malaysian manufacturing scene is that the majority of the firms were small in terms of the number of people employed.

1. Among others see, for example, The U.S. Department of Commerce, *Factors Limiting U.S. Investment Abroad*, Washington, D.C., 1953; H. J. Robinson, *The Motivaion and Flow of Private Foreign Investment*, Stanford Research Institute, Menlo Park, 1961; R. S. May, 'Direct Investment in Less Developed Countries . . .', *Journal of Development Studies*, April 1968, especially pp. 420–2; R. B. Stobaugh, Jr., 'How to Analyse Foreign Investment Climate', *Harvard Business Review*, September–October 1969, pp. 100–8; and C. P. Kindleberger, 'Restrictions on Direct Investment in Host Countries', in J. Bhagawati and R. Eckaus, eds., *Development and Planning: Essays in Honour of Paul Rosentein-Rodan*, George Allen and Unwin, 1972, pp. 201–9.

2. *Overseas Economic Survey, 1952*, HMSO, pp. 86–7.

3. *First Malaysia Plan, 1966–70*, p. 131.

4. FIDA, *Malaysia: Your Profit Centre in Asia*, 1970, p. 20.

5. This statement was largely true until the recent announcement about the need to direct the movements of the private foreign investor in the country; see *Malaysia Industrial Digest*, Vol. 7(1), First Quarter, 1974.

6. *First Malaysia Plan, 1966–70*, pp. 129–36, and *Second Malaysia Plan, 1971–75*, pp. 147–62.

7. According to informants interviewed during field work, the foreign ownership of commercial fixed assets, when the companies not covered by the official survey are taken into consideration, constitute about 60–65 per cent of the total value in 1970.

8. See *First Malaysia Plan, 1966–70*, p. 131, and *passim*.

9. The Partai Sosialis Rakyat Malaysia and the Democratic Action Party are opposed to private, particularly foreign investment. See also Mr. Fan Yew Teng, letter to

the editor, *The Times*, 22 September 1973. Among others who have expressed concern over foreign capital are Wheelwright, Puthucheary, Kanapathy, and Hirschman; see Bibliography.

10. See among others H. F. Bell, 'Attitudes to Overseas Investment', *Australian Quarterly*, Vol. 32(3), September 1960, pp. 49–57; The Task Force Report, *Foreign Ownership and the Structure of Canadian Industry*, Ottawa, Privy Council Office, 1968; and N. *Guide*, and U.S. Department of Commerce, *Overseas Business Report (71-0044)*, Washington, D.C., October 1971.

11. FIDA, *Malaysia: Your Profit Centre In Asia*, 1970, p. 16.

12. The Chartered Bank, *Malaysia, A Business Guide*, Kuala Lumpur, Chartered Bank Berhad, 1971, p. 27.

13. See Allen and Donnithorne, *Western Enterprise in Indonesia and Malaya*, pp. 50–1, Chapter XV, and *passim*.

14. *First Malaysia Plan, 1966–70*, p. 9.

15. See evidence in *Industrial Digest*, Vol. 2(2), Fourth Quarter, 1969; P. J. Drake, 'The New-Issue Boom in Malaya and Singapore, 1961–64', *Economic Development and Cultural Change*, Vol. 18, 1970, pp. 73–91; The Chartered Bank, *Malaysia: A Business Guide*, and U.S. Department of Commerce, *Overseas Business Report (71-0044)*, Washington, D.C., October 1971.

16. FIDA, *Malaysia: Your Profit Centre in Asia*, p. 18.

17. With the approval of the Minister, a company may be given pioneer status which entitles it, among other things, to a tax holiday with a maximum of ten years, provided it fulfils the requirements laid down in the *Investment Incentives Act* (Part II, Chapter I, Clauses 3 to 12). Basically it must bring in at least $1 million capital; produce priority products (defined in the Act, Clause 3 a–c); be located in a development area, and make use of locally available raw materials. The minimum tax holiday period is four years.

18. See C. T. Edwards, *Public Finance in Malaya and Singapore*, and J. H. Power in B. Balassa, *et al.*, *The Structure of Protection in Developing Countries*.

19. *Mid-Term Review of the First Malaysia Plan, 1966–70*, pp. 76–8.

20. ibid.

21. Two of the areas designated as FTZ are located at Bayan Lepas Airport in Penang, and at a place near Kuala Lumpur International Airport. One is located at Tanjung Keling, Malacca.

22. *Second Malaysia Plan, 1971–75*, p. 162.

23. Local partners can be foreigners resident in the country.

24. This is part of the Malaysianization scheme. See report in *The Straits Times*, 17 May 1972.

25. In this connexion, at the time of writing, the government was formulating the introduction of an export insurance scheme under the proposed Malaysian Export Credit Insurance Corporation (MECIC). The scheme was eventually formed in October 1978. It is called Malaysian Export Credit Insurance Berhad (MECIB).

26. See Edwards, op. cit., and S. A. Lee, 'Fiscal Policy and Political Transitions: the Case of Malaya, 1948–60', *Journal of Southeast Asian Studies*, Vol. 5(1), March 1974, pp. 102–14. By and large, the article although statistically referring to the pre-1960 period is applicable to the decade following 1960 as well. See also Bank Negara, *Quarterly Economic Bulletin*, Vol. 6(1), March 1973, pp. 41–3.

27. See Chapter 9 below.

28. Export earnings grew at an annual rate of 6.3 per cent in the period 1966–70, and 10 per cent in the period 1970–3.

29. *Mid-Term Review of the Second Malaysia Plan*, p. 44.

30. Although economic growth has been questioned lately by the Club of Rome, see D. H. Meadows, *et al.*, *The Limits to Growth*, Pan Books Ltd., 1972. For counter arguments, see W. Beckerman, *In Defence of Economic Growth*, Jonathan Cape, 1974.

31. For a comparison of Investment Incentives in South-East Asia, see the *Asia Research Bulletin*, September 1973, pp. 2140–2. If it is merely a simple question of tax concession Thailand seems to offer better concessions than Malaysia. See G. A. Marzouk,

A Case Study of Thailand: Economic Development and Policies, Rotterdam University Press, 1972.

32. The British corporation tax introduced in 1965 penalized British companies investing abroad in the sense that the Inland Revenue took away from the companies benefits they derived from tax reliefs obtained in the underdeveloped countries. See analysis in *Overseas Investment—Why and How?*, Confederation of British Industry, October 1967, pp. 26–7, and *passim*. See also J. B. Bracewell-Milnes, 'Overseas Development and British Taxation', in P. H. Ady, ed., *Private Foreign Investment and the Developing World*, Praeger, 1971, pp. 87–139.

33. The amounts involved were not known exactly, but an estimate can be made thus:

(a)	Estimated profits of five British companies enjoying tax relief in 1970	$46 mil.
(b)	40 per cent tax on (a) representing revenue loss of say	$18 mil.
(c)	Income tax revenue collected in the year, approximately	$877 mil.
(d)	Revenue loss, (b) as percentage of (c) for the year	2.1%

Hence, by giving a tax relief of $18.4 million, approximately £2.5 million, the Malaysian Inland Revenue forwent that amount of revenue equivalent to 2.1 per cent of revenue collected in that year. Part of the revenue forgone in Malaysia benefited the U.K. Inland Revenue.

34. Details are given in the *Investment Incentives Act, 1968*, Chapter 3, Clauses 26 (1) to (7).

35. The tax relief scheme also provides a carry-forward arrangement of losses, but it is limited to companies enjoying 'pioneer status' as defined by the Act. The tax credit scheme is open to companies not qualified to be, or by choice preferred not to be, granted 'pioneer status'. To most interviewees whose companies did not enjoy 'pioneer status', the tax credit scheme was therefore the more accessible of the two concessions.

36. For a technical demonstration of the working of the Investment Tax Credit scheme, see M. K. Mathai, 'Incentives for Investment In Malaysia', *Bulletin for International Fiscal Documentation*, Vol. 23 (11), November 1969, p. 509 et seq.

37. For items permissible for deductions see *Investment Incentives Act, 1968*, Part III, Chapter 1, Clause 27. An export credit insurance scheme had been proposed and would be set up in the mid-1970s. See *Mid-Term Review of the Second Malaysia Plan, 1971–75*, p. 143. See footnote 25 above.

38. Accelerated depreciation was first introduced in the U.K. Budget, 1945. See A. R. Prest, 'Taxes, Subsidies and Incentives in Government', in A. T. Peacock and G. Hauser, eds., *Government Finance and Economic Development*, Paris, OECD, 1965, p. 118.

39. This can be illustrated thus: the accelerated depreciation rate allowed is 40 per cent. If a company incurred an expenditure on capital of $100,000 the writing-off of the expenditure would be:

in the first year, 40% of $100,000	–	$40,000
second year, 40% of $ 60,000	–	$24,000
third year, 40% of $ 36,000	–	$14,400
fourth year, 40% of $ 21,600	–	$ 8,640
fifth year, 40% of $ 12,960	–	$ 5,184

giving a total allowance in five years of $92,224, which is effectively 92.2 per cent of the original capital expenditure, written off under the scheme.

40. The deductions for export promotion expenses are quite straightforward. The export allowance is not. It is calculated according to the formula: VE-AV3/GS x 20 cents, where VE = value of export sales in base period, AV3 = average of export sales for three preceding years, and GS = gross sales for base period. For details, see *Investment Incentives Act, 1968*, Chapter 3, Clauses (1) to (6).

41. The Government is concerned about the under-representation of Malay people in the private sector, particularly in commerce and industry, an aspect of the country which has been the subject of concern of politicians like Dr. Mahathir Mohamad, Minister of Education in 1974, and now (1978) Deputy Prime Minister. See M. Mahathir, *The Malay Dilemma*, Singapore, Donald Moore Asia Pacific Press, 1970, Chapter 4. Basically 'the strategy for restructuring' the economy refers to the attempt of the gov-

ernment to increase the participation of the Malay people in the modernization of the economy. See detailed descriptions in the *Second Malaysia Plan, 1971–75,* Chapter III, and the *Mid-Term Review of the Second Malaysia Plan, 1971–75*, pp. 8–17.

42. PERNAS is a limited company which had a capital of about $100 million when it was established in 1969. The capital is provided by the government in the form of loans. In 1970 the company had seven wholly-owned subsidiaries engaged in insurance, construction, property development, trading, engineering, securities, and joint-venture manufacturing activities. By design the company is intended to promote the interests of the indigenous peoples in the various of economic activities. All viable ventures initiated by PERNAS will be turned over to the public at large, with share allocations to the Malay people. See 'Interview with Pernas Chairman', *Malaysian Business*, December 1972, p. 16 et seq.

43. *Straits Times*, 21 June 1972.

44. Until October 1974 when the government issued a request on the racial proportion of industrial employment.

45. In 1969, Malays owned less than 2 per cent of all share capital of publicly quoted companies. Chinese owned 22.8 per cent, and foreigners owned 62.1 per cent of the estimated total $4,678 million share capital of publicly quoted companies in the country. See details in *Second Malaysia Plan, 1971–75*, p. 40, Table 3.1.

46. What happened according to some representatives was that some Malays were used as front-men by non-Malays who provided funds to acquire the share allotments to the Malays. This arrangement, colloquially known as the 'Ali-Baba' deal (the 'Ali' being a Malay and the 'Baba' being a non-Malay, usually a Chinese), led to a situation where, after the share allotment transactions were completed, the Malay would transfer 'his' share to the non-Malay for a small fee. The net effect was that, even if initially it appeared that the Malay had acquired share capital in industry, eventually it was the non-Malay who owned the shares. The 'Ali-Baba' deals have not been fully researched and the extent of the practice, though commonly known to exist, is not known.

47. See details in the *Second Malaysia Plan, 1971–75*, p. 41, *passim.*

48. In practice company representatives believed that the government is quite flexible in the question of Malay equity participation. In the experience of some companies, the policy is not what the members of the government will rigidly impose on the private sector. In this context, the deterring effect of the stipulation of the plan is more apparent than real. It is nevertheless a deterrent in so far that it irritates the private investor who may be led to believe that he is being ordered to do specific acts which he considers discriminatory. Some foreign companies have as a matter of policy the practice of keeping of ownerships of their share capital to themselves. The question of local equity participation then involved a much broader issue than just giving shares to Malays.

49. The newly established firms were American and Japanese companies mainly in the industry manufacturing electrical and electronics components largely for overseas markets. See various issues of the *Malaysia Industrial Digest*, 1970–4, particularly Vol. 5(4), 1972; Vol. 6(1), 1972; Vol. 7(1), 1974; and *Malaysian Digest* (Ministry of Foreign Affairs), 31 March 1974, p. 2.

50. The situation, according to the informants, led to firms either looking elsewhere in the region for their plant location or, as in several cases, to install automated plants.

51. The economic case for industralization is made in the *Rueff Report, 1963*, p. 8, and *passim*; T. R. McHale, *Rubber and the Malayan Economy*, University of Malaya Handbook Series, 1967, pp. 1–8; R. Ma and P. S. You, *The Malayan Economy in Transition*, Singapore, Institute of Management, 1965; and the *First Malaysia Plan, 1966–70*, p. 123, pp. 41–64, and *passim.*

52. *First Malaysia Plan, 1966–70*, p. 44.

53. Loc. cit., pp. 9 and 27.

54. See details in N. S. Choudhry, *Socio-Economic Sample Survey of Household; Employment and Unemployment, Malaysia 1967–68*, Kuala Lumpur, Department of Statistics, 1970.

55. *First Malaysia Plan, 1966–70*, p. 35; and *Second Malaysia Plan, 1971–75*, p. 96. The Minister of Finance estimated unemployment to be about 9 per cent. See *Budget Speech*, 1971.

56. *First Malaysia Plan, 1966–70*, p. 129, and *passim*; and *Second Malaysia Plan, 1971–75*, p. 155.

57. *First Malaysia Plan, 1966–70*, p. 15, and *passim*.

58. *Second Malaysia Plan, 1971–75*, p. 153. Employment under the First Plan period did not expand as fast as the labour force. Consequently there was the need to look for avenues of employment creation in all sectors of the economy, including the industrial sector.

59. *Second Malaysia Plan, 1971–75*, p. 154. The idea is that with regional dispersion of industries, a more balanced geographical development can be achieved so that the modernization process brought along with industrialization will be more widely diffused. The break up of Pakistan into West Pakistan and Bangladesh in 1971 was a lesson on the short-sighted policy of locating all industrial development in one geographical area of the country to the neglect of the other. Malaysian planners are conscious of the sensibility of developing both the West and East Malaysian backward areas.

60. *First Malaysia Plan, 1966–70*, pp. 123–4.

61. The concept of linkages is described in Chapter 9, and more fully dealt in A. O. Hirschman, *The Strategy of Economic Development*, Yale University Press, 1959, Chapter 6.

62. See discussion in S. Y. Lo, *The Development Performance of West Malaysia*, Kuala Lumpur, Heinemann Educational Books, 1972; and D. Lim, *Economic Growth and Development in West Malaysia, 1947–70*, Kuala Lumpur, Oxford University Press, 1973. The growth of industry due to growth of the domestic market is also referred to as the 'final demand' linkage, as distinct from the backward and forward linkages, mentioned earlier, resulting from the technical relationships between input and output of firms.

63. *Second Malaysia Plan, 1971–75*, p. 15.

64. ibid.

65. *Mid-Term Review of the Second Malaysia Plan, 1971–75*, pp. 55 and 142.

66. ibid, p. 142.

67. Loc. cit.

68. ibid, p. 46.

69. See Ridzuan bin Akil, 'Growth, Structural Change, and Employment Creation in Malayan Manufacturing Industries since Independence', unpublished Ph.D. thesis, University of Hull, 1972; Lo, op. cit., and *Economic Report 1972–73*, Kuala Lumpur, The Treasury, 1972.

70. See *Mid-Term Review of the Second Malaysia Plan, 1971–75*, p. 72.

4 How British Firms Evaluate this Climate and their Motivations to Invest

INTRODUCTION

THE purpose of this chapter is threefold: first, to analyse the reasons why British firms have invested in Malaysia and compare evidence arising from this inquiry with existing theories of international capital movements; second, to explain why British investors have chosen Malaysia as a place of operation; and third, to account for the location of manufacturing units within the country.

The methodology involves asking companies to rank ten possible reasons that led them to decide to invest in manufacturing in Malaysia. An analysis of this ranking is given in Table 4.1.

THE MOTIVES FOR INVESTING IN MALAYSIA

While several companies ranked two or more of the motives listed in Table 4.1 as of equal importance, the overwhelming significance of three or four factors is clearly shown. The most important single reason given for the decision to invest was 'to take advantage of markets already established'. Such markets were established by direct export from the U.K., either through the companies' marketing affiliates or through agents resident in Malaysia. About 56 per cent of all respondents regarded taking advantage of their established market as a crucial motive for investing in manufacturing in Malaysia, while 21 per cent mentioned it as an important consideration, and 23 per cent thought it was of some importance. The respondents believed that unless they began local production their markets would be seriously eroded by competitive suppliers from America, Japan, and other European countries.

Thus it would appear that there was a preponderance of motives related to protecting a stake in a market that was built through export trade. This aspect of the motivation suggests, as will be seen in Chapter 5, that British manufacturing interests in the coun-

TABLE 4.1
SUMMARY OF THE MOTIVES OF U.K. COMPANIES FOR INVESTING IN MANUFACTURING FACILITIES IN MALAYSIA
(by per cent)

Motives for Investment	*Motives Ranked as:* *A*	*B*	*C*	*D*	
Market Consideration					
1. To take advantage of market already established	56	21	23	–	N = 103
2. To take advantage of expected growth of market	35	61	3	1	N = 103
3. To gain access to the South-East Asian market	–	8	67	25	N = 101
Cost Consideration					
1. To avoid/reduce freight charges	4	46	39	12	N = 103
2. To take advantage of other lower cost conditions	–	–	51	49	N = 103
Tariffs and Other Incentives Consideration					
1. To overcome expected rise in tariffs	15	49	14	22	N = 103
2. To take advantage of government incentives	–	1	26	73	N = 88
Policy and Other Considerations					
1. To follow company practice of investing in growth areas	–	24	70	7	N = 102
2. To follow an attractive proposal by a local agent	–	14	8	78	N = 98
3. To invest as a matter of policy to diversify the company's investment areas	–	–	19	81	N = 98
Other motives	–	–	100	–	N = 29

Source: Compiled from data gathered at interviews.
Notes: (i) A = Crucial; B = Important; C = Of Some Importance; D = Not Important.
(ii) Some firms ranked two or more motives as of equal importance, while some did not rank some of the factors.
(iii) Percentages may not add to 100 because of rounding off.

try grew out of their earlier trading activities.[1] However, this motivation by itself does not explain why British firms have actually become involved in manufacturing, since the market could have continued to be served by exports from U.K. factories, possibly in conjunction with a local firm to undertake any necessary after-sales service. More than one-third (35 per cent) of the respondents gave as their main reason 'to take advantage of the expected growth of the market'. This factor was also rated as important by 61 per cent of the company representatives. Another

3 per cent regarded it as of some importance, while 1 per cent thought the factor was unimportant.

The desire to gain access to the South-East Asian market was regarded as a very important motivating factor by only 8 per cent of companies interviewed, although 67 per cent thought it of some importance, and one-quarter of the respondents regarded it as unimportant. Of those firms which began manufacturing in Malaysia in order to gain access to the South-East Asian market, about half regarded Malaysia as the base from which they hoped to expand into the neighbouring countries. Many regarded Malaysia as a training ground for their younger executives who eventually would establish their firms' activities in other countries of the region, or would help to man their establishments elsewhere in the developing countries. Why the firms chose Malaysia from among the countries of South-East Asia will be discussed later.

The desire 'to avoid and/or reduce freight charges' was a prime consideration for 4 per cent of respondents, and a further 46 per cent regarded it as important. Some 39 per cent believed it of some importance, while 12 per cent did not believe them to be important at all.

In Malaysia, as in many developing countries, low wages did not necessarily yield low labour costs. Thus, of the firm representatives who were asked to rank their motivation to invest in the country 51 per cent thought 'to take advantage of lower Malaysian cost conditions' an important factor, but not crucial to their investment decision. The remaining 49 per cent regarded it as either a supplementary or an unimportant motivating factor. Although company representatives believed that industrial land, water, electricity, and internal transport service were generally cheaper in the country than elsewhere in the region, this belief did not extend to labour costs. The interviewees found that Malaysia as a whole was very short of managerial and supervisory staff from the foreman level upwards. They found that there was a high labour turnover, with managers and skilled labour moving from one firm to another where they could get better pay.

Since skilled labour was scarce, most companies had to train their own labour forces, unless they could attract people trained by other firms. There were numerous unskilled workmen, but many companies experienced initial problems of poor time-keeping, frequent absenteeism, unwillingness to work overtime near festival days, and general untidiness of work benches. None of the firm representatives, however, made derogatory remarks about the local workers' qualities and there was no suggestion that local employees were indolent, failed to respond to incentives, or were unsuited to working with Western technology, and the general opinion was they were capable of attaining the efficiency levels of their U.K. counterparts.

Company representatives did not consider Malaysia to be a low labour cost area in view of the type of labour that industrial firms employed. The companies interviewed had no special inducement to use labour-intensive production techniques for at least two reasons. First, the machines in use in Malaysia were designed and manufactured in Britain and in use there, where factor costs were quite different from those existing in Malaysia. The type of labour input used in British manufacturing did not necessarily favour the type of unskilled labour which was in relative abundance in Malaysia. Companies found that labour had to be trained to operate British equipment. Second, companies interviewed expressed the belief that automatic machines in their factories had definite advantages. Automatic machines, they claimed, saved on raw materials and generally improved appearance and quality of the products. Primitive techniques were thought to produce primitive products which could not compete in the quite sophisticated Malaysian domestic market. Moreover, representatives thought that firms with the most highly mechanized processes were the ones with the fewest factory problems and the ones most able to survive in the competitive product market.

The skilled labour required by factories was not easily obtainable, and was relatively expensive compared to other Asian countries. This is borne out by data in Table 4.2 which shows the comparative wage levels in selected Asian countries in five selected occupations.

It is clear from the Table that if labour cost was a prime consideration for the foreign investor, countries such as Indonesia, Thailand, the Philippines, and South Vietnam, would be preferable areas of operation. Even semi-skilled workers such as truck drivers in Malaysia earn more than their counterparts in India or Indonesia. Most skilled workers are by Asian standards expensive to hire in Malaysia. As for unskilled labour, other neighbouring countries have lower wages than Malaysia, as indicated by the International Labour Office (ILO) data Table 4.3 which shows the average earnings of wage earners in manufacturing, in selected Asian countries, in 1960 and 1969.

To the British firm, labour cost formed only a small part of their total unit cost of production,[2] while raw materials which were mainly imported constituted the bulk of the cost.

TABLE 4.2
COMPARATIVE WAGE LEVELS IN SELECTED ASIAN COUNTRIES IN SELECTED INDUSTRIAL OCCUPATIONS, 1972

	Mechanical Engineer		*Senior, or Executive Secretary*		*Technical Salesmen*		*Skilled Worker*		*Truck Driver*	
1. Malaysia	656	(100)	305	(100)	326	(100)	70	(100)	58	(100)
2. India	224	(34.1)	185	(60.7)	385	(118)	59	(84.3)	23	(39.7)
3. Indonesia	364	(55.5)	217	(71.1)	104	(31.9)	62	(88.6)	51	(87.5)
4. Philippines	101	(15.4)	145	(47.5)	153	(46.9)	78	(111.4)	69	(119)
5. Taiwan	176	(26.8)	181	(59.3)	157	(48.2)	78	(111.4)	102	(175.9)
6. Thailand	399	(60.8)	282	(92.3)	272	(83.4)	114	(168.9)	70	(120.7)
7. S. Vietnam	179	(27.3)	139	(45.6)	107	(32.8)	59	(71.4)	62	(106.9)

Source: Calculated from data in *Asia Research Bulletin*, Vol. 12 (11), March 1973.

Notes: (i) Bracketed figures represent indices with Malaysian figures as bases.
(ii) Amounts in US$ per month, adjusted for cost of living variations to render the figures comparable.

TABLE 4.3

ESTIMATED AVERAGE EARNINGS OF WAGE EARNERS IN MANUFACTURING IN SELECTED ASIAN COUNTRIES, 1960 AND 1969

(in US$ equivalent)

	Average Earnings Per Hour		*Average Earnings Per Day*	
	1960	*1969*	*1960*	*1969*
1. Malaysia	0.280	0.330	2.24	2.64 (100.0)
2. Philippines	0.264	0.258	2.10	2.10 (79.5)
3. Thailand	0.154	0.187	1.23	1.49 (56.4)
4. Taiwan	0.087	0.178	0.69	1.42 (53.8)
5. South Korea	0.018	0.165	0.14	1.32 (50.0)

Source: U.N., International Labour Office, *Year Book of Labour Statistics, 1970.*

Notes: (i) Bracketed figures represent indices with Malaysian figure as base for the year 1960.

(ii) Earnings relate to average earnings of wage earners in manufacturing industries. Earnings include bonuses, cost of living allowances, taxes, social insurance contributions payable by the employed person, and in some cases, payments in kind, but excluding social insurance contributions payable by the employers, family allowances, and other social security benefits.

(iii) Calculated on the basis of an eight-hour day.

(iv) Wage earners covered by the ILO were not necessarily unskilled, but certainly not highly skilled.

The most important single motive was to overcome tariff barriers, 15 per cent of the respondents regarding it as most important, while another 49 per cent considered it important; 14 per cent thought it was of some importance, and 22 per cent did not find it important. Among the latter were those firms that supplied the Malaysian public sector with duty-free goods. Many company representatives emphasized the importance of the expected increases in Malaysian tariffs, about which they seemed to know a great deal.[3] Before the 1960s there was no compulsion to overcome tariff barriers because tariff protection, as mentioned in Chapter 3, was then negligible. The increases in tariffs since the mid-1960s seemed to have impelled many manufacturers to start local production.

Table 4.4 shows tariff increases proposed in 1972/3 for some products already manufactured by British firms in Malaysia.[4] Most of the import duties are on an *ad valorem* basis, and a few items are subject to duties of more than 35 per cent. Company representatives who regarded adequate protection by tariffs as important in their decision to begin manufacturing indicated that they

TABLE 4.4

EXPECTED CHANGES IN IMPORT DUTIES OF SOME SELECTED MANUFACTURED ITEMS ENTERING MALAYSIA, 1972–1973

Items	Ad Valorem *Duty* (%) *Existing*	*Proposed*
Products with high local content		
Rubber goods* and all items made of rubber	nil	35
Table ware, kitchen ware, china pots and pans	15	50
Brooms and brushes*	10	30
Electrical fuses, plugs, and sockets	20	35
Electrical filaments*	nil	40
Products for use by local industries		
Motor vehicle spare parts and accessories*	nil	35
Electric motor parts and refrigerator parts*	20	35
Parts of electric motors and appliances for domestic use*	nil	35
Electric transformers*	nil	25
Fuses, switchgear, carbon filaments, resistors, diodes, etc.	nil	35
Products of other light engineering		
Hand tools*	15	35
Spanners and small tools*	nil	35
Torchlights	15	40

Source: *Malaysian Industrial Digest*, Vol. 5 (2), Second Quarter, 1972; and interviews.
Note: *Denotes involvement of U.K. firms producing item in question.

themselves had been instrumental in seeking the required protective tariff from the government. The government itself was seemingly reluctant to raise trade barriers, unless it was convinced of the viability of the industry which sought protection.[5]

The connexion between rising tariffs, the rapidly growing market, and the decision of U.K. manufacturing companies to invest in Malaysia is best summed up by one company representative who said:[6]

> Our company long held a good export market in Malaysia. Coming into the country would be the logical step to follow so that the market might be preserved, or even enhanced, in the light of imminent rising import duties . . . [sic]. It is the trend with developing countries to raise tariffs in order to make manufacturing in these countries more attractive than supplying [manufactured goods] from overseas [U.K.]. Personally I imagine no British company, such as ours, would establish manufacturing in Malaysia, if the Malaysian market could be supplied from our bigger affiliates. The problem, of course is that someone [a competitor] will establish a factory in the Malaysian market

and secure high tariffs for its own benefits and to our disadvantage, if we do not come in first. We [therefore] came in before we were confronted by rising tariffs.

However, even the prospect of protection, the representative added, might not be sufficient inducement for a foreign company to establish manufacturing facilities without the existence of the local market.

Very few companies—only 1 per cent of all those interviewed—regarded government incentives as an important factor in their decision to invest.[7] About 26 per cent thought government incentives of some importance, but the majority (73 per cent) considered incentives of marginal significance only; and 14.5 per cent of all companies consulted did not attempt to rank the factor at all. It would appear that the effect of state-created incentives on the decision to start production in the country was only marginal.[8]

No attempt is made here to evaluate whether or not the industrial incentives have been worthwhile from the Malaysian government's standpoint. Given the unsolicited nature and limited effectiveness of investment incentives, there is good reason to believe that it will probably be preferable for the government to devote attention to improving its organizational efficiency and to put less emphasis on financial incentives to the foreign investors. An improvement in government efficiency, by reduction of bureaucratic procedure, will probably stimulate a higher rate of economic growth, and will certainly remove one of the deterrents to private foreign investment.

An important motivating factor for at least 24 per cent of the British firms interviewed was 'To follow company practice of investing in growth areas'. About 70 per cent regarded this as of some importance; 7 per cent considered it unimportant. This suggest that the opportunity to compete freely had been an incentive for some firms who were confident of their growth potential. The greatest attraction to the investor was the opportunity provided for him in a protected market, where he was able to create and consolidate a potentially profitable production base, relatively unaffected by the local activities of rival foreign firms.

Agency houses, as will be seen in Chapter 5, had (and many still have) important functions in promoting foreign participation in Malaysian manufacturing. As distributing agents they played a significant part in establishing markets for British goods, and in some cases it was they who suggested to their principals that local production facilities should be established in Malaysia. Nevertheless, as shown in Table 4.1, only 14 per cent of company representatives thought that 'to follow an attractive proposal by a local agent' was an important factor in their investment decision, while it was a factor of some importance to another 8 per cent. To the majority (78 per cent) of respondents the factor was unimportant, and 5 per cent of the total number did not consider it a motivating factor at all. This is partly because some companies had marketing affiliates in Malaysia, and also partly because they had plans to begin overseas manufacturing before being prompted by their agents. The large and multinational enterprises[9] had a satisfactory knowledge and experience of the Malaysian market, and were likely to be the least affected by an outsider's suggestion concerning the location of their plants.

It is fairly obvious that U.K. firms did not rank Malaysia as an important area in which they would readily expand and diversify their manufacturing activities. This is illustrated by the low importance attached to the factor 'To invest as a matter of policy to diversify the company's investment areas', regarded as of some importance by only 19 per cent of the executives interviewed. The majority thought it was an unimportant factor in their decision to invest in Malaysia, while 5 per cent of the total number did not rate it as a motivating factor at all.

MOTIVES ANALYSED ACCORDING TO COMPANY GROUPS

The motivations of companies were analysed according to whether the representatives belonged to either 'small', 'medium-sized', or 'large' companies. The objective of the analysis was to find out if there were significant variations from the general pattern of motivation previously discussed. The results, not significantly different from the broad description above, are summarized in Table 4.5.

Group I: Small Companies

About one-half of this group had built up markets for their products in Malaysia through the agency houses before the 1960s. The majority viewed their manufacturing investments in Malaysia as an experiment in a growing economy. Thus 71 per cent of the respondents in this group gave as the most important motive for investing in the country 'taking advantage of the expected growth of the Malaysian market'. The next very important motive was 'to take advantage of markets already established', which 29 per cent of the respondents rated as crucial to their investment decisions. More than one-half (54 per cent) of this group also considered this

TABLE 4.5
MOTIVES OF COMPANIES (CLASSIFIED INTO GROUPS) FOR INVESTING IN INDUSTRY IN MALAYSIA
(by per cent)

Motives for Investment	*Group I* *Motives Ranked as:* *A*	*B*	*C*	*D*		*Group II* *Motives Ranked as:* *A*	*B*	*C*	*D*		*Group III* *Motives Ranked as:* *A*	*B*	*C*	*D*	
1. To take advantage of established market	29	18	54	—	(N = 28)	61	21	18	—	(N = 61)	86	14	—	—	(N = 14)
2. To take advantage of expected growth of Malaysian market	71	21	—	7	(N = 28)	26	74	—	—	(N = 61)	14	64	21	—	(N = 14)
3. To gain access to S.E. Asian market	—	26	52	22	(N = 27)	—	7	72	22	(N = 60)	—	—	50	50	(N = 14)
4. To avoid/reduce freight charges	4	64	32	—	(N = 28)	5	40	38	16	(N = 61)	—	50	50	—	(N = 14)
5. To take advantage of other lower cost conditions	—	—	54	46	(N = 28)	—	—	56	44	(N = 61)	—	—	—	100	(N = 14)
6. To overcome expected rise in tariffs	18	18	21	43	(N = 28)	13	61	10	16	(N = 61)	29	50	21	—	(N = 14)
7. To take advantage of government incentives	—	5	24	71	(N = 28)	—	—	19	81	(N = 59)	—	—	88	13	(N = 8)
8. To follow company practice of investing ahead of competitors	—	41	33	26	(N = 27)	—	16	82	2	(N = 61)	—	29	64	7	(N = 14)
9. To follow an attractive proposal by local agent	—	36	12	52	(N = 25)	—	5	3	92	(N = 59)	—	—	50	50	(N = 14)
10. To invest as a matter of policy to diversify company's investment areas	—	—	11	89	(N = 28)	—	—	26	74	(N = 61)	—	—	100	—	(N = 9)
Other motives	—	—	100	—	(N = 12)	—	—	100	—	(N = 10)	—	—	100	—	(N = 7)

Source: Compiled from data gathered at interviews.

Notes: (i) Company group classification as explained in the text, and in the Introduction.

(ii) A = Crucial; B = Important; C = Of Some Importance; D = Not Important.

(iii) Some companies ranked two or more motives as of equal importance, while some did not rank some of the factors.

(iv) Percentages may not add to 100 because of rounding off.

second motive as of only some importance, while 18 per cent thought it was important. More than half (57 per cent) viewed tariff considerations as either crucial, important, or of some importance in their decisions to invest, while 43 per cent thought tariff considerations did not significantly influence their decisions. Avoiding freight charges was quite an important factor to at least 68 per cent of the companies in the group. The majority (74 per cent) regarded the motive of 'following company practice of investing in growth areas ahead of competitors' as either important or of some importance. To 78 per cent the factor 'to gain access to the South-East Asian market' was also either important or of some importance. Although the pattern was by no means exclusive to firms in Group I, there were some elements of entrepreneurial mobility and aggressiveness in their investment move into Malaysia. They wished to enter what seemed to them to be a new and growing market; but without suggestion from their agents (regarded as either important or of some importance by 48 per cent), they might not have begun manufacturing in Malaysia.

In common with the firms in Group II and Group III, few companies (29 per cent) in Group I regarded 'taking advantage of government incentives' as of any real importance. The majority (71 per cent) of the group viewed government incentive as unimportant. Just over one-half (54 per cent) considered 'taking advantage of other lower Malaysian cost conditions' of some importance.

Group II: Medium-sized Companies

Some of the old-established British firms were in this group. Many representatives had had very long personal and business connexions with Malaysia. However, the pattern of motives ranked as crucial by the group as a whole does not differ significantly from the general pattern discussed above. Hence, four motives considered crucial by the group were: 'to take advantage of the market already established', rated very important by 61 per cent of the group; 'to take advantage of the expected growth of the Malaysian market', rated very significant by 26 per cent; 'to overcome the expected rise in tariffs', considered vital by 13 per cent of the respondents, and 'to avoid/reduce freight charges', ranked crucial by 5 per cent of the companies in the group.

Other important motives of the group were 'to follow company practice of investing ahead of competitors', rated important by 16 per cent of the respondents in the group; 'to gain access to the South-East Asian market', considered important by 7 per cent;

and 5 per cent rated the motive 'to follow an attractive proposal by local agent' as an important motive, although the majority (92 per cent) did not consider this motive important in influencing their decisions. 'To follow company practice of investing ahead of competitors' was a factor of some importance to 82 per cent of the respondents, and 'to gain access to the South-East Asian market' was also a motive of some importance to the majority (72 per cent) of the representatives in the group.

It is clear that government incentives were unimportant as an instrument for attracting foreign investment. In common with the other company representatives interviewed, very few of them invested in manufacturing facilities in the country 'as a matter of policy' to diversify the geographical areas of their overseas investments.

As will be discussed in Chapter 5, diversification of activities into manufacturing was one of the reasons why agency houses in the group participated in the manufacturing sector. This motive was linked with their desire to gain access to the neighbouring South-East Asian markets where they had trading channels. Considering the length of commercial and trading associations of the group in Malaysia and the broad pattern of ranking of their motivations, it seemed that their major intentions were related to attempts to preserve markets which in the first place had been obtained by export trade. The expected rise in tariffs and the opening of the Malaysian market to competitive suppliers threatened the existing markets of these firms. Hence their motive to begin manufacturing in Malaysia may be regarded as a defensive measure to preserve their market interest. At the same time, there was also some element of aggressive investment motive when these firms were trying to capture the growing domestic market.

Group III: Large Companies

Broadly the pattern of motivation of large companies to invest in Malaysian industry was similar to those firms in the other groups. The factors considered crucial by these companies were 'to take advantage of their established market'; 'to overcome expected rise in tariffs'; and 'to take advantage of expected growth of the Malaysian market'. In addition, they also considered important 'to avoid/reduce freight charges' and 'to follow company practice of investing ahead of competitors' in influencing their decisions to begin manufacturing in the country. Additional factors regarded as of some importance were 'to gain access to South-East Asian market'; 'to follow an attractive proposal by local agents'; 'to invest as a matter of policy to diversify company's investment (geographical) areas'; and 'to take advantage of government incentive', as well as other factors related to the favourable investment climate of the country.

With regard to government incentives, 6 out of 14, nearly 43 per cent of representatives in the group, did not rank the factor as a consideration in their move to invest in Malaysian industry. Of those that ranked the factor, seven representatives thought it was of some importance and one did not think it was important, as an inducement to invest in industry. As previously mentioned, it would appear that the effect of state-created incentives, in themselves, on the decision to start production in the country was marginal.

The respondents in this group were more attracted to Singapore where they thought the government was more efficient, and the geographical location of the city-state ideal for them to supply the South-East Asian region. The creation of the Asia-Dollar Market in 1968 in Singapore was certainly part of the attraction of Singapore to the foreign investor. What seems clear from the standpoint of the companies in this group is that in the absence of tariff barriers in Malaysia, most companies in the group would not have come to Malaysia whose market they could easily supply from their plants in Singapore.

AN EVALUATION OF THE MOTIVES TO INVEST IN MALAYSIA

The pattern of the motives to invest in the Malaysian industry was nearly the same for all groups of firms. As expected, market considerations featured most prominently in the motives of the companies. Taking advantage of their established market and the expected growth of the domestic market constituted the crucial factors in influencing the companies' decision to begin local manufacturing. Investment opportunities grow with rising incomes and changing patterns of demand. For instance, according to Engel's Law, the proportion of income spent on basic food tends to diminish as income increases, whilst growth in income induces a higher proportion to be spent on non-basic food and manufactured items.

Available evidence seemed to indicate that in Malaysia in the early 1960s there were rapid increases in consumption of durable consumer goods, such as motor vehicles, household appliances, and the like,[10] some of which were manufactured locally. It seems clear that any growth in income is likely to have very favourable repercussions on the market for consumer goods, and hence create investment opportunities to manufacture them locally.

Underlying the motivations to invest was the immediate profit motive. Executives stressed that the level of profit[11] they expected to get in Malaysia must be higher than that which they could get in the U.K. in order for them to feel compensated for the trouble and risk of investing abroad.[12] There were of course other motives,[13] besides the profit motive, as outline in Tables 4.1 and 4.5.

The desire of the industrialists to preserve their established markets and to capture additional shares of the growing market formed what can be called the defensive and aggressive aspects of investment motives.[14] The companies would not have established local production facilities had they been able to supply the market by exports from the home country. Therein lies the significance of the factor 'to overcome the expected rise in tariffs' which, in the views of the executives, was a threat that could exclude them from the market. Of course there were instances when the investor, having decided to begin local manufacturing, asked for tariff protection to exclude potential competitors. Those British companies which had hitherto been engaged in agricultural, mining, and trading activities found circumstances surrounding their businesses were such that they could improve their profitability by going into local manufacturing. This will be examined in Chapter 5.

The low level of importance attached to incentive created by the state had a definite policy implication: companies found government financial incentives to investment less attractive than the opportunities to expand production in a growing domestic market.

WHY CAPITAL MOVES INTERNATIONALLY

Professor Arndt (1954)[15] among others suggested that direct investment was explainable in terms of the marginal efficiency of capital (or the profitability of the investment). However, the position of British industrial investment in Malaysia seems more completely explained by Hymer's thesis (1960)[16] that direct investments occur when firms have, and wish to exploit overseas, some 'quasimonopolistic powers' or 'major advantage over their competitors' arising from patents, products, or other unique technological and managerial advantages.

Direct foreign investments have also been explained in terms of the theory of industrial organization. Territorial diversification of investment by firms is thought to be one explanation of direct investment.[17] After an initial investment abroad, subsidiaries of foreign firms tend to develop entities of their own which enable them to keep on growing,[18] independent of the parent firm. British investment in Malaysia can be explained in these terms, as they tend to be self-perpetuating, and grow with the economy in which they operate.[19]

The move by British firms to come to Malaysia can also be explained in terms of a theory advanced by R. Z. Aliber (1970).[20] According to him, direct investments involve the acquisition of plant and equipment for production in selected currency areas, other than the area in which the firm is domiciled. Direct investments, according to this theory, take place in areas whose currencies are preferred by the investors. Reference was made to the stable and strong Malaysian currency in Chapter 3. Company respondents also mentioned the influence of Malaysia's currency on their decision to invest in Malaysia. It seems clear that part of the explanation for British companies' preference to locate their plants in Malaysia was their preference for holding assets denominated in Malaysian currency.[21]

Professor R. E. Caves'[22] extension of the theory of industrial organization explained foreign investments by 'vertical' and 'horizontal' integration of firms across national boundaries. A discussion of Caves' ideas will be made in connexion with the multinational enterprises in Chapter 7. Briefly, according to this line of explanation, corporations make 'horizontal' investments to produce abroad the same lines of goods as they produce in their home market; other corporations undertake 'vertical' direct investments to produce abroad raw materials or other factor inputs for their manufacturing operations.

In addition, it is also plausible to view British capital inflow into Malaysian industry in terms of J. H. Dunning's[23] analysis. Dunning suggested that, where the additional cost of producing a certain quantity of output for export to a particular country, plus distribution and marketing costs, was greater than the cost of producing this same product in the country concerned, it would pay the exporting company to set up local production facilities. The tendency would be accentuated when the company was confronted by a threat (e.g. by rising tariffs and/or from other competitors) that would cut it off from an expanding market. Provided the company in question possessed some form of special advantages (in S. Hymer's sense) and wished to exploit them, the company would establish a manufacturing plant abroad. Conversely, if a company did not export, and did not have any special advantages to exploit, it would not invest abroad.

There remain two important, though not often realized, aspects of British manufacturing investment in Malaysia. By the standard of developing countries, the Malaysian market for manufactured products is thought to be sophisticated.[24] It is worthwhile for investors to begin manufacturing in the country to take advantage of such a market. Also British firms there find the country a good training ground for their young executives who in time will manage the firms' interests elsewhere in the developing world.

In general it was the agreeable foreign investment climate discussed in Chapter 3 that made Malaysia an obvious choice for British investment over other countries of South-East Asia.

The considerations that are dominant in all cases appeared to be:

1. the long commercial association between Britain and Malaysia;
2. the similarities in the judiciary and other government institutions of the two countries;
3. the political and financial stability of Malaysia;
4. the fact that Malaysia is a very pleasant place to live in and the English language is generally understood in the commercial sector;
5. the potential market growth and the commitment of the government to economic development;
6. the favourable attitude of the government towards foreign, especially British, investors;
7. the convertibility of Malaysian currency and the high external reserves maintained by Malaysia in the U.K.;
8. the readiness of the government to protect local manufacturing;
9. the few restrictions and the absence of special regulations concerning the ownership of foreign business in the country;
10. the existence of established brand names for British goods in Malaysia, and
11. the 'social premium' of being British in Malaysia[25] —'being British is a mark of having adequate resources, and being commercially and politically acceptable'
12. the good infrastructure, and facilities available for the needs of expatriate executives.[26]

The executives interviewed believed that Malaysia offered the greatest advantages of location within the region without appearing to have any major drawbacks of other countries. Besides, Malaysia also maintained friendly ties not only with countries of the region but also with the countries in the Middle East, North and East

Africa.[27] A large proportion of manufactured items from Malaysia exported to these countries were products of British firms, or products of domestic firms marketed by British firms.

Many firms hoped that as a result of the much-discussed ASEAN common market,[28] they would be in a position to expand within a wider market from their Malaysian base. Some firms had already made use of their Malaysian personnel to manage and train local people to man their establishments in the other ASEAN countries. Such a move had the obvious advantage of saving on the cost of employing additional expatriate personnel from Britain and of eliminating any possible cause of friction in places where expatriates were less welcome.

To most British firms that had been trading in Malaysia for a long time the question of choosing Malaysia *vis-à-vis* the other countries in the region did not arise. They turned to manufacturing as a means of preserving their established market. To these firms, manufacturing in Malaysia in the late 1960s represented the apex or superstrata of their business which they have built on foundations laid early in the beginning of the twentieth century.

THE NATURE OF THE MARKET FOR MANUFACTURED PRODUCTS IN MALAYSIA

IBRD Report (1955)[29] pointed out that the smallness of the country's domestic market by standards of modern industrial output had been one of the constraints on industrial development. The Rueff Report (1963)[30] suggested that the formation of Malaysia would enlarge the domestic market for the manufacturing sector.

In the 1960s, at least three separate markets existed to provide opportunities for Malaysia's industrial development: the home market for consumer goods, the home market for intermediate and capital goods, and the export market for processed local primary materials, e.g. rubber, tin, palm oil, and timber. Malaysia also stood to gain external markets for her manufactured goods with the improvement of prospects in regional co-operation such as ASEAN,[31] and the cultivation of friendly relations with the developing countries of Africa and Asia. It has appeared from Table 3.9 above, that the scope for expanding local manufactures was supplied by imports. In the following sections, the broad outline is drawn of the pattern of demand for manufactures.

THE SIZE OF THE MARKET IN MALAYSIA IN THE PERSPECTIVE OF OTHER SOUTH-EAST ASIAN COUNTRIES

In terms of all market indicators (population, GNP, income per capita, steel consumption, etc.)[32] tabulated in Table 4.6, the Malaysian domestic market was quite small. The total population of the country in 1969 was less than 1 per cent of the population of the Asia and Pacific region. Of the 10.5 million, less than one million people lived in the urban areas. In all the other countries more than one million people live in urban areas. Malaysia's urban population represented about 0.5 per cent of the total population of the region.

Although Malaysia's GNP in 1969 represented only about 1.1 per cent of aggregated GNPs in the region, per capita income of US$284 was higher than the average of US$264 for the region. Private consumption expenditure in Malaysia represented 1.5 per cent of all private consumption expenditure in the region. By way of contrast, the aggregate private consumption expenditure of Indonesia, the Philippines, and Thailand was 3.8 per cent, 3.7 per cent, and 2.8 per cent respectively of the private consumption expenditure of the region; although in terms of per capita private consumption expenditure these countries had in 1969 low private consumption levels compared to Malaysia.

Production of electricity and steel consumption in Malaysia each represented less than 1 per cent of the total production of electricity and consumption of steel in the Asia-Pacific region in 1968 and 1969. Cement production in the country in 1969 represented a little over 1 per cent of all cement production in the region. At best, Malaysia's domestic market might represent less than 1.5 per cent of the market for goods and services in the region, with Indonesia, the Philippines, Thailand, South Korea, South Vietnam, and Taiwan each providing a much bigger domestic market.

In terms of GNP, income per capita, production of electricity, steel consumption, and size of private consumption expenditure, Japan, Australia, and New Zealand, the three most developed countries in the region, accounted for over one-half of the region's market even though in terms of population the three nations constituted only 10 per cent of the whole population of the area. On the basis of the indicators shown in Table 4.7 it is clear that the Malaysian domestic market was small in relation to the total Asia-Pacific market, and the markets of the other developing countries of South-East Asia. As in many small countries where the

TABLE 4.6

INDICATORS OF MARKET SIZE FOR MALAYSIA AND SOME SELECTED COUNTRIES OF ASIA AND THE PACIFIC REGION

Countries / Region	*1. Population Total 1969*		*2. Urban Population*		*3. Gross National Product 1969*		*4. Per Capita GNP 1969*		*5. Private Consumption Expenditure*	
	(million)	*(%)*	*(million)*	*(%)*	*(US$ billion)*	*(%)*	*(US$)*	*(%*)*	*Per Capita in 1969 (US$)*	*as Per Cent of Total for the Region*
1. Burma	27.0	(2.4)	1.1	(0.6)	2.10	(0.6)	66	(0.8)	56	1.0
2. Hong Kong	4.0	(0.4)	3.5	(2.1)	3.18	(1.0)	686	(10.1)	109+	1.0
3. Indonesia	116.0	(10.2)	9.5	(5.6)	12.50	(3.8)	96	(2.8)	49+	3.8
4. S. Korea	31.1	(2.7)	8.7	(5.1)	7.00	(2.1)	190	(10.2)	133+	2.8
5. Malaysia	10.5	(0.9)	0.8	(0.5)	3.69	(1.1)	284	(5.5)	208	1.5
6. Philippines	37.2	(3.3)	4.9	(2.9)	8.14	(2.5)	182	(5.4)	182	3.7
7. Singapore	2.0	(0.2)	2.0	(1.1)	1.63	(0.5)	724	(6.0)	500+	0.7
8. Taiwan	13.8	(1.2)	4.6	(2.7)	4.76	(1.4)	268	(11.0)	185	1.7
9. Thailand	34.7	(3.0)	2.1	(1.2)	6.29	(2.0)	151	(7.8)	120	2.8
10. S. Vietnam	17.9	(1.6)	2.2	(1.3)	4.46	(7.3)	207	(7.3)	187	2.3
Sub-total	294.3	(25.8)	39.4	(23.0)	53.75	(16.3)	183	–	118	21.3
Japan	102.3	(9.0)	53.7	(31.4)	166.40	(50.4)	1288	(10.4)	733+	50.3
Australia	12.3	(1.1)	7.2	(4.2)	31.20	(9.5)	2041	(5.3)	1510+	12.3
N. Zealand	2.8	(0.2)	1.3	(0.7)	5.24	(1.6)	1612	(3.4)	1085+	1.9
Sub-total	117.4	(10.3)	62.2	(36.4)	202.84	(61.5)	1374	(9.8)	822	64.4
Other Asian Countries@	726.8	(63.9)	69.4	(40.6)	73.25	(22.2)	101	–	101	14.1
Total	1,138.5	(100.0)	171.0	(100.0)	329.84	(100.0)	241	(6.8)	264	100.0

(Continued)

TABLE 4.6 (*Continued*)

Countries / Region	*6. Production of Electricity: 1969* (*bil. KWH*)	(%)	*7. Steel Consumption: 1968* (*'000 metric tons*)	(%)	*8. Production of Cement 1969* (*'000 metric tons*)	(%)
1. Burma	0.6	(0.1)	87	(0.1)	182	(0.2)
2. Hong Kong	4.0	(0.8)	469	(0.7)	378	(0.4)
3. Indonesia	1.8	(0.3)	249	(0.4)	—	
4. S. Korea	8.1	(1.7)	886	(1.3)	4,872	(5.5)
5. Malaysia	3.0	(0.6)	391	(0.5)	973	(1.1)
6. Philippines	6.3	(1.3)	1,080	(1.5)	2,304	(2.6)
7. Singapore	1.9	(0.3)	—		—	
8. Taiwan	11.4	(2.3)	1,084	(1.5)	4,092	(4.7)
9. Thailand	4.1	(0.8)	762	(1.1)	2,404	(2.7)
10. S. Vietnam	1.1	(0.2)	201	(0.3)	—	
Sub-total	42.3	(8.9)	5,209	(7.4)	15,205	(17.3)
Japan	302.1	(63.5)	49,908	(71.0)	50,964	(57.9)
Australia	51.2	(10.7)	5,884	(8.4)	4,344	(4.9)
New Zealand	12.7	(2.6)	758	(1.1)	803	(1.0)
Sub-total	366.0	(76.9)	56,550	(80.4)	56,111	(63.8)
Other Asian Countries@	67.4	(14.2)	8,545	(12.2)	16,603	(18.9)
Total	475.7	(100.0)	70,304	(100.0)	87,919	(100.0)

Source: United Nations, *Statistical Year Book*, 1970 and 1971; *Demographic Year Book*, 1970 and 1971; *Year Book of National Accounts*, 1970 and 1971; *Monthly Bulletin of Statistics* and *ECAFE Bulletin*, various issues.

Notes: * Average annual rate of increase per annum over the previous five years.

\+ 1968 data.

@ Excluding Communist China, North Korea and North Vietnam.

— Not available.

Steel consumption refers to production plus imports less exports of crude steel.

Private Consumption Expenditure refers to the value of final expenditure by households and private non-profit institutions on current goods and services, less sales of similar goods.

TABLE 4.7

MALAYSIA, EXPENDITURE ON GOODS AND SERVICES
(at current prices), 1962–1972
($ million)

	1962	*1963*	*1964*	*1965*	*1966*	*1967*	*1968*	*1969*	*1970*	*1971*	*1972**	*Increase 1962–72 (%)*	*Average Annual Growth (%)*
1. Total private and public consumption expenditure	5,693	6,157	6,616	7,041	7,533	7,925	8,161	8,540	9,208	9,987	10,711	88.1	6.4
2. Total gross capital formation	1,193	1,235	1,299	1,411	1,498	1,602	1,670	1,571	2,055	2,227	2,657	122.7	8.3
3. Aggregate domestic expenditure	*6,886*	*7,393*	*7,915*	*8,452*	*9,031*	*9,527*	*9,831*	*10,111*	*11,263*	*12,214*	*13,368*	94.1	6.8
4. Imports of goods and services	3,585	3,749	3,953	4,166	4,208	4,097	4,417	4,686	5,300	5,598	5,803	61.9	4.9
Total Expenditure on Goods and Services	10,471	11,141	11,868	12,618	13,293	13,624	14,248	14,797	16,563	17,812	19,171	83.1	6.2

Source: Calculated from GNP data provided by the Department of Statistics as quoted in Bank Negara Malaysia, *Quarterly Economic Bulletin*, Vol. 6 (1), March 1973, p. 51.

Note: *Provisional.

domestic market alone was insufficient to form the sole basis for industrialization,[33] external markets were sought. The importance of the outward-looking industrial strategy for the country will be mentioned in Chapter 9.

AGGREGATE DOMESTIC DEMAND

Estimates of expenditure on goods and services between 1962 and 1972 are presented in Table 4.7. The aggregate domestic expenditure on goods and services in 1962 was $10,471 million, and in 1972 $19,171 million, thus giving an approximate total increase of 83.1 per cent over the period 1962–72, equal to a growth rate of 6.2 per cent per annum.

Such growth was likely to have favourable repercussions on general domestic demand and on the market for manufactured goods that were either imported or locally made. Indeed as shown in Table 3.9, the market for manufactures in Malaysia increased by about 146 per cent between 1961 and 1971, from $1,536 million to $3,781 million. As already mentioned, the dominant position for manufactures opened possibilities for import substitution. The changing composition of import demand shown by Table 4.8 is partially a reflection of the beginning of such import-substitution industry.

From Table 4.8, it can be seen that the import of food, beverages, and tobacco had declined from 25.6 per cent in 1967 to 20.4 per cent in 1970, as a result of the establishment of local production. On the other hand, under the pressure of development programmes and the resultant import requirements of new industry, the shares of inedible crude materials for industry as well as machinery and transport equipment had expanded from 27.1 per cent in 1967 to 35.6 per cent of imports in 1970. This same pattern is repeated when imports are classified as consumer, intermediate, and capital goods. The share of consumer goods had fallen from 38.3 per cent in 1967 to 28.0 per cent of imports in 1970; while the aggregate share of capital and intermediate goods had risen from 55.4 per cent in 1967 to 63.0 per cent in 1970. This distribution of imports was reflected in Malaysia's industrial production for the period, more than two-thirds of which consisted of consumer goods.[34]

The domestic market for manufacturers had grown considerably in the late 1960s. In 1963 imported and domestically produced manufactures amounted to $1,893 million, which was equivalent to 25.6 per cent of aggregate domestic expenditure of $7,392

TABLE 4.8
THE COMPOSITION OF IMPORTS, 1967–1970

By SITC Group	*1967*		*1968*		*1969*		*1970*	
	$ mil.	%	*$ mil.*	%	*$ mil.*	%	*$ mil.*	%
0 + 1 Food, beverages, and tobacco	852.2	(25.6)	844.1	(23.8)	814.5	(22.6)	884.5	(20.4)
2 Crude materials	165.8	(5.0)	284.2	(8.0)	302.6	(8.4)	322.3	(7.5)
3 Mineral fuels	446.2	(13.4)	500.7	(14.1)	485.7	(13.5)	518.8	(12.0)
5 Chemicals	248.2	(7.5)	239.5	(6.7)	274.7	(7.6)	314.7	(7.3)
6 Manufactures classified by materials	592.5	(17.8)	613.5	(17.3)	624.2	(17.3)	773.1	(17.9)
7 Machinery and equipment	735.8	(22.1)	792.7	(22.3)	840.9	(23.3)	1,214.7*	(28.1)
8 Miscellaneous manufactures	193.5	(5.8)	188.4	(5.3)	182.8	(5.1)	204.2	(4.7)
Other imports	90.2	(2.8)	88.5	(2.5)	79.6	(2.2)	91.0	(2.1)
Total	3,325.0	(100)	3,551.6	(100)	3,605.0	(100)	4,323.0	(100)

(*Continued*)

TABLE 4.8 (*Continued*)

By Use: **								
(0 + 1 + 8) Consumer goods	1,291.0	(38.8)	1,275.1	(35.9)	1,138.5	(31.6)	1,212.0	(28.0)
(3 + 4 + 5 + 6 + 8) Intermediate goods	1,028.7	(32.5)	1,156.7	(32.6)	1,356.7	(37.6)	1,572.2	(36.4)
(7 + 8) Capital goods	759.4	(22.9)	750.2	(21.1)	741.6	(20.6)	1,150.8	(26.6)
(0 – 8) Imports for re-export	182.8	(5.5)	332.3	(9.4)	340.4	(9.4)	360.4	(8.3)
Imports not allocated	9.1	(0.3)	37.3	(1.0)	27.8	(0.8)	27.9	(0.7)
Total	3,325.0	(100)	3,551.6	(100)	3,605.0	(100)	4,323.3	(100)

Source: Department of Statistics, *Statistics of External Trade* (various issues).

Notes: * Including aircraft purchased by Malaysia-Singapore Airline, valued at $54.3 million.

** Classified according to nature of item, e.g. consumer goods include food, beverages, tobacco, and consumer durables; intermediate goods include materials for agriculture, construction, and industry; while capital goods include machinery, equipment, metal products, and transport equipment such as trucks and other commercial vehicles. Included in the category of 'imports for re-export' are items considered as consumer, intermediate, and capital goods are included in the category of 'imports not allocated'.

Import figures do not include military equipment and ammunition.

TABLE 4.9

AGGREGATE DOMESTIC EXPENDITURE AND ESTIMATED DOMESTIC MARKET FOR MANUFACTURED GOODS, 1963–1971

	1963	*1966*	*1970*	*1971*	*Growth 1963–71*
1. Aggregate domestic expenditure, in $ million	7,392	9,031	11,263	12,214	6.4
2. Value of imported manufactured goods, in $ million	1,346	1,595	2,172	2,310	7.0
3. Locally manufactured goods, value in $ million	547	779	1,354	1,471	13.2
4. Estimated domestic market for manufactured goods	1,893	2,376	3,526	3,781	9.0
5. 4 as percentage of 1	25.6	26.3	31.3	31.0	

Source: As for Table 4.8.

million for the same year. In 1971, imported and locally produced manufactured goods amounted to $3,781 million, which was 31 per cent of the $12,214 million aggregate domestic expenditure in that year (see Table 4.9).

Expenditure on manufactured goods constituted an increasing proportion of aggregate domestic expenditure for the period 1963 to 1971. Whereas the aggregate domestic expenditure grew at an annual rate of 6.4 per cent, the estimated market for manufactured goods expanded at an annual rate of 9.0 per cent. Both the growth rate of imported manufactures and that of locally manufactured goods shown in Table 4.9 were higher than the growth rate of aggregate domestic demand in the 1960s. This situation was indicative of the growth in the country's aggregate domestic demand at about the time when British firms commenced local manufacturing. Broadly, this supported the companies' claim that they commenced manufacturing to take advantage of the expected growth of the market for manufacturers.

MARKET CHARACTERISTICS

To discover the characteristics of the Malaysian market it is necessary to consider individual consumer behaviour. By examining household budget studies, one can obtain an idea of how demand patterns, and hence opportunities for industrial investment, are likely to change with rising income. *The Household Budget Survey, 1957–58*[35] offers a guide to detailed expenditure figures for the following eleven groups of commodities:

1. Total Food, consisting of all kinds of foodstuffs including beverages and meals out.
2. Alcoholic Drinks, comprising all kinds of alcohol and spirits, including aerated drinks.
3. Tobacco, consisting of all kinds of tobacco and other smoking accessories, and including betel and areca-nut.
4. Clothing and Footwear, comprising all types of these including their repairs, and also including jewellery.
5. Household Goods, made up of household durable goods, furnishing materials, and kitchen equipment.
6. Fuel, including charcoal and firewood.
7. Power, defined as electricity only.
8. Transport, including all fares and charges for repairs and service.
9. Entertainment and Services, consisting of different kinds of entertainment and service, and including union and society subscriptions.
10. Sundries, consisting of miscellaneous personal requisites such as cosmetics and tooth-paste, medicines, stationery, reading material, and insurance.
11. Housing, including house repairs and purchase, and all kinds of rentals and rates.

The survey covered a sample of 2,760 households of three major racial groups, Malays, Chinese, and Indians both in rural and urban areas. Working from unpublished summary sheets of the survey, Dr. A. H. Ismail (1971)[36] computed expenditure elasticities for the eleven groups of items enumerated above. A summary of the expenditure elasticities, by rural-urban areas and by racial strata, is given in Table 4.10.

A cursory examination of the Table reveals that within the rural and urban areas, the elasticities for a given group of commodities generally differed slightly among the three racial groups for most of the commodity groups, although in many cases the magnitudes of these elasticities appeared to be of the same order. Similarly, if the corresponding columns of a given racial group in rural and urban areas are compared, there are considerable differences in the elasticities shown.

In general, however, in the rural areas the elasticities for total

TABLE 4.10
WEST MALAYSIA, EXPENDITURE ELASTICITIES FOR RURAL AND URBAN AREAS BY MALAY, CHINESE AND INDIAN RACIAL STRATA

Commodity Groups	*Rural Areas* (1) *Malay* (a)	(2) *Chinese* (a)	(3) *Indian* (a)	*Urban Areas* (4) *Malay* (a)	(5) *Chinese* (a)	(6) *Indian* (a)
1. Total food	0.967	0.626	0.761	0.788	0.503	0.717
2. Alcoholic drinks	1.039	1.021	1.400	(b)	0.912	0.991*
3. Tobacco	1.207	1.425	1.139	0.929	1.294	0.962
4. Clothing	0.928	1.204	1.019	0.921*	1.371	1.407
5. Household goods	1.106	1.175	1.258	(c)	1.111	0.800
6. Fuel	1.212	1.130	0.997	0.980	0.878	0.832
7. Power	0.381	0.761	(b)	0.546	0.968	0.640
8. Transport	0.862	0.923	0.966	1.595	0.913	0.871
9. Entertainment	0.931	1.217	1.167	1.228	1.068	0.967
10. Sundries	0.883	1.113	1.110	0.961	1.138	1.133
11. Housing	(c)	1.069	(b)	0.935*	0.921	1.082

Source: A.H. Ismail, *A Study of Total Expenditure Elasticities For West Malaysia*, Kuala Lumpur, The National University, 1971, Tables II (p. 20) and III (p. 22).

Notes: (a) Unless otherwise stated, all elasticities presented in the column are significant at the one per cent level. * elasticity significant at the 5 per cent level.
(b) Regression not computed as data were too few.
(c) Inconclusive result.

food, though their magnitudes varied, were less than unity for all racial groups. It appears also that for all racial groups, the elasticities were equal to or greater than unity for alcoholic drinks, tobacco, household goods, and fuel; and less than unity for power (elasticity for Indian power expenditure not computed), and transport. In the urban areas the elasticities for total food were less than unity for all races.[37] It was also apparent that the elasticities of expenditure on fuel, power, and alcoholic drinks were less than unity.

The urban Malay (column *4*) shows relatively high elasticities for food, fuel, transport, and entertainment. The urban Chinese (column *5*) has the highest elasticities for tobacco, household goods, power, and sundries; while the urban Indian (column *6*) has the highest elasticities for clothing and housing.

By comparing the elasticities for each racial group between its rural and urban locations (i.e. comparing columns *1* and *4*; *2* and

5; *3* and *6*) it can be seen that for the Malays the elasticities are higher in the rural areas for food, tobacco, and fuel; and lower for power, transport, and entertainment (column *1*). The rural Chinese (column *2*) has higher elasticities for total food, alcoholic drinks, tobacco, fuel, entertainment, and housing. To Indians in the rural areas (column *3*) higher elasticities are in total food, alcoholic drinks, tobacco, household goods, fuel, transport, and entertainment.

On balance, for each of the racial groups, especially the Chinese and Indian, the rural sector has higher elasticities for a large number of commodity groups, including food, than has the urban sector. This situation is consistent with the survey finding that for all races, the average monthly income and total expenditure per person was lower in the rural areas than in the urban areas.[38] If the survey adequately reflects the income and expenditure patterns in the country, one may expect, *ceteris paribus*, that as levels of income of rural communities rise, income elasticities of demand generally began to fall. But the household budget survey which was the basis of the expenditure elasticities summarized in Table 4.10 covered only West Malaysia, and one may not be warranted in inferring from the survey the consumption behaviour of people living in East Malaysia. Nevertheless, assuming the same consumption functions applied to all parts of Malaysia, one may expect the general level of income elasticities of demand in East Malaysia to be relatively higher than levels in West Malaysia since income and purchasing power were lower in the former. It would follow that as levels of income rise in East Malaysia, the income elasticities of demand there would fall.

The foregoing discussion of the various elasticities suggests that the market for manufactured products in the country was segmented. The root of the phenomenon of market segmentation lay in the low level of all incomes, the general differences in income levels of the various races and the differences in incomes of the rural and urban areas. There was not a single demand for a great many manufactured products, but a number of demands, perhaps for varying qualities of the products at different prices. In other words, there was market segmentation which called for product differentiation which in turn affected the size of the market for industrial products.

The differences in incomes are reflected in the mean and median monthly household incomes shown in Table 4.11.

Segmentation of the market required different marketing techniques in order to realize the full potential of the market. Any

TABLE 4.11
WEST MALAYSIA, HOUSEHOLD INCOMES FOR RURAL AND URBAN AREAS, BY MALAY, CHINESE, AND INDIAN GROUPS, 1970
($ per month)

	Mean Household Income	*Median Household Income*
Rural Household		
1. Malay	154.5	111.7
2. Chinese	332.6	254.4
3. Indian	237.2	220.3
4. Other	563.4	87.9
Urban Household		
1. Malay	328.1	227.3
2. Chinese	464.3	289.9
3. Indian	441.5	241.9
4. Other	1,491.7	1,139.5
Total		
1. Malay	178.7	122.3
2. Chinese	387.4	271.1
3. Indian	310.4	195.5
4. Other	950.5	324.3
National Total	268.7	168.6

Source: *Mid-Term Review of the Second Malaysia Plan, 1971–75*, Table 1–2.

growth in income and lessening of the segmentation of the market was likely to have favourable repercussions on the domestic market for standardized, mass-produced factory-made goods.

THE MARKET FOR CONSUMER GOODS

As a result of the market segmentation referred to above, the demand for standardized, mass-produced goods was limited. With limited purchasing power accentuating market segmentation, poorer members of the population will often choose inexpensive low quality imported products or products manufactured by indigenous small-scale industries. As shown in Table 4.12 below, more than one-half of all households in 1970 belonged to the income ranges below the (national) mean household income of $268.7 per month.

Over one-half of households provided a market for low priced low quality consumer goods. The situation allowed the small-scale entrepreneur to gain experience and perhaps accumulate capital

TABLE 4.12
WEST MALAYSIA, PERCENTAGE DISTRIBUTION OF HOUSEHOLDS BY INCOME RANGE AND RACE, 1970

Income Range ($ per month)	*Malay*	*Chinese*	*Indian*	*Other*	*Total*
1 – 99	33.9	2.6	1.3	0.2	27.1
100 – 199	19.1	7.8	4.4	0.1	31.4
200 – 399	10.4	11.9	3.5	0.1	25.9
400 – 699	3.0	5.3	1.2	0.1	9.6
700 – 1,499	1.1	2.9	0.6	0.1	4.7
1,500 – 2,499	0.2	0.7	0.1	0.1	1.1
3,000 and above	*	0.1	0.1	0.1	0.3

Source: *Mid-Term Review of the Second Malaysia Plan, 1971–75*, pp. 3–4.
Notes: Income includes cash income, imputed income for earnings in kind plus transfer receipts.
*Negligible in relation to the total. The (national) mean household income for 1970 was $268.7 per month.

before entering the higher quality market of the higher income households, in competition with the larger-scale manufacturers who were usually foreigners. British and other foreign firms dominated the higher priced and quality-conscious consumer market provided by the 6 or 7 per cent higher income groups. The sub-market of the lower income groups were predominantly the domain of small-scale enterprises, or cheap imports.

A few examples to illustrate the segmentation of the market may throw light on the character of the domestic market for consumer items. Canned meats, fish, beans, bottled sauces, and other similar food preparations originally imported from the United Kingdom but now manufactured locally, mainly for consumption by British and Commonwealth servicemen, foreign residents, and higher income local people were beyond the means of the majority of Malaysians. Local people from the lower income groups patronized similar, but low priced, foodstuffs made by local firms, or imported from Taiwan or Communist China. Dunlop tyres, tubes, and other rubber products virtually monopolized the high quality market, but tyres, tubes, and other rubber goods made (in Selangor) by smaller-scale local firms such as Shum Yip Leong and Fung Keong sold in the low quality market at prices about 60 per cent below those of products of Dunlop Malaysian Industries Bhd. The higher priced soap market, the aerated water, and bottled drinks as well as bread and dairy food markets were respectively supplied by Lever Brothers, Fraser and Neave, and Cold Storage. At the same time, local smaller-scale enterprises also supplied similar goods of inferior quality but in the lower priced end of the market. The quality work in the job printing and book publishing business was dominated by British firms, but local printing works predominated in the moderate to low quality printing and publishing jobs. Similarly, while British firms supplied the higher income consumers with household appliances and durable goods, cheaper varieties either made locally or imported, sold among the poorer section of the population.

Although at first the segmented market appeared to be the limiting factor for the large-scale production of consumer goods, the existence of sub-markets had promising implications for long-term economies of scale. A large-scale firm that can reduce costs could capture the low priced sub-market and might find that the segmented markets need not be a permanent hindrance to the growth of output. In reality there are firms which produce on a large scale that do practise product differentiation and price discrimination to enlarge the market for their manufactures. The scope of such practices is affected by the ease of transfer of goods between the segments of the market. In broad terms, British firms found most of their customers among the top 15 per cent (Table 4.12) of Malaysian households. In terms of total value of the consumer goods market, British companies controlled about 50 per cent of the market in 1970. In absolute amounts, British business in that year supplied an estimated $700–$800 million worth of consumer goods. The general opinion of executives interviewed was that by the standards of developing countries, the Malaysian market was 'probably uniquely sophisticated'.[39]

PRINCIPAL BRITISH CONSUMER GOODS IN THE MALAYSIAN MARKET

Table 4.13 shows the principal imports of consumer goods from the U.K. into West Malaysia in 1962, the year before the formation of Malaysia, and in 1967, the year which marked the establishment of the majority of British industrial concerns in Malaysia. Import figures for 1970 are also shown to provide a comparison. The inclusion of imports into East Malaysia and the output of British manufacturing establishments in the country, of course,

TABLE 4.13

PRINCIPAL IMPORTS INTO WEST MALAYSIA OF CONSUMER GOODS FROM THE UNITED KINGDOM

($ million)

Commodity Groups	1962 (1) Total$^{\phi}$	1962 (2) From U.K.	1962 (3) (2) as % of (1)	1967 (1) Total$^{\phi}$	1967 (2) From U.K.	1967 (3) (2) as % of (1)	1970 (1) Total$^{\phi}$	1970 (2) From U.K.	1970 (3) (2) as % of (1)
1. Food and foodstuff	279.5	44.6	16.0	268.4	25.4	9.5	673.1	29.7	4.4
2. Passenger cars (built up)	61.4	31.7	51.6	72.9	14.5	19.9	201.8*	107.5+	53.2
3. Clothing and apparel	30.9	1.5	4.7	30.0	0.9	2.9	32.3	2.3	7.1
4. Books, magazines, stationery	28.0	8.2	29.3	37.6	17.2	45.7	35.7	10.0	28.0
5. Cosmetics and toilet goods	26.2	9.1	34.6	17.5	6.4	36.5	71.9	19.7	27.4
6. Rubber tyres and tubes	24.2	14.7	60.6	5.5	0.8	13.9	4.5	0.1	2.2
7. Cigarettes and tobacco	17.2	10.5	61.1	9.8	1.7	17.3	8.2	2.3	28.0
8. Motor-cycles and parts	16.7	2.6	15.5	25.7	0.3	1.1	33.6*	...	
9. Radios, tape recorders, etc.	15.8	1.2	7.9	23.7	3.0	12.5	15.2	0.8	5.3
10. Paper and glass	12.7	4.9	38.6	25.1	4.8	19.2	109.5	10.3	9.4
11. Refrigerators, air-conditioners	7.1	1.3	18.0	10.6	0.8	7.7	24.6	3.4	13.7
12. Toys and sports equipment	6.5	1.4	21.1	9.1	1.9	20.6	11.9	1.3	10.9
13. Furniture and household goods	5.5	2.3	41.6	5.7	1.2	21.0	2.5	0.5	20.0
14. Footwear, travel and leather goods	5.3	1.7	32.3	7.4	1.5	20.1	4.9	0.4	8.2
15. Cutlery, kitchenware and stoves	4.3	1.6	38.1	7.2	1.6	22.4	12.3	1.8	14.6
16. Sandles, matches and small goods	1.4	0.3	20.5	4.2	0.9	22.5	10.7	0.4	3.7
17. Lenses and optical goods	0.5	0.1	28.4	0.8	0.1	11.5	0.8	...	
Total Principal Consumer Goods	543.3	137.6	25.3	561.2	82.9	14.8	1,253.7	190.5	15.2

Source: Department of Statistics, *Annual Statistics of Internal Trade*, Kuala Lumpur (various issues).

Notes: ϕ Total amount of import.
+ Including special purpose vehicles.
* Including completely-knocked-down vehicles, parts and accessories.
. . . Amount negligible, and included elsewhere.

would show a larger share of British consumer goods in the Malaysian market.

An estimated 90 per cent of the sales of U.K. consumer goods in the Malaysian market between 1962 and 1970 consisted of items in the seventeen groups shown in Table 4.13.

Throughout the 1960s the marketing of imported goods, particularly goods from the U.K. was mostly conducted by 'agency houses'[40] with headquarters either in Singapore or Kuala Lumpur, and with sales outlets in principal towns throughout the country. Only a small amount of international trade was conducted by branches of foreign manufacturing firms, or directly between suppliers and local importers and distributors. As importers and distributors the agency houses started their activities supplying the requirements of the rubber plantations, tin mines, and later, the British and Commonwealth forces in the country. An agency house might represent several hundred British as well as other foreign suppliers, and it might be involved in the marketing of several thousand individual products. Through its sales' outlets the agency house sold to other local enterprises operating wholesale and retail outlets, or sometimes to government agencies owning and operating public facilities.

The wholesalers and retailers dealing with the agency houses might be called their accredited sub-agents who, like the agency houses, might provide service and spares for the consumer goods they sold. In addition to performing their normal wholesale and retailing trade the accredited sub-agents took orders from customers. Thus, the agency houses with their sub-agents provided the full array of marketing service; they imported for their own account; they maintained stocks of goods and spare parts; they provided maintenance services; they sold to intermediate and final consumers and lately, since the mid-1960s, they have conducted market research for manufacturers.[41]

There were other variations in the distribution pattern of U.K. consumer goods in Malaysia. A department store, such as Robinson (M) Sdn. Bhd., operated as a direct importer and retailer of British consumer goods in the 1950s and 1960s importing direct from British manufacturers usually through its London agent, or through indent orders placed with an agency house. Dealers and distributors such as Weld Supermarket Bhd. specializing in food, liquor, and tobacco followed the same procedure as the department store. Specialist retailers in pharmaceutical items, cosmetics, and other shelf goods ordered direct from suppliers in Britain. There were also instances of local sales branches maintained by

British manufacturers who staffed them with local management and technical personnel, who in turn provided sales and services facilities.

British consumer goods listed in Table 4.13 were more expensive than locally produced goods because of shipping costs. This priced them out of reach of the lower income groups. In spite of higher prices, however, some British products earned a special reputation in the local market for quality and performance on the basis of consumption experience (e.g. Dunlop products) or gained wide acceptance through trade promotion and advertising (e.g. Rothmans cigarettes), or achieved a preference through long and successful exposure in the market (e.g. Brand's Essence of Chicken). Most of these items gained what might be called a 'brand name reputation' and found a market outside the more exclusive higher income groups.

In 1962, the total amount of consumer goods from Britain valued at $137.6 million occupied a little over one-quarter of the principal consumer import market. For some items such as rubber tyres and cigarettes, British goods constituted over 60 per cent of the West Malaysian imports of the items concerned. More than one-half of the value of passenger cars imported in 1962 were from Britain. So were over one-third of pharmaceuticals, cosmetics, paper and glass articles, household goods, travel and leather goods, footwear, kitchen ware, and more than 20 per cent of all imported books, magazines, and stationery, toys, games and sports equipment, optical goods, candles, matches, and small goods.

In 1967, however, the British share of consumer goods imports dropped to a mere $83 million, constituting approximately 15 per cent of total value of imports for the year. The individual imported commodity groups which showed significant decreases in absolute amounts as well as in relative market shares between 1962 and 1967 were drinks and foodstuffs, rubber tyres and tubes, cigarettes and tobacco, paper and glass articles, together with refrigerators and room air-conditioners. The period from 1962 to 1967 coincided with the local production of items formerly imported by such firms as Guinness Malaysia Bhd. (beers and stouts), Cold Storage Holdings Bhd. (dairy products), Dunlop Malaysia Industries Bhd. (tyres and rubber products), Rothmans of Pall Mall (Malaysia) Bhd. (cigarettes and tobaccos), Malayan Containers Bhd. (glass and plastic containers), and Electrical and Allied Industries Bhd. (refrigerators and air-conditioners).

The import of British consumer items such as passenger cars, motor-cycles, household furniture, footwear and travel goods, and clothing declined between 1962 and 1967 owing partly to the arrival of competing suppliers mainly from Japan and Europe; and partly to the setting up of local production of many of these items by foreign and local competitors. British motor-cars and motor-cycles faced competition from vehicles from Japan (Datsun, Toyota, Mazda, Honda, Suzuki, and Yamaha), Germany (Mercedes-Benz, Volkswagen, and BMW), France (Peugeot and Renault), Italy (Fiat and Alfa-Romeo), Sweden (Volvo and Saab), and Australia (GMH—General Motors-Holden). The problems that surround the British motor industry need not be considered here.[42] In Malaysia in the 1960s one of the main problems that handicapped the competitiveness of British passenger vehicles was the inability of British suppliers to meet demand in the small- to medium-size range of cars (0.85 to 1.6 litre class). The British car market was rapidly eroded by aggressive marketing tactics of other foreign suppliers,[43] a number of whom began to assemble their (imported completely-knocked-down) vehicles in Malaysia. Tariff protection and import restrictions limited the market for direct imports of all cars, although as Table 4.13 shows they did not decrease the total amount of cars imported. In spite of foreign competition the British share of the imported car market rose from about 20 per cent in 1967 to just over 53 per cent in 1970, largely as a result of increases in the imports of trucks, buses, land-rovers, and other special-purpose passenger vehicles.

In general, the declining British share of other imported consumer goods in the country in the 1960s coincided with the setting up of factories producing consumer items locally; the gradual withdrawal of British servicemen, their families and other civilian foreign residents who were major customers of imported British goods; and the arrival of very attractively priced consumer items from China, Taiwan, and Hong Kong. Manufacturers from the last two countries also came to manufacture locally in Malaysia, while a wide range of consumer products from China flooded the lower income range market.[44] The competitors of British consumer goods tended to be successful amongst low and middle income groups, while British suppliers continued to cater for higher income groups. At the same time, other competitors from the developed countries began to intensify their campaign to capture the market hitherto occupied by British goods. It was partly the realization that unless they retaliated against foreign competition the British imported consumer goods market might be in jeopardy that motivated British manufacturers to set up local production facilities in Malaysia.[45]

THE MARKET FOR INTERMEDIATE AND CAPITAL GOODS

In the 1960s, intermediate goods, i.e. partly processed goods and raw materials for industries, and capital or producer goods import requirements of Malaysia were enormous since the country produced only a limited range of materials for industry and virtually negligible amounts of technically sophisticated machinery for industry. The market for intermediate and capital goods was segmented into at least three divisions: the market for agricultural equipment and other machinery required by primary industries; the market for raw materials and equipment for construction and manufacturing industries; and the market for capital goods provided by the government, for use in public works.

Suppliers of intermediate and capital goods came particularly from Britain, Europe, and Japan. British suppliers in the early 1960s predominated in the capital goods market largely as a result of custom and familiarity of local users with British industrial and technical standards. Malaysian engineers and technicians trained in British institutions tended to favour the use of British machines. Where British technicians were employed in government departments, there was also a tendency to specify British standards in engineering and equipment requirements. British-owned rubber and palm oil plantations as well as tin mines were favoured markets for British capital goods suppliers. When British manufacturers established local production facilities in Malaysia, they naturally preferred British sources of intermediate and capital goods.

In the early 1960s British suppliers dominated over one-half of the local import market for intermediate and capital goods valued at about \$200–\$250 million annually. In the late 1960s the market had expanded, such that in 1970 the value of imported intermediate and capital goods estimated to be nearly \$1,900 million was over 700 per cent above the level in 1962. Suppliers from America, Europe, and Japan had made significant inroads into the market so that the British share of the import market for intermediate and capital goods declined from over 55 per cent in 1962 to about 14 per cent in 1970. In absolute terms, the amounts of British supplied intermediate and capital goods in 1970 constituted just over \$250 million, an increase of about 10.5 per cent over the amounts supplied in 1962.

THE PRINCIPAL BRITISH INTERMEDIATE AND CAPITAL GOODS IN THE MALAYSIAN MARKET

The position of imported intermediate and capital goods from Britain between the years 1962 and 1970 is summarized in Table 4.14. For certain goods such as telecommunication apparatus, switchgears, cables, and allied items British sources supplied more than 80 per cent of the import market in 1962. The situation changed drastically in the period 1963 to 1970. With the exception of electrical apparatus for industry, British imports and British suppliers in the market for imported industrial materials and equipment had decreased. Some comments on the market circumstances surrounding the demand for producer goods may throw some light on the nature of the market.

The reduction in the British import share of building and construction materials shown in Table 4.14 was largely due to Malaysia's growing capability of producing her own building materials. This ranged from almost total self-sufficiency in cement, crushed rocks, bricks, roofing materials (including ceramic and asbestos tiles), saw-mill products (including plywood, parquet, and hardwood flooring), and paints, to a major reliance on local production for the more common structural steel such as steel bars and rounds, architectural metal products, and window glass. There also was (and is) considerable local production of interior furnishings, including office and household furniture, ceramics, and sanitary ware. Several British firms, e.g. Malayan Cement Bhd. (a constituent of the Blue Circle Group), Crittall–Hope Malaysia Bhd., Shanks Malaysia Sdn. Bhd., and William Jacks Bhd., began local manufacturing of most building requirements previously imported. Local production of steel and iron by Malayawata Steel Bhd., and in Singapore by the National Iron and Steel Mills Ltd., helped to reduce the requirement for imported structural steel previously supplied by British Steel Corporation through its local agents.

The market for British-made transport equipment faced similar problems to those suffered by the British motor imports in Malaysia referred to earlier. Equipment of American, European, and Japanese origin competed vigorously in what was formerly an area of British domination (see Table 4.14).

Even the British share in the market for power generating and transmission equipment declined owing to two major circumstances. Firstly, the government (LLN, the National Electricity Board) purchases of power-generating and transmission gear which

TABLE 4.14

PRINCIPAL IMPORTS INTO WEST MALAYSIA OF INTERMEDIATE AND CAPITAL GOODS FROM THE UNITED KINGDOM

($ million)

Commodity Groups	1962 (1) Total ϕ	1962 (2) From U.K.	1962 (3) (2) as % of (1)	1967 (1) Total ϕ	1967 (2) From U.K.	1967 (3) (2) as % of (1)	1970 (1) Total ϕ	1970 (2) From U.K.	1970 (3) (2) as % of (1)
1. Building and construction materials	54.2	23.7	43.7	61.2	23.6	38.6	83.3	16.7	20.0
2. Transport equipment, including spares and parts	24.9	12.9	51.8	40.9	12.8	31.3	150.7	10.5*	7.0
3. Lifts, winches, pumps and industrial air-conditioners	24.2	14.7	60.7	38.8	5.0	13.0	162.6	39.0	24.0
4. Office, printing and related machines	23.6	10.1	42.8	34.0	8.6	25.3	21.0	5.3	25.2
5. Switchgear, cables and allied items	20.8	18.7	89.9	29.5	16.7	56.6	53.2	26.2	49.2
6. Power generating machinery	15.3	8.2	53.6	23.8	8.4	35.3	61.2	19.1	31.2
7. Telecommunication gear	13.7	11.5	83.9	15.2	6.5	42.8	16.5	3.0	18.2
8. Chemicals and semi-processed materials for industry	12.8	7.1	55.5	15.9	2.6	16.4	882.8	85.6	9.7
9. Other electrical goods	10.3	5.0	48.6	7.2	1.9	26.4	13.3	8.5	63.9
10. Petroleum products	9.8	4.0	40.8	20.8	8.6	41.3	215.4	6.5	3.0
11. Materials and machinery for agriculture	8.5	4.2	49.5	13.4	6.6	49.3	157.6	29.9	19.0
12. Miscellaneous equipment	4.7	1.8	32.3	5.4	0.3	5.6	17.4	2.9	16.7
Total	228.8	121.9	54.7	305.8	101.6	33.2	1,835.0	253.2	13.8

Source: As in Table 4.13.

Notes: ϕ Total amount of import.
* Excluding trucks and buses.

accounted for 85 to 90 per cent of the total purchases of such equipment, and which in the early 1960s has been financed by arrangements with British suppliers, were partly financed under the Malaysian development plans (1966–75) by the IBRD and ADB loans. These loans required that government purchases should be obtained from suppliers through competitive bidding on a world-wide basis. Hence competitive suppliers from Japan, Germany, and the United States seized the opportunity to erode the traditional British equipment market in Malaysia. Secondly, import requirements for mining and other private enterprises were mainly for the smaller to medium-sized petrol or diesel engine-powered generating units with the related transmission gear for which suppliers from Japan and Germany had been concentrating their marketing effort in the country. Since the mid-1960s, for example, one Japanese firm had been active in the marketing of multi-purpose portable generators into rural areas, and this represented an entirely new market not previously considered by other foreign suppliers.

It should, however, be noted that the decrease in the import of electrical cables and related items from U.K. suppliers was also partly due to the local establishment of Malayan Cables Bhd., a subsidiary of British Insulated Callendars Cables Ltd. (BICC), manufacturers of cables for all purposes. Also, the establishment of Federal Cables, Wires and Metal Manufacturing Bhd., further reduced the need for imported wires, cables, and metal products. At the same time, the firm also met increased local competition in the electrical cable and wire markets.

The loss of the U.K. share of the imported telecommunication equipment market was mainly the results of inroads made by a large U.S. supplier into the Malaysian market. Other suppliers from Germany, Sweden, the Netherlands, and Japan also contributed towards the diminution of the long-time British market stronghold.

To some extent, the reduction in the import of chemicals and semi-processed materials for industrial use was connected with the local production of these items by such companies as Chemical Company of Malaysia Bhd. (CCM, a member of the Imperial Chemical Industries), Malayan Oxygen Bhd., Mega Chemicals Bhd., and Pacific Chemicals Bhd. The development of Singapore into the centre for the petroleum products in the region too, had reduced the import of some industrial chemicals and petroleum products from U.K. into Malaysia. Shell Refining Co. (F.O. Malaya) Bhd. began production in the country in the early 1960s thus cutting further the need to import petroleum products, although crude petroleum had to be imported mainly from Bahrain, Kuwait, and Saudi Arabia.[46]

The opening of land under the Federal Land Development Authority (FELDA) generated demand for imported agricultural machinery. Similarly the development of the palm oil industry also created a demand for oil processing plants and other related equipment. The introduction of double- and treble-cropping rice farms as well as the increase in average of rice-growing lands resulting from the success of the drainage and irrigation schemes induced some demands in small farm machinery which was largely met by Japanese suppliers.

As for miscellaneous machinery and equipment for industry, e.g. machinery for processing, packaging, and canning food products, their imported amount of $1.8 million from the U.K. in 1962 (Table 4.14) accounted for about one-third of the total imported that year, but in 1970 the share of U.K. imports which rose to $2.9 million was only about 17 per cent of total imports of miscellaneous machinery at $17.4 million.

The position of British-supplied intermediate and producer goods in the Malaysian market was similar to that of consumer goods. In the beginning, British suppliers were supreme when the country was a British territory. The initial and continuing access to British goods helped by large, well-financed, and competent British agency houses enabled British manufacturers to serve the market by exports.

The arrival of other foreign suppliers in the early and mid-1960s provided keen competition. Unlike the British suppliers who were market preservers, the other foreign suppliers were market penetrators, sparing little effort in exploring new marketing ideas, and relying less on foreign distributing agents but more on local distributors[47] with numerous retail outlets. The success of the other foreign suppliers appeared to have been based on their understanding of the segmented nature of the Malaysian market. Accordingly, they shaped their marketing policies to penetrate the hitherto unexplored segments by emphasizing such factors as price, credit, quality, delivery, and service. Japanese suppliers concentrated more effort on testing and demonstrating their goods, equipment, and machines in the market, and they were quick to adapt their products to local requirements.

A combination of well-planned marketing tactics and the growth of the local market has aided the foreign non-British penetration of the Malaysian market. The strategy of the traditional

British suppliers being to defend their position in the Malaysian market, they began producing locally some of the products formerly imported.

THE EXPORT MARKET

In the 1960s very few of Malaysia's exports were in the form of crude and unprocessed raw materials. The bulk of the primary products exported was in the processed form. The significance of exports of processed primary materials to the economy of the country is already well known.[48] More recent in the development of Malaysia is the growth of the export manufactured products. The growth of manufactured exports is briefly discussed here and will be dealt with again in Chapters 5, 7 and 9.

During the period 1963 to 1967, total exports of products manufactured in Malaysia (excluding rubber, palm oil, and tin metal) doubled to $419 million (see Table 4.15 below).

Exports of manufactured products (excluding re-exports but including shipment to East Malaysia) grew at an average annual rate of 19.2 per cent. As a share of total exports, exports of manufactured products increased from 8.6 to 15.1 per cent.

TABLE 4.15

WEST MALAYSIA, EXPORTS OF MANUFACTURED PRODUCTS 1963–1967 ($ million)

	1963	*1965*	*1967*	*Increase 1963–7*
1. Total exports	2,428	2,940	2,778	350%
2. Manufactured exports*	208	337	419	211
3. Share of manufactured exports in the total exports	8.6%	11.5%	15.1%	–
4. Average annual growth rates	*1963–5*	*1963–7*		
Total exports	10	3.4%		
Manufactured exports	27	19.2		

Source: *Mid-Term Review of the First Malaysia Plan, 1966–70*, p. 72.

Note: *Manufactured food, textiles, and footwear, wood products, rubber products, chemical and chemical products, non-metallic mineral products, metal products and machinery, and miscellaneous products of manufacturing industries (excluding processed rubber, palm oil, and tin).

In the period 1966 to 1970 manufactured exports grew at an average annual rate of 12.8 per cent[49] giving an estimated value of $515 million of exported manufactured goods in 1970.[50] Exports of manufactured products as a whole had been growing at the rate of about 18 per cent per annum, twice the rate of total exports in the period 1968 to 1972.[51] Over the same period, manufactured exports constituted about 10 per cent of total exports.[52] Further development had occurred in the early 1970s. Net manufactured exports between 1970 and 1973 accounted for about 22 per cent of total exports, and in absolute amount manufactured exports in 1973 were estimated to be $1,550 million.[53] The average annual rate of growth of export of manufactured products in the early 1970s was around 18.8 per cent.[54] It is clear that the export market for Malaysian manufactured products had been growing rapidly.[55] In contrast to the experience of other developing countries, industrial development in Malaysia was not merely catering for the domestic market; it was also export oriented. In other words, it was part of the industrialization strategy that manufacturing industry be outward-looking.[56]

In 1970, Malaysian-made goods were exported to more than seventy countries all over the world. Just over 40 per cent of the value of manufactured exports went to the industrially developed countries. The neighbouring countries absorbed about 20 per cent of Malaysia's manufactured exports in that year, while the remainder went to other developing countries including Communist countries. Manufactured products ranged from those that had high local content (e.g. canned pineapples and timber products) to those that had high import content (e.g. machinery and equipment) and those that had moderately high skill content (e.g. electronic goods and precision instruments). Thus the manufactured exports consisted of a broad range of consumer, intermediate, and producer goods.

1. This was the case with British industrial investment in Singapore. See H. Hughes and P. S. You, eds., *Foreign Investment and Industrialisation in Singapore*, Canberra, Australian National University Press, 1969, p. 179.

2. As will be seen in Chapter 9, in terms of value added the cost of domestic labour constituted not more than 3 per cent on average for the companies surveyed, during the period 1963–70.

3. Industrial development in Malaysia since the mid-1960s follows the familiar infant industry strategy. Many of the respondents who have business connexions in Africa, Latin America, and other countries, were aware of the strategy.

4. The Tariff Advisory Board, the body responsible for advising the government on the application of protective tariffs as recommended by the Rueff Report, was fully

constituted in June 1964. As an instrument of industrial development, the tariff protection was used only after the late 1960s, i.e., since the announcement of the 'New Industrial Development Strategy'. See FIDA, *A New Industrial Development Strategy*, 1969, pp. 10–11.

Empirical studies on industrialization of many countries such as Brazil, Australia, and Nigeria showed that tariffs did play an important role in luring foreign investment in manufacturing. See L. Gordon and E. L. Grommers, *United States Manufacturing Investment in Brazil*, Boston, Harvard University Press, 1962; D. T. Brash, *American Investment in Australian Industry*, Canberra, Australian National University Press, 1966; and P. Kilby, *Industrialization in An Open Economy: Nigeria, 1945–66*, Cambridge University Press, 1969.

5. See evidence in the *Mid-Term Review of the First Malaysia Plan, 1966–70*, pp. 76–8. In the late 1960s, an industrialist seeking tariff protection had to approach the Tariff Advisory Board with regard to the protection required. The Board would conduct a public hearing on the matter, and thereafter put up a report to the government which would decide on the basis of the report. If the government was unconvinced of the viability of the project in question it would delay or even refuse the request. Since the abolition of the Tariff Board in 1970, the procedure has been reversed: the government decides on the identification of viable projects and the levels of protection it is prepared to give. Such projects are then announced to the private sector. Interested entrepreneurs may then decide whether or not to take up the projects.

6. Quotations throughout this study have been slightly edited, without altering the original sense, in order to transpose the spoken to written expressions.

7. See Chapter 3, Section 7, above.

8. This agrees with the findings of Hughes and You. See Hughes and You, eds., *Foreign Investment and Industrialisation in Singapore*, p. 183.

9. The multinational enterprises or the transnational enterprises as they are also called will be discussed in Chapter 7.

10. On the basis of the magnitude and composition of imports, between 1960 and 1970, there had been considerable increases in the domestic market for manufactured goods. Between these years, the imports of machinery and equipment grew at an annual rate of 11.7 per cent; that of manufactured items classified by materials, 6.2 per cent; and that of all manufactures was 8.4 per cent. The growth of import of food, beverages, and tobacco was only 1.5 per cent per annum. Domestic production of these items has also increased. See *Economic Report*, The Treasury, Kuala Lumpur, 1972, pp. 23, 90–1, and 98–9.

11. The subject of profits of British companies is discussed in detail in Chapter 8.

12. See Chapter 8. The prerequisite of a higher profit abroad than at home as underlying the investors' decisions to go overseas is universal. See H. J. Robinson, *The Motivations and Flow of Private Foreign Investment*, Stanford Research Institute, California, 1961, p. 2.

13. The older executives who may be sentimentally attached to Malaysia remarked that they wanted to play a part in the economic development of the country. Others also mentioned that the process of industrialization itself is an attraction to the foreign investor.

14. A classification of aggressive and defensive motivations is to be found in H. P. Gray, *The Economics of Business Investment Abroad*, Macmillan, 1972, p. 77, and *passim*.

15. H. W. Arndt, 'A Suggestion for Simplifying the Theory of International Capital Movements', *Economia Internationale*, Vol. VII, 1954, pp. 469–79.

16. S. H. Hymer, 'The International Operations of National Firms: A Study of Direct Investment', M.I.T. Ph.D. thesis, 1960, as quoted in C. P. Kindleberger, *International Economics*, Illinois, Irwin, 1963 (3rd ed.), and in C. P. Kindleberger, ed., *The International Corporation: a Symposium*, The M.I.T. Press, 1971.

17. See E. T. Penrose, 'Foreign Investment and The Growth of the Firm', *Economic Journal*, Vol. 66, 1956, pp. 220–35.

18. ibid. Firms tend to grow indefinitely, and there is continuity in the 'history' of firms. See E. T. Penrose, *The Theory of The Growth of The Firm*, Oxford, Basil Black-

well, 1972, p. 22 et seq., and *passim*. In contrast to Penrose's suggestion that there is a limit to the expansion of the firm as provided by the capacities of its management, British firms in Malaysia, as will be evident later in this study, appear to have no such limit. The agency houses in particular have been extending their activities into numerous kinds of industrial activity which are often unrelated. Similarly, other firms have also diversified their activities into areas of industry not directly related to their original activities.

19. Available evidence shows that British firms expanded considerably during the period covered by the present study. In certain cases, it was clear that the growth of their output and sales was aided by the growth of the domestic economy. See Chapter 9.

20. R. Z. Aliber, 'A Theory of Direct Investment', in C. P. Kindleberger, ed., *The International Corporation*, The M.I.T. Press, 1971, pp. 17–34.

21. During the world currency crisis in 1971, about US$35 million came into Malaysia (as reported in the *Far Eastern Economic Review*, 1 April 1972, p. 106). The origin of the currency inflow is not exactly known, but information gathered during field work suggests that a substantial amount came from holders of currencies that were devalued during the year. International investors prefer to have currency that does not fluctuate in value, such as the Malaysian dollar.

22. R. E. Caves, 'International Corporations: The Industrial Economics of Foreign Investment', *Economica* (*New Series*) Vol. 38 (149), February 1971, pp. 1–27.

23. J. H. Dunning, ed., *International Investment*, Penguin Books, 1972, pp. 9–23.

24. 'Doing business in Malaysia: The View of a British Industrialist', Paper presented at the Conference on Business Opportunities in South-East Asia, London, 1972.

25. The informant added that British investors realized that they should come (and they do) on the merit of their investment proposals, and not merely banking on their British nationality.

26. 'Doing Business in Malaysia: The View of a British Industrialist'.

27. Additionally, Malaysia also trades with countries in the Eastern and Western Blocks, which are becoming increasingly important trading partners. Malaysia has a great potential in terms of market prospects for exports of Malaysian-made manufactures to these countries.

28. ASEAN, the Association of South-East Asian Nations, comprises Indonesia (population 1972, 118 million), the Philippines (population 37 million), Thailand (population 36 million), Malaysia (population 10 million) and Singapore (2 million). Such a market in the region is worthwhile planning for, and anticipation of it led many British investors to consider Malaysia as a springboard to enter what will certainly be a profitable area.

29. *IBRD Report, 1955*, p. 31.

30. *Rueff Report, 1963*, p. 25.

31. Malaysia exports to these countries; see Chapter 9.

32. These indicators were chosen because companies interviewed considered them reasonably reliable pointers to the approximate measure of national markets. Other sets of market indicators may also be used.

33. Taiwan, Hong Kong, and Singapore, for example, gear their industries for export. See G. K. Helleiner, 'Manufactured Exports from Less Developed Countries and Multinational Firms', *The Economic Journal*, March 1973, pp. 21–47.

34. See Chapter 3 (Section 10, Table 3.7, and *passim*); see also D. Lim, *Economic Growth and Development in West Malaysia, 1947–1970*, p. 250, and *passim*.

35. Department of Statistics, Kuala Lumpur (n.d.). For details, see the Survey, pp. 9–13.

36. A. H. Ismail, *A Study of Total Expenditure Elasticities for West Malaysia*, Paper No. 1, Kuala Lumpur, The National University, 1971.

37. Except for meat which has an elasticity of demand of 1.26, and animal fats 1.66. Other elasticities are rice 0.18, cereals 0.45, vegetables 0.84, fruits 0.91, milk 0.90, vegetable oil 0.66, and all food for all races 0.67. For details, see M. J. Purvis, *Research Report on the Food Economy of Malaysia and Brunei*, Cornell University, Department of Agricultural Economics, 1965, and P. R. Crosson, *Economic Growth in Malaysia*, Washington, D.C., National Planning Association, 1966, pp. 165–80.

38. On the rural-urban differences in incomes, see L. L. Lim, *Some Aspects of Income Differentials in West Malaysia*, Kuala Lumpur, University of Malaya, 1971, and the *Mid-Term Review of the Second Malaysia Plan, 1971–75*, p. 4 et seq.

39. See 'Doing Business in Malaysia: The View of a British Industrialist'.

40. Chapter 5 discusses the participation of the agency houses in the involvement of British capital in Malaysian manufacturing.

41. Chapter 5 describes other activities of the agency houses.

42. For a general review of the problems of the British motor industry, see Simon Caulkin, 'British Cars—What's Wrong?', *Management Today*, December 1973, p. 74 et seq.

43. While British cars were mainly distributed by the British agency houses and their accredited sub-agents in the larger towns, the agencies of most foreign cars in the 1960s were held by local companies with numerous retail outlets. Some of these retail outlets were operated on very low margins which enabled them to offer lenient payment terms to their customers. Japanese cars sold in the market had cassette players and/or stereophonic radios as standard fittings. Some Japanese cars in the 1.6 litre range had factory-fitted air-conditioning units which made them very attractive in the tropical climate. Mercedes-Benz and Peugeot cars had factory-fitted diesel engines which made them popular with taxi operators in Malaysia where petrol was expensive. Of all the foreign motor vehicle suppliers, the Japanese were the most determined to capture as much of the local market as possible. The vehicles they sold were competitively priced, were very much differentiated, and designed to cover as wide a range of the market as possible.

44. The Communist Chinese mounted an intensive market development programme overseas in the late 1960s. Communist Chinese goods were at first sold in huge emporiums (department stores) in the cities and in general merchant shops in the smaller towns. Later these goods competed side by side with imported goods from other countries, in many large shops.

45. Other motivations have been discussed at the beginning of this chapter.

46. The petroleum industry in Malaysia deserves a separate study. Although the estimated crude petroleum production (in 1970) was around 70,000 barrels a day, very little of it was refined locally. The big petroleum companies have not been on friendly terms with the oil-producing countries of the Middle East since the Suez crisis of 1956 and the Arab-Israeli War in 1967. As part of their world-wide strategies, the companies arranged for the Middle East oil to be refined in Malaysia, a country which is friendly with the Arab oil producers, while good quality low-sulphur content crude oil from Malaysia is exported to be refined overseas.

47. Locally-owned distributing outlets without established market concentrated on giving good service to create customer goodwill.

48. See D. Lim, *Economic Growth and Development in W. Malaysia*, and J. T. Thoburn, 'Exports and Economic Growth in W. Malaysia', *Oxford Economic Papers*, Vol. 25 (1), March 1973, pp. 88–111.

49. *Second Malaysia Plan, 1971–75*, p. 148.

50. Loc. cit., p. 147.

51. Government of Malaysia, *Economic Report, 1972–73*, The Treasury, Kuala Lumpur, 1972, p. 13.

52. ibid.

53. *Mid-Term Review of the Second Malaysia Plan, 1971–75*, p. 142.

54. ibid.

55. This situation again confirms the vision of the companies interviewed when they said they came to begin manufacturing in Malaysia in anticipation of market growth; see Table 4.1.

56. See Chapter 9. Briefly it refers to the importance of international trade considered in the planning of the development. Conversely, an inward-looking strategy is one that does not emphasize the role of trade; instead, the industrial development of countries with such a strategy focuses mainly on the domestic market.

5 The Agency System

INTRODUCTION

THIS chapter examines the role of the agency houses and the growth of British capital in the manufacturing sector in Malaysia. The term 'agency house' is synonymously used with 'export-import firm', 'managing agent', 'merchant house', 'managing agency house', or just 'agency firm' to refer to the expatriate merchant firms which carry on a host of entrepreneurial activities including the provision of technical, scientific, financial, and marketing services. Because of the complex and comprehensive nature of their business, these firms cannot be called by any one term that can adequately describe their operation. Throughout the chapter a specific agency house will be called after its popular name (e.g. Sime Darby Holdings Ltd. will just be referred to as Sime Darby; Syarikat Harper Gilfillan Berhad as Harper Gilfillan; Boustead Holdings Berhad as Boustead; Kumpulan Guthrie Sendirian Berhad as Guthrie; and William Jacks & Co. Malaya Berhad as William Jacks, and so on).

Studies by Kidron (1965)[1] and Kilby (1969)[2] have attributed the involvement of British capital in local manufacturing, in India and (to a lesser extent) in Nigeria respectively, to the British merchant firms which dominated the external trade of these Commonwealth countries. However, Puthucheary (1960)[3] and Wheelwright (1965)[4] argued that these British merchant firms would not favour the development of local manufacturing in Malaysia because of their vested interests in agriculture, mining, and external trade of the country. Any local industries would, according to Puthucheary, compete with imported goods, thus taking away profits from the agency houses. Therefore, Puthucheary concluded, it could hardly be expected that agency houses would invest in local manufacturing, nor favour anyone else doing so.[5] There was a clear conflict of interest, according to Wheelwright, between manufacturing development and the big British importing houses in the country.[6]

The objective of this chapter is to examine empirically[7] the extent of conflict, if any, between British manufacturing interests and those of the agency houses, to discover the business associations of the agency firms with the manufacturing firms in Malaysia, and to evaluate their role in the country's industrialization programme in the 1960s.

THE ACTIVITIES OF THE AGENCY HOUSES

Originally the operators of the agency houses were merchants trading in European goods in the East, and Asian produce in Europe.[8] Later in the days of British Malaya they also became managing agents of plantations and mines, and around their trading and managing agency activities they built up other commercial activities such as shipping, insurance, and the provision of finance. Today their activities are so complex that it is difficult to unravel their engagement in every branch of the Malaysian economy without running the risk of oversimplification. In broad terms, it can be said that the agency firms were involved in every aspect of trade, commerce, and industry, dominating the scene of every area of economic activity, and virtually controlling the external trade of the country.

The position of the agency house in the Malaysian economy is best illustrated as in Figure 5.1. In the 1950s, for example, agency houses controlled 65 to 75 per cent of the export trade and 60 to 70 per cent of imports into the Malaysian area.[9] Between 1960 and 1970, the proportions fell to about 60 per cent of exports, and over 55 per cent of imports. In the period 1960 to 1970, ten of the largest agencies (in terms of market capitalization)[10] handled an estimated 70 per cent of British manufacturers, and an estimated 40 to 50 per cent of all manufacturers supplying the Malaysian market. Most of the agency houses also had equity interests in the large foreign companies in which the agencies were frequently regarded as the 'local' partners.[11]

Agency houses were continually reorganized into bigger units of operation so that they could provide the diversified activities shown in Table 5.1. Prior to 1960 they were mostly managing firms serving the interest of mainly British proprietary companies in the Malaysian region. As managers they facilitated the flow of British capital into the primary industries of the region.[12] At the same time they were also active in trade; they were 'importers of general merchandise and dealers in and shippers of tin, rubber and tropical produce . . .'.[13] Over the years they transformed their

FIGURE 5.1
THE POSITION OF THE AGENCY HOUSES IN THE MALAYSIAN ECONOMY

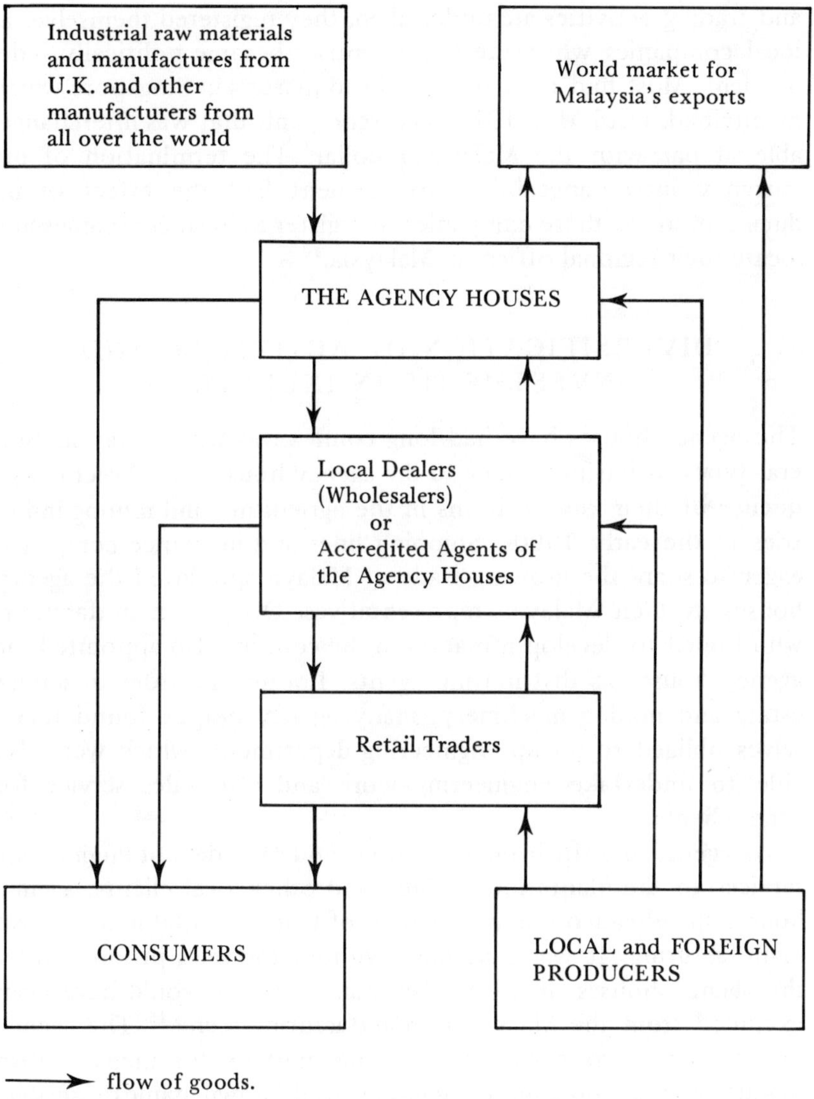

Source: Interviews.

organizational structures by take-overs, by mergers, and less frequently by new issues, from managing and trading concerns to complex holding companies with numerous affiliates.

A great deal of reorganization took place within the agency houses in the period 1960 to 1970. Since most of them were, to begin with, incorporated in London, they had to register themselves as locally incorporated companies.

In Malaysia and Singapore, where most of their management and trading activities are undertaken, they registered themselves as local companies when the two countries became politically independent. Most had their regional headquarters in Singapore which maintained, until May 1973, a currency unit that was interchangeable at par with the Malaysian dollar. The termination of the currency interchangeability arrangement had the effect of inducing more of these companies to register as local companies and locate their regional offices in Malaysia.[14]

DIVERSIFICATION OF ACTIVITIES AND INVESTMENTS IN INDUSTRY

The agency houses have had long connexions with Malaysia. Several types of business came to the agency houses as a direct consequence of their key positions in the agriculture and mining industries in the early 1900s. Shipping lines and insurance companies eager to share the growing trade of Malaya appointed the agency houses as their Malayan representatives. Overseas manufacturers who hoped to develop a market in the country also appointed the agency houses as distributing agents. Locally, in order to service estate and mining machinery, many agency houses found themselves obliged to set up engineering departments which were also able to undertake engineering work and after-sales service for other clients.

As agents of British manufacturers and providers of engineering services to the plantations, mines, and other local clients, agency houses spearheaded the involvement of British capital in Malaysian manufacturing. It was said that, without the sales promotion by the agency houses, many British manufacturers would have been excluded from the Malaysian manufacturing scene.[15] The agency houses were responsible for creating markets for many British manufacturing companies, including well-known names like Beecham, British Leyland, British Insulated Callendars Cables (BICC), British American Tobacco (BAT), Guinness, Imperial Chemical Industries (ICI), Shanks, and Shell. There were numerous other branded goods (e.g. packaged and tinned foods, toilet preparations, clothing, and medicines) as well as other manufactured commodities (e.g. cement, flour, and sugar) manufactured by British firms that were distributed by the agency firms. By employing imaginative advertising techniques these agency firms built up a strong market preference for British goods. As was discussed in the previous chapter, many firms which came to invest in manufacturing in Malaysia were motivated by the desire to take advantage of markets already established. To the extent that agency houses were instrumental in creating those markets, it can be said that their role in the process of British capital participation in manufacturing in Malaysia was crucial. By themselves, the agency houses were also involved in manufacturing as part of their diversification programme.

The involvement of these houses in manufacturing might take several overlapping forms. Firstly, the agency house concerned might expand its engineering works into manufacturing metal products, as in the case of Harper Gilfillan's expansion of activities into the manufacture of road tankers in aluminium alloy and steel aviation refuellers, articulated semi-trailers, coach bodies, and mineral treatment equipment. Secondly, the agency firm might expand by the acquisition of existing factories as in the case of Sime Darby's take-over of various ice factories supplying the public and the fishing industry. Thirdly, some firms might become involved in manufacturing as a result of the integration of their businesses, as in the cases of Harper Gilfillan, James Warren, and Sime Darby which seized the opportunities (arising from the government economic plans in the 1960s) to supply the agriculture, fishing, and timber industries with machinery and equipment.[16]

The building boom of the 1960s induced the involvement of the agency firms in manufacturing in yet another way; by going into partnership with their principals, the British manufacturing firms (and in one or two cases with non-British firms), for example Sime Darby (PAR Paints Berhad), and William Jacks (Critall-Hope Malaysia Berhad, Pillar-Naco, and Shanks Malaysia Sendirian Berhad) diversified into building materials manufacture. Hotels and business premises also provide customers for subsidiaries of Sime Darby (Chubb Malaysia Berhad) and William Jacks (Wismer Automation Berhad) which manufacture and install security systems, automatic doors, and certain building accessories.

The growth of the market for consumer goods induced a subsidiary of Inchcape Berhad (A. S. Watson Sendirian Berhad) to manufacture cosmetics and pharmaceutical products. Another of Inchcape's associates (Federal Industries Berhad) began manufacturing sanitary products for hospitals and rural clinics. Several other subsidiaries (e.g. Champion Motors Sendirian Berhad, Borneo Motors Sendirian Berhad, Motor Investments Berhad, and Orchard Motors Sendirian Berhad) which originally acted as motor vehicle distributors began local assembly of cars and the manufacture of car parts and accessories. Trebor Malaysia Sendirian Berhad, an associate of Boustead which started manufacturing sweets in the late 1960s, provided another example of an agency house entering the consumer industry.

Another form of diversification involved vertical integration of activities of the agency houses which, as mentioned above, have had very close associations with primary industries. Such integration took the form of either the manufacture of parts of machines, or the manufacture of products required or produced by the industries with which the firms have had long connexions. Subsidiaries of Harper Gilfillan, Sime Darby, James Warren, and William Jacks had gone into the manufacturing of spares and parts of machines and equipment required by industry. A subsidiary of Inchcape's (the Borneo Agrichemicals Sendirian Berhad) processes fertilizers and agricultural chemicals for the rubber and palm oil estates; another subsidiary, the Borneo Timber Company Sendirian Berhad manufactured timber mouldings from timber produced by yet another of Inchcape's subsidiaries, Austral Sendirian Berhad. An associate of Harrisons & Crosfield, the Wilkinson Process Rubber Company Berhad manufactured industrial rubber goods from latex produced in the plantations of the parent firm. The processing of edible oils (mainly from palm oil) was also carried on by an associate within the Harrisons & Crosfield organization, which also expanded into the business of manufacturing machines and equipment required by the primary industries in Malaysia through its affiliates, J. Whyte Malaysia Sendirian Berhad, Harrison Lister Engineering Berhad (in conjunction with Hawker Siddeley), and Bradken Malaysia Sendirian Berhad. A subsidiary of Harper Gilfillan's processed non-ferrous ores and refined tin from products of local tin-mining companies. Another example of vertical integration of activities is provided by an associate of Kumpulan Guthrie Sendirian Berhad, Guthrie-Pullen Limited which, in 1966, pioneered the development of crumb-rubber processing machinery which was very much in demand by the rubber industry. Other companies in the Guthrie group manufactured agricultural products (e.g. Guthrie Rubber Processing Sendirian Berhad, Guthrie Palm Products Sendirian Berhad, and Guthrie Latex Sendirian Berhad—in conjunction with Wm. Symington and Son Ltd.).

There were other miscellaneous forms of entry of the agency houses into manufacturing, but generally the pattern seemed to follow two broad stages. Firstly, the agency firms assembled the

TABLE 5.1

SELECTED AGENCY HOUSES AND THEIR INTERESTS IN MALAYSIA, BETWEEN 1960 AND 1970

Agency (major reorganizations/ new names)	*Commencement of Contact with Malaysia*	*No. of Companies Managed (1965)*	*No. of Rubber+ Estates Managed (1966) (No.)*	*Acres*	*Other Activities*
T. Barlow (Barlow Boustead Estates Agency Sdn. Bhd.)	1820s	19	42	111,600	A, I, M.
Guthrie (Kumpulan Guthrie Sdn. Bhd.; Guthrie Waugh and Guthrie Boustead*)	1820s@	22	39	213,980	A, I, M, S, T.
Boustead-Buttery (Boustead Holdings Sdn. Bhd.; Sandilands Buttery Bhd., and John Buttery*)	1827@	37	58	148,250	A, I, M, S, T.
Harrisons & Crosfield Sdn. Bhd.	1844	42	111	360,430	A, I, M, S, T.
*R.E.A. Cumberbatch*ø	1850s	37	55	120,310	A, I, M, S.
Plantation Agencies Sdn. Bhd.	1850s	10	29	55,030	A, I, S.
Borneo (Inchcape Berhad)	1860s@	63	...	...	A, I, M, S, L.
Harper Gilfillan Berhad	1886@	16	18	37,790	A, I, M, S, T.
*Oriental Estates*ø	1890s	14	19	69,210	A, I, S.
James Warren (M) Sdn. Bhd.	1890s	16	21	30,230	A, I, M, S, T.
*Ethelburga*ø	1900s	1	9	30,660	A, I, S.
*Whittal*ø	1900s	22	28	47,410	A, I, S.
Paterson, Simons and Ewart	1900s	5	7	23,450	A, I, M, S, T.
William Jacks & Co. (M) Bhd.	1900s@	5	...	...	A, I, M.
Sime Darby Holdings Ltd.	1902@	23	30	81,400	A, I, M, S, T, L.

Sources: *Straits Times Directory*, various issues; Stock Exchange of Malaysia and Singapore, Company Reports; and *Manual of Rubber Planting Companies*, John and Leigh Hunt (Private publication), 1960.

Notes:
+ Including palm oil and other crops.
@ Listed on the Malaysia-Singapore Stock Exchange.
* Complicated reorganizations into many companies.
ø Interests either sold or now managed by Meagl Sdn. Bhd.
A = Import/Export Agency: provides all facilities connected with trade (e.g. warehouse, transport, etc.).
I = Insurance and agency.
M = Owning or managing manufacturing establishments.
S = Having shipping agency and other international forwarding agencies.
T = Managing mining companies.
L = Having interests in the timber industry.
... = Not known.

TABLE 5.2

SELECTED AGENCY HOUSES WITH SELECTED INDUSTRIAL INVESTMENTS, 1968

Agency House	*Name of Industrial Firms*	*Main Products*	*Agency House Equity* (%)
Borneo Berhad (renamed Inchcape Berhad, 1971)	Austral Sdn. Bhd.	timber products	100
	Borneo Agrichemicals	fertilizer	70
	Champion Motors	motor cars	100
	Duncan Roberts	office equipment	100
	Quink Co. Sdn. Bhd.	writing ink	89
	A.S. Watson Sdn. Bhd.	pharmaceutical products	100
Boustead Holdings Bhd.	East English Sdn. Bhd.	machinery	100
	Trebor Sdn. Bhd.	confectionery	24
Guthrie Sdn. Bhd. (renamed Kumpulan Guthrie in 1971)	Guthrie Latex Sdn. Bhd.	processed latex	100
	Guthrie Palm Products	palm oil products	100
	Guthrie Pullen Ltd.	machinery	100
Harper Gilfillan Berhad	Hargill Engineering Berhad	transport equipment	100
	Edgar Sdn. Bhd.	handling equipment	100
	Paterson Candy Sdn. Bhd.	water-treatment plants	100
Harrisons & Crosfield	Harrison Lister	heavy machinery	100
	Wilkinson Process	rubber goods	100
William Jacks	Jacks Hardwood Ltd.	wood products	100
	Wismer Automation	electrical control gear	52
	Components International	electronics components	75
	Shanks Malaysia	sanitary ware	35
Paterson Simons	Sincere Match	matches and tobacco	100
Sandilands Buttery	Novakey Sdn. Bhd.	pipes and conduits	70
	Ansul Sdn. Bhd.	agricultural chemicals	50
Sime Darby	Chubb Malaysia	security equipment	49
	Par Paints	paints	50
	Tractors Malaysia	agricultural equipment	75
	Malaysian Bitumen	bitumenous products	99
	Malaysian Ice	ice	100
	Devon Instrument	precision instruments	100
James Warren	Malayan Casting Bhd.	cast-iron products	50
	Stay Board Ltd.	cement additives	50

Sources: Interviews and company reports.

final products from imported knocked-down parts, and secondly, the imported products or parts of the products were replaced by products manufactured either by the engineering departments of the agencies or by their associates in Malaysia.

As shown in Table 5.1, the majority of British agency houses have manufacturing interests, and as indicated by the examples of Boustead (Fig. 5.2) and Sime Darby (Fig. 5.3) these firms had also diversified into other non-industrial activities such as shipping, insurance, and the provision of services to commerce and industry. Table 5.2 shows selected industrial firms in which some agency houses have management and equity interests. It can be seen from the Table that in the majority of cases, the industrial concerns are wholly-owned subsidiaries of the agency firms. It can also be seen from the range of products manufactured, that the agency firms do not specialize in any particular industry.

In essence the agency houses were conglomerates, in the sense that their business organizations consisted of holding companies and groups of subsidiary companies engaged in several unrelated activities. The diversified and unrelated nature of their activities was reflected in the composition of their average turnover shown in Table 5.3 below. Over the years there had been a shift in the activities of these firms towards manufacturing, and the supply and servicing of machines and equipment.

TABLE 5.3

COMPOSITION OF THE AVERAGE TURNOVER OF TEN AGENCY FIRMS OPERATING IN MALAYSIA, 1962 AND 1971 (per cent)

	1962	*1971*
1. General merchanting, importing and exporting	38.0	26.0
2. Supply and servicing of machines and equipment	21.0	50.0
3. Plantation and general management	18.0	3.5
4. Technical contracting	10.0	6.0
5. Other services	6.2	2.5
6. Local manufacturing	1.8	10.0
7. Investment, interest, and other income	5.0	2.0
	100.0	100.0

Source: Interviews.

FIGURE 5.2

AN ILLUSTRATION OF THE ORGANIZATION OF COMPANIES BELONGING TO AN AGENCY HOUSE: BOUSTEAD HOLDINGS BERHAD, 1973

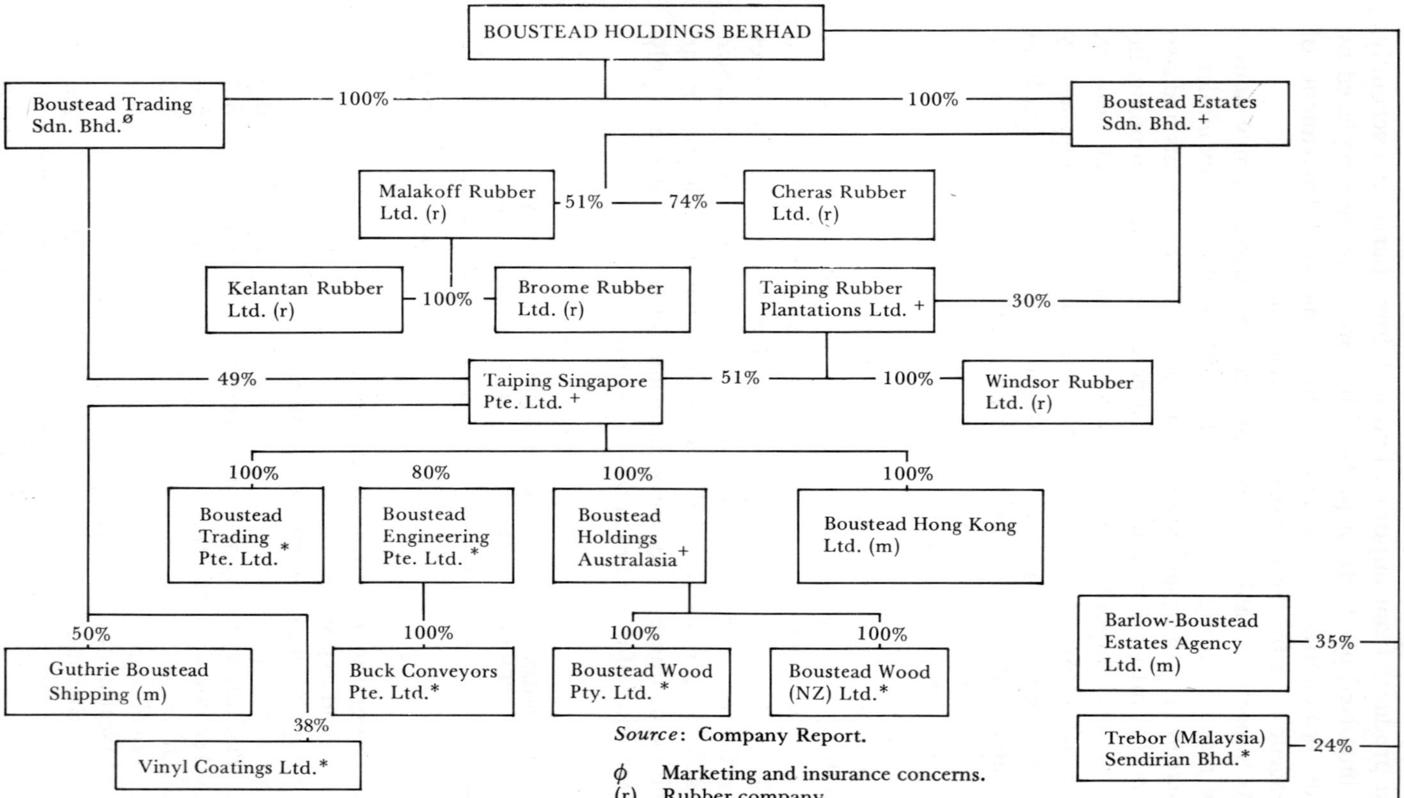

Source: Company Report.

ϕ Marketing and insurance concerns.
(r) Rubber company.
(m) Management firm.
* Manufacturing concerns.
\+ Intermediate holding company.

FIGURE 5.3

AN EXAMPLE OF AN AGENCY HOUSE THAT HAS TURNED INTO A CONGLOMERATE: SIME DARBY, 1972

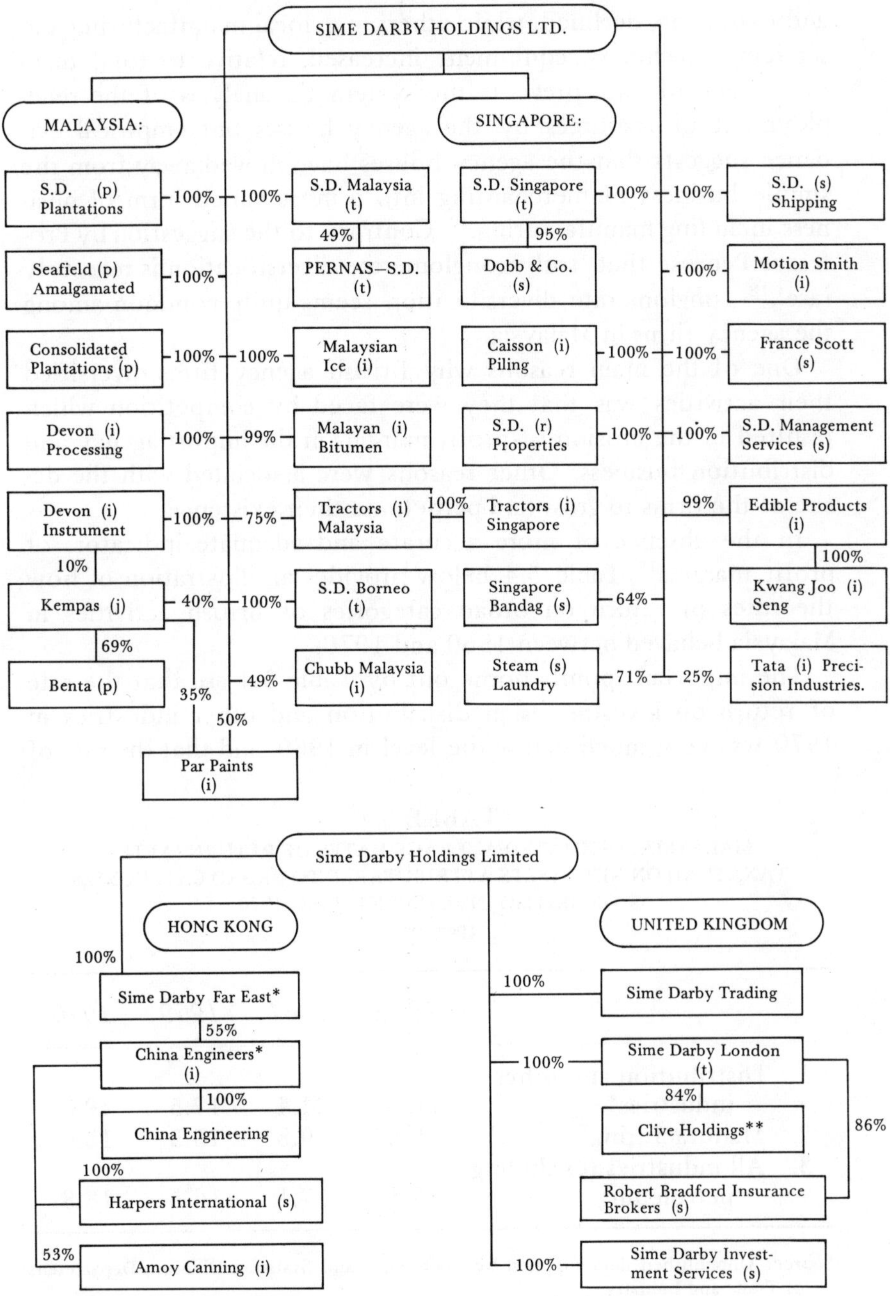

Source: Chart based on company reports.

Notes:
(p) = Company primarily involved in plantation business, i.e. rubber estates and oil palm.
(t) = Trading is the main activity of the company.
(i) = Industrial company.
(s) = Company is either a service company or is mainly involved in service industry.
* = Intermediate holding company.
** = Discount house.
(r) = Company involved in real estate business.

Although in absolute terms all components of turnover shown in Table 5.3 increased between the two years, the proportions of certain categories of turnover, e.g. general merchanting, importing, and exporting, declined, while others, e.g. local manufacturing and servicing machinery equipment increased, relative to total turnover. Lack of data prevents the systematic analysis of the redeployment of resources by the agency houses but empirical evidence suggests that the agency houses have moved away from the simple business of merchanting into a more varied form of business including manufacturing.[17] Contrary to the suggestion by Professor Penrose that 'truly conglomerate diversification is relatively rare',[18] conglomerate diversification seems quite common among the agency firms in Malaysia.

One of the main reasons why British agency firms diversified their activities was that they were faced by competition which resulted in the erosion of profit margins in the import agency and distribution business. Other reasons were associated with the desire of the firms to grow and perpetuate their existence.

In the absence of more accurate and adequate indicators of profit margins[19] Table 5.4 below provides an illustration of how the rates of return on broad categories of British activities in Malaysia behaved between 1960 and 1970.

The important points borne out by Table 5.4 are that the rate of return on investments in distribution and other industries in 1970 was very much below the level in 1960, and that the rate of

TABLE 5.4

MALAYSIA: ESTIMATED AVERAGE RATES OF RETURN (AFTER TAXATION) ON NET ASSETS ATTRIBUTABLE TO BROAD CATEGORIES OF BRITISH INVESTMENT, 1960–1970

(per cent)

	1960	*1961*	*1969*	*1970*
1. Distribution and other industries*	26.0	24.4	17.5	19.0
2. Manufacturing+	9.6	9.8	15.5	18.6
3. All industries (excluding petroleum)	17.8	17.1	16.5	18.8

Source: Unpublished data supplied by Economics and Statistics Division, Department of Trade and Industry.

Notes: * Including agriculture, construction, and mining.

\+ Electrical, mechanical and marine engineering, vehicles, and miscellaneous manufacturing.

return on investments in manufacturing in 1970 was almost double that of 1960. It was the recognition of the flagging import agency business that partly induced many agency houses to diversify into other activities including manufacturing.

The British agency houses found they had to contend with American, Japanese, and other European manufacturers. Even though the Malaysian market for manufactures in the 1960s still preferred goods from Britain, the agency firms began to find it was unprofitable to cater for the market purely by relying on the reputation of 'British-made' labels. Cheap consumer goods from China, Taiwan, and Hong Kong, machinery, equipment, and consumer durables from American, Japanese, and other European suppliers, imported by competitors to the British agency houses, shown in Table 5.5 were challenging British-made goods in Malaysia.

Some foreign manufacturers appointed British agencies as their accredited distributors in Malaysia, but the majority appointed non-British agents or local traders partly to dissociate themselves from the image of 'neo-colonial collaborators'[20] and partly because British agency houses held agencies of their competitors.

Many of the non-British agency firms listed in Table 5.5 were instrumental in penetrating the Malaysian market with foreign goods in competition with British-made goods. It was apparent to the British agency houses that they could not retain any monopoly of the import and distributive trade for very long, in spite of their critical position in the Malaysian external trade as portrayed in Figure 5.1. Some British manufacturing companies found that a number of British agency firms were too ambitious and were handling too diversified a range of manufactured goods. As a result, the agencies were unable to maintain the necessary technical and service staff and facilities for the great number of British manufacturers they endeavoured to represent.[21] As a result, several manufacturers appointed non-British firms as their distributors, while others set up their own distributing companies. Many manufacturers realized they had to adopt a counter strategy in the face of competition from other non-British sources. Part of the strategy was to set up local manufacturing facilities as a means of retaining their share of the market, as discussed in Chapter 4.

There was no doubt that the British agency houses advised some of their principals to manufacture locally. Those manufacturers that agreed with such advice received further assistance from the agency firms, a number of which, as noted before, became the 'local' partners of the manufacturers and which provided services

TABLE 5.5
SELECTED NON-BRITISH AND OTHER TRADING COMPANIES IN THE DISTRIBUTIVE TRADE IN MALAYSIA, *c.* 1967

Name of Firm	*Types of Activities*		*Number and Nationality of Manufacturers Represented; Nature of Products*
Foreign			
1. Behn Meyer Ltd.	A, B, C, and D.	*	over 60; mainly German; ϕ
2. Clouet & Co. Ltd.	A, B, C, and D.	*	over 50; mainly French; f, m
3. Daiichi Bussho Ltd.	A, B, C, D, and E.		over 20; mainly Japanese; ϕ
4. Diethelm Ltd.	A, B, C, D, and E.		over 100; European; ϕ, m
5. East Asiatic Co. Ltd.	A, B, C, D, E, F, and G.	*	over 80; Danish, Italian, German; ϕ, m, f, h
6. Jebsen & Jessen Ltd.	C, and D.	*	over 20; German; ϕ
7. Lindeteves-Jacoberg Ltd.	A, B, C, D, and E.	*	over 20; German, Dutch and Italian; ϕ, h
8. Societa Commissionaria di Exportazione/Importazione	A, and B.	*	? Dutch and Italian; ϕ, h
9. Sumitomo Ltd.	A, and B.		? mainly Japanese; ϕ, m
10. Swedish Trading Co. Ltd.	A, and C.	*	? mainly Swedish; ϕ, m
11. Toyo Manka Kaisha Ltd.	A, B, and D.		over 10; Japanese; ϕ, m, h
12. Vevasseur Ltd.	A, B, C, D, E, F, and G.		? mainly European; ϕ, m
Malaysian			
13. Asia Trading Ltd.	A, B, C, and D.	*	? all nationalities; ϕ, m, f
14. General Trading	A, and B.	*	? all nationalities; m, f
15. Cycle & Carriage Ltd.	A, D, and E.	*	? mainly German; ϕ, h
16. Naina Mohamed Ltd.	A, B, C, and D.	*	over 20; ϕ, m
17. Sim Lim Ltd.	A, B, and D.	*	over 20; ϕ, m
18. United Motors	A, B, D, and E.	*	over 10; ϕ, h

Source: *Straits Times Directory of Malaysia*, 1965, 1967, and 1968.

Notes: A = Importing.
B = Exporting.
C = General Merchanting.
D = Manufacturers' Representative.
E = Manufacturing.
F = Shipping Agent.
G = Insurance Agent.
ϕ = Consumer durables.
f = Foodstuffs.
m = Miscellaneous manufactures.
h = Heavy machines and equipment.
* = Company also handles British-made goods.
? = Number of manufacturers represented not known exactly.

in the form of assistance in company formation,[22] and in some cases, the provision of finance as well. Agency houses also extended such services to non-British manufacturers who wished to make use of them.

Having been in the country for some time and having interlocking interests in many branches of the country's economy,[23] the agency houses possessed the stamp of credit-worthiness and easy access to capital. For example in the late 1960s directors of Inchcape and Sime Darby were represented on the Court of Directors of the then largest bank in Malaysia, the Chartered Bank.[24] Prominent agency houses had associations with merchant bankers (e.g. Gray, Dawes and Company Limited in Inchcape; Clive Holdings Limited in Sime Darby) which provided assistance in company promotion and finance, and with management service companies which also gave assistance in company promotion and management. These ancillary services were partly the result of the diversification of activities of the agency houses, and partly they were created in response to the demand for such services. In other words, the ancillary services of these firms were both a manifestation and an instrument of diversification of activities.

TABLE 5.6

ESTIMATED EXTENT OF AGENCY HOUSES' INTERESTS IN BRITISH INDUSTRIAL INVESTMENTS IN MALAYSIA, 1968

	(1) Total Number/ Amount Attributable to All British Interests	*(2) Agency Houses' Interest*	*(3) (2) as % of (1)*
1. Total number of firms and number in which agency houses had an interest	112	62	54
2. Estimated value of net assets committed to industry in $ million	159	87	55
3. Estimated value added in $ million	181	99	55
4. Estimated gross sales in $ million	585	309	53
5. Estimated number of full-time paid employees	9,186	3,850	42

Source: Based on *Census of Manufacturing Industries, 1968*; and information derived from interviews.

THE INTEREST OF AGENCY HOUSES IN BRITISH INDUSTRIAL INVESTMENTS

The extent of association between the agency houses and British industries in Malaysia in 1968 is given in Table 5.6.

More than one-half of the number of companies and value of assets attributable to British industrial interests were either controlled or managed by an agency house. At the same time 55 per cent of value added and 53 per cent of gross sales of all British industrial firms originated from firms in which the agency houses had some interest.

Not all were involved in manufacturing, but certainly the large ones were. Some of those not directly involved in manufacturing had trade investments in industry, and many of those not involved had followed other opportunities, e.g. acquiring the distribution of non-British manufactures and participating in the service industries which appeared to them less risky and did not require a radical break with their traditional agency and merchanting activities.

THE AGENCY HOUSES AS DISTRIBUTORS OF MALAYSIAN MANUFACTURES

The agency houses formed a loose federation of consumer-selling and export organizations in which they acted as distributors for products of local industries. This was one of their very important functions in the economy. They distributed products manufactured not only by British but also other foreign and local-owned firms in the country. Table 5.7 shows a select number of industrial firms whose products were handled by the agency houses in 1970. Industrialists generally preferred to make use of the services of these established agency houses because of their world-wide connexions, experience, knowledge, and reliability. It was also advantageous for industrialists to engage the services of the agencies since the latter were in a good position to give financial advances. Moreover, ancillary services of agency houses such as storage, shipping, and insurance were an added convenience and economy of arrangement for those who engaged them.

In the export business, the agency which had a marketing organization in a particular country or region handled the distribution of Malaysian manufactures in that particular area. However, the same manufactured products might be distributed by another agency in another area.

Empirical evidence suggests that the agency houses had little

TABLE 5.7
SELECTED BRITISH AGENCY HOUSES MARKETING SELECTED PRODUCTS OF LOCAL INDUSTRIAL COMPANIES, 1970

Agency House	*Name of Company*	*Main Products*
1. Borneo (Inchcape)	Borneo Agrichemicals S.B.*	chemical fertilizers
	Borneo Timber Co. S.B.	timber mouldings
	Champion Motors S.B.	motor vehicles
	Duncan Roberts S.B.	office equipment
	Federal Industries S.B.	sanitary products
	A. S. Watson S.B.	pharmaceutical products
2. Boustead	Beecham (M) S.B.	pharmaceutical products
	Best Products S.B.	glucose
	Crescent Manufacturing	baking powder
	Health Products S.B.	insecticides
	Kelantan Match S.B.	safety matches
	Malayan Industrial Plastics	PVC materials
	Nestlé (M) Ltd.	dairy food products
	Tasek Cement	cement
	Trebor (M) S.B.	confectionery
3. Guthrie	Cement Paints (M) S.B.	concrete products
	Concrete Products (M) Ltd.	roofing tiles
	Hume Industries (M) Ltd.	pipes and culverts
	Insulations (M) Ltd.	foam polystyrene
	Johore Pipes Co. Ltd.	glazed stoneware
	John Lysaght (M) Ltd.	roofing materials
4. Harper Gilfillan	Ansul (M) S.B.	herbicides
	Federal Plastics Ind. Ltd.	plastic goods
	Federal Tiles Ltd.	tiles
	Hargil Engineering	transport equipment and heavy machinery
	ICI Paints (M) Ltd.	paints
	Malayawata Steel Bhd.	steel and iron
	Malayan Batteries Bhd.	batteries
	Malayan Cables Bhd.	electric cables
	Malayan Ve-Tsin S.B.	gourmet powder
	Paterson Candy (M) S.B.	water treatment plants
	Tamco S.B.	engineering products
5. Harrisons & Crosfield	Capricorn (M) Ltd.	springs and locks
	Fisons (M) Ltd.	Fison chemicals
	Harrison Lister S.B.	heavy equipment and machines
	J. Whyte (M) Ltd.	engineering products
	Wilkinson Rubber	rubber foams
6. William Jacks	Bok Kee S.B.	parquet flooring
	Chubb (M) S.B.	safes
	Maltronics S.B.	electronic goods
	Pacific Engineering Bhd.	water heaters
	Pakai Industries S.B.	plastic cisterns
	Shanks (M) S.B.	sanitary wares
	Tropical Veneer Bhd.	plywood and veneer
	Wismer Automation Bhd.	electrical and mechanical control gears

(*Continued*)

TABLE 5.7 (*Continued*)

7. Paterson Simons	IT & T (M) Ltd.	telecommunication gear
	Malayan Weaving Mills Ltd.	textiles
	Sincere Match & Tobacco	matches and tobacco
8. Sandilands Buttery	Ansul S.B.	agricultural chemicals
	Joyce Brothers S.B.	spring mattresses
9. Sime Darby	Glaxo-Allenburys S.B.	pharmaceutical products
	Rothmans of Pall Mall S.B.	cigarettes and tobacco
10. James Warren	Chop Jin Chong S.B.	sprayers
	Malayan Casting S.B.	cement additives
	Stayboard S.B.	cast iron pipes

S.B. = Sdn. Bhd. = Sendirian Berhad, the equivalent of 'private limited'.

Source: *Straits Times Directory*, 1971.

conflict of interest with manufacturing development in Malaysia, because the development of industries enabled them to secure additional business. No data are available to show how much the agency houses suffered reductions in income from the loss of their import agency as a direct result of the growth of local manufacturing. Nevertheless this is an important issue. The representatives of these agency houses interviewed believed that the growth of local industries as well as the expansion of their own business had more than compensated for losses that might have arisen from reductions in their import agency activities. Certainly, whatever temporary losses they might have suffered, their profit trends in the 1960s were not adversely affected; and this is supported by evidence.

Admittedly between 1963 and 1967 the profit level of the agency houses in Malaysia fluctuated, but this was partly due to the bad trading situation arising from the uncertainties brought about by the Indonesian 'confrontation' and no agency made significant losses during that period. As Table 5.8 shows, some agency firms continued to make profits throughout the 1960s. Executives interviewed said that they achieved what they considered as satisfactory levels of profits[25] in Malaysia in the 1960s. In individual cases, such as Inchcape Berhad and Harper Gilfillan, there were rapid increases in profits towards the end of the 1960s. It would appear that no agency house had any significant conflict of interest with the import-substitution industrialization programme in the country from 1960 to 1971. The general view of the

TABLE 5.8

TRENDS IN AFTER-TAX GROUP PROFITS OF SELECTED AGENCY HOUSES IN MALAYSIA, * 1962–1971

Company Year End	*Harper Gilfillan* ($'000)	*Guthrie* (£'000)	*Harrisons & Crosfield* (£'000)	*Inchcape Berhad* ($'000)	*Sime Darby* (£'000)	*J. Warren* (£'000)
1962	...	...	600	...	980	115.1
1963	...	...	626	...	1,148	153.4
1964	...	...	668	...	1,095	93.2
1965	...	...	902	...	997	83.7
1966	...	...	1,015	...	1,033	110.6
1967	722	1,662	1,260	...	1,152	140.7
1968	932	1,894	1,519	2,404	1,465	80.7
1969	1,040	2,571	1,478	2,461	1,650	104.5
1970	1,662	3,321	1,982	4,183	2,076	176.7
1971	2,650	3,676	2,361	14,617	2,645	132.7
Per cent increase	267	121	294	508	170	15
Annual rate of growth	38.4	22.0	17.6	83.0	11.7	1.5

Source: Company reports.

Notes: * The average yearly profit originating directly from the Malaysian region for the period was approximately 49 per cent. The remaining 51 per cent came from their activities in not less than ten other countries including the U.K.

... Not available.

representatives interviewed was that on the whole, the industrialization programme resulted in a situation favourable to the agency houses and was congruent with their market protecting strategy.

Contrary to assertions of Puthucheary and Wheelwright that agency houses did not favour the development of local manufacturing, the empirical evidence cited in the foregoing sections suggests that the agency firms not only favoured economic development in the country but also assisted in the process of development by either promoting the entry of foreign manufacturers into local industry or by getting directly involved in manufacturing themselves.

SOURCES AND USES OF FUNDS

Historically the agency houses had always arranged for the provision of their own capital not only for initial capital expenditure, but also for subsequent reorganization, extension, and modernization, as well as working capital. In the beginning they organized their finance in several ways: by themselves subscribing to the share capital of the new companies; by getting friends and relatives to subscribe to the share capital; by arranging loans from banks and pledging their guarantees for the loans; by attracting deposits from the public on the strength of their reputation and standing in the business world; and by a combination of the foregoing. Agency houses also pooled their own private resources to be used by their businesses at agreed rates of interest. In the 1960s, the firms resorted more to providing capital partly from reinvestment of their profits and partly from bank borrowing. Technically, the agency houses were (and are) able to borrow capital from financial institutions in the countries in which they have branches. In Malaysia, the capital requirements of the Malaysian branch of the agency houses had frequently been met by local borrowings. In general the agency houses would borrow in countries where the cost of borrowing was low, but they had been known to borrow locally in Malaysia even when interest rates were lower elsewhere. This was especially done at times of political crisis when the companies felt the need to conserve their external assets and minimize their net asset holdings in Malaysia. After 1971, when opportunities for local investments in the country improved, they made a considerable amount of local reinvestment consistent with their resource redeployment referred to earlier.

Table 5.9 shows the sources of funds employed by selected agency houses in 1967 and 1971. It can be seen that paid-up capital constituted less than one-third of total capital employed in 1967, and in 1971 it constituted only about 23.4 per cent of total capital employed. That the agency houses were able to use some considerable amounts of loans and overdrafts (27 per cent in 1967 and 32.4 per cent in 1971 of total) reflected their borrowing power and credit-worthiness in the eyes of the lending institutions.

By virtue of their credit-worthiness (and the interlocking directorates—see Chapter 6), the agency firms in the 1960s raised as much funds as possible from local sources. It can be seen from Table 5.9 that overdrafts and long-term loans constituted about 27 per cent in 1967, and in 1971 nearly one-third of the total sources of funds employed. If gearing is defined as the relationship between the funds provided to a company by its ordinary shareholders and the long-term sources of funds carrying interest charges[26] then it can be seen that the structure of capital in the agency houses was highly geared—68 per cent in 1967, and just over 80 per cent in 1971. At the same time, Table 5.9 also shows

TABLE 5.9
SOURCES OF FUNDS BY TEN SELECTED AGENCY HOUSES IN MALAYSIA, 1967 AND 1971

	1967		*1971*	
	$ mil.	(%)	*$ mil.*	(%)
Total funds employed of which	548.8	(100)	1032	(100)
(a) Shareholders' interest consisting of	*324.9*	*(59.5)*	*572.5*	*(55.5)*
(i) ordinary share capital	180.6	(33.1)	241.7	(23.4)
(ii) capital reserves	73.6	(13.5)	177.3	(17.2)
(iii) revenue reserves	70.8	(13.0)	153.4	(14.9)
(b) Group liabilities	*220.9*	*(40.5)*	*459.5*	*(44.5)*
(i) long term loans (and debentures)	64.5	(11.8)	162.1	(15.7)
(ii) overdrafts	82.4	(15.1)	172.8	(16.7)
(iii) other funds carrying fixed interest charges	74.0	(13.5)	124.7	(12.1)
Gearing or leverage: (b) / (a) x 100	68%		80.3%	

Source: Based on data from company reports and interviews.

that agency firms had been able to generate internally a substantial proportion on their funds. In 1967 for instance, reserves constituted about 26.5 per cent of capital employed; in 1971 the proportion was 32.1 per cent. The situation provided a contrast to the situation in the 1950s when much of the capital used by these firms was borrowed.[27] Individual agency firms in the 1960s were able to generate large cash flows.[28] This was partly because of their profitable operations and partly because of other factors such as efficient management of firms and the fact that there were few defaulting clients. In the opinion of many executives it was not difficult for companies to raise capital in Malaysia,[29] and because of this most companies shifted their sources of borrowing away from British to non-British (mostly Malaysian) sources.[30] This probably accounted for the small British capital inflows into Malaysian industry at this time, as discussed in Chapter 2.

Changes in the capital structure of the agency houses had been frequent, and sometimes intricate. Since their involvement in local manufacturing in the 1960s, most agency firms had undergone extensive capital reconstruction as outlined above. The broad pattern of the structural changes in the paid-up capital of agency firms quoted on the Malaysian stock exchange is shown in Table 5.10.

TABLE 5.10

SUMMARY OF CHANGES IN THE ISSUED AND PAID-UP CAPITAL OF AGENCY HOUSES QUOTED ON THE MALAYSIA-SINGAPORE STOCK EXCHANGE, 1967–1971

		$ *mil.*	%		$ *mil.*	%
1967,	Issued and Paid-up Capital, capital changes attributable to			(a)	162.9	(53)
	(i) Acquisition and Mergers	31.1	(40)			
	(ii) Public issues	26.9	(35)			
	(iii) Bonus and Rights Issues	19.2	(25)			
	Total increase in capital			(b)	77.2	(47)
1971,	Issued and Paid-up Capital, (a) + (b)				240.1	(100)

Source: The Stock Exchange of Malaysia and Singapore.

There was an estimated 47 per cent increase in the paid-up capital of the quoted agency houses during the period 1967 to 1971, thus increasing the paid-up capital from $163 million in 1967 to about $240 million in 1971. Approximately 65 per cent of the total increment of $77.2 million (item (b), Table 5.10), had been internally generated, while the remaining 35 per cent (item ii), came from public subscriptions. The one important point that emerges from the changes illustrated in the above Table is that the agency houses rarely floated new issues, mainly because the directors wanted to retain ownership and control of the firms.[31] This point will be substantiated in the section analysing the shareholdings below.

The changes in the employment of funds by the agency houses between 1967 and 1971 are shown in Table 5.11.

The most significant change was in the amounts of stocks and work-in-progress which was around $148 million, equal to 27 per cent of funds employed in 1967 and about $349 million in 1971, almost 34 per cent of funds employed in that year. Fixed assets made up 29 per cent of funds employed in 1967, while in 1971 they constituted one-quarter of funds employed. In absolute terms, there was an increase of over 64 per cent in the fixed assets of the companies between the two years. Most of these increases were

TABLE 5.11
EMPLOYMENT OF FUNDS BY TEN SELECTED AGENCY HOUSES IN MALAYSIA, 1967 AND 1971

	1967		*1971*	
	$ mil.	*%*	*$ mil.*	*%*
Employment of funds in				
1. Fixed assets*	157.8	(28.9)	257.8	(25.0)
2. Net current assets:				
Accounts receivable	158.1	(29.0)	292.6	(28.4)
Stocks and works-in-progress	147.5	(27.0)	249.2	(33.8)
Trade investments	52.5	(9.6)	61.4	(5.9)
Cash and bank balances	22.6	(4.1)	64.1	(6.1)
Miscellaneous uses	7.4	(1.4)	6.8	(0.8)
Total Funds Employed	548.8	(100)	1031.2	(100)

Source: As for Table 5.9.
Note: Land, buildings, plant, machinery, equipment, and vehicles.

attributable to the acquisition of plant and machinery for industrial production.

Trade and other investments declined from about 10 per cent of resources employed in 1967 to about 6 per cent in 1971. A substantial proportion of trade investments was increasingly placed in industrial investments of subsidiaries and other local manufacturing companies. Small amounts were put into government securities. Accounts receivable, i.e. debtors less creditors, formed about 28–29 per cent of resources employed from 1967 to 1971. The remaining 5–6 per cent of resources were in the form of cash balances and miscellaneous items such as goodwill and deferred expenditure.

SHARE OWNERSHIP POLICY

Most agency firms supported the broad aim of the government's 'New Economic Policy',[32] which encouraged local people to have equity participation in foreign-owned concerns and to have more local people employed at the high executive levels. A number of the agency firms was actively trying to identify themselves with Malaysia by having their shares quoted on the local stock exchange, appointing Malaysians to their boards of directors and generally recruiting an increasing number of local executives. The process of identifying themselves with the country has been referred to as part of their 'localization' policy. This localization process is summarized in Table 5.12 below.

The picture which emerges from Table 5.12 is that British agency firms were trying to change their image from one of entirely British-dominated organizations to one where local people could acquire some ownership, and participate in the employment created by these firms.

However, as these companies had been profitable the directors wished to retain their ownership and control of the firms. Of those companies listed in the Malaysian stock exchange only a small proportion of their equity was freely traded in the 1963–70 period. Examination of the shareholders' register showed that in general Malaysian equity holders constituted about one-third of the total ordinary shareholders of the agency firms. The largest company and the most ardent supporter of the government industrialization programmes,[33] Sime Darby Holdings Limited had, in 1972, about 38.8 per cent non-British (mostly Malaysian) ordinary

TABLE 5.12

'LOCALIZATION' OF SELECTED AGENCY HOUSES, 1963 AND 1970

	(1) Listing at the Local Stock Exchange		*(2) Appointment of Malaysian Directors*		*(3) Percentage of Malaysians Employed at Executive Levels*	
	1963	*1970*	*1963*	*1970*	*1963*	*1970*
Borneo (Inchcape)	No	Yes	No	No	39	80
Boustead	Yes	Yes	Yes	Yes	31	60
Guthrie	No	Yes	No	Yes	29	63
Harper Gilfillan	No	Yes	Yes	Yes	28	80
Harrisons & Crosfield	No	No	Yes	Yes	13	75
William Jacks	Yes	Yes	No	No	19	68
Paterson Simons	No	No	Yes	Yes	30	47
Sandilands	No	No	No	No	35	63
Sime Darby	Yes	Yes	Yes	Yes	1	62
James Warren	No	No	No	No	50	55

Source: Compiled from information derived at interviews.

Note: Executive level defined as employment of people as salaried officers, at Branch, Divisional Office, Office Manager, Accountant, Chemist, Engineer, and other professionally qualified job levels.

TABLE 5.13

SIME DARBY HOLDINGS LTD.: ORDINARY SHAREHOLDERS AS AT 12 MAY 1972

		Number of Shares		(%)
I. *United Kingdom Register*				
Shares held by banks*		24,511,953		30.5
Shares of other institutional investors		26,801,742	(ii)	33.4
Shares held by private persons		29,017,326		36.1
Total on U.K. Share Register		80,331,021		100.0
II. *Malaysian Register*				
Shares held by banks*		19,872,031	(i)	29.6
Shares of other institutional investors		20,772,964	(ii)	30.9
Shares held by private persons		26,594,134	(iii)	39.5
Total on Malaysian Register		67,239,129		
III. *U.M. and Malaysian Registers (I + II)*				
Shares held by banks*		44,383,984		30.1
Shares of institutional investors		47,574,706	(ii)	32.2
Shares held by private persons		55,611,460		37.7
Total number of shareholders (a)		147,570,150		100.0
IV. Breakdown of (a)				
British interests				
as in U.K. Share Register ϕ		80,331,021	)	
as in Malaysian Register:				
British banks*	2,568,720		)	
Other institutions	4,718,073		)	
British persons	2,746,757	9,033,550	)	
Total British interests		89,363,571		61.2
Total non-British interests		57,205,579		38.8
		147,570,150		100.0

Source: Shareholders' Registers.

Notes:
* Including bank nominee holdings.
(i) Including shares held by British banks and bank nominees.
(ii) Insurance companies, pension funds, and charitable institutions.
(iii) Further classified in Table 5.14.
ϕ Including a small portion of European and Eurasian interests.

shareholders, while the remaining 61.2 per cent consisted of mainly British interests as shown in Table 5.13.

As a whole banks and institutional investors constituted about 69.9 per cent of the total shareholders while private persons made up about 30.1 per cent of all shareholders. When the ownership of shares by private persons on the Malaysian register is further classified, the picture is as represented in Table 5.14.

The Chinese (86.3 per cent) followed by the British (10.3 per cent) were the majority private shareholders of Sime Darby in 1972. Indian shareholders constituted 2.5 per cent while Malay shareholders formed less than 1 per cent. Viewed in the total perspective of Sime Darby's ordinary shares, the Malay interest was insignificant. It seems inconceivable that Malay interests in the agency houses[34] could come anywhere near the '30 per cent level within two decades' of 1971 as envisaged in the Second Malaysia Plan.[35]

What seems certain is that British ownership and control as exercised through management and equity holdings (private and

TABLE 5.14

BREAKDOWN OF ORDINARY SHARES OF SIME DARBY HOLDINGS LTD. HELD BY PRIVATE PERSONS ACCORDING TO THE MALAYSIAN SHARE REGISTER AS AT 12 MAY 1972

Shares Held By	*Number of Shares*	(%)
(i) British	2,746,757 (1)	10.3
(ii) Chinese	22,937,979 (2)	86.3
(iii) Indians	671,243 (3)	2.5
(iv) Malays	238,155 (4)	0.9
Total shares held by private persons as per Malaysian Register (see item marked (iii), Table 5.13)	26,594,134	100.0

Source: As for Table 5.13.

Notes: (i) The amount may be overstated since the basis of classification was the name of the person on the Share Register. It may well be that some Malaysians with British names may have been included in this group.

(ii) This group includes Chinese from Hong Kong, and other parts of South-East Asia.

(iii) This group may have been understated since some Indians with English and/or Malay names may well have been included in (i) and (iv).

(iv) This is excluding MARA provident funds and Malaysian Muslim Pilgrim Savings Trust (in which there are Malay interests) classified under institutional investors. The amount given may well have been overstating the Malay share to the extent to which there are Indians with Malay names.

institutional holdings) of the agency houses will continue. This will arise for a number of reasons: the profitability of these firms, the fact that only a limited number of shares are freely traded on the stock exchange in Malaysia, the frequency of bonus and rights share issues, and the generally high market price of their shares.[36] Moreover, most of the debentures and other preference shares of these companies are in British hands: and the British directors are usually the holders of many of the ordinary shares (registered under the category of shares held by private persons in Tables 5.13 and 5.14) while Malaysian directors who are mostly invited to be on the boards of directors by the British directors, hold very few shares.[37] Although executives interviewed had no objection to local equity participation in principle, in practice most of the share-holdings of the agency houses from 1963 to 1972 were British.

THE AGENCY HOUSES IN THE 1970s

In the 1970s the name 'agency house' is a misnomer because the agency houses are no longer solely merchandizing and managing agents but holding companies with business interests that are as diversified as they are comprehensive. In organization they are conglomerates. They have handled and continue to handle a wide range of imported goods—from pins to computer hardware, from perambulators to aircraft, and virtually every kind of industrial raw material, equipment, and machine. They provide management expertise over a wide range of enterprises from rubber estates, tin mines, financial institutions, and real estate, to complicated industrial holding companies. They provide finance and assist in company promotions as well as in the marketing of the products of industrial companies. They handle a wide range of exports from Malaysia—from latex to electronic goods, and from processed wood to mining and transport equipment. In sum, there is no major economic activity in the country in which the agency houses have no interest.

Originally agency houses were merchants in the East, but in the 1970s the geographical areas of their operations are as wide as their range of activities. Table 5.15 outlines the world-wide connexions of the agency houses.

As pointed out above (Tables 5.1 and 5.2) the agency houses are engaged in a wide range of unrelated activities so that in fact each agency house is a conglomerate. They have expanded their activities mainly from internally generated resources (Table 5.10),

TABLE 5.15
SELECTED AGENCY HOUSES IN MALAYSIA AND THEIR WORLD-WIDE CONNEXIONS, 1970

Agency House	*Status/Parent Firm*	*Area/Country of Operations and Number of Subsidiaries or Associates**
Borneo (Inchcape)	Intermediate holding company of the Inchcape Group.	Africa, 9 s. Australia, 9 ws. Canada, 3 s. West Indies, 3 s. Hong Kong, 11 s.
Boustead	Holding company for Malaysian operations of E. Boustead & Co. Ltd.	Argentina, 2 a. Australia, 5 s. Canada, 1 s. Columbia, 1 a. France, 1 a. Italy, 1 a. India, 3 a. New Zealand, 3 a. South Africa, 1 a. Switzerland, 2 a. U.S.A., 4 a.
Guthrie	A constituent of Guthrie Corporation Ltd.	Australia, 1 s. Canada, 1 s. France, 1 s. S. Africa, 1 s.
Harper Gilfillan	A holding company associated with Blyth, Greene, Jourdain & Co.	Australia, 3 s. Canada, 5 s. Mauritius, 3 s. Rhodesia, 1 s. S. Africa, 1 s.
Harrisons & Crosfield	Subsidiary of Harrisons & Crosfield Ltd.	Africa, ? s. Australia, 1 s. Canada, 1 s. India, 1 a. New Zealand, 1 s. U.S.A., 3 s.
William Jacks	Holding company for Malaysian operations of W. Jacks & Co. Ltd.	Africa, ? s. Australia, 1 s. India, 1 s. Germany, 1 s.
Paterson Simons	Associate of Paterson, Simons Ewart and Co. Ltd.	Canada, ? a. U.S.A., ? a. Europe, ? a.
Sime Darby	Holding company operating in Malaysia, associated with R.G. Shaw Ltd.	Hong Kong, ? as. Europe, ? as. U.S.A., ? a.
Sandilands Buttery	An associate of the Henry Gardner Group.	Africa, ? as. Canada, ? a. U.S.A., ? a. Europe, ? a.
James Warren	Subsidiary of J. Warren & Co. Ltd.	Africa, 4 s. India, 1 s.

Sources: Based on annual reports of the companies and the *Straits Times Directory*, 1971.

Notes: Figures refer to the number of associate or subsidiary.
* = Excluding subsidiaries and associated companies in the United Kingdom, Ireland, Singapore, and other countries of South-East Asia.
a = Associated company in which the agency firm has equity interest.
s = Subsidiary company controlled by the agency firm.
ws = Wholly-owned subsidiary.
? = Exact number not known.

and they have expanded their geographical areas of operations as shown in Table 5.15.

As illustrated in Table 5.8, the agency houses have achieved very rapid rates of growth over the last decade. In view of the variety of management expertise within their organizations, it would seem that there may be no limit to their expansion. However, Professor Penrose postulated that there is a limit to the rate at which any firm can grow, a limit provided by the capacities of its existing management.[38] The agency firms in Malaysia provide examples of firms that can grow beyond the capacities of their original managements. This has been done by their continual recruitment of new managerial talents. The keynote of the expansion of activities in the agency firms has been entrepreneurship and managerial flexibility. The directors of the firms have been alert to investment opportunities and willing to recruit diverse managerial talents. For example, in the 1960s when the government in Malaysia initiated the industrial development programme, agency houses were among those firms that reorganized themselves to take advantage of the opportunities to engage in investment in industry. The operators of these firms, who were originally merchants, recruited a variety of talents in the form of accountants, bankers, chemists, economists, engineers, quantity surveyors, scientists, and technologists, as well as numerous other professionally qualified people. A combination of opportunity and talents provided the means of expansion of business.

It is beyond the scope of the present study to make an extensive examination of the role of entrepreneurship in the growth of the agency firms.[39] A brief mention may be made of the characteristics of the directors of the agency firms. For instance, almost every director has, or has had, long connexions with Malaysia. Several of them served in the British Colonial Service in the country and elsewhere in the Commonwealth. Many of them have friends among members of the government; this is useful in providing a channel of communication about matters of mutual business interest. A number of the directors are also people trained in the various professions and, supporting them with ideas and skills are young recruits with managerial, scientific, and technological training. A number of directors are also directors of financial institutions, insurance companies, and numerous other commercial concerns.[40] A few directors are versatile in the sense that they are equally at home in the rubber plantations and in the mines; in Kuala Lumpur and in London; as well as on the factory floor and in the city.

Crucial to the successful running of conglomerates is the role of management. New management techniques are employed, and managers are well paid. Equally important has been the fact that these organizations never had any labour problem.[41] Most agency houses in Malaysia completed their major reorganizations and capital reconstructions in the 1960s. The stage is set for them to achieve higher rates of growth in output, sales, and exports in the 1970s than in the previous years.[42]

AN ASSESSMENT OF THE ROLE OF THE AGENCY HOUSES

As agents for distributing and selling British manufacture the agency houses helped to build markets for British goods in Malaysia. In the process, the commercial interests of the agency houses became very closely associated with those of their principals, the manufacturing companies in Britain. Competition threatened the established markets of British manufactures, a situation adversely affecting the income of the agency houses originating from their traditional trading activities.

There arose the need for resources redeployment in the agency houses if they wished to retain the market they had helped to create for their principals. To the principals in Britain there was the obvious need to set up production facilities in Malaysia in order to maintain the competitiveness of their products and retain their markets. It was the market retention strategy adopted by both principals and agents in the mid-1960s that resulted in the more intensive involvement of British capital in local manufacturing.

The role played by the agency houses was crucial in that they not only created markets and influenced manufacturers to set up manufacturing in Malaysia, but also offered their managerial, financial, and marketing services to the newly established firms in the manufacturing sector. The agency firms' involvement in industrial investments was part of their diversification process. In addition to industry, they also had other interests in almost every branch of the economy. They were conglomerates consisting of industrial holding companies and groups of companies with a wide range of unrelated activities. As conglomerates they recruited diverse managerial talents which no doubt increased their capacity to grow with the economy.

Agency houses did not hinder industrial development in Malaysia by virtue of their dominant interest in the import trade. On the contrary, they spearheaded British participation in local manufacturing. They recognized the economic pressures surrounding the future of British manufactures. They advised their principals on the appropriate steps to be taken to avoid being squeezed out of the market. By virtue of long connexion with Malaysia, agency firms (and their directors) were in a position to know business practices and customs in the country, inspiring the confidence of a number of British manufacturers who knew little about the local conditions. The range of services offered by the agency firms was comprehensive, even in the early 1960s. Their already established distribution facilities, trading reputations, connexions with other companies, the civil service, and financial institutions made them an effective vehicle for increasing the participation of British (and other foreign) firms in Malaysian manufacturing.

The world-wide connexions of agency houses made them a useful vehicle for international trade. In fact, local manufacturers rely on the international marketing services of the agency firms to export locally-made goods. In broad terms, the agency houses provided all services associated with company promotion, management, and product marketing. Their interests in banking, insurance, and shipping were an added attraction. Their ability to generate resources internally with little recourse to public issues provided a very attractive proposition to those foreign companies that looked upon the agency firms as the 'local' partners. Internally-generated funds enabled these companies to expand without alienating their ownership and control over these concerns.

As a rough measure of the importance of the agency firms it can be said that without the services offered by them, British manufacturers, who were largely unfamiliar with market conditions in Malaysia, would have lost more ground to the more aggressive foreign manufacturers (from Japan, America, and Europe) who employed the services of rival (non-British) agency firms. As mentioned in Chapter 4 other foreign manufacturers were market penetrators determined to erode the market supremacy of the British in Malaysia. The British agency houses provided assistance to British goods. What was even more important was the fact that the agency firms also gave both domestic and export marketing assistance to Malaysian manufactured products. Clearly these were valuable contributions of the agency firms to Malaysian industry.

On their own account agency firms had formed manufacturing companies, but there were also instances when they were engaged in joint ventures with their principals. As a whole, the direct involvement of the agency firms in the manufacturing sector constituted about one-half of the total involvement of British capital in industry, in terms of assets committed to industry, industrial output, and sales. It seems obvious that the agency houses in Malaysia, as in India[43] and to a smaller extent in Nigeria,[44] have been instrumental in assisting British capital involvement in industry. They have also been partly responsible for the growth of the industrial sector.[45]

There is little doubt that the British agency firms with their entrepreneurship and managerial flexibility exerted a strong influence on the structure and organizational characteristics of British industry in Malaysia.

1. M. Kidron, *Foreign Investments in India*, Oxford University Press, 1965.

2. P. Kilby, *Industrialisation in an Open Economy Nigeria, 1945–1966*, Cambridge University Press, 1969.

3. J. J. Puthucheary, *Ownership and Control in the Malayan Economy*, Singapore, Eastern Universities Press, 1960.

4. E. L. Wheelwright, *Industrialization in Malaysia*, Australia, Melbourne University Press, 1965.

5. Puthucheary, op. cit., pp. 154–5.

6. Wheelwright, op. cit., pp. 97–8.

7. The primary sources of information for this chapter are interviews with directors and representatives of the agency firms in London.

8. In addition to Puthucheary, op. cit., and Allen and Donnithorne, *Western Enterprise in Indonesia and Malaya*, see also K. G. Tregonning, *The British in Malaysia*, Tucson, The University of Arizona Press, 1965, Chapter VIII; and for a detailed study of one of the agency firms see S. Cunyngham-Brown, *The Traders*, Guthrie and Company (U.K.) Ltd., 1971. The available studies, however, do not deal with the engagements of these merchant firms in industry which is a recent development in the agency houses.

9. See Puthucheary, op. cit., pp. iv, xiv, and *passim*.

10. i.e. market value of the issued shares; this is derived by multiplying the number of shares outstanding by the quoted price of shares.

11. Wheelwright, op. cit., p. 48, and *passim*. The companies interviewed regarded the agency houses as 'local' primarily because the latter have been in the country for a very long time. The agencies were considered the experts in 'local matters', i.e. dealing with government departments, interpreting local customs and commercial conventions and the like. Sometimes, as a result of their dominance in the economy the agency firms were referred to as cartels. Politicians, in their misunderstanding of the entrepreneurial functions of the agency firms and the superb marketing network of these firms, have referred to commerce and industry in Malaysia as being cartel-ridden. See report in *Straits Times*, 9 August 1973.

12. See Sir E. Macfadyen, 'Managing Agents in the Eastern Plantation Industry', *Tropical Agriculture*, Vol. 13(4), 1954; and also Allen and Donnithorne, op. cit.

13. *Boustead & Co. Ltd., East India Merchants, Established 1828*, London (no date), private publication of the company, *passim*.

14. As mentioned in Chapter 4, British firms prefer to locate their regional head offices in Singapore. British agency firms with headquarters in Singapore quite naturally pooled their profits into the island leaving the surrounding areas as rural hinterland deprived of the major spin-off effects of the profits. Viewed in this perspective, the final separation of the currency ties between Malaysia and Singapore in May 1973 was probably beneficial to the former.

15. This was, according to CBI representatives interviewed, probably true of other countries also. See Report of the South-East Asian Trade Delegation, *A Trade in Transition*, Confederation of British Industries, 1961.

16. At first the machines and equipment were imported in knocked-down form, and assembled locally. Later, spares and parts were manufactured locally by the agency firms' subsidiaries.

17. The agency and distribution business of the agency houses constituted the major activity of these firms in the years before 1960. In the late 1960s this aspect of the firms' business was only about one-quarter of their total source of income. According to the agency firms interviewed, only about one-fifth of their resources (i.e. fixed assets and management time) was considered to be directly engaged in the traditional activity of agency and distribution.

18. E. T. Penrose, *The Theory of the Growth of the Firm*, Oxford, Blackwell, 1972, p. 143.

19. A more refined indicator would be the rate of returns, net of tax, on capital employed in each line of activity in each enterprise. DTI data do not allow for such calculations to be made. Executives interviewed confirmed the broad trends shown by the DTI data.

20. This was the slogan of President Soekarno during the 'confrontation' years 1963–7.

21. This point, mentioned by several executives of manufacturing companies interviewed, was also raised in the Federation of British Industries 1960 visiting delegation report; see their report *A Trade in Transition*. In their defence, the agency firms said they took over additional agency of manufactures whenever they found their traditional manufactured products could not hold their market, and whenever their principals were not keen to begin local manufacturing.

22. The agency firms were familiar with local procedure of company formation. The presence of a number of local prominent citizens, usually lawyers or accountants, on their boards of directors was an additional advantage.

23. See Chapter 6 about Interlocking Directorates.

24. Loc. cit.

25. The question of the profitability of British companies is more fully discussed in Chapter 8.

26. There is of course more than one way of defining and calculating the gearing ratio, see R. H. Parker, *Understanding Company Financial Statements*, Pelican Library of Business and Management, 1972, p. 71.

27. In the 1950s and throughout their earlier times in the East, according to Allen and Donnithorne, op. cit., p. 204, the agency houses relied substantially on bank credits to finance much of their overseas operations.

28. Sime Darby for instance (according to information derived from the company's Annual Report, 30 June 1971, p. 23, and *passim*), generated an annual average cash flow (retained profits plus provisions for depreciation) of about £500,000 during the period 1962 to 1971. Several other agency firms were also able to generate nearly half as much as Sime Darby's cash flow in the same period.

29. Many British companies found that their share capital offers to the public were several times over-subscribed. See FIDA, *Malaysia: Your Profit Centre in Asia*, 1970, p. 18; and P. J. Drake, 'The New Issues Boom in Malaysia and Singapore, 1961–1964', *Economic Development and Cultural Change*, Vol. 18, 1970, pp. 73–91.

One British industrialist even remarked that '[if British companies] can contribute the necessary expertise, Malaysia can provide almost everything else . . .' see 'Doing Business in Malaysia: The View of a British Industrialist', Paper presented at a Conference on Business Opportunities in South-East Asia organized by *The Financial Times* (1972), London.

30. Initially many of the borrowings were from such British banks as The Chartered Bank and Hongkong and Shanghai Bank; but in the 1960s an increasing proportion was borrowed from locally-owned financial institutions. At the same time there was a net reduction of borrowing in London where as will be seen in Chapter 8, the cost of borrowing was higher than in Malaysia.

31. This objective is well served by bonus and rights issues. Such issues also entail less expense on the part of the firms compared to public offers for subscription to new issues. Bonus issues involve capitalizing reserves—which were quite substantial according to Table 5.9 above; and such capitalizations imply that management is confident of more profits in the future. Rights issues give existing shareholders the first chance to subscribe to new issues. Shareholders may either exercise their rights or else sell the rights. In the bullish share market of the 1960s, selling the rights probably benefited the existing shareholders.

32. See report of Prime Minister's outline of the policy in the *Straits Times*, 11 August 1972.

33. Based on assets committed to manufacturing; and claims of company representatives.

34. The Malay equity holdings in other agency houses besides Sime Darby were even more insignificant. In a number of cases, Malay equity holding in the period up to 1972 was nil. The position may well have changed since the announcement of the 'New Economic Policy' (of the *Second Malaysia Plan, 1971–75*, p. 158).

35. *Second Malaysia Plan, 1971–75*, p. 158; see also report of the Prime Minister, 'New Economic Policy', in the *Straits Times*, 11 August 1972.

36. In 1973 for instance, the highest market price of Sime Darby's ordinary 10p share was $14.60; that of Inchcape was $12.80 (nominal $1.00), and that of Boustead (nominal $1.00) was $11.00. Throughout the period 1963 to 1972, the market prices of the ordinary shares of the agency houses according to the records of the Stock Exchange of Malaysia and Singapore ranged from 3 to 23 times their nominal values. With such prices, the number of Malaysians able to purchase these shares was limited, bearing in mind the generally low income levels of the population referred to earlier.

37. With very few exceptions, local dignitaries invited to be present on the boards of directors of the agency houses in 1973 owned insignificant numbers of shares in the companies. Of those Malaysian directors who had shares, their shareholdings constituted on average less than 3 per cent of the shareholdings of the British directors. In terms of total shareholdings, the shares held by the Malaysian directors were unimportant; and thus it was unlikely that these local directors could assert any influence on ownership and control by virtue of their equity holdings.

38. Penrose, *The Theory of the Growth of the Firm*, p. 263.

39. An example of an intensive study of the history of an agency firm is provided in Cunyngham-Brown, op. cit. The book gives a chronological account of Guthrie from the birth of Alexander Guthrie in 1796 to the Guthrie Corporation of the early 1970s.

40. Almost all of the industrial companies in Malaysia, as will be pointed out in Chapter 6, are inter-connected through linked directorships. Most of the commercial companies and a great deal of the rubber and tin companies are concentrated in not more than thirty directors. As a whole, company directorships in the country are in the hands of fewer than thirty people. Concentration of directorship in the agency houses is even more intense because the conglomerate organizations of these companies bring about a situation where directors of the holding companies are frequently directors of the subsidiary and associated companies also.

41. In the 1960s, according to the executives interviewed, no agency firm suffered from work stoppage resulting from labour disputes. There were minor disputes about wages and over-time rates, but in general labour employed by the agency firms cause employers no major problems.

42. In the period 1970 to 1973 many agency firms achieved high rates of growth compared to the previous years. A number of industrial firms in the Harper Gilfillan and Inchcape groups increased output by nearly 90 per cent in the period. Exports and profits of the two groups doubled in the same period. In the period 1970 to 1972, group turnover for agencies consulted increased generally, ranging from 30 to 120 per cent. Although the results in the later part of the 1970s might not be as spectacular as the early 1970s, executives interviewed believed that on the whole their growth of output, sales, and exports would be higher than achieved in the past.

43. Kidron, op. cit.

44. Kilby, op. cit.

45. See Chapter 9. The activities of the agency houses in Malaysia provide some basis to refute the commonly held view that British companies are averse to modernization—H. D. Willey, 'Growth Patterns and Export Performance: Britain and Germany', in P. B. Kenen and R. Lawrence, eds., *The Open Economy: Essays on International Trade and Finance*, Columbia University Press, 1968.

6 Structure and Organization of U.K. Investment in Manufacturing

INTRODUCTION

COMPREHENSIVE sources of statistics covering British manufacturing investments in Malaysia are few and inadequate. The Department of Trade and Industry (DTI) in the U.K. for instance has published regularly since 1964 estimates of book values of U.K. direct investments overseas,[1] but unfortunately the published estimates pertaining to Malaysia do not present details in respect of those individual investments which amount to less than £250,000.[2] Such a limitation is serious, since most investments in industries in Malaysia in the 1960s had initial book values of less than £250,000. The 1968 *Census of Manufacturing Industries* published by the Department of Statistics in Kuala Lumpur is by far the most comprehensive available source of information on manufacturing in the country. However, because of the definition of ownership adopted in the census, the published figures underestimated the extent of foreign capital in Malaysian industry. The census categorized ownership of firms according to citizenship of the majority shareholders such that if in a company 60 per cent of the capital was held by Malaysians and 40 per cent by British, the ownership was reported as Malaysian even if the control of the company resided in the 40 per cent. If a company was jointly owned (e.g. 40 per cent British, 30 per cent Malaysian, and 30 per cent Singaporean) the company was classified as owned by 'Others'. In either case the net result was an understatement of British ownership and control in the manufacturing sector in the country. The census data, which referred to manufacturing establishments and not companies, also understated the actual situation because not all establishments of companies were covered. It is therefore necessary to supplement published data with information gathered from interviews with company representatives.

THE INITIAL INVESTMENTS

When companies were asked to indicate how their initial investment in industry in Malaysia had taken place it proved impossible for many of them to decide what constituted their initial investment. Very few companies began with fixed amounts of imported capital. In many wholly-owned subsidiaries,[3] the initial share capital was only a small fraction of the parent companies' initial investment. Very often the total value of imported capital of each concern was much less than £250,000 (i.e. approximately $1.9 million). Many manufacturing branches incorporated in the country began as marketing subsidiaries with very small initial capital, often using leased premises for their registered offices. In the case of the agency firms, described in Chapter 5, their initial industrial investments could not be accurately ascertained. Such investments were so much intertwined with their other activities in the country that few representatives could accurately recall the actual initial amount of capital involved. As agents of British manufacturers, these firms had been involved with servicing plants, machinery, and equipment and other manufactured goods long before the country's industrialization programme was first conceived. In at least three cases, the initial industrial ventures began with the principal U.K. manufacturers providing servicing equipment, while in other cases the industrial venture began with the principal U.K. manufacturers supplying technical information and machinery. Other companies used imported second-hand machinery from the U.K. parent companies. In some cases British managers and technicians came together to make the initial investment, supplemented with funds from local sources such as British-owned financial institutions.

It was difficult for companies to place accurate values on their original imported capital. The book values of imported second-hand machines from the U.K. parent might be nil; the historical costs of equipment were often out of date and meaningless. There might not be any realistic replacement values, and frequently firms could not accurately determine the prices at which the capital equipment could be valued. Moreover, the cost of dismantling, reconditioning, transporting, and re-erecting second-hand machines were not usually exactly known, but firms assumed, perhaps sometimes incorrectly, that costs were less than those of new plant. No values could be accurately assigned to managerial and technological expertise, access to parent or principal company technology, research and development, or to entrepreneurial skills devoted to the original investments.

In addition to initial tangible capital, U.K. manufacturing concerns setting up operations in Malaysia frequently used credit facilities from local financial institutions, or from intra-company sources. Market interest rates for these credit facilities were often not accounted for in the books of the affiliates, and for accounting convenience they were regarded as costs by the parent firm.[4] It was not easy to define and calculate accurately the net worth (i.e. assets less liabilities) of the initial manufacturing investment.

Some cases of initial investment by companies are mentioned here to show the problems associated with trying to define how much capital was brought in when industrial investments started. It is true that many U.K. firms have drawn on Malaysian funds for a substantial part of the resources needed to commence their Malaysian operations.[5] In some cases the investing companies were incorporated first as private companies and later turned public. Others were incorporated as private limited companies and continued to be so. The authorized share capital ranged from $1 million to $50 million, but the paid-up capital, in the initial stages of the companies' investments in the country, varied in amounts ranging from one-thirtieth to one-half of their authorized amounts.

There was no hard and fast rule stipulating the amounts of capital that foreign investors might bring in;[6] but a limited liability company seeking to be listed on the stock exchange (founded in 1963) must in addition to complying with the Malaysian Companies Act 1965 satisfy certain requirements, one of which was that the paid-up share capital of the company in question be at least $1 million.[7] There was no law governing the gearing of capital, and companies were therefore at liberty to devise their own means of capital gearing.

In two cases, firms in their initial year of investing in industry raised loans equivalent to their issued capital, while in another case a company borrowed locally a sum equal to more than twice its issued capital. Two firms started with equipment supplied by parent firms and loans secured from the Malaysian Industrial Development Finance Ltd. Another two used local funds to finance their entire initial investments. Having established a holding company in the country, the firms borrowed locally to purchase majority holdings in a number of locally-owned companies. Dividends from the companies purchased were used to pay off loans borrowed locally. Several marketing affiliates developed into manufacturing concerns funded by equipment, technical information, and goods from the main companies in the U.K. In the initial period of formation it was not unusual for such firms to have intra-company debts as large as (and in a few cases larger than) their paid-up capital. One firm with a paid-up capital of about $6 million had a number of loans of over $20 million from intra-company sources and nearly as much from local sources. One other firm with less than $1 million paid-up capital was operating entirely on credits raised from local and overseas sources totalling nearly $7 million.

In spite of the various ways in which U.K. parent companies could avoid sending cash to Malaysia, it remained true that a great many U.K. affiliates were established in the country with managerial, technical, and sometimes financial assistance from British parent firms. It was difficult for representatives to put any value on managerial and technical expertise, but the general belief was that at least one-half of the estimated net worth of their initial investment was met by the parent firm, both in cash and equipment.

ORGANIZATION AND CONTROL

Table 6.1 outlines the forms of organization of industrial investment by estimated numbers and book values of their invested capital, i.e. assets less liabilities, in 1965 and 1968. Until 1967, not many affiliates published separate accounts and annual reports. Information on their Malaysian operations was condensed in the parent companies' consolidated reports and statement of accounts. Consequently little statistical information was obtainable on these companies relating to the early 1960s.

Table 6.1 shows that the most common form of business organization employed by the large investing companies was the branch, which in 1965 accounted for about 41 per cent in number, and in 1968, 29 per cent. The net book values of the branches of companies made up 70 per cent and 62 per cent of total book values of all U.K. industrial investments in the country in 1965 and 1968 respectively. The next common form of organization was the subsidiary which, in 1965, accounted for 18 per cent in number and value. In 1968 company subsidiaries made up about 24 per cent in number and 29 per cent in value. A number of small investments in the form of associates which were normally regarded by the parent firms as trade investments constituted the remainder. Such affiliates were mainly marketing outlets of manufacturing companies.

With the exception of agency houses and some notable firms (e.g. Fraser and Neave, established in 1883; United Engineers,

TABLE 6.1
FORMS OF ORGANIZATION OF BRITISH INDUSTRIAL INVESTMENTS IN MALAYSIA BY ESTIMATED NUMBERS AND BOOK VALUES, 1965 AND 1968

	1965				*1968*			
	No.	(%)	*Value (£ mil.)*	(%)	*No.*	(%)	*Value (£ mil.)*	(%)
I. *Large Investing Companies*								
(a) Branches	62	(41.2)	13.9	(69.8)	49	(29.3)	13.4	(62.0)
(b) Subsidiaries	27	(18.1)	3.5	(17.5)	40	(24.0)	6.2	(28.6)
(c) Associates	26	(17.3)	1.5	(7.5)	24	(14.4)	0.4	(2.0)
All Affiliates of Large Companies	115	(76.7)	18.9	(94.8)	114	(67.7)	20.0	(92.6)
II. *Small Investing Companies*	35	(23.3)	1.1	(5.2)	55	(32.3)	1.6	(7.4)
Total	150	(100.0)	19.9	(100.0)	168	(100.0)	21.6	(100.0)

Source: DTI, as for Table 2.6.

Notes: (i) Large Investing Companies are defined by the Department of Trade and Industry as those firms where the total of the book values of net assets amount to £¼ million or more. Small Investing Companies are those with less than £¼ million book values of net assets.

(ii) By 'branch' is meant 'permanent establishment' as defined for the purpose of United Kingdom tax in the relevant Double Taxation Agreements. 'Subsidiaries' are defined in Section 154 of the *Companies Act, 1948*, and 'associates' are companies which are not subsidiaries but in which the investing companies have interests which they regard as 'trade investment'.

(iii) The values of all company affiliates above refer to net book values of industrial assets only. Several companies were in fact affiliates of companies with substantial assets in agriculture, mining, and trading activities.

(iv) The affiliates referred to in the table do not include oil, insurance, and banking concerns.

1912; Wearne Brothers, 1912; Wilkinson Process Rubber, 1926; Metal Box, 1949; Malayan Cement, 1950, and Malayan Cables, established in 1957), most industrial affiliates of British companies in Malaysia were incorporated in the 1960s, although they may have been selling products in the Malaysian market for a long time prior to their formation. With rare exceptions like Raleigh Cycles (Malaysia) Berhad and Pernas-Plessey Berhad, which are joint-ventures, British industrial firms in the 1960s were predominantly owned and controlled by British nationals even after their incorporation dates as public companies in the country. As shown in Table 6.2, almost three-quarters of the equity capital of publicly-owned U.K. industrial companies in Malaysia in 1972 were owned by British interests, notably companies and other institutional investors. A little over one-quarter of the equity capital was owned by non-British interests, mainly Singaporean and Malaysian institutional investors, and individuals. In terms of proportions between institutional and individual investors among the non-British interests, a little over one-half (14.4 per cent) of non-British equity interests belonged to nominee companies, insurance companies, and pension funds. In total, it seemed that individual investors accounted for less than 23 per cent of all equity capital of British industrial companies in Malaysia.

TABLE 6.2

OWNERSHIP PATTERNS OF CAPITAL IN U.K. AFFILIATES IN MALAYSIAN MANUFACTURING, 1972

	*Per cent Ownership**	*Total (%)*	*Capital as % of Total Funds*
I. *Equity Capital*			
British interests, consisting of		73.8	
(a) Banks and nominee companies	16.6		
(b) Other institutional investors	46.8		
(c) Private persons	10.4		
Non-British interests, consisting of		26.2	
(a) Institutional investors	14.4		
(b) Private persons	11.8		
Total	100.0	100.0	30.5
II. *Debt Capital*			
Originating from:			
(a) Local financial institutions of which		73.2	
British-owned banks and other concerns	42.1		
Other financial institutions	31.1		
(b) Intra-company sources	10.0	} 26.8	
(c) Other sources (non-Malaysian sources)	16.8		
Total	100.0	100.0	69.5

Source: As for Table 5.9.

Note: *Based on forty affiliates, as not all companies were able to provide information on their respective ownership percentages. Equity Capital here means Ordinary Shares, including Reserves. Debt Capital includes preference shares, debentures, and overdrafts.

The vast majority of U.K. firms preferred to retain for themselves the bulk of shares in their Malaysian affiliates, although as Table 6.2 shows, a considerable portion (73.2 per cent) of debt capital was raised from local sources.

When British firms began their manufacturing in the 1960s there was no capital gearing regulation, and neither was there pressure nor inducement for companies to form joint-ventures. Brooks and Remmers[8] stated that joint-ventures were widespread in the developing countries as a means of reducing the risk of discrimination, investment restriction, or other unfavourable reactions to foreign investment. This was certainly not the case with British industrial investments in Malaysia in the 1960s. Companies interviewed did not find they were discriminated against for not forming joint-ventures, and as stated earlier there was no special regulation governing the foreign sector in Malaysian industry, although foreign companies forming joint-ventures with local partners were (and are) welcome.

According to company representatives, there was no special merit in a joint-venture project over a sole venture and they believed that the former was inferior in its uses of economic resources to the latter. It should be noted that in Africa the joint-venture enterprise has provided an example that it can be a useful way of getting foreign and local capital to co-operate in industry.[9] In principle the companies in Malaysia did not seriously object to the idea of joint-venture, but in practice the companies preferred sole venture.[10] A number of reasons were given to explain this preference.

An important reason was that most British companies either had sales or marketing subsidiaries in Malaysia long before they became incorporated locally as industrial concerns, or had established their markets (brand names) through their export trade. There was no really compelling reason for British companies to combine their manufacturing side with local partners to form joint-ventures in order to extend their sales outlets.

Another important consideration was that British overseas manufacturing investment represents a 'package' of inputs including technology, products, capital, and management. In common with other foreign investors from the industrialized countries, investing British companies preferred to take advantage of their 'package' within their corporate structure, especially through their wholly-owned subsidiaries or branches over which they exercised full control.[11] They would have had less than complete control over the advantages of the 'package' if they had substantial local minority shareholdings, joint-ventures, or licensing arrangements. Company representatives believed that full control was essential to companies with large expenditure on research and development, as well as to firms where intra-company transactions were considered vital to the achievement of corporate objectives.

Most firms with international dealings or those with organizations spanning many countries would wish to retain the flexibility of being able to shift company profits to places where they wanted to expand. This is done usually through the 'transfer pricing' mechanism.[12] Company representatives admitted that the desire of the investing companies to remain flexible in their operations might conflict with local shareholders' interests. Consequently, companies preferred to have sole ventures in which there was no (or little) potential conflict with shareholders' interests.

The question of dividend policy and technical fees was also thought to be a possible source of conflict of interests if there was a considerable proportion of local shareholders. One company representative mentioned that local shareholders seemed to have a 'traders' mentality' by which he meant that the local shareholders were more interested in quick returns on their initial investments than in long-term growth. With rare exceptions, the general opinion of company representatives was that in the 1960s there was no special advantage in having a large number of local shareholders and they viewed the government's attempt to encourage local equity participation as a possible deterrent to foreign investments, particularly in manufacturing where the companies preferred their subsidiaries wholly-owned.

Since 1968, several U.K. (and other foreign) firms have appointed prominent local citizens to their boards of directors who provided useful services to the companies. For instance, they served as channels of communication between the companies and other institutions (e.g. the government, banks, insurance, shipping, and other companies) in the economy.[13] One of the main reasons for appointing local directors concerned the resident status of these companies. It is essential for foreign companies to acquire 'resident company' status if they wish to enjoy some of the benefits of the *Investment Incentives Act, 1968* (as amended). When a company's control and management were exercised from abroad (as was usual with all British companies in Malaysia), the company was, for the purposes of the *Investment Incentives Act*, a 'non-resident' company. To be considered a 'resident company', directors' meetings, formulation of policies, and management of the company must be carried out in Malaysia. This was where the appointment of local directors, who were very often local dignitaries, became useful.

The effective control exercised by U.K. parent companies or their subsidiaries was facilitated by good communication systems between Kuala Lumpur, the location of most U.K. subsidiaries, and London, the location of most parent firms. It was possible to telephone direct from London to Kuala Lumpur, and the large firms had Telex machines to record instantaneous written communication between firms in the two countries. Board chairmen of parent companies who were ordinarily resident in the U.K. travelled regularly to the affiliates in Malaysia.[14]

Owing to the imperatives of technology in manufacturing, the U.K. parent companies exercise control over their affiliates through the supply of technical information, material inputs, and personnel. When a company had branded products, it also possessed some leverage over its affiliates as a result of its monopoly of technical know-how, trade marks, and patent rights. In fact, when a firm employed a certain amount of technical information in its operations, the head of production would normally be a British citizen appointed by the head-office and co-opted to the local board. It was also quite common for the chiefs of the marketing departments to be head-office appointments; and the heads of marketing were sometimes on the local board of directors.

The average number of members of the local board of directors of U.K. firms in Malaysia from 1963 to 1971 was seven, including at least one Malaysian. In 1970, several U.K. companies had Malaysians as their board chairman or vice-chairman, although no Malaysian was a managing director. The managing director was the pivot of control from the U.K. head-office, assuming the role of the chief executives and making crucial operational decisions. The chairman's position on the other hand was usually non-executive, and confined to presiding over board meetings as well as to making business and social contacts for the firm.

It was also common for British companies to have Malaysian company secretaries, the post of a company secretary being usually occupied by someone qualified and competent in local company law. Most British firms were audited by an international firm of accountants like Price Waterhouse and Company, Cooper Brothers and Company, Peat, Marwick, Mitchell, or Turquand Youngs and Company, although a few were audited by smaller firms of accountants. The reason for their preference for big international firms of accountants was that these firms were able to provide world-wide service and standardized reporting of accounts.

INTERLOCKING DIRECTORATES

An interlocking directorate exists where two or more firms are joined by virtue of their having directors in common. The subject of interlocking directorates is very important since it can lead, in some circumstances, to a reduction of competition.[15] The subject has not been studied in detail in Malaysia,[16] and is outside the scope of the present study.

Broadly, an interlocking directorate, as distinct from a multiple directorate in which a person is a director of a number of companies—a common phenomenon in the Malaysian economy, exists only where the links provided by directors are of benefit to the companies involved. It is difficult to ascertain whether directorship links of companies definitely benefit the companies involved, but on the basis of empirical evidence most of the links between companies in Malaysia are of some benefit to the companies linked through the directors.[17]

Table 6.3 outlines the types of interlocking directorates, based on twenty-one British holding companies in the country. The types were not mutually exclusive, and there were instances when a director, by virtue of his directorships of many companies, provided all four kinds of interlock.

Two or three prominent Malaysians on the boards of British companies were also on the boards of local and other foreign companies. Thus they provided the connexions of local, British, and other foreign companies in the country. The connexions are best illustrated by Figure 6.1 which shows the tie-up of manufacturing, construction, transport, mining, agriculture, petroleum, hotel, engineering, and financial companies. Through the interlocking of directorates, the majority of big companies and subsidiaries in Malaysia are in the hands of not more than two dozen company directors.[18]

The twenty-one groups of companies[19] on which Figure 6.1 and Table 6.3 are based had about 126 directors in 1972. Twenty-five directors (19.8 per cent of the total number) served on the boards of more than one group of companies. On average, each of the 126 directors served on the boards of 2.5 companies (usually affiliates).[20] It would appear that British companies without any form of interlocking directorships were few in number.

The existence of a large number of interlocking directorships cannot, in itself, be interpreted as grounds for considering them harmful to the competitive structure of the Malaysian economy. In fact, without further field investigation, no definite assertion

TABLE 6.3

TYPES OF INTERLOCKING DIRECTORATES IN SELECTED BRITISH COMPANIES IN MALAYSIA, 1971–1972

Type	*Outline of Link*	*Nature of Interlock*
Type A	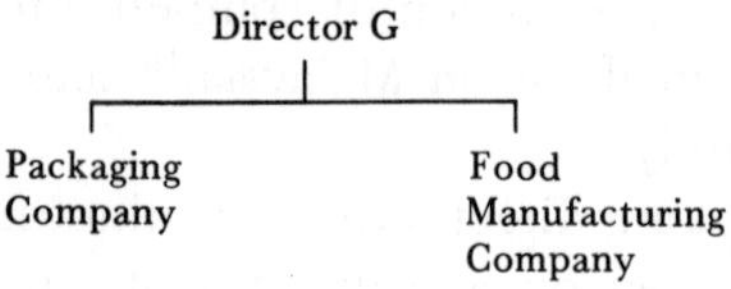	interlock with supplier
Type B	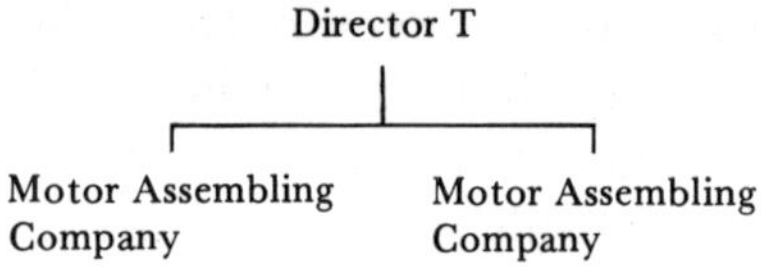	interlock with competitors
Type C	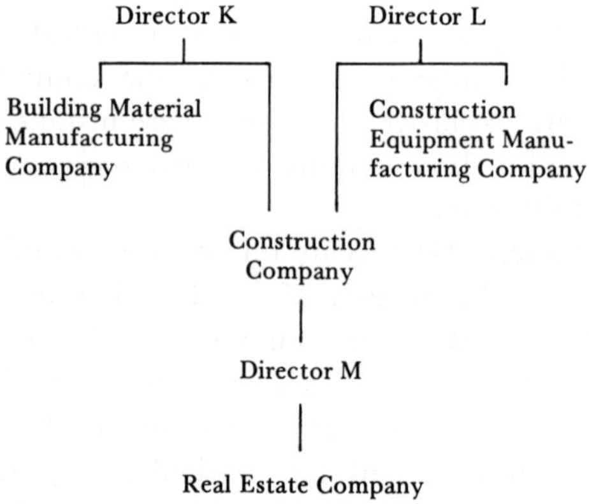	interlock with customers and suppliers
Type D	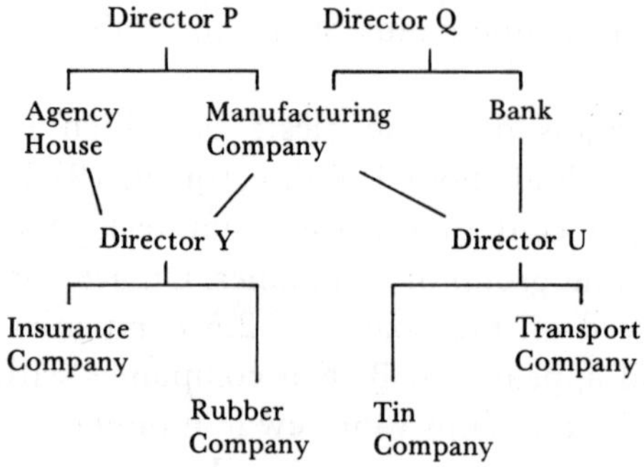	interlock with suppliers, customers, competitors, financiers and other companies

Source: Compiled from data in *Stock Exchange of Malaysia and Singapore Handbook*, 1973.

FIGURE 6.1

INTER-CONNEXIONS OF SELECTED COMPANIES IN MALAYSIA THROUGH LINKED DIRECTORSHIPS, 1971–1972

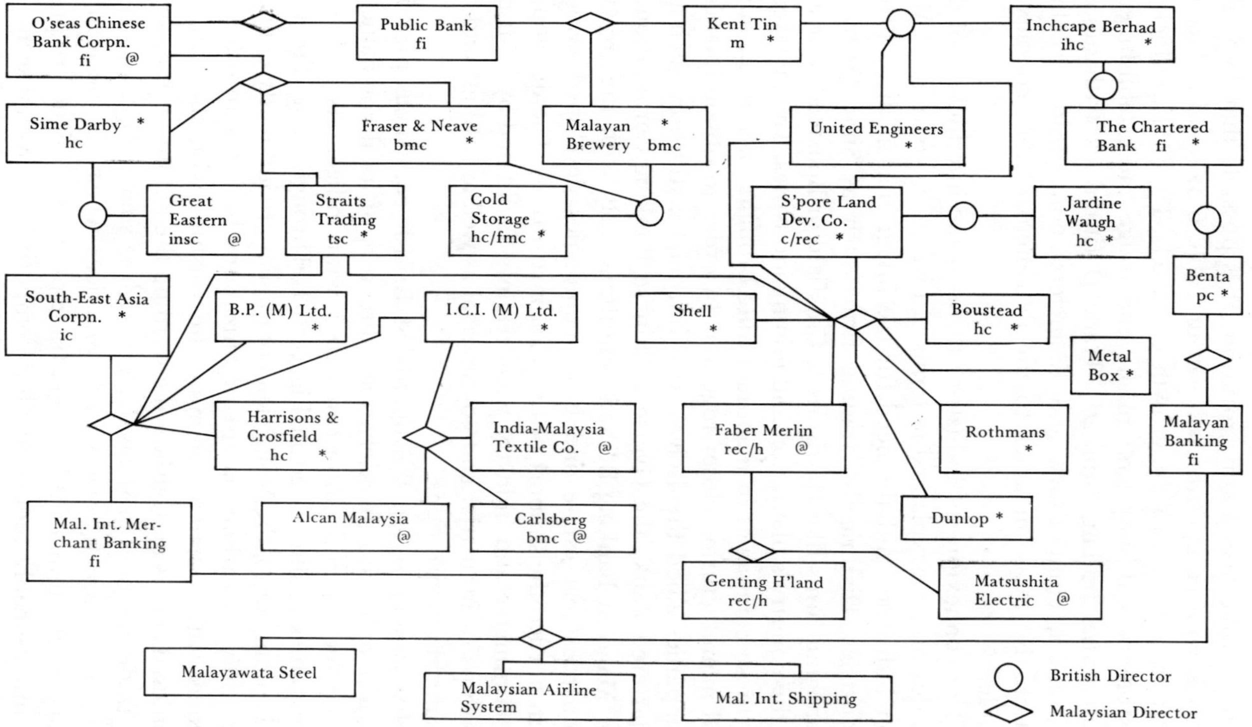

Source: As in Table 6.3.

Notes:

tsc	= tin smelting company.	bmc	= beverage manufacturing company.	m	= mining company.
@	= Other foreign company.	c/rec	= construction/real estate company.	pc	= plantation company.
*	= British company.	rec/h	= real estate/hotel company.	ic	= investment company.
fi	= financial institution.	hc	= holding company.	insc	= insurance company.
		ihc	= intermediate holding company.	fmc	= food manufacturing company.

can be made on the effect of interlocking directorships on competition in the economy. Nevertheless it is crucial to consider the potential reduction of the competitive process in the present position of directorship concentration. It is possible that Type B (interlock with competitors) shown in Table 6.3, could reduce competition and lead to the growth of cartels. Type C (interlock with customers and suppliers) might encourage the establishment of preferential trading. Similarly Trade D (interlock with suppliers, customers, competitors, and financiers) could lead to collusive actions by the companies to the detriment of the economy as a whole.

The connexions of industries through the interlocking of directorates may be explained in terms of historical evolution of Malaysian industries and the need for the integration in the control of industries. Historically, trading firms such as Sime Darby, and managing firms like Harrisons & Crosfield or Boustead were active in the country's plantation and mining industries. The involvement of these companies in manufacturing brought plantation, mining, and manufacturing closer together. In order to obtain finance the companies allied themselves with financial institutions such as the Chartered Bank, the Overseas Chinese Banking Corporation, and the Malayan Banking Berhad. Simultaneously with the growth of industries real estate and hotel companies developed—which in turn needed the support of financial institutions. The development of commerce and industry was certainly facilitated by joint directorships of industrial and commercial as well as banking and other financial organizations.

By appointing to the boards of British companies prominent local people who themselves are directors of local companies, the companies became inter-connected with indigenous and foreign companies as illustrated in Figure 6.1. Through some directors of U.K. companies, the Malaysian companies are indirectly connected not only to various parent organizations but also to other companies which shared common directorships with the U.K. companies. There is no legislation governing the nature of directorships or trade practices in Malaysia, although in some countries[21] regulations exist which govern trade practices which are deemed contrary to the public interest: i.e. trade practices designed to prevent or unreasonably reduce or limit competition. It would seem possible, in the absence of regulations about interlocking directorships and trade practices, that companies might collude in a manner detrimental to competition and the whole economy. It would seem necessary to introduce legislation regulating trade practices and to reduce the interlocking directorates that could directly curb competition.[22]

INDUSTRIAL DISTRIBUTION OF INVESTMENTS

In 1968 British manufacturing companies in Malaysia were well spread over a wide variety of industries. Numerically more than one-half (and, in terms of employment concentration, over 60 per cent) of manufacturing establishments were in the groups covering the processing of agricultural commodities, in food, drink, and tobacco manufacturing, chemical, metal, and rubber products manufacturing. In general, British firms dominated the modern and research-intensive industries.

For the purpose of exposition, manufacturing industries are classified according to Dunning's two main groups: (a) research-intensive, or technologically advanced group; and (b) other industries, or less research-intensive group.[23] Examples of research-intensive industries in Malaysia are those concerned with petroleum and coal products, chemical and chemical products, rubber products, transport equipment, electrical goods, and machinery manufacturing. Examples of the latter group are those in the manufacture of food, drink, tobacco, basic metals, metal products (except machinery), textiles, and other miscellaneous products not included in (a).

In practice little fundamental research has been carried out by British firms in category (a) above. On the other hand, industries in category (b) are technologically advanced in comparison to the indigenous industries of the same category. Local research which is limited to product adaptation and quality control is undertaken in the country by several firms of both categories. British firms which are classified as research-intensive pay royalties and service charges to their parent firms which conduct research and development activities for all their affiliates. No details of such payments made by British affiliates in Malaysia were available. Nevertheless, in 1968 an estimated $14 million, approximately 7 per cent of gross sales, were paid in royalties alone by U.K.-owned research-intensive industries in Malaysia to their headquarters in Britain.[24]

Given the broad classification of industries into (a) and (b) above, Table 6.4 shows the structural distribution of U.K. manufacturing affiliates in Malaysia in 1968. The Table emphasizes a marked concentration of British firms participating in the research-intensive sectors of industry. In 1968, a little over one-half of the capital stake of British manufacturing affiliates (columns *1*

TABLE 6.4

INDUSTRIAL DISTRIBUTION OF FIXED ASSETS AND GROSS SALES OF U.K. MANUFACTURING AFFILIATES, 1968

Industrial Category	*(1)* *Assets of U.K. Companies* *$ m.*	*(2)* (%)	*(3)* *Assets of All Companies* *$ m.*	*(4)* (%)	*(5)* *Sales of U.K. Companies* *$ m.*	*(6)* (%)	*(7)* *Sales of All Companies* *$ m.*	*(8)* (%)	*(9)* *Col. 1 / Col. 3*	*(10)* *Col. 5 / Col. 7*
a) *Research-Intensive Industries*	107.3	51.7	296.0	33.3	181.7	31.0	697	22.6	36.3	26.1
Petroleum and coal products	38.0	18.3	75	8.4	83.0	14.2	175	5.7	50.7	47.4
Chemicals and chemical products	40.0	19.3	109	12.2	37.0	6.3	210	6.8	36.7	17.6
Rubber products	16.4	7.9	40	4.5	39.4	6.7	110	3.6	41.0	35.8
Transport equipment	3.7	1.8	35	3.9	2.4	0.4	82	2.7	10.6	2.9
Machinery (except electrical)	4.5	2.2	18	2.0	2.7	0.5	63	2.0	25.0	4.3
Electrical machinery	4.7	2.3	19	2.2	17.2	2.9	57	1.9	24.7	30.2
b) *Other Industries*	100.0	48.3	594	66.7	404.3	69.0	2,382	77.4	16.8	17.0
Food, drinks, and tobacco	58.6	28.3	190	21.3	250.0	42.7	980	31.8	30.8	25.5
Basic metals	18.6	9.0	159	17.9	8.8	1.5	175	5.7	11.8	5.0
Other	22.8	11.0	245	27.5	145.5	24.8	1,227	39.9	9.3	11.9
All manufacturing	207.3	100.0	890	100.0	586.0	100.0	3,079	100.0	23.3	19.0

Sources: Assets and Sales of All Companies derived from *Census of Manufacturing Industries, 1968*, Kuala Lumpur; U.K. companies' figures are estimates arrived at during field work.

Notes: (i) No official statistics are available for the exact assets and sales of U.K. manufacturing affiliates in Malaysia. Consolidated balance sheets for the census year seldom show separate figures attributable to manufacturing activities.

(ii) Fixed assets cover all goods that have a normal economic life of more than one year. Their values shown refer to year end values according to the books of accounts. Amounts include additions during the year and exclude disposals during the year; they are net of depreciations.

(iii) Gross Sales values shown refer to ex-factory values of goods manufactured and repaired during the year. The amounts exclude export duties and excise taxes paid on sales.

(iv) Columns *9* and *10* show the share of assets and sales accounted for by U.K. affiliates, i.e. their 'participation coefficients'.

and *2*), and 31 per cent of their sales (columns *5* and *6*) were in these sectors. The corresponding share of the net assets of all manufacturing companies in the country was about one-third (columns *3* and *4*), while the proportions of sales of all manufacturing establishments in the research-intensive industries was about 23 per cent (columns *7* and *8*).

Columns *9* and *10* of Table 6.4 calculate the participation coefficients,[25] or the share of the total assets and sales accounted for by British manufacturing affiliates. Table 6.4 shows that over one-third (36.3 per cent) of all assets and over one-quarter (26.1 per cent) of all sales belonged to British manufacturing affiliates in the research-intensive sectors of Malaysian industry. Of the assets and sales in all the other (non-research-intensive) sectors, approximately one-sixth was attributable to British affiliates.

Among the research-intensive group of industries, participation coefficients of British affiliates were highest in the petroleum and coal products industries (columns *9* and *10*). About one-half of all assets and 47 per cent of sales in the petroleum and coal products industry in 1968 were accounted for by British firms such as Shell, Castrol, and British Petroleum (BP) and Malayan Bitumen.[26] The dominance of Dunlop and Wilkinson Process in the rubber products industries in Malaysia helped to account for the high participation coefficients (41 per cent of assets and 36 per cent of sales) of British firms in rubber products manufacturing. Similarly, the commanding positions of Malayan Oxygen—a subsidiary of British Oxygen—and the Chemical Company of Malaysia—a constituent of ICI—in the industrial gases, chemicals and chemical products industry explained the high concentration of British-owned assets in the industry. About 37 per cent of assets in the industry was British.[27] Other British chemical and pharmaceutical companies, e.g. Beecham, Boots, Brand, Burroughs Wellcome, and Glaxo-Allenburys were also prominent in the production and supply of patent medicines in the country. Lever Brothers, a wholly-owned subsidiary of Unilever, was in control of the market in branded soap and washing powder.[28]

Petroleum, chemicals, and rubber products together made up 45.5 per cent of all British industrial investments in the country in 1968. The capital intensity of production, the technical links with parent firms and the world-wide organizations of leading British firms in these products were likely to ensure the importance of these industries in Malaysia for a long time.

The pattern of foreign investment which exist in these sectors of industry in Malaysia appears to be similar to those existing in many countries receiving foreign investments at a certain stage of their development. In India, for example, petroleum and chemicals and allied products constituted 48.6 per cent of foreign investments in 1961,[29] while in Australia[30] in the period 1957 to 1960, over 30 per cent of foreign investment was in chemicals and oil refining. In Canada[31] nearly 35 per cent of U.S. and other foreign direct investments in 1965 were in chemicals and petroleum industries. Even in Britain[32] in the early 1950s American foreign investment in the chemical and allied trades was quite important. Likewise, foreign investments in Ceylon[33] (Sri Lanka) and in Thailand[34] in the 1960s tended to concentrate in petroleum and chemical and chemical products industries.

In 1968 about one-quarter of all assets in industries producing machinery (except electrical) and electrical appliances in Malaysia belonged to British firms, notably the Electrical and Allied Industries Bhd.—a member of the GEC-EE group—and United Engineers. The market for electrical appliances and machinery was very competitive, and British firms encountered tough competition. In the Malaysian climate, with its high temperature and high humidity, there was a great demand for refrigeration and air-conditioning equipment. Rivals of British firms (e.g. International Air Conditioning and Pan Electric) were established earlier than the British-owned Electrical and Allied Industries. British firms had to contend with fierce competition from these rivals who were subsidiaries of other foreign companies. For example, in the field of electrical appliances, British firms had to compete vigorously against such rival firms as Matsushita Electric (M) Bhd., Sanyo Industries Bhd., Toshiba Sdn. Bhd., and Acma Electrical Industries.

In food, drink, and tobacco industries, the combined aggregates of U.K. firms owned about 31 per cent of the assets and accounted for a little over one-quarter of all sales in 1968 (Table 6.4, columns *9* and *10*). Although Cold Storage and its twenty-five affiliated companies dominated about 40–50 per cent of the dairy and frozen food industries, the retail prices of such foods were still too high for the market provided by the lower income demands. Similarly, although in 1968 Guinness Bhd. controlled the stout and lager beer market, such brewed drinks were still out of reach of the lower income groups. Malayan Tobacco, a member of the British-American Tobacco Co. Ltd., and Rothmans of Pall Mall (M) Bhd. had been able, by a combination of product differentiation and price discrimination, to capture over three-fifths of the cigarette and tobacco market in the country.

In the manufacture of transport equipment, the low participation coefficient of British firms in 1968—about 11 per cent of all assets in the industry belonged to British interests—might be accounted for by their late entry into the market, although as discussed earlier (Chapter 4) British motor vehicles had earlier dominated the Malaysian market. Wearne Brothers Ltd. joined forces with Inchcape in establishing an assembly firm, Motor Investments Berhad in 1970. Rival concerns (e.g. Asia Automobile Industries, Cycle and Carriage, and Swedish Motor Sdn. Bhd.) were by that date also in production. In the manufacture of bulk-transport equipment (road tankers, coaches, articulated trucks, and trailers) the British firm Hargill Engineering Sdn. Bhd., a subsidiary of Harper Gilfillan, was the only important company in the industry in 1968. However in the same year, there was no British manufacturing interest of importance in the country in certain industries like textiles,[35] footwear, furniture, paper and paper products, even though some large British firms imported these products into Malaysia. British paper manufacturers like Spicers, a subsidiary of Reed International, and Wiggins Teape however had marketing subsidiaries in the country, and between them supplied an estimated 60–70 per cent of the country's paper requirements. British-made furniture in the 1960s was available through Robinsons department store which also retailed a variety of British footwear and other apparel.

In printing, publishing, and allied industries, leaders in the production of English language publications were the Straits Times group of companies, Longman (M) Sdn. Bhd., and Oxford University Press. Of the three, only the Straits Times—which also publishes the country's popular daily newspapers, *The Straits Times*[36] (morning, circulation *c.* 300,000), *Berita Harian* (morning, circulation *c.* 40,000) and *The Malay Mail* (*c.* 30,000), as well as a number of magazines—had printing, lithographic, engraving, binding, and packaging plants in the country. The other two usually subcontracted their publishing works either in Malaysia or overseas. In 1968 in the non-metallic mineral products industry, Malayan Cement, a constituent of the Associated Portland Cement Blue Circle Group, provided nearly 70 per cent of the country's cement requirements. Being associated with the real estate business, the company also produced nearly one-half of the building materials supplied to the construction industry. British firms were not extensively involved in the production of basic metals. Apart from the foundries of James Warren and United Engineers and others associated with the mining industry, most of the companies in the basic metal industry were indigenously owned. Changes might have occurred in the detailed distribution of assets of U.K. manufacturing affiliates since 1968, but the broad distribution seemed to indicate that British manufacturing companies were concentrated in the research-intensive and technologically advanced sectors of industry.

U.K. CAPITAL ENJOYING 'PIONEER' STATUS

'Pioneer' companies are those which are given a combination of tax and other incentives by the Ministry of Commerce and Industry upon the fulfilment by these firms of conditions and stipulations laid down in the *Investment Incentives Act, 1968*.[37] As shown in Table 6.5 British companies which enjoyed pioneer status in 1970 were concentrated in the technologically advanced sectors of Malaysian industry conforming to the broad picture outlined in the previous section[38] above. Over three-quarters of British capital enjoying pioneer status was in the rubber manufacturing, chemical, and petroleum industries. Almost 16 per cent of British capital investment with pioneer status was in the food and beverage manufacturing industries. The remainder was distributed among other sections of industry, e.g. in the manufacture of electrical machinery, transport equipment, non-metallic minerals, and miscellaneous products.

By way of contrast, only about 22.2 per cent of locally-owned capital in pioneer industries in 1970 was engaged in the technologically advanced sectors of rubber manufacturing, chemical, and petroleum industries. The respective percentages of other foreign-owned capital and total capital invested in these industries (Table 6.5, columns *3* and *4*) were approximately 37 per cent and 37.9 per cent. The marked concentration of U.K. capital participation in the more research-intensive or technologically advanced sectors of Malaysian manufacturing industries enjoying pioneer status is emphasized in columns *5*, *6*, and *7* in Table 6.5. In total, the $79.7 million U.K. capital enjoying pioneer status in 1970 constituted about 16.9 per cent of total capital of pioneer companies in the country. By December 1973, although British capital enjoying pioneer status increased in actual value to $91.2 million, the proportion had fallen to approximately 9.2 per cent of total capital of pioneer companies in that year.[39]

AN EXPLANATION OF INDUSTRIAL STRUCTURE

Ridzuan bin Akil,[40] S. Y. Lo,[41] and J. T. Thoburn[42] have explained the existing structure of manufacturing in Malaysia in

TABLE 6.5

INDUSTRIAL DISTRIBUTION OF U.K. CAPITAL ENJOYING PIONEER STATUS IN MALAYSIA, 1970

Industry Group	(1) *U.K. Owned* $m.	(%)	(2) *Locally Owned* $m.	(%)	(3) *Foreign Owned** $m.	(%)	(4) *Total* $m.	(%)	(5) (1) *as % of* (2)	(6) (1) *as % of* (3)	(7) (1) *as % of* (4)
Food, beverage	12.6	(15.8)	38.6	(21.3)	50.5	(23.9)	101.7	(21.6)	32.6	25.0	12.4
Textile, garment	0.7	(0.9)	26.2	(14.5)	18.6	(8.8)	45.5	(9.6)	2.7	3.8	1.5
Wood products	—	—	20.5	(11.3)	2.9	(1.4)	23.4	(5.0)	—	—	—
Paper and printing	—	—	4.1	(2.3)	2.0	(0.9)	6.1	(1.3)	—	—	—
Leather, rubber	12.2	(15.3)	6.0	(3.3)	3.7	(1.8)	21.9	(4.7)	203.3	329.7	55.7
Chemicals	25.4	(31.9)	16.4	(9.1)	21.9	(10.4)	63.7	(13.5)	154.9	116.0	39.9
Petroleum	22.7	(28.5)	17.8	(9.8)	52.3	(24.8)	92.8	(19.7)	127.5	43.4	24.5
Minerals	1.8	(2.3)	6.6	(3.6)	11.3	(5.4)	19.7	(4.2)	27.3	11.3	9.1
Basic metals	—	—	29.7	(16.4)	24.0	(11.4)	53.7	(11.4)	—	—	—
Metal products	—	—	3.0	(1.7)	9.8	(4.6)	12.8	(2.7)	—	—	—
Machinery and transport equipment	1.1	(1.4)	2.4	(1.3)	3.5	(1.7)	7.0	(1.5)	45.5	31.4	15.7
Electrical machinery	3.1	(3.9)	5.7	(3.2)	9.5	(4.5)	18.3	(3.9)	54.4	32.6	16.9
Miscellaneous	0.1	(0.1)	4.0	(2.2)	0.8	(0.4)	4.9	(1.0)	2.5	12.5	2.0
Total	79.7	(100.0)	181.0	(100.0)	210.9	(100.0)	471.6	(100.0)	44.0	37.8	16.9

Source: Data source, from compilation of Federal Industrial Development Authority (FIDA), Kuala Lumpur.

Notes: There would be some minor discrepancies due to rounding off. Amounts refer to paid-up and loan capital as at year end.

*Other Foreign Owned capital belongs to companies from Singapore, United States, Japan, Hong Kong, West Indies, Australia, Canada, Holland, Taiwan and smaller companies from other countries.

terms of natural locational advantages and backward and forward industrial linkages. But why the British industrial capital stake in Malaysia assumed the structural distribution mentioned in the previous two sections cannot entirely be explained in terms of locational advantages and industrial linkages. Two general propositions based on empirical observations may be made here to account for the industrial composition of U.K. investments in Malaysian industries. Firstly, manufacturing companies as a rule invested in the country in those areas of manufacturing activities where both the growth and/or profit potential were favourable to them. As pointed out in Chapter 4, British companies had a strong motivation to set up manufacturing establishments in Malaysia in order to preserve and enhance their share of the Malaysian market.

Secondly, manufacturing companies tended to invest in those industries where they had the greatest comparative advantages *vis-à-vis* local or indigenous firms. Their comparative advantage was due to several factors, such as their possession of established branded products, technological know-how, sophisticated marketing facilities, and modern management techniques, as well as access to sources of capital. As can be seen from those industries where U.K. participation coefficients were high (Table 6.4), the content of productive knowledge in them was important, and in the specific cases of petroleum and chemical industries the cost of entry was high.

Data limitations do not permit a more rigorous testing of these propositions, but general pointers may be obtained by recalling that in the 1960s industries that had contributed highly to growth were, among others, chemicals, petroleum, rubber products, food, beverages, and tobacco manufacturing: and as suggested by Tables 6.4 and 6.5, British companies were distributed precisely in those industries where growth in the 1960s was high.

British firms in Malaysia being affiliates of well-developed parent firms in the U.K. had a great comparative advantage over local firms which had all the limitations associated with indigenous industry in an underdeveloped economy. General considerations of the disadvantages normally associated with investing in a foreign country would also lend credence to the argument that British companies as foreign investors in Malaysia must have substantial advantages of some kind over host-country firms in order to remain in the modern sector of the economy.[43] When foreign firms ceased to possess any advantage in the form of product brands, technical know-how, or conversely if host-country firms could gain all the advantages the foreign firms had, there was no reason why host-country firms could not dominate the modern industrial sector in Malaysia.

There are other specific explanations as to how British firms assumed their positions in Malaysian manufacturing. In tobacco and cigarette manufacturing for instance a British enterprise was first to start local manufacturing. Being first on the scene, the firm in question enjoyed the protective effect of tariff on imported manufactured tobacco. Seven years after the first company was in production another British firm with established brands came. Ten years later yet another British tobacco firm came into the country. Between them, these firms controlled a substantial portion of the market. In the case of building materials and cement manufacturing a British firm also first began local production, and its growth was enhanced by the building and construction boom of the late 1950s and 1960s. In the case of food manufacturing, a British company was also first to start local manufacturing of dairy and frozen foods. Cold Storage Holdings Ltd., a prominent firm in the food industry, began in the early 1900s,[44] at first catering for the needs of Europeans and other foreigners but later branching into food processing which catered for the country as a whole. Over the years this company developed into an integrated manufacturing firm having, by 1972, more than twenty subsidiaries and affiliates. A British company was also first to begin local manufacturing in the light-engineering industry. Among the multinational enterprises, British-based concerns again were the first to commence local manufacture. Companies that were first in the market had to maintain their leading position by continuously improving their already comparatively high level of technology. Supported by the parent companies' research and development, the British subsidiaries in Malaysia tend to remain in the technologically advanced sector.

DISTRIBUTION OF MANUFACTURING ESTABLISHMENTS BY SALES SIZE GROUP

Table 6.6 presents the distribution of manufacturing establishments by size of sales.[45] It can be seen that a little over 60 per cent of U.K. manufacturing establishments were distributed among the larger groups of firms having sales over $3 million, whereas only about 13 per cent of all firms in the country belonged to those groups. About one-fifth of U.K. industrial firms were among those medium-sized groups of firms with sales between $0.5 million and $3 million, but only about 17 per cent of

TABLE 6.6
DISTRIBUTION OF MANUFACTURING ESTABLISHMENTS BY SALES SIZE GROUP, 1968
(as per cent of number of establishments)

Sales Size Group	*U.K.-owned*	*All Establishments*
Under $400,000	8.5	49.9
$400,000 – $499,999	10.6	20.5
$500,000 – $999,999	4.3	10.2
$1,000,000 – $2,999,999	15.9	6.5
$3,000,000 – $4,999,999	37.3	12.6
$5,000,000 and over	23.4	0.3
	100.0	100.0

Sources: *Census of Manufacturing Industries, 1968*, and interviews.

all manufacturing establishments were in this group. By contrast, over 70 per cent of the country's manufacturing concerns in 1968 belonged to the smaller groups of firms with sales below $0.5 million, and only about 19 per cent of British manufacturing concerns were in this category. The general picture that emerges from the above Table is that British industrial establishments were mainly distributed among the group of firms with high sales, and they were clearly the leaders in the Malaysian industrial sector as far as sale sizes are concerned.

Changes might have occurred in the detailed distribution of British companies and their respective sales positions since 1968. The broad picture of the situation in the 1960s suggested that British companies dominated the respective sub-sectors of the economy they were in. In the majority of cases (as illustrated by examples noted earlier), each company controlled over one-third of its market. In terms of the definition of monopoly in the *(U.K.) Fair Trading Act, 1973* (which considered a firm as a monopoly when it controlled more than one-quarter of the market) British companies in Malaysia were (and some still are) in monopolistic positions in the economy.

EMPLOYMENT CHARACTERISTICS IN U.K. MANUFACTURING CONCERNS

In 1968 about 9,200 full-time paid workers[46] of varying levels of skills and education were employed in British manufacturing establishments covered by the census of manufacturing industries. The aggregate full-time employment in British manufacturing concerns represented about 7.6 per cent of all employment in the manufacturing sector, or approximately 0.3 per cent of the estimated 2.8 million total working population in 1968. In terms of employment directly created by British industry, the number of full-time paid workers was by no means large, but the variety of employment offered was wide.[47]

About one-quarter of the total employment was in the manufacture of food, beverages, and tobacco; one-fifth was in the processing of agricultural commodities; just under 17 per cent was in the manufacture of rubber, chemicals, and chemical products; 12 per cent was in the manufacture of metals, machinery, and electrical goods, and the remainder was in petroleum, printing, nonmetallic mineral, and miscellaneous industries.

The value of fixed assets per full-time employee in U.K.-owned establishments is higher than that of the average of firms in Malaysian industry as can be seen from Table 6.7 below.

On the whole, the value of assets per full-time employee in all British-owned industrial establishments in Malaysia was nearly three times that of the average for all manufacturing establishments in the country. In some specific cases, e.g. beverages, tobacco, and rubber products manufacturing, the value of assets per employee in British establishments was very much higher than that

TABLE 6.7

FIXED ASSETS AND VALUE ADDED PER FULL-TIME EMPLOYEE IN SELECTED INDUSTRIAL ESTABLISHMENTS, 1968 ($'000)

Industry	*Assets per Employee*		*Value-Added per Employee*	
	U.K. Establishments	*Average for All Establishments*	*U.K. Establishments*	*Average for All Establishments*
Food manufacturing	22.1	7.2	21.7	7.8
Beverage manufacturing	51.9	15.0	33.3	15.9
Tobacco products	26.7	7.2	56.1	14.8
Rubber products	16.0	4.8	21.4	6.1
Chemicals and chemical products	41.9	19.9	51.5	14.6
Machinery (non-electrical)	9.8	3.1	4.3	4.3
Electrical machinery	15.1	9.2	12.8	10.2
All Industries	20.8	7.4	19.7	7.2

Source: Calculated from data in the *Census of Manufacturing Industries, 1968*, and information gathered during field work.

of the average establishment in Malaysia, and the value added per employee in British-owned concerns was also higher compared to that in the average industrial firm, as shown in Table 6.7.

In almost all British manufacturing establishments the technical processes employed were highly capital intensive,[48] embodying the most advanced technologies available in their respective fields. The firms' choice of technology within the competitive Malaysian market had been governed by the motive of sales maximization with a satisfactory rate of return.[49] The common consideration which led management to adopt automated production techniques was the ability to supply the market with an uninterrupted flow of goods and the belief that automated production techniques enable them to expand capacity and output rapidly. The use of labour-intensive production and handling techniques was thought likely to lead to greater vulnerability to interruptions than was the case with automated production. Moreover, the majority of representatives with whom this point was raised believed they had little choice in the types of machines they could use in the first instance, because the machines and equipment used in their Malaysian affiliates were made in the U.K. where Malaysian factor proportions were not an important consideration. British manufacturing affiliates in Malaysia did not even have a choice of suppliers of equipment and machines since the parent firms decided what should be supplied to the affiliates. The equipment and machines supplied generally reflected the conditions of relative costs of factors of production in the parent companies. Consequently, the production techniques in use in British affiliates in Malaysia did not result in high employment creation. In 1968, although British manufacturing establishments accounted for over one-fifth of all industrial value added, they contributed to less than 8 per cent of industrial employment. In contrast, indigenous industrial establishments, which in the same year accounted for about 52 per cent value added in manufacturing, accounted for more than 69 per cent of industrial employment.[50]

Data reflecting the structure and skill content of employment in U.K.-manufacturing affiliates are difficult to obtain. On the basis of information gathered during interviews it would appear that the skilled manpower requirements for operating mechanized establishments were, with some exceptions, generally quite modest, at least at the operative and junior supervisory level. In the 1960s U.K. nationals constituted the majority (about 80–85 per cent) of the technical, managerial, and higher professional personnel. By 1972 the position had changed since, as a rule, most British companies were progressively replacing expatriate employees with locally-recruited personnel.

As Table 6.8 shows, the educational levels of the vast majority of local employees of British-owned establishments—the wage-earners—were no higher than lower secondary school level. Many workers at that level of employment had in fact only primary education.

In many U.K. affiliates training was usually available through working with a skilled operator. The worker might get a rise in position and remuneration with seniority, experience, and demonstrated ability. Some larger concerns arranged their own training programme consisting of a number of short formal courses in machine operation and maintenance, general supervision, and marketing. In a few instances middle management employees were sent to attend courses at the government-sponsored National Productivity Centre (NPC), or at the local Institute of Management.[51]

Almost three-fifths of the technical, professional, and managerial employees entered British firms as new recruits. They were usually graduates of local and foreign (mainly U.K. and Australian) institutions of higher learning; the other two-fifths had risen through the ranks. In 1972 British firms did not experience any shortage of candidates for available vacancies, although many candidates had only limited industrial experience. Training new recruits for higher levels of employment in the firms consisted of usually rotational assignments in the affiliates, and a short course (normally three months) in the U.K. Sometimes the candidates were sent to a longer established branch of the firm in the region, e.g. in Singapore. Candidates intended for top level technical and management assignments were trained in the plant of the parent firms in the U.K. for periods of up to two years.

British nationals, as indicated in Table 6.8, constituted about one-third of the total employees of all British-owned firms. Their tenure of office was decided by the head-office and ranged from a few months to five years. A few might rise to the local board of directors though local employees did not usually attain such positions. However, in a number of the multinational enterprises, Malaysian personnel at higher levels of management were selected to be part of the management teams to spearhead the development of overseas branches in South-East Asia (see Chapter 7).

On the whole it is not possible to measure accurately the contribution made by British firms in training Malaysian workers in industrial techniques.[52] Those employees who might be in a position to learn some industrial techniques (by virtue of their training

TABLE 6.8

THE STRUCTURE OF EMPLOYMENT IN U.K. AFFILIATES, 1970

Level of Employment	*Per Cent of Number Employed*		*Education/Experience Requirements*
I. *Local Citizens*		*66*	
i) Wage earners (e.g. general labour, machine operators, sectionmen, watchmen, etc.)	75		Primary schooling, or Lower Certificate of Education
ii) Salaried employees			
a) Juniors and middle management (e.g. foremen, supervisors, clerks, etc.)	11		School Certificate or its equivalent
b) Technical and professional (e.g. technicians, accountants, etc.)	8		Technical or professional qualifications
c) Managerial or higher professional (e.g. personnel, finance, sales, and production managers)	5		University degree, or professional qualifications and experience
d) Higher management (e.g. works directors, general managers, sales directors, etc.)	1		As in (c) and by promotion from (c), or by special parent company appointments
	100		
II. *U.K. Nationals*		*34*	
None for employment levels i) and ii) (a) above			
ii) b. Technical and professional	10		By parent company assignment
c. Managerial or higher professional	40		
d. Higher management	50		
	100		

Source: Based on interviews.

and educational qualifications) were small in number. The vast majority of employees may have learnt very little from their jobs, because the techniques involved in the capital-intensive British firms were almost invariably specific to the particular firms concerned, with the result that the simple skills demanded of production-line workers were of little direct use in other sectors of the economy, except perhaps in a similar industry with an equally high level of technology. It is not possible to say whether such a situation could lead to the extensive development of broadly based local entrepreneurship or management to 'spin off' truly Malaysian enterprises. There are of course examples, as will be mentioned later in Chapter 9, where ex-employees of British concerns set up their own firms on their own account.

As noted previously in Table 6.7, value added per employee in U.K.-owned industrial firms is higher than that of the average for all firms in the country, in general being over two and one-half times. Wages and salaries per employee in British-owned firms are also higher than those for the average industrial firm. In 1968 the average remuneration of production workers in the manufacturing sector as a whole was $2,210 per annum; whereas the average remuneration of each production worker in British-owned manufacturing concerns was about $4,060 per annum.[53] The total remuneration paid to workers by British companies was $37.3 million which was approximately 14 per cent of all salaries and wages paid to all employees in the manufacturing sector in that year.[54]

The generally high level of payment to employees in U.K. companies compared to those in indigenous firms was accounted for by the high level of productivity in the former relative to the latter.

SOURCES AND USES OF FUNDS

According to Gethyn Davies,[55] U.K. companies in Singapore were generally expected to generate their own cash to finance their local operations. This was achieved largely from sales of the products they manufactured. This arrangement was also true in British industrial firms in Malaysia. As noted in Chapter 5, the agency firms provided the bulk of their own funds for industrial activities. By and large, British firms in Malaysia provided over one-half of their yearly financial requirements from internally generated funds. If intra-company finance is considered as part of the internally generated source of funds, then the proportion of funds provided by these firms to finance their own operations was certainly considerable, as can be seen from Table 6.9.

In 1964 and 1965, unremitted profits constituted over 45 per cent of the total sources of funds for British firms in Malaysia. In 1966 and 1967, funds originating from unremitted profits and provisions for depreciation together constituted more than 60 per cent of the sources of funds, while in 1970, unremitted profits only constituted about 30 per cent of the source of funds of the British affiliates. Intra-company sources of funds were also quite

TABLE 6.9
SOURCES OF FUNDS IN BRITISH AFFILIATES IN MALAYSIA
(per cent)

Year	*Unremitted Profits*	*Provision for Depreciation*	*Intra-company*	*Take-overs*	*Other*@	*Total*
1963	34.0	*	22.9	*	43.1	100
1964	45.1	*	35.5	12.1	19.4	100
1965	40.7	7.3	*	*	52.0	100
1966	90.3	*	*	*	9.7	100
1967	14.3	50.8	22.2	*	12.7	100
1970	30.1	*	48.0	16.9	5.0	100

Source: Based on information gathered at the Economics and Statistics Division of the Department of Trade and Industry.

Notes: @ New capital, credits and long-term borrowings.
* Not available, separately; included in 'Other'.

important, ranging in proportion from 22 per cent to 48 per cent of total sources of funds in the period 1963–70.

Take-overs or mergers (i.e. net acquisitions of shares and loan capital of established firms)[56] in Malaysia had been used as one of the sources of financing new investments by British-owned firms (e.g. Cold Storage, Sime Darby, Inchcape Berhad, and United Engineers).

In general, internally generated sources of funds in British affiliates were very important in financing operations,[57] and companies faced little problem in attracting funds for investment.

Turning to a study of the use of funds, of the seventy companies that provided information on this for the period 1970 to 1971, about 30 per cent of funds was employed in expenditure on fixed assets; 34 per cent on net current assets (mainly accounts receivable and stocks and works-in-progress), and the remaining 36 per cent on miscellaneous uses such as cash, trade investments, provision for taxation and workers' retirement benefits, as well as reserves for dividends and other purposes. The pattern of uses of funds in British affiliates in Malaysia is similar to that of British affiliates in other developing countries.[58]

THE GROWTH OF U.K.-OWNED COMPANIES

As far as the parent firms were concerned their overseas affiliates must not only be self-financing but also provide an ever increasing income to the parents.

TABLE 6.10

DIVERSIFICATION OF ACTIVITIES AND INCREASES IN PROFITS OF SELECTED INDUSTRIAL COMPANIES IN MALAYSIA, 1968–1970

Company/Year of (Establishment), Year of Commencing Production, Main Products at Establishment Year	*Products/Activities in 1973:*	*Reported Profits* 1968 (1) ($'000)	1968 (2) ($'000)	1968 (3) (%)	1970 (1) ($'000)	1970 (2) ($'000)	1970 (3) (%)	*Per Cent Increase in Pre-Tax Profits 1968–70*
Chemical Company of Malaysia (ICI-Group), (1963), 1965, chemicals and fertilizers.	5 subsidiaries and associates, producing ICI products.	(2,279)	–	–	6,133	6,133*	(20.4)	see (i)
Cold Storage Holdings Ltd. (1900), 1901+, dairy and frozen foods.	25 subsidiaries and associates. Engineering, Pharmaceuticals, Detergents, in addition to food processing.	7,061	4,410	(21.3)	11,238	6,587	(28.2)	59.2
Dunlop Malaysian Industries Bhd. (1961), 1962, rubber tyres.	4 subsidiaries, producing a variety of Dunlop products.	6,338	6,288	(35.2)	10,566	6,187	(58.7)	66.7
Fraser and Neave Ltd. (1883), 1960+, aerated water, cordials.	21 subsidiaries and associates engaged in a variety of activities associated with the beverage industry. Plywood, Dairy Foods	12,559	6,803	(40.0)	14,774	8,516	(41.0)	17.6
Guinness Malaysia Bhd. (1964), 1965, Guinness stouts.	4 subsidiaries brewing lager and pilsner beers additional to stouts.	4,134	4,131*	(51.7)	4,355	4,276	(43.6)	5.3
Malayan Tobacco Bhd. (1956), 1957, cigarettes.	3 subsidiaries management and computer services, prawn fishing in addition to manufacture of tobaccos.	19,918	10,744	(44.3)	23,867	13,157	(53.0)	19.8

(*Continued*)

TABLE 6.10 (*Continued*)

Company/Year of (Establishment), Year of Commencing Production, Main Products at Establishment Year	*Products/Activities in 1973:*	*Reported Profits* 1968 (1) ($ '000)	1968 (2) ($ '000)	1968 (3) (%)	1970 (1) ($ '000)	1970 (2) ($ '000)	1970 (3) (%)	*Per Cent Increase in Pre-Tax Profits 1968–70*
Metal Box Bhd. (1949), 1963+, cans and tin containers.	3 subsidiaries engaging in lithographic and plastics industries.	3,887	1,932	(28.7)	5,412	3,032	(40.1)	39.2
Straits Times Bhd. (1959), 1960+, newspapers.	11 subsidiaries engaging in all aspects of printing and publishing.	7,656	3,898	(55.5)	9,450	5,781	(68.6)	23.4
Electrical and Allied Ind. (1965), 1967, refrigeration and air-conditioning equipment manufacture.	Began local production of a wide range of GEC-EE electrical appliances.	(8)	–	–	329	329*	(25.9)	see (ii)
United Engineers Ltd. (1912), 1966+, servicing of machines and equipment.	4 subsidiaries engaging in all aspects of workshop and light engineering activities. Pharmaceutical prod. manufacturing.	1,901	1,201	(14.6)	3,111	1,407	(19.1)	63.7
Wearne Brothers Ltd. (1912), 1964+, importers of motor vehicles.	19 subsidiaries and associates engaging in the assembly and service of all kinds of vehicles. Rubber products manufacturing.	6,221	2,839	(20.7)	11,646	5,952	(38.9)	87.2

Source: Company reports.

Notes: (i) The $6 million profit was made in the second year the company earned profits since commencing production. Amount represented increase of 41.7% over 1969 earnings.

(ii) The $329,000 represented profit earned in the second year the company made profits since commencing production. Profit in 1969 was $108,000.

*Tax exempted under provision of *Investment Incentives Act, 1968*.

+Company started production units in Singapore at earlier dates.

(*1*) Pre-tax;

(*2*) Post-tax;

(*3*) Gross earnings as per cent of paid-up share capital.

Table 6.10 outlines the growth and diversification[59] of selected firms in a variety of industries. It shows that, for most firms, growth was attained by branching out into new fields by increasing the product range and exploiting entirely new growth opportunities. In four cases, diversification was partly a means of investing accumulated profits since the establishments concerned had excess capacity which limited the extent to which ploughing back of profits could be made.

Evidence suggests that diversification of activities was often associated with the entrepreneurial inclination of the chief executives who, when confronted with a limited internal market, had to think of other ways of increasing earnings. In general, the initiative to diversify and reinvest funds originated in the local management and the chief executive. The head-office seldom disapproved of well conceived projects when the chief executives were convinced of their viability. There is some basis for arguing that U.K. affiliates in Malaysia were increasingly developing their separate entities although the parent companies did scrutinize their development.

Professor E. T. Penrose (1959) has argued that, in the absence of a markedly unfavourable environment, there was a strong tendency for a business enterprise to grow, and diversification was one of the means of achieving growth.[60] The expansion of British affiliates in Malaysia into diverse activities supports the above arguments.[61]

1. *Board of Trade Journal*, 7 August 1964; 30 June 1967; 26 January 1968; 19 July 1968; 9 May 1969 and 23 September 1970. See also *Trade and Industry* 15 November 1973, and *Business Monitor*, M4., Overseas Transactions, April 1972 and 1974.

2. Some unpublished information was available from the Economics and Statistics Division of the DTI. The following sections will use this source of information supplemented with data verbally communicated during field work.

3. Manufacturing investments are organized into branches, subsidiaries, and associates, described collectively as 'affiliates'. For definitions of terms, see notes in Table 6.1.

4. The accounting treatment of promotional expenses and related outlays of companies in Malaysia has not been fully studied and it is outside the scope of the present study to do so. Evidence from field work suggested that there was a variety of practices in the treatment of outlays that were expensed and those that were capitalized. This complicates the attempt to quantify the initial investments accurately.

5. This is also true of all other foreign firms.

6. For the general requirements for establishing business including branches of foreign companies in Malaysia, see The Chartered Bank, *Malaysia: A Business Guide*, Kuala Lumpur, 1971.

7. See detail in *Listing Manual*, The Stock Exchange, Kuala Lumpur.

8. *The Strategy of Multinational Enterprise*, Longman, 1970, p. 293.

9. The experience of the United Africa Group, a wholly-owned Unilever company, in Nigeria and Ghana provides examples of successful joint-ventures. See E. Hallett, 'Joint-Ventures in Developing Countries' in P. Ady, ed., *Private Foreign Investment and the Developing World*, Praeger, 1971, pp. 231–2.

10. A general discussion on issues relating to joint-ventures is found in the International Chamber of Commerce, *Joint-Ventures in Developing Countries*, Geneva, 1968.

11. i.e. full power to exercise control which is derived from the ownership of shares. The word 'control' used in this sense implied that when the majority shares of a company are owned by entities other than the investing firm, there is dilution of control over the administration of the company by the investing firm. There are of course other aspects of control over a company which are not necessarily related to the possession of majority shares; see O. S. Hiner, *Business Administration, An Introductory Study*, Longman, 1972, pp. 36–41.

It was possible for British companies to control their Malaysian affiliates by means other than full ownership of shares (e.g. by capital gearing, vote gearing, agreements, etc.) but the overwhelming majority of them exercised control via ownership of shares and appointment of chief executives.

12. See Chapter 7. See also S. Lall, 'Transfer Pricing by Multinational Manufacturing Firms', *Bulletin of the Oxford University Institute of Economics and Statistics*, Vol. 35(3), August 1973, for details of the mechanism.

13. Local directors represented vital links with all sorts of companies in the country, as shown in Fig. 6.1.

14. Some large firms have special appointments known as either area manager or area co-ordinator to look after the progress and well-being of the overseas affiliates. The area co-ordinator commutes regularly between the affiliates and the parent firm. Three companies employed retired executives as their 'advisers' on the affairs of their Malaysian subsidiaries. These advisers monitored closely the performance of the Malaysian companies and accordingly advise the U.K. boards of directors on matters pertaining to the overseas affiliates.

15. See, among others, P. C. Dooley, 'The Interlocking Directorate', *American Economic Review*, Vol. 59, June 1969; and G. Fogelberg and C. R. Laurent, 'Interlocking Directorates: A Study of Large Companies in New Zealand', *Journal of Business Policy*, Vol. 3(2), 1973.

16. A brief non-analytical account of interlocking directorates in Malaysia is found in Puthucheary, *Ownership and Control in the Malayan Economy*.

17. Company representatives interviewed said that companies at least benefit through exchange of information among directors.

18. This is not uncommon in underdeveloped countries. See for instance L. J. White, *Industrial Concentration and Economic Power in Pakistan*, New Jersey, Princeton University Press, 1974.

19. A group of companies consists of a holding company, a number of intermediate holding companies and several branches, subsidiaries, and affiliates.

20. Not all of the affiliates are manufacturing companies. A number of companies may be non-trading companies; several of the affiliates are marketing companies and others are service companies.

21. New Zealand for example has a Trade Practices Act (1958) which prohibits practices that prevent, reduce, or limit competition. See Fogelberg and Laurent, op. cit., p. 16.

22. It is not possible to state whether British companies in Malaysia have been engaged in trade practices detrimental to competition in the economy. But according to Malaysian businessmen interviewed, it was fairly certain that in the case of international shipping, the steep rises in shipping costs of Malaysian exports (see *Economic Report* of the Malaysian Treasury, 1972, pp. 13–14) in the period 1969–72—aside from rising fuel costs—was due to the collusion of shipping companies in the Far Eastern Freight (Shipping) Conference (FEFC) which has the monopoly of international shipping in Malaysia.

23. This categorization of industries follows that of J. H. Dunning, *United States Industry in Britain*, Economic Advisory Group, Business Research Study, *The Financial Times*, 1973, p. 37.

24. Information privately obtained from DTI.

25. The concept is derived from Dunning, *United States Industry in Britain*, p. 16. The technique of analysing industries used here is based on Dunning.

26. Malayan Bitumen is a subsidiary of Sime Darby. Only Shell has a refinery and lubricants blending plant although Castrol and BP have many retail outlets. BP was in 1973 negotiating for a refinery to be built in the country.

27. In the field of industrial chemicals, chemical fertilizers, and paint, the ICI group was in 1968 in control of over three-quarters of the market. The low sales participation coefficient shown was due to distortion brought about by the definition of chemicals in the census which treated refining of vegetable oils and animal fats under chemical products. The dominance of ICI in many parts of the world is not surprising; see G. Foster, 'Complicated Chemistry of ICI', *Management Today*, May 1973, p. 70 et seq.

28. Lever Brothers also manufacture frozen foods, over 50 per cent of the market of which it controlled in the country in 1972.

29. M. Kidron, *Foreign Investments in India*, Oxford University Press, 1965, p. 243.

30. E. L. Wheelwright, 'Overseas Investment in Australia', in A. Hunter, ed., *The Economics of Australian Industry*, Melbourne University Press, 1963, p. 164.

31. K. Levitt, *Silent Surrender, The American Empire in Canada*, New York, Liveright, 1971, p. 60.

32. J. H. Dunning, *American Investment in British Manufacturing Industry*, G. Allen and Unwin, 1958, pp. 58–64.

33. L. E. N. Fernando, 'Some Aspects of Private Foreign Enterprise in Ceylon', unpublished Ph.D. thesis, University of Hull, 1971.

34. C. Isarangkun, 'Manufacturing Industries in Thailand', unpublished Ph.D. thesis, Australian National University, 1970.

35. J. & P. Coats set up a thread manufacturing subsidiary in 1973. See report in *Malaysia, Industrial Digest*, Vol. 6 (I), First Quarter, 1973.

36. In 1974 renamed *The New Straits Times* following a reorganization of the Straits Times Group.

37. The conditions for the pioneer status award are laid out in the *Investment Incentives Act, 1968*, Part II, Chapter I. In broad terms a firm in Malaysia can be granted pioneer status if: (i) it may be represented to the Minister (of Commerce and Industry) by any person that (a) any industry is not being carried on in the country on a commercial scale suitable to the economic requirements or development of Malaysia, and (b) there are favourable prospects of further development of the industry including development for exports; or insufficient facilities in Malaysia to enable the industry to be carried out on a commercial scale suitable to the economic requirements or development of the country including development for export; and (ii) it is expedient in the public interest to encourage the development (including development for export) or establishment of the industry in Malaysia by the making of a statutory order declaring the industry to be pioneer industry, and any product or products of the industry to be a pioneer product or pioneer products. See details in Chapter I, Clause 3(I) to (5) of Part II of the *Investment Incentives Act, 1968*.

The pioneer status gives a combination of tax holidays, tax deductions, and other exemptions from statutory obligations.

38. British capital with pioneer status is not technically distinct from the total industrial investment; it forms part of the total.

39. The total amount of capital enjoying pioneer status in 1973 was $996 million, $508.3 million (51 per cent) of which belonged to local companies. Besides the U.K., other foreign countries investing in pioneer companies in that year were: Singapore ($139.8 million or 14 per cent), the United States ($91.7 million or 9.2 per cent), Japan ($48.7 million or 4.9 per cent), Hong Kong and West Indies respectively $44.4 million (4.5 per cent) and $35.4 million (3.9 per cent); see *Malaysia, Industrial Digest*, Vol. 7(I), First Quarter, 1974.

40. Ridzuan bin Akil, 'Growth, Structural Change and Employment Creation in Malayan Manufacturing . . .'.

41. S. Y. Lo, *The Development Performance of W. Malaysia*.

42. J. T. Thoburn, 'Exports and the Malaysian Engineering Industry: A Case Study

of Backward Linkage', *Bulletin of the Oxford Institute of Economies and Statistics*, Vol. 35(2), May 1973, pp. 91–118.

43. This idea is after C. P. Kindleberger, as quoted by R. Z. Aliber, 'A Theory of Director Foreign Investment', in C. P. Kindleberger, ed., *The International Corporation*, The M.I.T. Press, 1971, p. 19.

44. Cold Storage developed from a Singapore-based company, The Singapore Cold Storage. See historical account in K. G. Tregonning, *The Singapore Cold Storage*, Singapore (private publication of the company), n.d.

45. Other sets of statistics such as number of employees, assets, value added, or net profits may also be used, but sales would be more appropriate since British concerns are generally more capital-intensive than other concerns in the country. Rowthorn for instance considered sales as a reliable measure of size; see R. Rowthorn, *International Big Business 1957–67*, Cambridge University Press, 1971, pp. 13–14.

46. In 1968 part-time workers constituted about 275, or about 3 per cent of total employees; most of them were in ancillary services not directly involved in the manufacturing process.

47. The establishment of such diverse firms as Rothmans, Shell, Guinness, Chemical Company of Malaysia, Malayan Cement, Electrical and Allied Industries, Cold Storage, United Engineers, Champion Motors, and Raleigh Cycles, added variety to the types of manufacturing employment available. Industrial employment in British concerns was well distributed over a number of industrial categories.

48. British firms are under-represented in labour-intensive industries, and the emphasis seems to be more on automated plant.

49. The subject of rate of return is dealt with in Chapter 8.

50. Based on *Census of Manufacturing Industries, 1968* data.

51. Many top personnel of British firms take an active part in running the Malaysian Institute of Management.

52. The question of transfer of skill is dealt with in Chapter 9.

53. All figures calculated from data in the *Census of Manufacturing Industries, 1968*.

54. As in footnote 53. Remuneration in British industrial firms represented about 0.4 per cent of GNP in 1968.

55. See G. Davies in H. Hughes and P. S. You, eds., *Foreign Investment and Industrialization in Singapore*, p. 51.

56. British companies in the early 1970s have been acquiring controlling interests in a wide range of companies. For instance, one company acquired an insurance company, which in turn took over an engineering company and a real estate company, which in turn took over a tin mining company and an industrial holding company.

Most of the company take-overs in Malaysia were not even reported. Since companies taken over seldom changed their names, members of the public were not aware of changes of ownership of companies in the country. Slater, Walker Securities Ltd. had taken over several companies, the most notable being Haw Par International Ltd. which was originally a pharmaceutical firm. Following the acquisition of the company in June 1971, Slater, Walker Securities Ltd., reorganized the company into an investment company with seventeen subsidiaries engaged in investment banking, insurance, manufacturing, property development, tin mining, timber extraction, and rubber plantations, through the holding company (incorporated in Singapore) and the subsidiaries, the acquiring British company has spread throughout South-East Asia. The most significant aspect of the take-over is that one of the companies in the group is a financial institution which is a principal operator of the Asia Currency Unit in the Asia-Dollar Market.

57. See Chapter 5, 'Sources and Uses of Funds'. See also Chapter 8, 'Profit Appropriation and Internal Finance'.

58. According to Remmers, as quoted by W. A. P. Manser, U.K. affiliates in developing countries, in the period 1964 to 1968, on average annually used their funds thus: 32 per cent on fixed assets; 30 per cent current assets; 37 per cent on miscellaneous uses—reserves, cash, trade investments, etc.; see details in W. A. P. Manser, *The Financial Role of Multinational Enterprises*, Cassell Associated Business Programme Ltd., 1973, pp. 58–9.

59. Diversification here means increase in the variety of final products produced,

increase in vertical integration, and increase in the number of affiliates and areas of production in which the firm operates. On the various meanings of diversification, see E. T. Penrose, *The Theory of the Growth of the Firm*, pp. 107 et seq.

This is illustrated in the case of General Motors-Holden in Australia. See details in E. T. Penrose, 'Foreign Investment and the Growth of the Firm', *Economic Journal*, Vol. 66, June 1956, pp. 220–35. Foreign-owned firms tend to have advantages in management, technology and capital. These advantages tend to allow them to grow faster than domestic firms.

60. There are, according to Penrose, fine distinctions between diversification in response to specific opportunities, diversification to solve problems of demand, and diversification as a general policy for growth. In practice they are inextricably intertwined, and often the same act of diversification can be explained with reference to any one of these motives, or to all three together; see details in E. T. Penrose, *The Theory of the Growth of the Firm*, p. 144, and *passim*.

In the case of the agency houses, discussed in Chapter 5, their expansion into manufacturing may be regarded as both diversification in response to specific opportunities and diversification to solve problems of demand. The manufacturing affiliates, including the affiliates of the agency houses, diversify for all the three reasons suggested by Penrose above; but executives interviewed claimed that diversification was a general policy for growth. The general belief was that it would be essential to diversify to continue to be profitable. In many cases, firms found that it was more profitable for them to diversify than to specialize.

61. Under Malaysian company law, tax on profits may be off-set against losses in branches and subsidiaries. It is therefore possible also that some companies open as many diverse affiliates as they can, partly in order to gain tax advantages; but companies interviewed were reluctant to comment on this.

7 British Multinational Manufacturers

INTRODUCTION

THE existence of companies operating internationally is not a novel phenomenon,[1] but the emergence of the multinational corporation, as this term is generally understood to describe a company with many production facilities and with an intricate structural organization straddling the boundaries of many nations, is associated with the propagation of new technology in the industrially advanced countries, particularly the U.S.

The presence of internationally organized business is not new to South-East Asia either,[2] but what is relatively new is the presence of multinational enterprises engaged in manufacturing there. For the purpose of this chapter a multinational enterprise (MNE) is one in which at least one-quarter of its foreign content (sales, production, investment, and employment) originates in overseas subsidiaries, and where the composition of the top executives reflects the range of countries in which the enterprise operates. Table 7.1 shows some of the world's MNEs.

This chapter attempts firstly to identify some of the U.K.-based multinational enterprises and describe their nature, and secondly to examine some of their effects on the Malaysian economy.

BRITISH[3] MULTINATIONAL ENTERPRISES

The problems encountered in applying the above idealized definition of the MNEs to British companies are the lack of data on their overseas operations and insufficient knowledge of the nationalities of their executives. To overcome these problems an alternative approach is taken. Where there is insufficient information to establish the multinationality of an enterprise on the above definition, the enterprise may be regarded as an MNE if it has production units in at least six countries. This alternative proce-

TABLE 7.1

SIXTY LARGEST INDUSTRIAL COMPANIES IN THE WORLD, 1972

Name of Company and Country		*Sales (in US$ billion)*	*Assets (in US$ billion)*	*Name of Company and Country*		*Sales (in US$ billion)*	*Assets (in US$ billion)*
General Motors	U.S.A.	30.4	18.3	International Harvester	U.S.A.	3.5	2.6
Ford Motors	U.S.A.	20.3	21.6	Eastman Kodak	U.S.A.	3.5	3.8
General Electric	U.S.A.	10.2	7.4	Matsushita Electric	Japan	3.3	3.2
Chrysler Motors	U.S.A.	9.8	5.5	Bayer	Germany	3.3	4.1
I.B.M.	U.S.A.	9.5	10.8	British Leyland	U.K.	3.3	2.1
Unilever	U.K./Netherlands	8.9	4.7	Union Carbide	U.S.A.	3.3	4.8
I.T.T.	U.S.A.	8.6	8.6	Tenneco	U.S.A.	3.3	3.7
Western Electric	U.S.A.	6.5	4.3	Swift	U.S.A.	3.2	1.0
Philips Gloeilampenfabrieken	Netherlands	6.2	6.9	AEG Telefunken	Germany	3.2	2.3
Nippon Steel	Japan	5.4	8.6	Kraftco	U.S.A.	3.2	1.2
U.S. Steel	U.S.A.	5.4	6.6	Bethlehem Steel	U.S.A.	3.1	3.6
Westinghouse	U.S.A.	5.1	3.8	Thyssen-Hutte	France	3.1	2.6
Volkswagenwerk	Germany	5.0	3.5	Tokyo Shiburu	Japan	3.9	4.5
Siemens	Germany	4.7	4.3	Dunlop-Pirelli	U.K./Italy	2.9	2.9
Hitachi	Japan	4.4	6.3	Firestone Tyre	U.S.A.	2.7	2.5
Du Pont	U.S.A.	4.4	4.3	Greyhound	U.S.A.	2.7	1.2
I.C.I.	U.K.	4.2	5.5	McDonnel Douglas	U.S.A.	2.7	2.4
Toyota Motors	Japan	4.2	3.1	Ugine Kuhlman	France	2.6	1.9

(*Continued*)

TABLE 7.1 (*Continued*)

Name of Company	*and Country*	*Sales (in US$ billion)*	*Assets (in US$ billion)*	*Name of Company*	*and Country*	*Sales (in US$ billion)*	*Assets (in US$ billion)*
Daimler Benz	Germany	4.2	1.6	G.E.C.	U.K.	2.6	2.5
Nestlé	Switzerland	4.1	3.3	Caterpillar	U.S.A.	2.6	1.9
Hoechst	Germany	4.1	4.7	Nippon Kokai	Japan	2.6	3.8
Mitsubishi Heavy Industries	Japan	4.0	7.3	Litton Industries	U.S.A.	2.6	2.1
Nissan Motors	Japan	4.0	4.8	Lockheed	U.S.A.	2.5	1.6
R.C.A.	U.S.A.	3.8	3.1	British-American Tobacco	U.K.	2.5	3.2
BASF	Germany	3.7	3.9	Pont-a-Musson	France	2.5	3.1
Montedison	Italy	3.6	5.8	Xerox	U.S.A.	2.4	2.5
British Steel	U.K.	3.6	3.5	General Food	U.S.A.	2.4	1.6
Proctor & Gamble	U.S.A.	3.5	2.4	Dow Chemical	U.S.A.	2.4	2.5
LTV	U.S.A.	3.5	1.8	Boeing	U.S.A.	2.4	2.5
Renault	France	3.5	1.6	Beatrice Foods	U.S.A.	2.4	1.0

Source: Compiled from *Fortune*, Vol. 87(5), May 1973; and Vol. 88(3), September 1973.

Notes: The list excludes the petroleum companies listed in the sources. Assets means total assets employed by the business (less depreciation) at the companies' year ends. Sales refers to consolidated sales excluding taxes and custom levies. Fifty per cent of each company's sales must be derived from manufacturing and/or mining in order for the company to be listed. Only companies with sales over US$2.4 billions are listed.

dure of classifying enterprises is similar to the one used by The Conference of The Atlantic Council (of the Committee for Atlantic Co-operation) mentioned in Rolfe and Damm.[4] Using a combination of this definition and the alternative one, Table 7.2 is constructed to show a selection of British MNEs.

Most of the enterprises in the Table are still identifiable with Britain from the composition of equity holding, management, and organization of production. An overwhelming majority of the firms are, in Pelmutter's term,[5] ethnocentrically organized. During the interviews, a few firms have shown some degree of polycentricity in their Malaysian operations. Two or possibly three firms are geocentrically organized in the sense that they have a good mixture of nationalities in the high ranks of their executives and heads of production. Strictly speaking, Shell and Unilever are not identifiable with any one nationality; they are Anglo-Dutch. Approximately two-thirds of the shareholdings of the two groups are in the hands of nationals of Britain and the Netherlands, while the other third is held by citizens of various nationalities.

A common characteristic of the British MNEs in our selection is their size. Each of them, for instance, had in 1970–1, a net turnover of more than £100 million. Shell, Unilever, BP and ICI each had a turnover exceeding £1,000 million, as indicated in Table 7.3.

WHY DO MULTINATIONAL ENTERPRISES INVEST OVERSEAS?

The reasons why British investors came to Malaysia have been dealt with in Chapter 4. In general, the MNEs came to Malaysia to protect their already established markets and to explore new market opportunities. It has also been suggested that MNEs go abroad to exploit their inherent advantages and power which, according to the Economist Intelligence Unit,[6] lie in their scale of production, marketing, finance, research and development (R & D), and in their organizational flexibility, as well as in their skill in exploiting the 'international product cycle'.

Professor Vernon, among others,[7] attempted to 'explain' the global spread of the MNEs, particularly U.S.-based MNEs, in terms of what may be called the 'product cycle' theory.[8] In the case of some British MNEs, notably in the electrical industry, their moving into Malaysia conforms to some of the traits of the product cycle as expounded by Vernon. In many other cases, the move to invest in Malaysia cannot be strictly explained in terms of the standard concept of the product cycle theory.

TABLE 7.2

A SELECTION OF BRITISH MULTINATIONAL ENTERPRISES, 1970–1971

Companies whose Principal Products or Activities are in*						
Chemicals, Fibres, Rubber, and Pharmaceutical Manufactures	*Food and Tobacco*	*Engineering, Machinery, Vehicles, and Equipment*	*Metal, Glass, Paper, and Cement*	*Construction and Civil Engineering*	*Extractive Industry/ Mining*	*Electrical Products*
ICI	Unilever	British Leyland	Tube Investments	G. Wimpey	Shell	GEC
Courtaulds	BAT	J. Lucas	Bowater	Taylor Woodrow	BP	BICC
Dunlop	Imperial Group	Hawker Siddeley	Amalgamated Metal	Laing	RTZ	EMI
Albright & Wilson	RHM	Ford (U.K.)	Reed International	Tarmac Derby	Burmah Oil	Plessey
Coats Patons	Cadbury-Schweppes	Vickers	Dickinson	Babcock & Wilcox	Lonrho	Philips (U.K.)
Fisons	Gallaher	Chrysler (U.K.)	Metal Box		Consolidated Goldfields	ICL
Beecham Group	Reckitt & Colman	GKN	A.P. Cement			Smiths Ind.
Glaxo	Brooke Bond	British Oxygen				
	Leibig					

Notes: *Companies are listed according to their popular or abbreviated names. Full names are given in *Who Owns Whom*, Roskill, 1968.

The enterprises listed constitute an incomplete list which is offered only as a general guide. The basis for inclusion of enterprises in the list are, either that at least 25 per cent of the foreign content (respectively production, sales, investment and employment) of each company originates in overseas subsidiaries, or that at least six production units must be in countries other than the U.K. All the MNEs listed have either a production unit or a marketing organization in Malaysia.

Sources: The information for compiling the list is derived from field work; *The Times 1000 Leading Companies in Britain, 1970–72*; S. E. Rolfe and W. Damm, eds., *The Multinational Corporation in the World Economy*, Preager, 1970; and W. B. Reddaway, *et al.*, *Effects of U.K. Direct Investment Overseas* (Interim Report), Cambridge University Press, 1967.

TABLE 7.3

SIZE AND PERFORMANCE OF SELECTED LARGEST BRITISH MNEs, 1971

Company	*Main Activity/ Product*	(*1*) *Total Turnover* (*£'000*)	(*2*) *Capital Employed* (*£'000*)	(*3*) *Net Profit* (*£'000*)	(*3*) *as % of* (*1*)	(*3*) *as % of* (*2*)
Shell Group*	oil	2,352,250	1,909,593	335,435	14.3	18.9
BP	oil	2,242,800	1,769,000	384,300	17.1	25.1
BAT	tobacco and cosmetics	1,467,140	659,210	140,870	9.6	23.2
ICI+	chemicals	1,355,100+	1,581,000	198,600	14.7	13.2
Unilever	detergents and foods	1,144,800	548,000	68,600	6.0	12.6
GEC	electrical engineers	898,200	606,469	71,433	8.0	11.8
Dunlop	rubber goods	495,000	298,121	36,116	7.3	13.4
RTZ	mining	338,046	574,830	80,852	23.9	16.1
Tube Investments	general engineers	294,491	246,829	22,353	7.6	10.9
Rank Organisation	entertainment and xerox	237,094	179,138	59,015	24.9	37.9

Sources and *Notes*:

The companies are selected to show a variety of activities they engage in. All companies appear in the *Fortune* magazine (September 1973) listing of the world's 300 largest companies outside the United States in 1972.

Capital employed means total tangible assets less current liabilities and sundry provisions employed by the companies, at their year ends. Turnover refers to consolidated sales net of custom levies, except in the case of Shell figure which includes them. Net Profit refers to the company's accounting profit before charges in interest and tax. Information derived from *The Times 1000 Largest Industrial Companies, 1970–71*, and *Fortune*, September 1973.

* Shell Transport & Trading

\+ inclusive of Imperial Metal Industries

A new approach by Professor Caves[9] attempts to account for the spread of the MNEs in terms of a combination of international trade theory and that of industrial organization.

Caves's argument is that foreign direct investment occurs mainly in industries characterized by certain market structures in both the host and home countries. In terms of industrial organization, oligopoly with product differentiation[10] normally prevails where corporations make 'horizontal' investments[11] to produce abroad the same lines of goods as they produce for the home market. Oligopoly, not necessarily differentiated, in the home market is typical in industries which undertake 'vertical' direct investments[12] to produce abroad a raw material, or other input, for the production process at home. 'Direct investment tends to involve market dependence—the essence of oligopoly—beyond national boundaries.'[13] The choice between production at home and abroad by the corporation will be affected by national comparative advantage and the corporation's special advantages, as well as by transport costs and tariffs.

The link between the oligopolistic firm with differentiated products and direct investment is, according to Caves, explained thus: the successful firm producing a differentiated product controls (technological) knowledge about serving the market that can be transferred to other national markets for this product at little or no cost. This is so far the patented goods or products embodying certain characteristics (which Caves called 'a particularly apt bundle of traits'—e.g. physical design and fabrication or 'style'), which may be the result of world-wide advertising. When it is advantageous to the firm to service its overseas markets itself, instead of by alternative means, e.g., licensing, it will produce the product in the host country market abroad.

The MNEs listed in Table 7.2 suggest that not all of their investments abroad can be attributed to their product differentiation which is central to the thesis put forward by Caves. However, it is known (from Table 7.4) that the multinational enterprises in Malaysia are those firms with differentiated products, e.g. those producing consumer goods like cigarettes, and consumer durables like electrical appliances, as well as those producing chemicals and other intermediate goods. In addition to the motives discussed in Chapter 4, field investigation also shows that the MNEs chose to invest in Malaysia because they preferred to exploit their own technologies in servicing the host country market instead of supplying the market through other means. The MNEs in Malaysia dominate the sectors or sub-sectors they are in, in that they are not only large in terms of the capital they employ but also in the sense that they control substantial portions of the market for their categories of products. The MNEs in Malaysia are effectively monopolies as the majority of them control more than one-quarter of the market in their respective products.[14] The presence of these MNEs in the country may be viewed in terms of the analysis put forward by Caves.

Some companies however do not perfectly fit the analysis. For example the presence of Shell, Dunlop, and Lever Brothers in the country cannot be explained solely in terms of 'oligopolistic firms with differentiated products'—the crucial idea in 'horizontal' investment mentioned above. The overseas investments of these firms may also be interpreted in the light of 'vertical' investments as explained by, among others, Penrose.[15] These firms took into consideration in their move to Malaysia, the prospect of being nearer to both their sources of raw materials and their consumers.

Some companies came to Malaysia because they were induced by the presence of others who use their products as manufacturing inputs—such was the case of Metal Box which provided packaging materials for other firms, and the case of ICI subsidiaries whose products were used by companies in the manufacturing and the agricultural sectors.

Another theory, the 'product cycle' theory, is discussed here to see its relevance in explaining the presence of MNEs in the country.

At the risk of over-simplication, Figure 7.1 is used to illustrate the ideas of the product cycle theory. It is assumed that the cycle has four stages, and that one can begin tracing the cycle where product innovations in the home country are nurtured by technological capability, effective market demand and well-organized supporting factors of production. When a new product is 'discovered' it is mass produced for the home market, as well as for export.

Conceivably, the technology embodied in the new product is only known to one company or a group of companies which initially dominates the market and enjoys elements of monopoly profits, which may induce competitors to imitate the new product. In phase one, therefore, the mass market is located in the home country (country *A*). In the meantime, the demand for the product in the export market grows. The export markets for new products are usually in the relatively more advanced countries where entrepreneurs from the home country begin to explore the possibilities of setting up production. When production starts in the overseas market (country *B*) the products will have matured

FIGURE 7.1
THE 'PRODUCT CYCLE': AN ILLUSTRATION

New Product	Maturing Product		Standardized Product
Phase 1	*Phase 2*	*Phase 3*	*Phase 4*
New Product 'discovered' in country *A* (the home country of the enterprise)	Enterprise in country *A* invests in country *B*	Product previously imported, now locally manufactured in country *C*	Product components manufactured in country *D* for export to home or other countries
Product mass-produced for home market and export	Product attains further maturity		
Overseas markets serviced by exports	Mass production for local and export markets	Enterprise becomes international	
Product becomes widely known	Competitors gain knowledge of product technology	Product attains more maturity	Components may be assembled for export to home or other countries
Export market grows, justifying production overseas	Standardized product may also be exported to country *A*	More competitors in possession of technology product	
	Meanwhile, export grows		
	Production in country *C* desirable	Enterprise will manufacture abroad where cost is lowest, possibly to supply home and other markets	At Phase 4, the enterprise becomes multinational. Enterprise integrates production and marketing on world-wide basis. Other competitors may follow footsteps of the first enterprise. Matured product will complete 'cycle'
	Enterprise decides to invest in country *C*	Products which can be subdivided into components are manufactured where cost is lowest	

and the second phase in the product life cycle is entered in the host country, where the products are subjected to a new set of market forces. Some of the products may find their way back to the home country while some will be exported to a third country (country *C*), or group of countries. Competitive factors may, in time, force the entrepreneurs, possibly with the assistance of secondary entrepreneurs (i.e. entrepreneurs from subsidiaries in country *B*), to think about servicing country *C* by locating production facilities there. When production begins in country *C*, the product cycle will have entered the third phase in which there will be more producers of the same product as the technology becomes more widely used. There is a distinct possibility—if labour-cost differences can offset transport costs—that a product made in country *C* may be imported into the home country (country *A*), the second country (country *B*), or other groups of fourth countries, countries *D*, *E*, etc.

In the third phase, the enterprise in question will have become international, or possibly multinational as defined previously. All the while, the product in question attains maturity in the sense that many producers will have acquired the production technology, in which case the original entrepreneur will face competitors. If the production involves the manufacture of various components of the finished product, the original entrepreneur will look for ideal locations all over the world where the components may be cheaply manufactured. Hence in the case of electrical and electronics industries, a fourth phase may emerge in which components may be manufactured in overseas countries for supplying the whole enterprise in the various locations chosen during the previous phases. When these components are imported by the home country, the product will have completed the cycle as roughly illustrated in Figure 7.1; and the enterprise innovating the product will have become an MNE.[16]

SIZE AND INDUSTRIAL DISTRIBUTION OF MULTINATIONAL ENTERPRISES IN MALAYSIA

In terms of capital employed, the British MNEs in the country in 1971 were small compared to their parent organizations in the U.K. while the smallest represented about 0.2 per cent. Compared to industrial companies in Malaysia, however, the smallest of the MNEs' subsidiaries was, in 1971, larger than the average indigenous industrial company. In their own respective sub-sectors, the MNEs are dominant in respect of size of capital employed and

TABLE 7.4
INDUSTRIAL DISTRIBUTION OF MNEs, 1971

Industrial Groups		*Distribution of Capital Employed (%)*
MIC Code and Description		
32	Manufacture of tobacco products	15
40	Manufacture of rubber products, chemicals	
41	and chemical products	29
42	Manufacture of petroleum	19
43	Manufacture of non-metallic minerals	
44	basic metals	30
45	metal products	
46	Machinery except electricals	
47	electrical machinery	
	Other manufacturing and non-manufacturing	7

Source: Compiled from company reports.

share of the market. In 1971 for instance, although the capital employed by Lever Brothers and Chemical Company of Malaysia (ICI) respectively constituted 1 per cent and 0.6 per cent of their parent companies' capital, they were among the largest companies in the country, and were estimated to be in command of over one-half of the market for their respective industries.

An idea of the MNEs' industrial distribution, categorized according to broad industrial groups by the amounts of capital they employed in 1971 is given in Table 7.4 above.

OWNERSHIP STRUCTURE AND POLICY

With few exceptions, the MNEs' subsidiaries are either wholly-owned or majority-owned by their parent companies. Table 7.5 shows the percentage of equity held in the subsidiaries.

Of those MNEs whose shares are traded in the local stock and share market, only a small portion of their shares is freely traded. The reason put forward by the MNEs is that they wish to retain the majority control of these enterprises. However, the latest government guidelines for foreign investment[17] announced a move to encourage foreign companies to introduce, and increase, local equity participation in foreign enterprises that are presently wholly-owned, and controlled from overseas.

TABLE 7.5

OWNERSHIP PATTERN IN SELECTED MNE SUBSIDIARIES, 1972–1973

Parent Company in U.K.	*Name of Subsidiary in Malaysia*	*Per Cent of Equity of Subsidiary Controlled by the Parent*
Shell Group	Shell Malaysia Bhd.	100
	Shell Refining Co. S. Bhd.	75
	Sabah Shell Bhd.	100
	Sarawak Shell Bhd.	100
	Shell Borneo Bhd.	100
GEC	The GEC (M) S. Bhd.	100
	Electrical & Allied Ind. Bhd.	80
ICI	ICI (M) S. Bhd.	100
	Chemical Co. of Malaysia Bhd.	51
British-American Tobacco	Malayan Tobacco Co. Bhd.	80
Dunlop Co.	Dunlop Malaysian Industries Bhd.	75
Metal Box	Metal Box of Malaysia Bhd.	75
BICC	Malayan Cables Bhd.	80
Glaxo	Glaxo-Allenburys (M) Bhd.	100
Tube Investments	Raleigh Cycles Malaysia Bhd.	55
British Oxygen	Malayan Oxygen Bhd.	100

Source: Based on Company House search.

Note: Bhd. = Berhad, the equivalent of Ltd. = Limited.

The government is in favour of joint-ventures of the types pioneered by Tube Investments in Raleigh Cycles Bhd., and by Plessey in Plessey–Pernas Bhd. These ventures are relatively new, and judging from the equity distribution and policy determination in them, they are not yet radically different from the rest of the U.K.-controlled enterprises. The understanding in the ventures is that in time the equity and policy of the enterprises will truly reflect a joint-venture in which the local and foreign interests are equal. We will consider below why MNEs are less willing to participate in joint-ventures.

In contrast to the non-MNEs (e.g. William Jacks, Sime Darby, Harper Gilfillan, Inchcape, and United Engineers) which in 1971 traded between 30 and 50 per cent of their shares in the local equity market, the MNEs as noted above are reluctant to trade their shares more freely in the open market for they do not wish to abandon their majority control over their companies. Other reasons may be put forward to account for such a tendency. First, there was the virtual absence of an articulate Malaysian public opinion in the 1960s pressing for a greater local equity participation in the MNEs. Those Malaysians who were in a position to own shares in them, and were in fact already owning some shares, were not critical of the ownership policies of the MNEs. Most of these people were either executive employees of the MNEs, or were politically influential members of the community closely associated with the government whose policy, as we have discussed in Chapter 3, until very recently had been very lenient towards foreign investors generally.[18] In support of the government policy it may be argued that the ownership policy of the MNEs has not been shown conclusively to be detrimental to the industrial growth of the country.[19] Besides, it was possible that if the government were to insist on majority local equity participation in the very beginning, the MNEs would not have set up production facilities locally in the first place. As noted in Chapter 3, one of the attractions of Malaysia for the foreign investors was the acceptance of the presence of wholly foreign-owned enterprises. Companies interviewed maintained that it is their basic principle to control their foreign investments. If the control is not reflected in the equity ownership it will be exercised through other means such as through technical contracts and export market restrictions. (The typical comment was: 'If we do not have control of the subsidiary's equity, our attitudes towards it would be different; we would tend to regard it as a foreign concern. Since it is dependent on us for equipment, technical expertise, and other factor inputs, it may not get these things in the manner they are supplied at present.')

The second argument put forward by the MNEs in support of their bias towards wholly-owned subsidiaries was their desire to avoid any possibility of conflict of interest with local shareholders who were, they thought, more concerned about getting larger dividends than the foreign investors themselves.

Many of the MNEs regard their operations in Malaysia as a stepping stone for them to enter the neighbouring countries. Evidence exists to show that operations in the neighbouring countries are financed and manned from the MNEs' subsidiaries in Malaysia. Metal Box, for instance, has interests in Indonesia and Thailand that are financed and manned from Malaysia. Dunlop has a similar arrangement with its Singapore subsidiary. The presence of local shareholders with substantial equity holdings may prevent such flexibility in the use of resources by the MNEs.

Multinational enterprises interviewed foresee that a more articulate body of local shareholders may question company practices (such as the shifting of temporarily idle cash to the Asia-Dollar Market—further discussed below) designed to achieve the companies' global and strategic objectives. Executives interviewed regarded it as an unnecessary extra effort—('It's a waste of expensive company time')—to justify every company policy measure to people other than those who decide for the firms.[20] In line with the question of flexibility there is also the issue of disclosure of information on the intricate marketing and financial arrangements on the MNEs, which they prefer to keep to themselves and which they feel may be exposed if there are substantial local interests. (The typical comment was: 'What is there to prevent a chap who acquired a dollar share in our company from attending our annual meeting where he could ask awkward questions about our business affairs? He could well be doing some market intelligence work for an interested party!'—a competitor.)[21]

The most compelling reason perhaps, why the MNEs are reluctant to have more local equity participation is the unwillingness of many of them to share the profit of their companies while they are still in control of substantial portions of the Malaysian market.

Multinational enterprises in Malaysia in the 1960s did not favour the idea of joint-ventures because of the presence of many alleged obstacles.

Among the obstacles in the way of increasing the number of joint-ventures, discovered in South-East Asia by the International Chambers of Commerce,[22] the following were the most widespread:

(i) *Excessive interference by local government.* The government closely examines the details of the joint-venture contracts and approval is not given quickly. In some instances the host government unilaterally orders joint-venture firms to export a part of their output, controls the selling price, and/or restricts imports of raw materials and machinery.

(ii) *Hasty replacement of foreign officers with local personnel.* Some governments tend to restrict the stay of the foreign staff, control their business activities, or replace foreign officers with local personnel before the latter are fully capable of taking over.

(iii) *Restrictions on payment of royalties, management, and other fees.* Most governments sometimes refuse to recognize technical know-how as an industrial property right, and hence refuse or restrict the payment of fees on it.

(iv) *Difficulty of raising required funds.* Adequate capital sometimes cannot be raised, either because of the underdeveloped local capital market or the inability of the host country to borrow internationally owing to its low credit rating.

(v) *Heavy tax burden*. Foreign personnel suffer from a high tax burden on their income. The ventures are often subjected to arbitrary government levy in countries where company laws are underdeveloped or non-existent.

To this list made by the International Chambers of Commerce may be added the lack of public pressure on the foreign investor to engage in joint-ventures as a pre-condition of doing business. In Malaysia in the 1960s the preoccupation of the authorities was to attract foreign investment and not to put restrictions on it. In the 1970s, and with the possible exception of the bureaucratic slowness of government action, none of the obstacles listed would appear to be a serious impediment to the foreign investor wishing to enter into a joint-venture. Having regard to the resources and facilities Malaysia has, as discussed in Chapter 3, it would seem likely that the country would be an agreeable place for MNEs to form joint-ventures. Nevertheless, the present investigation finds that the MNEs have not, as yet, been required to participate in joint-ventures as prerequisites for manufacturing in Malaysia.

The lack of official pressure[23] for national participation in the MNEs is regarded by them as a symbol of appreciation by the government of the need to allow the MNEs freedom to decide how they should manage their affairs. In so doing the government is regarded as having made a real attempt to improve the climate for foreign investment. (The typical comment was: 'It is certainly a plus point [*sic*] for the country when political leaders are businessmen first, and politicians second! [*sic*].')

The widely recognized proposals for greater participation of local interests in the ownership of the MNEs is viewed by many as one of the critical problems facing the MNEs in general.[24] However, many executives thought the pressure for more local equity participation is rooted more in the force of nationalism than in pure economic considerations. They felt that local equity participation cannot significantly affect the efficiency of the MNEs.

On the other hand, it can be argued that local participation has its advantages. It can, for instance, provide the MNEs with a much more local identity which itself is a hedge against any dormant anti-foreign investment feeling against the MNEs. In Malaysia, although the MNEs are enjoying the lenient attitude of the politicians currently in power, the latent force of nationalism is by no means totally absent.[25] It would seem sensible for the MNEs to encourage local participation, although it would mean that they would have to forgo a certain amount of ownership control. The cost of prolonged insistence on a hundred per cent ownership may exceed the short-term gains.

CONTROL AND ORGANIZATION

By virtue of their command of the equity, the MNEs exercise control over the organization, operations, and business policies of their Malaysian subsidiaries. As a rule, the overseas enterprise is created to form an integral part on the MNEs' total organization. Brooks and Remmers have broadly categorized the MNEs' organizations into types *A*, *B*, *C*, and *D*.[26] Briefly, type *A* MNEs (prevalent in single product, engineering, and food industries) have a central service organization at the head office which maintains links with the overseas subsidiary (Figure 7.2) through the chief executive or his deputy, and the functional executives of the central service who have constant communication with their opposite numbers abroad.

Type *B* MNEs (common in some multi-product chemical and engineering industries) have a product group organization at home and a geographical organization overseas. In this type the overseas operation usually began with product assembly and later manufacture. The management of the overseas company—which may be called the overseas holding company, or in U.S. terms, the international division—began as a responsibility of the export department of the home office. The overseas company is headed by a manager of similar status to the product group manager. Many of the British MNEs in Malaysia appear to be organized along the lines of type *B* (although a number are changing to type *D*). The impression derived from field investigation points to the tendency for a clash of interest to occur between the export division (of the home office) and the overseas production unit. The executives of the export division (in the home office) may not be in close touch with complex overseas market situations, and would therefore insist on maintaining the market through exports; much to the displeasure of the chief executive in the overseas company. This situation would tend to delay (as indeed it did delay GCE setting up in Malaysia),[27] the setting up of production facilities in the overseas market. The problem can be acute when the overseas production unit is wholly dependent on substantial technical support from the home office and the channel of communication is constricted by the executives in the export division.

The MNEs are aware of the problems mentioned. Often this

FIGURE 7.2
ORGANIZATIONAL STRUCTURES OF MULTINATIONAL ENTERPRISES

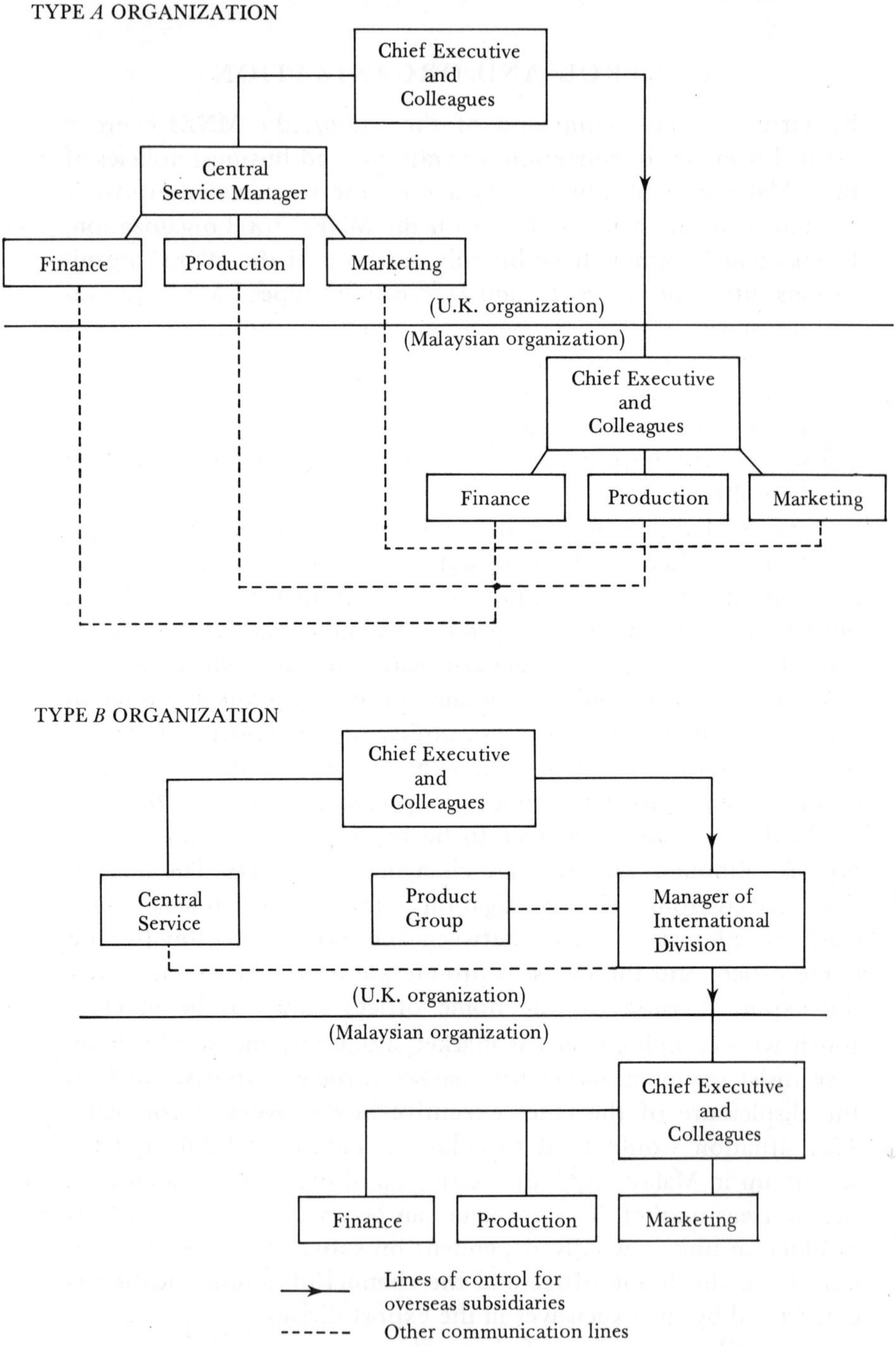

FIGURE 7.2 (*Continued*)

TYPE *C* ORGANIZATION

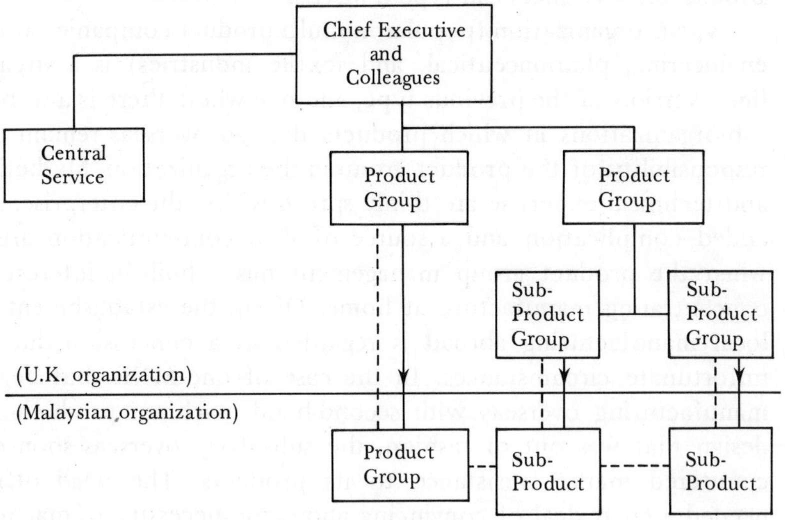

TYPE *D* ORGANIZATION

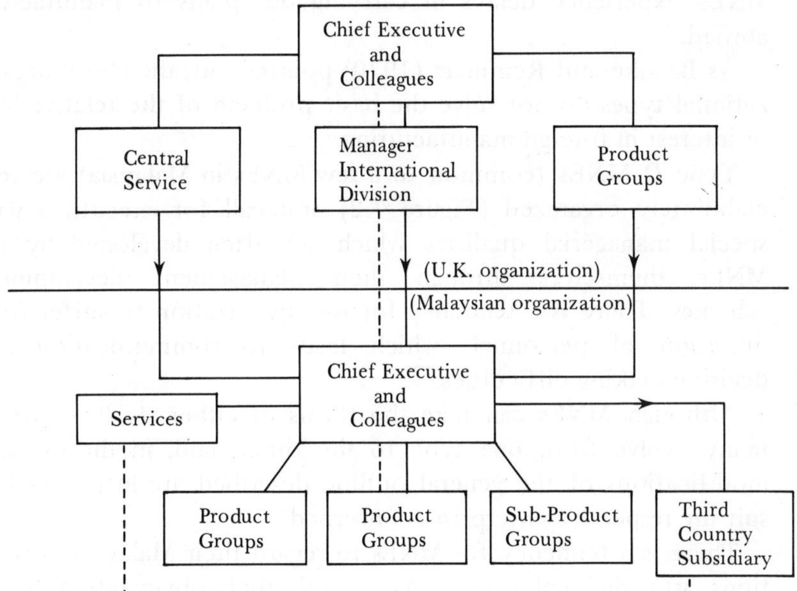

awareness led them to rearrange their home office export division in such a manner that their whole organization evolves into what Brooks and Remmers call type *C* MNEs.

Type *C* organization (popular in multi-product companies in the engineering, pharmaceutical, and textile industries) is a streamlined version of the previous type, and one where there is a web of sub-organizations in which products that go overseas remain the responsibility of the product group in the organization. Marketing and technical expertise are thinly spread within the enterprise. An added complication and a source of slow communication arises when the product group management has a built-in interest in concentrating manufacture at home. Often, the establishment of local manufacturing abroad is regarded as a concession due to unfortunate circumstances. In the case of one MNE that began manufacturing overseas with second-hand machines producing a design that was out of fashion, the subsidiary overseas soon encountered market resistance to its products. The head office needed a great deal of convincing about the necessity of machine conversion to incorporate new designs.[28] Like type *B*, type *C* MNEs experience delays in carrying out plans to manufacture abroad.

As Brooke and Remmers (1970) pointed out, the above organizational types do not solve the basic problem of the relative lack of interest in foreign manufacturing.

Type *D* MNEs (common to a few MNEs in Malaysia) are very elaborately organized (Figure 7.2) and call for executives with special managerial qualities which are often developed by the MNEs themselves through their management development schemes. There is a tendency for the organization to suffer from 'inflation of personnel' which leads to communication and decision-making difficulties.[29]

Although MNEs can take the forms of either *A*, *B*, *C*, or *D*, many evolve from one type to the other, and, in the process, modifications of the general outline described are introduced to suit the respective enterprises concerned.

There is a tendency for MNEs to regard their Malaysian operations as a regional centre. As a result their organizations there assume a form roughly similar to the home office organization (type *D*, in particular). In at least two cases it was found that the MNEs treated Malaysia as a training ground for their young executives, who in turn would be absorbed into the central organizations in the more advanced countries.

The increasing size and complexity of the MNEs in Malaysia has constantly led the top executives to seek new ways of making their organizations effective. There is room for local initiative in the overseas operations. The structure of organization often reflects the corporate strategy of the home office. Some regard their Malaysian subsidiaries as part of their world-wide product division, while others regard theirs as the area division. The distinction is by no means clear cut, but it appears that those which regard the Malaysian organization as part of their world-wide product division are the ones with diverse products, whereas those that treat their enterprises there as part of an area organization are the ones with a narrow range of products.

ASSETS STRUCTURE, SOURCES, AND USES OF RESOURCES

As in all cases of British companies in the country the MNEs, as a matter of policy, arrange for their Malaysian business to be self-financing. It was normal for them to begin by shipping over some fully depreciated equipment from the U.K. and raising the liquid capital from a variety of sources locally—mainly by borrowing from local banks in the country where the interest rates were lower than those prevailing in the U.K. Because of their well-known names, and in many cases established products in the local market, their credit ratings were good. There was no problem in borrowing from local sources.

Once such companies are established in normal production and trading there seem to be no radical yearly changes in the structure of resources in their employment. Information gathered from a sample of ten MNEs (summarized in Table 7.6) suggested that in 1972, the MNEs in Malaysia had estimated consolidated assets of about $600 million: more than one-half (about 54 per cent) in the nature of fixed assets—land, buildings, plant, machinery, and equipment. The remaining 46 per cent of company resources was made up of net current assets, i.e. current assets (inventories, debtors, prepayments, and cash balances) less current liabilities (creditors, other payables, and provisions). The bulk of these resources was financed by equity capital (63 per cent). Retained profits accounted for about 30 per cent of the sources of finance. The remainder was financed from miscellaneous sources.

It can be seen from Table 7.6 that more than one-third of current assets of the MNEs was in the form of inventories, and 40 per cent was in the form of trade debtors. The MNEs made advances to their subsidiaries in the region, while at the same time,

TABLE 7.6

ESTIMATED USES AND SOURCES OF RESOURCES IN SELECTED MNEs, 1972

(per cent)

Assets Employed	
Fixed Assets	
land and buildings (net of depreciation)	20
plant, machinery, and equipment (net of depreciation)	34

Current assets		*Current liabilities*	
Inventories	38	Provisions for taxation	35
Trade debtors (less provisions for bad debts)	40	Trade creditors	32
Amounts due from related companies	19	Amounts due to parent and related companies	10
Cash and bank balances	3	Provisions for dividends	17
		Provisions for employee retirement benefits	6
	100		100

Ratio of current assets to current liabilities: 1.7: 1

Net current assets	46
Total resources employed	100
Financed by	
Equity	63
Revenue surpluses	30
Miscellaneous sources	7
TOTAL SOURCES	100

Source: Derived from company reports and information gathered at interviews.

they also received advances from the parent organizations as reflected in the amounts due to and from related companies. It is significant to note that the advances from the Malaysian operations were greater than the advances they received from their parent organizations. They are net lenders of funds within their world-wide organization. The cash and bank balances of the MNEs constituted a very small percentage of current assets, but in absolute terms in 1972 they amounted to at least $12 million.

On the liabilities side, provisions for taxation (35 per cent) and trade creditors (32 per cent) were the main items. Provisions for dividends and employee retirement benefits (23 per cent) constituted the next important elements, while inter-company debts made up about 10 per cent of current liabilities. The ratio of current assets to current liabilities was approximately 1.7:1.

THE IMPACT OF THE MULTINATIONAL ENTERPRISES ON MALAYSIA

The existence of the MNEs in the country affects the level of demand for and allocation of resources. Equally important are the spill-over or spin-off effects of these companies. The dissemination of knowledge and entrepreneurship either vertically (as when technical knowledge is passed on to local suppliers and consumers), or horizontally (in the nature of stimulus given to competition) are valuable contributions of the MNEs. No less important are the resultant qualitative contributions of these companies to industrial structure, production, employment, skills, consumption patterns, and merchandise exports.

THE NATIONAL ECONOMIC OBJECTIVES AND THE MULTINATIONAL ENTERPRISES

The industrial sector is regarded as economically strategic in that the government hopes the sector will be instrumental in carrying out its policy of modernizing and restructuring the economy. Industry, according to the Second Malaysia Plan, is to provide employment, diversify exports, help in the creation of a Malay commercial and industrial community, and stimulate activities other than the traditional ones of agriculture, mining, and other extractive industries.[30] Accordingly, the plan sets growth targets for industrial output, employment, and exports as, 12.5 per cent, 7 per cent, and 15 per cent respectively per annum.[31]

Among other measures designed to achieve these growth targets,[32] the government encourages the inflow of private foreign investment by means of establishing investment promotion centres in the industrialized countries. The government is prepared to sign investment guarantee agreements with foreigners certain of investing in the country, and to continue the policy of unrestricted repatriation of capital and earnings.

The alternatives to private foreign investment[33] are joint-ventures, licensing arrangements, importing, or having state-owned investments. We have discussed why joint-ventures are not popular with the MNEs. As for licensing arrangements, the MNEs do not regard them as a practical alternative to direct investment, primarily because of their reluctance to export production technologies which they prefer to exploit themselves. As for the alternatives of importing and doing without foreign investment, one can say, in the light of the planned objectives, they are not real alternatives in the Malaysian case. Apart from 'do-it-yourself' industrialization, the choice of alternatives is by no means clear for the country. Since, as a matter of policy, the decision to invest is left to the private investor, it seems obvious that the foreign investor prefers to set up production locally instead of using other means of exploiting the market. The real alternative for the MNEs was not to invest in the country at all;[34] but they chose to invest for reasons we have already considered. Had they not invested locally, they believed other firms would have done so.

Our data are not comprehensive enough to show conclusively whether or not the MNEs have achieved, or have contributed towards achieving, the national plan growth targets. Between 1971 and 1973 for example, most of the MNEs achieved annual output growth rates ranging from 15 to 25 per cent. We cannot say whether these firms will attain the national plan target of an annual output growth rate of 12.5 per cent for the period 1971 to 1975, but the MNEs expressed confidence in their ability to exceed the national industrial target, given the buoyant business atmosphere in the country in 1972 and 1973.[35]

The greatest problem was in the area of employment creation. The MNEs in 1972 employed about 5 per cent of the country's industrial labour force, and the estimated growth of employment in the MNEs was around 2 per cent per annum. They are in a position to increase their output substantially without a corresponding expansion in the labour force they employ. This is because of the under-utilized capacity they have. Nonetheless, the MNEs claimed that they might well be able to achieve an annual growth rate of about 5 per cent for the Second Plan period. It is evident, however, that the MNEs cannot be a source of accelerated employment growth.

As for the growth of exports as conceived in the national plan, the MNEs certainly have a positive role to play. As a group, they not only account for over one-half of the total exports in manufactured goods but are also responsible for the diversification of exports and markets. A substantial proportion of manufactured goods from Malaysia since 1965 has been accounted for by the MNEs. Table 7.7 highlights the important role they have played in the country's exports. Excluding exports in primary commodities—rubber, tin, palm oil, and timber—the value of manufactured goods exported by the MNEs in 1970 constituted about 32 per cent of the total value of manufactured exports of the country in that year. What is even more significant is the diversified nature of the products exported, ranging from cigarettes to power-

TABLE 7.7

ESTIMATED AMOUNTS OF MANUFACTURED PRODUCTS EXPORTED FROM MALAYSIA, BY SELECTED MNEs, 1970

Item (MIC Code and Description)	*Amount ($ mil.)*	*Amount as % of Total of Each Category*
1. *Beverages and Tobacco* (121/3, cigarettes, and manufacturing tobacco)	30.7	70
2. *Mineral Fuels* (331/2, petroleum products, natural and manufactured gases)	35.3	65
5. *Chemicals* (512/3; 515, manufactured chemicals, 533, paints; 541, medical and pharmaceutical items; 533, toilet preparations; 561, manufactured fertilisers; 571, explosives; and 599, unclassified chemicals)	39.1	65
6. *Manufactured Goods by Materials* (excluding tin metals) (621, fabricated rubber manufactures; 661, cement; 691, construction materials)	300.0	50
7. *Machinery: Equipment* (711, Power-generating equipment; 714, Office machines; 722, electrical machinery; 725/6/9, medical apparatus)	51.1	53
8. *Miscellaneous Manufactured Goods*	33.8	50
Total	503.0	32

Source: Data derived from *Monthly Statistics of External Trade*, December 1970, and estimates made during field work.

Notes: The estimated total of manufactured exports from the country for 1970 was $1,556.2 million. The $503.0 million shown in the Table refers to the estimated share of British MNEs only.

The amounts shown do not include imported goods which were subsequently re-exported, and small amounts of manufactured foodstuffs.

generating equipment. In almost all major groups of manufactured items the MNEs' shares are predominant. Thus, company representatives believed they would have little difficulty in exceeding the national target of an export growth rate of 15 per cent per annum.

An added net contribution of the MNEs towards exports is intensifying the diversified export markets they created through their world-wide marketing organizations. In 1965 at least 18 per cent of Malaysia's export of manufactures went to the advanced countries of North America, Western Europe including the U.K., Australia, South Africa, Japan, and New Zealand.[36] In 1970, these countries absorbed nearly 50 per cent of Malaysia's export of manufactured goods. In certain industrial products, e.g. petroleum, manufactured rubber, and chemicals, the MNEs are clearly dominant in the sense that they lead in the production and export of these products.

With regard to the national objective of modernizing and restructuring the economy, it seems reasonable to expect the MNEs, with their advanced technology and efficient management, to play an equally positive role. We have noted that they occupy the research- and capital-intensive sectors of the country's industry, that they are active in arranging management training for their executives, and that their senior executives are active in the Malaysian Institute of Management. Also, the MNEs have diversified, or are diversifying, their investments into related and unrelated fields. On the strength of these activities one may presume that the MNEs are behaving in full accord with the national policy.

Compared to other British companies the MNEs may be said to be sympathetic to the national objective of employing more Malays in industry. Representatives of the MNEs interviewed did not find such a national objective unreasonable, since MNEs all over the world are trying to absorb 'minority groups'[37] into their organizations. As the MNEs can afford to conduct training programmes for their executives they are in a better position to employ anybody capable of being trained.

The evidence we encountered leads us to conclude that, apart from the national employment objective, the MNEs have been consistently contributing positively towards the national plan objectives. It is perhaps unrealistic to expect them to be a direct source of large employment. By virtue of their technology and production methods, they cannot be expected to create directly a large amount of employment,[38] although, as will be pointed out later in Chapter 9, most industrial companies in the country indirectly create additional employment.[39]

OTHER EFFECTS OF THE MULTINATIONAL ENTERPRISES ON MALAYSIA

It has been suggested that the MNEs create conflicts in the host country as a result of their bringing in capital-intensive processes and inappropriate technologies.[40] They have also been criticized for the problems they create in the host country owing to their size, their foreignness, their 'statelessness', the flexibility and remoteness of their decision-making, their adverse impact on labour unions, and the alleged irregularities in their currency and other practices.[41]

Streeten[42] for instance wrote:

> Conflict between the multi-national enterprise and the host government may derive from four sources: from the fact that it is *private* and hence may clash with the social and national goals; that it is *large* and oligopolistic and hence possesses market and bargaining power which may be used against the interest of the host country; that it is *foreign*, particularly if it is American, and hence may be serving the national interests of a foreign nation; and that it is 'western' and hence may transfer inappropriate know-how, technology or management practices, or products designed with characteristics not needed in less-developed countries.

We shall discuss in turn these hypotheses which, though attributable to Streeten, are common in the literature cited (*passim*) in this chapter on the MNEs and the underdeveloped countries.

PRIVATE OWNERSHIP, SIZE OF MULTINATIONAL ENTERPRISES AND THEIR EFFECTS ON THE INDUSTRIAL SECTOR

In the foregoing sections we have argued that the MNEs do not appear to clash with the social and national objectives as delineated in the economic plan. Except for the employment issue for which the MNEs cannot be held responsible by virtue of their technological nature (previously argued, and to be followed up below) the MNEs have contributed towards the national objectives of the country. On the strength of our outline of their output performance and their contribution to Malaysia's exports, we may state that when the host country's economic policy is oriented towards private investment, and when the MNEs in the industrial sector perform according to the targets of the national plans, the potential clash of objectives between the MNEs and the host country is diminished.

We mentioned that the smallest subsidiaries of the MNEs, in terms of capital employed, rank among the largest industrial companies in the country. We also noted that in whatever sub-sector of industry they operate, the MNEs dominated the sub-sector and its market. Structurally (see Table 7.4) the MNEs are distributed in those areas of industry where production techniques involve high capital intensity in the manufacturing processes. The size of the MNEs, which is the source of their strength, is dictated by the minimum efficient scale of production. As Pratten has rigorously examined, the production plant in certain types of manufacturing (e.g. oil, chemicals, cement, bicycles and other manufactured goods), must be of a certain size to be efficient.[43] This is illustrated in Table 7.8. It is in the interest of scale economy, rather than the desire to bargain against the host country, that the MNEs are large relative to the average size—measured by capital employed—of manufacturing companies in the underdeveloped country. It follows from the size of the investments and their output capacities, that the MNEs tend to be oligopolistically positioned in the small domestic market of the host country.

We cannot say whether the oligopolistic tendencies of the MNEs would permanently distort the Malaysian market. Evidence indicates that the high profits the MNEs enjoy—partly from their oligopoly position—tend to attract new entrants into the economy thereby creating competition,[44] or countervailing forces. Thus, Shell has to compete with Esso Malaya, Caltex, and soon with Petronas. ICI has to share the market with rivals like Mega and Pacific, respectively a local company and a subsidiary of Dow. GEC's competition with the Japanese electrical firms of Matsushita and Sanyo is well-known. BICC's and Lever's markets in the country are each being eroded by at least two rivals. Dunlop will have to share the market with the Goodyear and Firestone tyre

TABLE 7.8
MINIMUM EFFICIENT SCALE FOR SELECTED INDUSTRIES

Industry	*Output Capacity of Plant*
Oil	10 million tons per annum
Heavy chemicals, e.g. sulphuric acid, ethylene, and dyes	300,000–1,000,000 tons per annum
Detergent powders	70,000 tons per annum
Soaps	10,000 tons per annum
Cement	2 million tons per annum
Bicycles	100,000 units per annum
Turbo generators and electric motors	An output of at least 6,000 m.w. per year
Domestic electrical appliances (producing a range of ten appliances)	500,000 units per annum
Electronic capital goods	1,000 units of production runs

Source: C.F. Pratten, *Economies of Scale in Manufacturing Industry*, Cambridge University Press, 1971.

companies in the late 1970s. In the semi-conductor industry competition among rival companies from all over the industrialized world is well-known, but it is more a matter of competition in the area of securing skilled labour than in securing a domestic market. The net effect, in what seems to be an oligopolistic industrial structure, is the arrival of many MNEs from several countries, and the eventual enlargement of industrial employment.

We were unable to find instances where the MNEs used their size—as measured both in terms of capital employed and sales in the market—against the interest of the host country (although there are other practices of the MNEs which we will discuss later) that may be construed as acting against the national interest. On the contrary, the presence of the MNEs has led to the strengthening of the government administration since, in the first place, the government receives revenues from them (mainly from taxes estimated to be around $117 million in 1972) and, in the second place, the government has to hire competent civil servants who can match the foreign investors in business negotiations.[45]

Through the Private Sector Advisory Panel (PSAP) the MNEs are in consultation with the government on the possible means of improving the investment situation. At least for the period 1962–73 little evidence was found to suggest that the MNEs have succeeded in using, or attempted to use, their power to protect their oligopolistic market positions. On the contrary, the government has succeeded in persuading the MNEs of the need to export.

The main complaint of the MNEs (also the common complaint of companies engaged in import substitution) was that the government allowed too many companies to come into the country, relative to the capacity of the local market to absorb their output at the minimum efficient scales of production. One can certainly argue that this should not be a real complaint if the companies could export an increasing proportion of their production that was superfluous to local demand.[46]

Conceivably, the MNEs may try to influence government decisions about matters (e.g. the question of protection) affecting foreign investment in the economy. For its part, the government is aware of the complexities of the international trading arrangements of the MNEs and, as a result, the International Trade Division of the Ministry of Trade and Industry which monitors the activities of the MNEs only encourages the development in the country of MNEs which conform to the national interest.[47]

The hypothesis that the MNEs can act in the economy against the national interest presupposes that the government is either weak and corrupt, or foolish, a premise that cannot be accepted in the light of the activities of the MNEs in Malaysia and their relationships *vis-à-vis* the government.

THE QUESTION OF 'WESTERN' TECHNOLOGY

According to the hypothesis stated previously, the technology of the MNEs is regarded as unsuitable to the underdeveloped country because the technology is 'Western', meaning the use of highly capital-intensive production techniques. The implication of the hypothesis is that the imported technology does not exploit the comparative advantage (mainly in non-scarce labour) of the host country. Having reviewed the industrial distribution of the MNEs in the present study it is difficult to see the validity of the hypothesis in the Malaysian case. The types of industry (Table 7.4) in which the MNEs operate are capital-intensive industries, for reasons of scale economy (as indicated by Table 7.8). The MNEs interviewed were not aware of an intermediate technology[48] that can be employed in the kind of manufacturing they are in.

In the literature on the MNEs in the underdeveloped countries, it is far from clear whether there are real alternatives to existing techniques of production as embodied in the plants owned by the MNEs. In the Malaysian case where the industrialization strategy is 'outward-looking', it seems essential that production techniques should be abreast of the technology developed in the industrialized countries. In addition to supplying the local market, the foreign investor is expected to produce goods that can be marketed on an international basis. In fact, as will be shown in Chapter 9, many of the locally manufactured goods (e.g. refined petroleum products, chemicals and chemical fertilizer, machinery and equipment, as well as a wide range of consumer durables) are being exported internationally. The MNEs interviewed claimed that part of the reason why they have been able to export from Malaysia is that their production technology in the country allows them to produce goods that can compete internationally. They thought that using a 'non-Western' technology (i.e. labour-intensive production techniques) might not produce goods of a quality acceptable in the international market.

Even in supplying the local market, the quality of a product has to conform to the internationally known quality or standard. An executive pointed out a case where he found that the product of a line discontinued in the home country but started in the host country could not sell, because a rival firm produced a more modern version of the product in question. In this example it is clear to the MNE concerned that it should be abreast of the latest technique and design if it wishes to ensure its competitiveness.

Conceivably, in some types of manufacturing, labour-intensive techniques may be feasible, but the MNEs, apart from those in the semi-conductor industry, do not usually engage in them. Even in areas of manufacturing where labour-intensive techniques of production are feasible, the use of such a technique may have serious limitations. An executive told of a case where his enterprise employed a semi-automatic machine to produce a certain range of products. It so happened that the market demand for the products increased faster than the capacity of the semi-automatic machine to satisfy demand. The result was that a competitor, known to be using a fully-automatic machine, was able to secure a greater portion of the increase in the market demand. Looking back, the executive thought that where market demand was increasing rapidly, and when an enterprise wanted to increase sales rapidly, there was a definite disadvantage in using inefficient techniques involving less capital per man.

TRANSFER OF FUNDS

Many writers have associated the MNEs with international currency speculation, and in instances where the host countries have weak balance of payment positions the shifting of funds by the MNEs can aggravate those positions. Here we consider some of the issues relating to the transfer of funds by the MNEs.

The most critical statement about the role of the MNEs in the international transfer of funds is made by Vogel (1972) who wrote: '. . . monetary policy of the host country's central bank is rendered ineffective by the internationalisation of financial institutions through the multinationals . . . (by shifting idle cash balances) . . . they reduce the effectiveness of monetary . . . and fiscal policies'.[49]

We examine here the relationship of the MNEs' role of managing their cash balances and the behaviour of the short-term capital market. We are unable to trace statistically the movement of funds specifically attributable to the MNEs because of lack of information, and officially because short-term capital movements are aggregatively treated as 'other short-term capital; errors and omissions' in the balance of payments.[50] These 'errors and omissions' are large relative to the net sum of the current and capital accounts; and according to the 1972 report of the Treasury[51] between 1963 and 1972 the annual 'errors and omissions' recorded averaged about $280 million. It is incorrect to regard the sum of $280 million, as some writers seem to,[52] as representing a net drain on the Malaysian economy, but it is certainly correct to view the movement as the responsibility of the private sector, in which the foreign investor is predominant. It is invidious to point an accusing finger at the MNEs as being responsible for the large movements of short-term capital in the country. It is unfair as well, because in the first place they are officially welcome, and quite naturally they will manage their affairs in a manner they consider consistent with their corporate goals. The line of approach here is to argue that the hypothesis put forward by Vogel is less relevant to the case of the MNEs in Malaysia, and that when the MNEs shift funds they do so for economic reasons.

First we shall argue in *a priori* terms. Later, we will examine our empirical evidence to support our arguments. One would expect that an efficient MNE would try to maintain its liquid capital at the minimum level consistent with the requirements of the business. The retention of an unnecessarily high level of liquid capital for any speculative purpose would render an MNE uncompetitive, since one would expect its comparative advantage to be more in manufacturing, unless it was specifically created to practise currency or commodity speculation (in which case it might not have been welcome to the underdeveloped country in the first place, unless of course that country happened to be a tax-haven territory). Conceivably, since the MNEs are large organizations able to employ experts in marketing and international finance, they may well deal in international commodities and finance. In imperfect market situations one would expect them to deal internationally (in commodities and in currencies) to protect their interests and those of their shareholders; that is, at least they should avoid making losses.

There is a subtle distinction between 'dealings' and 'speculations', according to the executives interviewed,[53] although the net effects may be similar. In 'dealings' the actions are defensive, that is the main intention in the first instance is to do something else, but events occur unexpectedly, so that an immediate action (dealing) has to be undertaken to avert the crises. In contrast to the temporary nature of actions involving dealings, 'speculations' are deliberate and an end in themselves. Hence, the MNEs consulted in this study are not real speculators in the above sense, in the international market.

There are at least four reasons to support the claim that the

MNEs are not speculators as they are conventionally understood. First, speculation is not their business—as defined in their Memoranda of Association—and it is not what their shareholders expect them to do. Second, speculation, in international currencies especially, leads to international crises which is an aberration of the conditions in which international business may be conducted. The MNEs are interested in international financial stability because most of their investments are long-term. Third, in the Malaysian situation where the currency is strong,[54] and where, as will be seen, returns on capital are high by world standards,[55] it appears unlikely that MNEs would prefer to dabble in the risky business of speculation rather than get on with something else (like manufacturing) for which they have a comparative advantage. It would seem most likely that those who are in the speculative business are the commodity brokers and institutions such as banks that deal in international currencies. Finally, host countries have all the legal powers to discourage any currency speculations which are not in their national interests.

Manser[56] discovered that the MNEs are not speculators in the conventional sense. This was also supported by Professors Robbins and Stobaugh who studied the MNEs intensively at the Harvard Business School.[57] We can say that in Malaysia the MNEs are not speculators. Our field work allowed us to support the statement. The MNEs like Unilever[58] were categorical in their denial of any speculation in currencies, although they deal in international currencies since they have business in many countries.

The proximity of Malaysia to the Asia-Dollar Market facilitates these dealings. The Asia-Dollar Market is in Singapore, to the south of Malaysia. It is not intended to describe the Asia-Dollar Market here.[59] It is an off-shoot of the Euro-Dollar Market whose functions are quite well-known and need no elaboration,[60] only the implications of the Asia-Dollar Market (hereafter referred to as the ADM) are considered briefly here.

Commercial banking practices in Malaysia, as in the U.K. are governed by, in addition to the prescriptions by the monetary authorities, bankers' gentlemen's agreements—or to use Professor Machlup's phrase 'cartel constraints'[61] whereby minimum and maximum rates on loans and deposits are determined. The bankers have their own methods of screening loans and they adjust their rates according to their own formulae. They seldom pay interest on call money; and the interest they pay on deposits is rigidly determined by their gentlemen's agreements. In 1971, for example, the Malaysian bankers' ruling was that each commercial bank should pay no more than 5¾ per cent on time deposits for 3–6 months, and 6 per cent for 9–12 months. Negotiations for loans are often lengthy, as managers of the banks are cautious about their prospective customers. The ADM on the other hand is free from all the restrictive conventions of the commercial banks. Its clients are selected from among wealthy individuals and large businesses like the MNEs. Clients are 'wired' to the market and are given codes identifiable only by the parties concerned. The ADM pays interest on call money. Its interest rates are more flexibly determined; and as shown in Table 7.9, the ADM rates are more competitive than those of the Malaysian commercial banks. It is economically sensible to put short-term deposits on the ADM. As the market also accepts call deposits with interest payments, many of the MNEs find that it is worth their while to use the ADM more or less as a current account[62] with the added advantage that the account so held is flexible, in the sense that it can be converted into any world currency at very short notice.

The ADM pays higher rates for prime deposits than those in Table 7.9–according to demand and supply conditions. The margin between deposit and loan rates in the ADM is lower (1–1¼ per cent) than that in the commercial banks (4–5 per cent), which in March 1971 charged borrowers between 8 and 10 per cent.[63] It seems clear to the MNEs that there are definite advantages in becoming customers of the ADM. They find it easier to deal with the ADM because of the technical simplicity of transactions.

TABLE 7.9

COMPARATIVE INTEREST RATES ON DEPOSITS IN THE ASIA-DOLLAR MARKET AND MALAYSIAN COMMERCIAL BANKS, 1971

Length of Deposit	*Rates at the Asia-Dollar Market (per cent)*		*Rates for Malaysian Commercial Banks (per cent)*
	US Dollar Rate	*Resident Sterling Rate*	
Call	4 3/8	7	0
1 month	4 7/8	7 1/8)	maximum of 5¼
3 months	5	7 3/4)	
6 months	5 9/16	7 5/16)	maximum of 6
12 months	6 3/16	7 5/16)	
	(rates prevailing on 25 March 1971)		

Source: Based on S. Y. Lee, op. cit., p. 50.

Customers can conclude transactions by wire in a matter of minutes, instead of having to engage in lengthy and often difficult discussions (involved in transactions with commercial banks) during which many intrusive questions are asked, and in which rigid terms are insisted upon.

Finally, it is advantageous for the MNEs to be customers of the ADM since it is linked to the Euro-Dollar Market which, in December 1971, had access to an estimated equivalent of US$100.4 billion of international currencies.[64]

The MNEs need not deposit just their cash balances which we estimated to be very small in amount ($12 million). They can, for instance, deposit virtually any of their funds for which they may have no immediate use, and should they need them they can be recalled within a few minutes' notice. The speed with which the ADM handles its transactions is a manifestation of its superiority over the conventional banks. The use of the ADM reflects business prudence on the part of the MNEs.

The existence of such market facilitates the seizure of any investment opportunity anywhere in the world.[65] The implication for Malaysia is threefold: first, it seems essential to keep track of all capital movements from the country, and the current practice of concealing short-term capital movements as 'errors and omissions' in the balance of payments is unsatisfactory. It calls for better trained statisticians who can keep up with developments in international finance. It seems obvious that the best way of getting the maximum advantage from the MNEs is first to know what they are doing and why. Then, they may be persuaded to do what is in their own interest and that of the host nation.

The second implication is that there is the need to accelerate the growth of the economy so that opportunities for investment occur. Thereby, funds from the ADM may be attracted into the economy. Since the MNEs are alert to market opportunities, the direction of planning effort should be towards improving the domestic market.

The other implication is that financial institutions in the country should be reformed and made more flexible in order to compete in the market for capital. Banking laws may be reformed to allow them to give as good a facility as the ADM offers its customers. While we do not propose to say how the reforms should take place, it is clear that initial steps should be taken to study the ADM system.

We are left with Vogel's thesis that the MNEs render the host country's monetary and fiscal policies ineffective. We are unable to verify Vogel's hypothesis because it is impossible to say whether the MNEs are solely responsible for the malfunctioning and inadequacies of the host country's internal policies. Even in the relatively well-developed Euro-Dollar market it was impossible to identify the party ultimately responsible for the international currency operations,[66] although it is known that MNEs use the Euro-Dollar Market. To blame the MNEs solely is to ignore the fact that the dealers in the market include powerful individuals and also governments.[67] In the Malaysian case the specific role of the MNEs affecting the country's monetary and fiscal policies has not been noticed. This is primarily because the ADM is a relatively new institution (established in 1968) and the amount of transactions in it is still small (1 per cent of the Euro-Dollar's transactions) and also, as we have mentioned, the MNEs have not been speculating in the market. More fundamental perhaps is the strength of the Malaysian currency and the high external reserves the country has maintained since its political formation in 1963. Additionally, one may add that the monetary policy has been along conservative lines in that inflationary finance so far has been avoided. The preoccupation has been to maintain internal price stability, and stability of the external value of the Malaysian currency.[68]

The fiscal policy has been equally conservative in that it is preoccupied with budget balancing rather than ambitious project building and borrowing.[69] The fiscal management has been geared to the avoidance of inflation at the expense of a high unemployment rate of about 7.3 per cent.[70] The tax system is formulated on the basis of raising revenue in a form least prejudicial to private enterprise.[71] As will be shown in Chapter 8 the corporation tax structure compares favourably to that of the home country of the MNEs, in that it gives an incentive to companies to retain or reinvest their profits locally. An executive interviewed pointed out that the stability of the Malaysian currency is an inducement for the MNEs to retain as much of their funds denominated in the local currency as they think proper. They are least likely to be interested in economic instability because it affects their investment horizon.

There is of course the danger that in their keenness to hold on to Malaysian currency, which is backed by gold and foreign exchange reserves to the extent of 200 per cent,[72] they may exert some pressure on it, by way of pushing up its exchange value and thus affecting the country's export prices. The absence of exchange control regulations and the proximity of the ADM may open the way to an easy outflow of capital. In such an eventuality it is possible that the MNEs in the ADM might render local monetary and fiscal policies ineffective.[73]

The evidence in the Malaysian case has not shown that the MNEs are deliberately trying to undermine the country's domestic policies which are aimed at maintaining stability. Our interviews with the MNEs leave us with the impression that where a country has an unstable economic situation the MNEs' international transactions may aggravate the problem. Where a country's internal policies are leading to an inflationary situation[74] (e.g. when a country tries to maintain full employment and at the same time has serious deficits in the balance of payments; or when a country embarks on ambitious projects for which it cannot provide the finance; or when a country resorts to unregulated credit creation) the MNEs are alert to signs of further uncertainty which may cause them economic losses. In their desire to avoid losses they may have to make a rapid currency deal, which in turn would aggravate the uncertain situation. The defensive measures taken by the MNEs may hurt their host countries.

Where the host country's policy is designed to maintain financial and general economic stability, the presence of MNEs that deal internationally has not been shown to have any adverse effect on these policies.

Where a country's monetary and fiscal policies are managed so that the stock of money in the country grows at a rate roughly equal to the rate of growth of output in the economy, there is a tendency for the economy to achieve a certain degree of stability, as in Malaysia. For example, between 1963 and 1972, real output in Malaysia grew at approximately 6 per cent per annum;[75] and money supply for the same period grew at approximately 7.1 per cent per annum.[76] The results, although not entirely attributable to the growth in money supply, seem to indicate that the country's internal stability is not aggravated by the external disturbances in the international monetary situation which Vogel seemed to attribute to the activities of the MNEs.[77] There is of course a little inflation in the country, but it is more the result of inflated import prices[78] than domestic policies. The tendency to stability of the Malaysian economy is perhaps best illustrated by a quotation from the Governor of Bank Negara—Malaysia's Central Bank—in an address to bankers at Zurich in March 1973:

> We in Malaysia of course had our share of the excitement during the latest international monetary crisis of the past few weeks. The devaluation of the U.S. dollar, the decisions to maintain the gold parities of the Deutschmark and

the French franc, the floating of the Japanese yen and the British decision to continue floating the pound, are now a matter of record. The economic, financial and monetary position of Malaysia was such that our government was able to decide not to alter the gold parity of the Malaysian dollar which remains unchanged at 0.290299 grammes of fine gold representing a revaluation of 11.1 per cent against the U.S. dollar.

I might add that since the Smithsonian realignment of currencies in December 1971, the Malaysian dollar has appreciated by 20.6 per cent in terms of the U.S. dollar. This latest decision by the Malaysian Government to maintain the parity of the Malaysian dollar reflects once again the basic strength and stability of the Malaysian economy and its underlying balance of payments . . . .[79]

It seems apparent that the MNEs' international dealings, as we have outlined above, had not disturbed the Malaysian internal policies directed towards achieving stability. We may conclude by saying that the MNEs long-term interest is in the host country's internal stability. Where policies are orientated towards achieving stability the MNEs do not appear to be acting against the policies.

THE FUTURE OF THE MULTINATIONAL ENTERPRISES IN MALAYSIA

The MNEs we interviewed see themselves to be in majority control of their enterprises when their profits are still high. They also foresee a levelling off of profits within the next decade or two when more competitors enter the local market. In the meantime they are reorganizing themselves mainly in three areas: the first is in the area of control. They are moving from a centralized to a less centralized form of control. We see evidence of this when at least three MNEs[80] have already appointed local people to be their chief executives in Malaysia.

Whether the appointment of local people as chief executives means in reality a lessening of head office control one cannot say definitely, because in the first place there are other areas of control as was mentioned earlier, and in the second place one cannot be certain that the locally-appointed executives are any different in outlook and behaviour from executives (at the same level) from the home country. Conceivably, these local people may be no different from the expatriates, by the time they have graduated through the organization. However, it is not unreasonable to expect local people to have the national interest as their prime concern.

The second area of reorganization is in the structure of both the industry and the management. Many of the MNEs in Malaysia have diversified, and some are diversifying, where feasible, into other economic activities in the country. Sometimes the diversification involved investments in neighbouring countries (see Chapter 6). In the composition of executives in the MNEs, an increasing number of local people are being recruited and trained for technical and managerial appointments. Representatives of the MNEs welcome the development of technical and management education in the country. An increasing number of the MNEs are giving financial support in the form of scholarships and annual prizes to institutions of higher learning in the country. Some MNEs provide vacation employment for technical and management students.

The third area of reorganization relates to managerial style. Local personnel are increasingly being given responsible roles. For example, local personnel are asked to investigate opportunities for setting up subsidiaries in the neighbouring countries. Previously such assignments were left primarily to expatriate personnel. An increasing number of MNEs are also publishing their annual reports and accounts in the national language. This will enable the more literate local people to follow the accounts and activities of the MNEs. Those with the necessary means may thus be able to participate (in the sense of either purchasing the equity of the MNEs or seeking employment in them) in the organizations of the MNEs.

The government for its part is very aware of the MNEs and their complex international organization. The existence of communication channels such as the Private Sector Advisory Panel (PSAP) enables the government to gauge the mood of the international business community. The presence of government investment promotion agencies in the industrialized countries should also allow the government to have access to information about the activities of the MNEs in the advanced countries. Such information is valuable in formulating policy objectives and measures affecting the MNEs.

Although at present joint-ventures are not widespread, the MNEs that are coming may have to accept joint-ventures as a condition of entry. They may also have to employ workers, at all levels, reflecting the country's racial composition, and they may also have to locate their factories in areas designated by the government as development areas. These conditions are laid out in the incentive programmes referred to earlier.

A recent development we observed is the organization of newly formed locally-owned enterprises organized along the lines of the MNEs. In some cases they collaborate with foreign firms, as in the many ventures organized by Pernas; in other cases, as in those businesses run by Mara, the management is patterned on that of internationally organized companies. They have, for instance, opened up marketing outlets in the developed countries; these outlets are manned by Malaysians who will feed back information on consumer and market preferences to the factories in Malaysia. The types of manufacture they engage in are those that use mainly locally available materials, as in the manufacture of handicraft items such as batik fabrics, knocked-down furniture, small luxury boats, and prefabricated wooden structures for huts, garages, and small houses.[81]

In the service industries, e.g. accountancy, law, and data processing, a number of local firms are organizing themselves into an international network so that the services they give to their clients (who are mainly MNEs) can be of uniform standard. Local state governments are conducting ventures in the raw material processing industries such as timber, also along the lines of the MNEs in terms of finance and marketing as well as technical production.[82] It seems apparent from the foregoing that the MNEs will continue to form an important part of the industrial sector. Equally significant is the trend for local entrepreneurs to emulate the business organization of the MNEs. It would seem that in the near future, 'business everywhere (will be) outgrowing national boundaries . . .'.[83]

1. See M. Wilkins, *The Emergence of Multinational Enterprise*, Boston, Harvard University Press, 1970; and D. E. Lilienthal, *Big Business: A New Era*, New York, Harper, 1953.

2. See H. G. Callis, *Foreign Capital in South-East Asia* (mimeo.), New York, Institute of Pacific Relations, 1942, p. 98 *passim*. See also E. P. T. Lim, ed., *Multinational Companies and their Implication for South-East Asia*, Singapore, Institute of S.E.A. Studies, February 1973.

3. The adjective 'British' denotes the home base of these enterprises and distinguishes them from say American, Canadian, German, or Japanese firms exhibiting multinational characteristics.

4. S. E. Rolfe and W. Damm, eds., *The Multinational Corporation in the World Economy*, Praeger, 1970.

5. H. V. Pelmutter, 'The Tortuous Evolution of the Multinational Corporation', *Columbia Journal of World Business*, January/February 1969.

6. *The Growth and Abroad of Multinational Companies*, Quarterly Economic Report, Special Issue, No. 5, 1971.

7. R. Vernon, 'International Investment and International Trade in the Product Cycle', *Quarterly Journal of Economics*, Vol. 89, 1966, pp. 190–207.

8. See L. T. Wells, Jr., *The Product Cycle and International Trade*, Boston, Harvard Business School, 1972, and the reference therein.

9. R. E. Caves, 'International Corporations: The Industrial Economics of Foreign Investment', *Economica* (New Series), Vol. 38 (149), February 1971, pp. 1–27.

10. A 'differentiated product' is a collection of functionally similar goods produced by competing sellers, but with each other's product distinguishable from its rival by minor physical variations, 'brand name' and subjective distinctions created by advertising, or difference in the ancillary terms and conditions of sale.

11 The firm investing 'horizontally' basically repeats or duplicates the home base production in the new geographical location.

12. 'Vertical' investment by a firm can be 'forward' (producing nearer to the consumer) or 'backward' (nearer to the raw materials) as explained in E. T. Penrose, *The Theory of the Growth of the Firm*, Oxford, Blackwell, 1972, pp. 145–9; and *The Large International Firm in Developing Countries,* George Allen and Unwin, 1968, *passim*. The latter deals in detail with the issue of vertical direct investments which will not be considered any further here.

13. Caves, op. cit., p. 1, and *passim.*

14. A firm is regarded by the (U.K.) Monopolies Commission as a monopoly when it controls one-third of the market; but according to the *Fair Trading Act, 1973*, a firm is regarded as a monopoly when it controls one-quarter of the market.

15. Penrose, *The Theory of the Growth of the Firm*, p. 227.

16. It is also possible that the enterprise becomes an MNE at Phase 3.

17. See *Malaysian Industrial Digest*, Vol. 7 (1), First Quarter, 1974.

18. This view is also expressed in P..P. Streeten, S. Lall, *et al.*, *Balance of Payments and Income Effects of Private Foreign Investment in Manufacturing: Case Studies of Columbia and Malaysia* (mimeo.), UNCTAD Secretariat, July 1973.

19. See Streeten and Lall, *et al.*, op. cit., for a different view, argued from the standpoint of hypothetical alternatives to foreign investment open to Malaysia.

20. A good illustration of Pelmutter's point on the ethnocentricity of some MNEs.

21. One executive mentioned the case of suspected leakage of marketing information (from an established British company through a shareholder, who later became a senior executive, and subsequently a director, of a company competing in the same business) leading to the British company losing a big portion of its market.

22. See details in the International Chambers of Commerce, *Difficulties Confronting International Joint Business Ventures—Asian Experience,* ICC Commission on Asia and Far Eastern Affairs, 1966.

23. The existing government pronouncement on local equity participation referred to in Chapter 3, is not a decree in the sense that the foreign investor not complying to the request can be legally sued in a Court of law.

24. See A. O. Hirschman, *How to Divest in Latin America and Why*, Princeton University, Essay on International Finance, No. 76, November 1969; U.N., *Multinational Corporation in World Development*, p. 36 et seq.; and D. Wallace, Jr. and H. Ruof-Koch, eds., *International Control of Investment*, The Dusseldorf Conference on Multinational Corporations, Praeger, 1974, Chapter 15, and *passim*.

25. See for example Mr. Fan Yew Teng, M.P. (Malaysia), letter to *The Times*, 22 September 1973. Mr. Fan's political party is against foreign capital in principle.

26. Brooke and Remmers, op. cit., Chapter 2.

27. Although GEC was in control of a substantial portion of the local market for electrical goods, it did not begin local manufacturing until 1967, after two non-British companies began manufacturing locally in 1965 and in 1966.

28. In one instance, the head office blamed the workers in the overseas subsidiary for not making the products attractive in appearance. A visit by an executive to the overseas plant led to the realization that there had been some misunderstanding about the overseas market situation. Consequently, the MNE in question was restructured into a type *B*.

29. In one instance cited by Brooks and Remmers (p. 35) an executive of an overseas subsidiary had as many as nineteen reporting centres to route his papers. Our field work seemed to confirm this example. In at least two cases the MNEs pointed out that their Malaysian operations had additional problems associated with manufacturing, under con-

tract, a foreign brand of products similar to their own. In the mid-1960s communication between London and Kuala Lumpur was less easy than it is today when the use of direct telex/telephone lines permits instantaneous contacts between executives of the subsidiary and the home office.

30. *Second Malaysia Plan, 1971–75*, Chapter X, pp. 147–62, and *passim*.

31. ibid., p. 153.

32. ibid., pp. 155–8.

33. See various contributions in P. H. Ady, ed., *Private Foreign Investment and the Developing World*, Praeger, 1971; and P. P. Streeten, *The Frontiers of Development Studies*, Macmillan, 1972.

34. They could have gone to the neighbouring countries, e.g. Thailand and Indonesia, but for the fact that Malaysia has additional attractions mentioned in Chapter 4.

35. According to the review of the second plan, the average annual growth rate in manufacturing output during the period 1971–3 was 16.1 per cent. See *Mid-Term Review of the Second Malaysia Plan, 1971–75*, p. 142, Table 8.1.

36. Based on information from *Monthly Statistics of External Trade* (various issues), Kuala Lumpur, Department of Statistics. See also Chapter 9 for a fuller analysis of the export market for Malaysian manufactures. Between 1965 and 1970 there has been an intensifying of the development of export markets for Malaysian manufactures.

37. The Malays are not a minority group in the usual sense; they are a minority in the industrial sector. For example, in 1973, nearly 70 per cent of gainfully employed Malays were in agriculture. Of the Malays in industry the majority were in the unskilled jobs; and of all employees at the professional and managerial levels only 7 per cent were Malays. See details in *Mid-Term Review of the Second Malaysia Plan, 1971–75*, pp. 9–10.

38. *The Second Malaysia Plan, 1971–75* (p. 155) does not actually specify that the MNEs should create, or are expected to create, large employment; the plan merely specifies that the manufacturing sector as a whole should play a key role in creating employment.

39. Even in the U.K. MNEs (individually) do not create large employment as compared to the individual public utilities. For instance, according to *The Times 1000 Leading Companies in Britain*, 1971 issue (p. 8), the Post Office and British Rail employed respectively 417,000 and 275,500 people in 1971; whereas ICI and GEC respectively employed 197,000 and 228,000 in the same year.

40. In addition to the works cited in footnotes below and elsewhere above, see also N. Girvan, 'Multinational Corporations and Dependent Underdevelopment in Mineral Export Economies', *Social and Economic Studies*, Vol. 19 (4), December 1970; A. T. Knopper's 'A Multinational Corporation in the Third World', *Columbia Journal of Business*, July/August 1970; D. W. Ewing, 'MNC on Trial', *Harvard Business Review*, May/June 1972; and W. Chudson, 'Africa and the Multinational Enterprise', in H. R. Hahlo, J. G. Smith, and R. W. Wright, eds., *Multinationalism and the Multinational Enterprise*, Leiden, Oceana Publications, 1973. These writers refer to the question of the inappropriateness of the technologies of the MNEs in the underdeveloped countries.

41. A very large proportion of the discussions on these issues have been couched in generalized and intuitive terms, as is evident in many of the references cited in footnote 40 above. See also J. O. Vogel, 'The Real Culprit in International Monetary Crisis—The Impact of the Multinational Corporation', *Business Horizons*, Vol. 15 (2), April 1972. For works based on empirical evidence, see G. E. Bradley, and E. C. Bursk, 'Multinationalism and the 29th Day' (interviews with IBM and General Electric), *Harvard Business Review*, January/February 1972; G. K. Helleiner, 'Manufactured Exports from Less Developed Countries and Multinational Firms', *Economic Journal*, March 1973, and S. M. Robins and R. B. Stobaugh, Jr., *Money in Multinational Enterprises*, Boston, Harvard Business School, 1973.

42. P. P. Streeten, 'Costs and Benefits of Multinational Enterprises in Less-Developed Countries', in J. H. Dunning, ed., *The Multinational Enterprise*, Allen and Unwin, 1971, p. 251 (original emphasis).

43. C. F. Pratten, *Economies of Scale in Manufacturing Industry*, Cambridge University Press, 1971.

44. The arrival of new entrants may not result in a freer competition if the companies collude to share the market between themselves to the exclusion of late-comers. Whether or not such a tendency occurs we shall not know until a further investigation is made of the evolution of the Malaysian market for industrial products.

45. Predictably, some civil servants, desirous of increasing their incomes, have drifted into the MNEs. This tendency has not been found detrimental to the government for it has since devised special remuneration schemes for those officers in departments that deal with foreign investment promotion.

46. According to the 12th Industrial Trend Survey (1974) many companies have reduced their under-utilized capacity by increasing their exports; see details in *Malaysia Industrial Digest*, Vol. 7 (2), July 1974.

47. *Mid-Term Review of the Second Malaysia Plan, 1971–75*, p. 148.

48. It is recorded in Turner, *Multinational Companies and The Third World*, pp. 162–3, that Dr. Schumacher and his Intermediate Technology Group are investigating low-cost equipment suitable for use in poor countries. The present writer, in a conversation with Dr. R. B. Salleh of Queen Mary College (in 1972), was informed that researches were going on in the field of small hydro-turbines, solar-powered air-conditioners, and multi-purpose basic transportation vehicles. It is possible that the production of these items will be using labour-intensive techniques but these products are not strictly comparable with those that the MNEs produce.

49. Vogel, op. cit., pp. 41–6.

50. Discussed more fully in Chapter 9.

51. *Economic Report 1972–3*, Kuala Lumpur, December 1972.

52. Puthucheary, *Ownership and Control in the Malayan Economy*, and Wheelwright, *Industrialization in Malaysia.*

53. See also Manser, *The Financial Role of Multinational Enterprises*, p. 134 n; and J. S. G. Wilson and C. P. Scheffer, eds., *Multinational Enterprises—Financial and Monetary Aspects*, Leiden, A. W. Sijthoff, 1974.

54. See exposition in M. A. Merican, 'Exchange Rate Experience and Policy in Malaysia Since World War II', in H. G. Grubell and T. Morgan, eds., *Exchange Rate Policy in South-East Asia*, Lexington Books, 1972, pp. 19–29.

55. See Chapter 8.

56. Manser, *The Financial Role of Multinational Enterprises.*

57. See special report in *Fortune*, September 1973; see also S. Robbins and R. Stobaugh, Jr., *Money in the Multinational Enterprise*, Boston, Harvard Business School, 1973.

58. See statement by E. Woodroofe, Chairman of Unilever, as reported in *The Times*, 9 May 1972.

59. Briefly, the Asia-Dollar Market is a system of money market, located in Singapore, in which a group of bankers accept and lend funds denominated in U.S. dollars, pounds sterling, Japanese yen, German marks, Swiss, French and Belgian francs, Dutch guilders, Italian lira, Swedish kroner, or any other convertible world currencies. In the banking fraternity, the currencies held by the ADM are known as the Asian Currency Unit which is equivalent to the Euro-dollars of the Euro-Dollar Market. See S. Y. Lee, 'The Asia Dollar Market in Singapore', *The Malayan Economic Review*, Vol. 16 (1), April 1971, pp. 46–56. Our discussion of the MNEs in the ADM is based on Lee, op. cit., on interviews of the executives of three banks delving in the ADM, and on discussions with representatives of the MNEs.

60. The working of the Euro-Dollar is fully described in P. Einzig, *The Euro-Dollar System*, Macmillan, 1973, 5th ed. A hypothetical example is given in Professor N. Friedman, 'The Euro-Dollar Market: Some First Principles', *The Morgan Guaranty Survey*, October 1969, pp. 4–14. A critique of Professor Friedman's analysis is to be found in F. H. Klopstock, 'Money Creation in the Euro-Dollar Market: A Note on Professor Friedman's Views', Reserve Bank of New York, *Monthly Review*, Vol. 52 (1), January 1970, pp. 12–15. An analytical examination of the Euro-Dollar Market is made in H. Mayer, 'Multiplier Effects and Credit Creation in the Euro-Dollar Market', *Banca Nazionale Del Lavoro, Quarterly Review*, No. 98, September 1971, pp. 233–64.

61. Professor F. Machlup, 'Euro-Dollar Creation: A Mystery Story', *Banca Nazionale Del Lavoro Quarterly Review*, No. 49, September 1970, p. 243.

62. Lee, op. cit., p. 47.

63. Lee, op. cit., p. 52. This means, although ADM customers may have to pay high interest rates for loans raised at the ADM, they would also get high interest on their deposits compared to what they would get in the commercial banks.

64. Einzig, op. cit., p. 211.

65. An executive expressed the opinion that the ADM represents an almost perfect capital market which enables funds to move internationally. It also enables companies and individuals to be flexible with their funds. The fact that it is located near Malaysia should be an added advantage to the country since it will enable large companies to notice what the economy has to offer.

66. Einzig, op. cit., p. 214, and *passim*.

67. ibid.

68. Merican, op. cit.

69. In addition to Merican, op. cit., see also Governor of Bank Negara, 'Currency, Banking and Fiscal Systems, Money and Capital Markets', Bank Negara, *Quarterly Econ. Bulletin*, Vol. 6 (1), March 1973.

70. *Second Malaysia Plan, 1971–75*, p. 96.

71. Governor of Bank Negara, op. cit., *Quarterly Economic Bulletin*, Bank Negara Malaysia, Vol. 6 (1), March 1973, p. 42.

72. Loc. cit., p. 41.

73. The mechanism by which an international money market such as the ADM can render the domestic monetary and fiscal policies ineffective is fully described in Einzig, op. cit. Basically, the fluctuation of the market can make it difficult for the underdeveloped national monetary and fiscal authorities to control the influx and efflux of (short-term) capital.

The ability of the market to expand or reduce its liquid resources independent of national authorities tends to make it difficult for the authorities to exercise effective control over the volume of the liquid resources in the domestic money market and the structure of interest rates.

The sensible move by the national authorities, according to the executives interviewed, is to execute a policy of maintaining the stability of the external rates of exchange of the national currency so that the market will be less interested in speculating in it. According to the executives, the greatest uncertainties of recent times stem from the desire of international speculators and dealers to avoid holding on to overvalued currencies of those countries with low rates of economic growth, deficits in their balance of payments, militant labour unions demanding full employment irrespective of productivity considerations, and those countries which try to export capital which they cannot finance. As a general rule, according to the interviewees, MNEs are not interested in speculation in currencies of those countries with characteristics opposite to those mentioned above.

74. It is not intended to enter into the debate about the issues of inflation as it is outside the scope of this study; nor do we want to discuss monetary and fiscal policy management in any detail. Our conversation with executives of the MNEs induced us to think that an inflationary situation is brought about, to a great extent, by the host government attitudes towards monetary expansion. While opinions differ on what causes inflation, in the Malaysian case we know that the relative absence of inflation seems to be the absence of excessive monetary expansion. The case seems to agree with Professor M. Friedman's ideas as to what ought to be a country's monetary policy. See M. Friedman, 'Monetary Theory and Policy', in R. J. Ball and P. Doyle, eds., *Inflation, Selected Readings*, Penguin, reprinted 1972, pp. 136–45.

75. Based on Bank Negara, *Quarterly Economic Bulletin*, Vol. 6 (1), March 1973, p. 39.

76. Based on The Treasury, *Economic Report, 1972–73*, p. 120.

77. See Vogel, op. cit, pp. 41–6.

78. Bank Negara, March 1973, op. cit., p. 3.

79. ibid., p. 41.

80. Shell, Dunlop, and Metal Box.

81. Very little detailed information on these projects is known as they are still in their infancy. Data from FIDA is limited to a listing of products.

82. In the processing of wood products (e.g. plywood and flooring materials) for the export market, emphasis is more on automated plants. They may conflict with the employment objective of the country's economic plan, but automated plants are thought better able to cope with quality of finish demanded by the international market. According to Malaysian businessmen met during field work, even in the textile industry the trend is towards the production of quality items (with emphasis on fashion and design) that can sell in the international market. The smallness of the domestic market led businessmen to explore world markets for Malaysian manufactures.

83. U.S. Department of Commerce, *The Multinational Corporation*, Vol. 1, Washington D.C., 1972, p. 4. The U.S. Department of Commerce goes so far as to suggest that the MNEs are laying the basis for a world economic and political community. The MNEs are viewed as 'a vehicle for uniting the diverse nation states . . . into a true world economy'; see *The Multinational Corporation*, p. 7.

8 The Profitability of U.K. Industrial Companies

PROBLEMS OF PROFIT MEASUREMENT

Two problems arise in the evaluation of profit as reported in the accounts of companies investing abroad: (a) practical problems arising from the limitation of company data, and (b) conceptual problems relating to the use of the term 'profit' in accounting calculations and in economic theory. Where the U.K. company is not publicly quoted in Malaysia the company tends to consolidate its accounts and hence its profit figures with those of the U.K. parent company. Where the parent company owns other commercial or industrial establishments elsewhere in the world, the task of obtaining the relevant data for the Malaysian-based enterprise can be very difficult. Similarly, where a company has considerable non-manufacturing interests in the country and its accounts are not sufficiently disaggregated, it is difficult to sort out the manufacturing profits accurately.

Accounts of diversified companies are generally insufficiently disaggregated and thus give limited information on most economic aspects of the companies in question.[1] Even when individual manufacturing accounts are available, many of the financial figures, including those purporting to represent past events (recorded as objectively as possible by accountants) are necessarily estimates. The determination of profit is especially affected by the difficulties of valuing stock or inventory, and the method adopted for measuring depreciation. Accepted accounting practice permits significant variations in the methods by which stock or inventory is valued,[2] and the methods and rates at which companies depreciate their assets.

Under-valuation of stocks and over-depreciation of assets can very substantially reduce reported profits. The fragmentary evidence available suggests that under-valuation of stocks and over-depreciation of assets are common in wholly-owned overseas affiliates which are not under any pressure from private shareholders to maintain a high level of reported profitability. Such affiliates have incentives to state their profits very conservatively in the interest of minimizing corporation tax liabilities, as well as avoiding political charges by the host country of making excessive profits.

Conversely, profits may be exaggerated by under-depreciation of assets and over-valuation of stocks. Companies with a significant proportion of overseas local shareholders who wish to see high reported profits and receive early dividends may resort to measures that show large profits in their accounts. Other circumstances such as tariffs, tax reliefs, and other government concessions given by the host country may also lead to high reported profits. Besides, in multinational companies the level of profit can be manipulated by intra-firm pricing devices.[3]

Such a mechanism enables firms to shift profits from a high tax country to a lower tax country. Changes in interest on loans and arbitrary allocation of centrally incurred costs, e.g. research and development, may also affect the accuracy of reported profits. Bearing these issues in mind, it would be dangerous to infer too much from the data on reported profits of companies investing overseas.

At the conceptual level there is the need to distinguish between the determination of profits in accounting calculations[4] and the treatment of profits in the economic sense.[5] In accounting terms, gross profit is total sales less payments for raw materials, wages and salaries, and other expenses. This residual represents the difference between receipts and money outlays incurred directly in carrying on the operation of the firm. Net profit is gross profit less interest on loans and depreciation charges. As reported in company accounts, net profit is the residual value arrived at after deducting all money costs and charges. After deduction of tax it represents the after-tax profit, a surplus available to the firm's owners as income and as a source of reserves and funds for new investments.

The economic concept of profit need not correspond to that of the accountant's because the latter has not deducted imputed costs in addition to the money outlays from the profit calculation.[6] Costs of inputs used by a firm in the case of economic profit are measured by their 'opportunity costs' defined as the best return an input could earn outside the business. In the case of accounting profit the costs of inputs are measured in terms of the actual money expenditure on those inputs. The accounting profit does not indicate whether the profit attained is normal profit (i.e.

profit sufficient to induce the entrepreneur to remain in the present business, or the opportunity cost of remaining in that business), or super-normal (excess) profit brought about by such factors as barriers to entry into the business. It is pertinent to mention that the accounting profession itself is searching for a definitive standard of reporting of accounts that will unambiguously define what profit is.[7] Notwithstanding the conceptual problems associated with the term 'profit', the term used here, unless stated otherwise, refers to the accounting profit as reported by the investing companies. In subsequent references profit is defined in the long-run accounting sense as the rate of return (*P*) on total funds (as opposed to average funds) invested, net of tax (*NA*). The return on net investment (*P*/*NA*) concept appears to be generally understood by companies in the present study, whereas the use of the term 'profit' in the economic sense was not so familiar to the executives interviewed.[8]

Because of the practical and conceptual issues mentioned above, the return on net investment (*P*/*NA*) used as an indicator of the efficiency of capital employed is not a perfect measure of the efficiency of firms in using resources. The question of efficiency of resource usage will be touched upon later in the chapter.

THE IMPORTANCE OF PROFIT TO THE INVESTING FIRM

Profit is important to the investing firm since the growth of the firm depends considerably on profits which provide internal finance for growth and attract additional external finance. Maximization of profit as the goal of firms has long occupied pride of place in economic textbooks, but profit maximization interpreted as the underlying goal of firms to maximize the present value of the profits expected from the firms' productive activities over a specific period has been questioned on both theoretical and empirical grounds.[9]

Cyert and March (1963)[10] maintain that in practice firms pursue a multiplicity of goals—production, inventory, sales, market shares, and profits—which they attempt to achieve to a satisfactory level of performance depending on their aspirations and experience.

In considering the role of profit and other goals of firms, one must mention the involvement of people who decide for the firms. Company objectives after all have their origins in personal objectives of executives who decide for the company. Very rarely have these objectives been stated clearly and explicitly. Where decisions involve a group of people, conflicting aims rather than definable composite objectives tend to emerge. The conflicting aims tend to produce restraints which effectively limit the area within which the firms can operate. Thus internal restraints, in addition to the widely recognized external restraints–legal, ethical, and economic–operate to define the firms' manner and scope of operation. The restraints ultimately influence the firms' profitability.

Some of the restraints associated with U.K. manufacturing companies in Malaysia are summarized below.[11]

1. Most companies stated that since they were not operating at full capacity when they first started, their immediate concern was to expand sales subject to a minimum profit constraint. ('Our concern is to maintain and/or increase our share of the market; but obviously we do not expand sales by making our price so low that costs could not be covered.')

2. The majority of companies interviewed required that all expansion of their overseas affiliates be financed from retained earnings.

3. Most companies expressed the desire to agree with broad Malaysian government industrial policy objectives and maintain a good public image. The typical comments were '. . . we sympathize with what the government is trying to do–about encouraging local people to be employed managing foreign firms–and that is why as far as possible we try to train suitable local people to run our works there'; '. . . as far as possible we use local materials and products of local industries' and 'we aim at a "fair" rate of profit in the long run. To do otherwise would be unfair to our customers and to ourselves . . . we may even attract the adverse regards [*sic*] –criticism–of local politicians'. Many companies try to avoid showing that they are making 'too much' profit.[12]

4. Many firms undertook manufacturing in Malaysia either to forestall competitors or to try out a new area of operation. In such circumstances their attention was primarily directed at gaining efficiency and consolidation of their market position.

5. The practice of many companies in diversifying into different projects often impinges on their short-term profitability. ('We are continuously looking for opportunities of spreading our investment activities. In doing so it would be unreasonable to expect our newer ventures to yield profits in the initial periods of operation; besides, not every project yields the expected profits.')

Accepting from empirical evidence that the above restraints on companies' profit-making exist, how important is the profit goal

TABLE 8.1
THE IMPORTANCE OF PROFIT AS A COMPANY OBJECTIVE

	Number of Companies	(%)
1. Company regards the ability of project undertaken to earn profit as a key factor to be considered.	33	(51.5)
2. Company regards the ability of project undertaken to earn profit as an important factor in its decision to undertake major projects.	62	(60.0)
3. Company must be assured of long-run and/or short-run profit before a project is adopted.	93	(95.0)
4. Company gives profitability consideration top priority when assessing the success or otherwise of a project after it has been undertaken.	72	(70.0)
5. Company does not consider profit at all.	0	(0.0)

Source: Interviews.
Notes: N = 103.
Some overlapping considerations occurred.

to the companies? An answer is indicated in Table 8.1 above.

We see that none of the companies neglected the profit factor when they made project evaluations. All the firms mentioned that long-run profit must be maintained.

The majority of firms adopted the rule of thumb approach, that in the short run their investments should generate an after-tax return that is at least equivalent to the prevailing rate of interest.

Some firms would, if it were clearly established that a project is essential for their long-term interest, accept moderate short-term losses. 'Moderate' losses were not clearly defined but were regarded as 'losses of a certain magnitude which do not endanger the survival of the firm'. In the long term, companies expect that their investments in the country show 'adequate' return. What companies meant by 'adequate' return will be discussed later.

The profit-seeking goal is indisputably important. Table 8.2 summarizes the executives' responses when they were asked to rank at least six operational goals of their companies as 'critical', 'desirable', or 'unimportant'.

Next to the profit-seeking goal, most companies regarded maintaining or increasing sales, increasing efficiency, and maintaining or increasing output as critical goals. One-half of the companies

TABLE 8.2
THE DOMINANCE OF PROFIT-SEEKING GOAL
(per cent)

Operational Goals	*Regarded as*		
	Critical	*Desirable*	*Unimportant or Not Applicable*
1. Profit-seeking goal	95	5	–
2. Maintain or increase sales	75	25	–
3. Increase efficiency	60	40	–
4. Maintain or increase output	55	45	–
5. Avoid making losses	50	50	–
6. Seek opportunities for diversification	10	55	35
7. Other goals	–	100	–

Source: Interviews.
Note: N = 103.

regarded the avoidance of losses as a critical objective; while the other half considered it a desirable goal for them to seek opportunities for diversification. It should be mentioned that the operational goals of a firm may change from time to time, and if changes occur frequently the value of a static survey such as this is limited. Accordingly firms were asked to list only those operational goals that would not change within a ten-year period after setting up production facilities in Malaysia. The operational goals discussed in the interviews varied somewhat in detail, but the overwhelming dominance of the profit-seeking goal is indicated by the nearly total unanimity of firms in regarding the goal as critical. Three-quarters of all firms interviewed considered maintaining or increasing sales as critical. The expansion of sales in Malaysia forms part of the global marketing strategy of British firms investing overseas.

As Baumol has argued,[13] firms would be placed in a disadvantageous position if their sales showed either absolute or relatively declining trends. Executives are themselves motivated to expand sales if their remuneration increases with growth in sales.[14] Most firms expect to promote sales as a means to further their other objectives—operational efficiency and ultimately profits.[15] Firms with falling sales would lose their share of the market, their competitive power, and their attractiveness in the money market.

Of the firms surveyed 60 per cent viewed increasing efficiency as another critical goal while 50 per cent of all firms in the survey viewed avoiding making losses as either critical or desirable. Seeking opportunities for diversification was thought to be a critical objective by 10 per cent of all firms, while 55 per cent thought it was a desirable operational goal.

Other operational goals considered desirable were, maximizing the local content of output, minimizing taxation, ensuring the survival of the firm, training local people, maintaining a policy of growth, maintaining goodwill, looking after the interest of shareholders, minimizing risk, and participating in the country's economic development. Clearly they indicated the existence of a complex set of sub-goals, but there can be little doubt that for the firms in this study profit remains a dominant operational goal.

WHAT IS 'ADEQUATE' PROFIT?

Having established that profit is important to the firm, the crucial question is what constitutes a 'fair' or an 'adequate' profit. Companies regarded as meaningless any exercise at pinpointing the adequate rate of return because overseas investment once made represented 'sunk capital' which means that any positive return however small would be regarded as better than no return at all. The 'fair' or 'adequate' return that firms attempt to get only refers to the minimum rate because as far as practicable firms do not set any ceiling on their earnings. Variations on what is considered as adequate profit occurred not only between industries but also within the same firm at different times. Broadly, the expected minimum return bears a relationship to the cost of capital which businessmen equate to the prevailing rate of interest on commercial bank loans and advances to the manufacturing sector.[16]

Between 1960 and 1970 the market rate of interest averaged between 7 and 8 per cent.[17] Although many firms considered that they had earned an 'adequate' profit if they could get a return on the capital they employed equivalent to the market rate, several firms required their profits to be 2 to 3 per cent above the market rate. Some firms even insisted on making at least double the prevailing market rate. The weight of empirical evidence suggested that firms regarded a 10 per cent return on capital employed after tax as 'fair' return. In practice the majority of firms had returns exceeding this figure. There had been instances where the rate of profit achieved was 30 to 40 per cent.

PROFITABILITY AND RETURN ON U.K. OVERSEAS INVESTMENT

To the investor, profits indicate how well the managers of the investment had been doing, that is how efficiently they had been employing the resources of the investing companies. On the basis of global studies of returns from overseas investment, U.K. investments in Malaysia have been profitable. The Reddaway Report for instance, pointed out that during the period 1955 to 1964 an additional £100 to net operating assets of U.K. investments in Malaysia yielded 18.8 per cent return after tax[18] in contrast to the marginal return of 5.5 per cent for companies in the U.K. during the 1950–64 period.[19] The post-tax profitability of U.K. capital in Malaysia for the period covered by the Reddaway study, illustrated in Table 8.3A, was 19.8 per cent per annum, a rate higher than the profitability of U.K. investments in any country in the world, except West Germany. According to the calculations by the Department of Applied Economics of the University of Cambridge, presented in Table 8.3B, the post-tax profitability of all groups of U.K. companies in Malaysia between 1955 and 1964 was substantially higher than the average post-tax profitability of U.K. companies in all other countries.

The position of Malaysia as a very high profit country for U.K. direct investment was also supported by a study of Professor Dunning who made use of Board of Trade data.[20] Dunning's calculations, summarized in Table 8.4, showed that the average rate of return on U.K. capital in Malaysia in the period 1960–5 was 15.9 per cent, comparable to the highest return of 16.2 per cent in West Germany. The rate of return on U.K. direct investment in Malaysia was almost twice the world rate of 8 per cent, and more than twice the individual rates for the E.E.C., North America, Western Europe, the EFTA, Commonwealth, and the developed countries.

Between 1963 and 1971, British direct investment in Malaysia continued to have high rates of return in spite of the small fluctuations shown in Table 8.5. The fluctuations were brought about by a number of causes: the Indonesian 'confrontation' with Malaysia between 1963 and 1966, the uncertainty in the Malaysian federation following Singapore's becoming a Republic in 1965, the devaluation of the pound sterling in 1967, and the accelerated withdrawal of British forces from Malaysia in the late 1960s. Notwithstanding these uncertainties, Table 8.5 shows that returns on British manufacturing investments for most of the years remained

TABLE 8.3A

RATES OF RETURN ON U.K. DIRECT INVESTMENT BY COUNTRY, 1955–1964

Country	(1) *U.K. Stake (Av. Annual) (£ mil.)*[1]	(2) *Average Post-tax Profitability of U.K. Stake* (%)	(3) *Average Annual Royalties and Management Fees* (%)	(4) *Average Annual Capital Appreciation*[2] (%)	(5) *Total Average Annual Return* (2) + (3) + (4) (%)
West Germany	27.8	22.8	1.4	11.7	35.9
Malaysia[3]	50.8	19.8	1.0	8.1	28.9
Italy	6.0	12.3	1.9	4.9	19.1
India	132.4	7.7	0.3	0.0	8.0
Ghana	24.1	13.4	4.0	–0.6	16.9
Brazil	24.0	5.3	1.2	4.5	11.0
South Africa	97.0	10.5	0.5	9.0	20.0
Australia	156.4	8.0	0.8	7.5	16.3
U.S.A.	211.8	8.6	1.0	2.6	12.2
Jamaica	5.2	8.4	0.5	–1.7	6.8
Canada	171.4	5.5	0.2	–0.6	6.3
Nigeria	49.5	4.7	1.9	1.1	7.7
Argentina	14.0	1.6	0.4	4.2	6.2
France	14.5	1.9	1.2	–1.7	1.4
Denmark	4.4	5.3	2.6	–0.3	7.6
Total for 15 countries	989.3	8.7	0.8	3.0	12.5
World	1,214.8	8.7	0.9	3.0	12.6

Source: Derived from Reddaway Report, Tables IV-5 (p. 358), IV-10 (p. 360), and XVI-1 (p. 216).

Notes: [1]Excluding investments in oil industry, plantations, banking, insurance and manufacturing companies with only marketing subsidiaries.

[2]Appreciation of operating assets controlled by U.K.

[3]The high profitability recorded for Malaysia naturally owes a good deal to mining concerns. However, this group accounted for only about one-third of the assets, and most of the other industrial groups showed a profitability rate which was considerably above their average for the world as a whole. See Reddaway Report, p. 45.

TABLE 8.3B

AVERAGE POST-TAX PROFITABILITY RATES OF U.K. GROUP OF COMPANIES IN WEST MALAYSIA AND IN ALL OTHER COUNTRIES, 1955–1964

(per cent)

Companies in Industry Groups	*Average Post-tax Profitability Rates of U.K. Group in West Malaysia, 1955–64*	*Average Post-tax Profitability Rates of U.K. Group in All Countries, 1955–64*
1. Food, drinks, tobacco, and household products	16.7	8.8
2. Chemicals and chemical products	14.0	7.7
3. Electrical engineering	10.1	5.4
4. Other manufacturing	24.4	8.5
5. Mining	41.4	14.4
6. Plantations	15.3	9.6
7. TOTAL (including plantations)	19.8	8.7
8. TOTAL (excluding plantations)	26.9	8.5

Source: D. Lim, *Economic Growth and Development in West Malaysia, 1947–1970*, Oxford University Press, 1973, p. 264.

above the average rate of return on industrial investment, as well as above the average earnings on all capital for each of the years.

The rates of return on the investments did not include incomes of companies derived from capital appreciation, royalties, and management fees estimated to be around an additional 10 per cent of the average annual total investment stake in the country.[21] It would appear then that the estimated average annual rate of return on manufacturing investment during the 1963–71 period was between 30 and 35 per cent, while that on all U.K. capital was between 20 and 29 per cent. This estimate must be interpreted with great caution because of the caveats noted earlier. For example, book values may be biased downwards because of the use of historical costs in recording assets; and reported earnings are affected by intra-firm pricing, by the allocation of centrally incurred costs such as Research and Development (R & D), by tariffs, tax, and other concessions, by changes in the interest rates on borrowings, and not least by accounting procedures.

It is not easy to account for the factors that may distort the balance sheet valuation of capital and accounting profits, but three points are noted here to suggest that in the case of manufacturing in Malaysia the distortion may not be serious. Firstly, since most U.K. industrial firms in Malaysia were set up fairly recently in the

TABLE 8.4
AVERAGE RATES OF RETURN ON U.K. DIRECT CAPITAL STAKE BY COUNTRY AND AREA, 1960–1965
(per cent)

Country/Area	*Average Rates of Return*
West Germany	16.2
Malaysia	15.9
Brazil	12.9
Ghana	12.3
South Africa	12.1
Switzerland	11.9
Canada	8.9
India	7.7
Argentina	7.7
United States	6.6
The E.E.C.	6.2
North America	6.6
Western Europe	6.5
EFTA	7.4
The Commonwealth	7.6
Developing Countries	9.0
Developed Countries	7.1
World	8.0

Source: Derived from J. H. Dunning, *Studies in international investment*, p. 57.
Note: Capital stake excluding investments in oil industry, banking, and insurance.

1960s when the country was inflation-free, it is reasonable to suppose that the book values of their assets may be nearer their replacement value in the years noted. Secondly, all manufacturing companies contributed towards their U.K. parents' R & D programme, although no firm was free to reveal the extent of such contributions.[22] In addition, the affiliates paid royalties for patent use and service charges to their parent companies. Such payment in 1970 alone amounted to £2.7 million.[23] Thus, even if U.K. manufacturing affiliates were receiving subsidized research and technical services, the subsidies would probably have been negligible.

Thirdly, regarding Anglo-Malaysian accounting procedures there was no reason to suppose that they were different from those adopted by British companies in the U.K., since British-trained

TABLE 8.5

RATES OF RETURN ON U.K. INVESTMENTS IN MALAYSIA, 1963–1971

	Investment in Manufacturing			*Other Investments*			*All Capital Stake*		
	(*1*) *Amount of Assets* (*£ mil.*)	(*2*) *Earnings* (*£ mil.*)	(*2*)/(*1*) (%)	(*1*) *Amount of Assets* (*£ mil.*)	(*2*) *Earnings* (*£ mil.*)	(*2*)/(*1*) (%)	(*1*) *Amount of Assets* (*£ mil.*)	(*2*) *Earnings* (*£ mil.*)	(*2*)/(*1*) (%)
1963	15.5	5.4	34.8	116.2	15.9	13.7	131.7	21.3	16.2
1964	17.4	4.7	27.0	121.0	17.7	14.6	138.4	22.4	16.2
1965	19.9	5.1	25.6	124.1	17.2	13.9	144.0	22.3	15.5
1966	19.8	6.2	31.3	124.6	18.2	14.6	144.4	24.4	16.6
1967	22.9	4.5	19.7	151.6	13.7	9.0	174.5	18.2	10.4
1968	21.6	6.6	30.6	151.0	15.0	9.9	172.6	21.6	12.5
1969	21.6	7.5	34.7	151.0	21.0	13.9	172.6	28.5	16.5
1970	19.2	7.4	38.5	163.6	27.0	16.5	182.8	34.4	18.8
1971	23.3	8.7	37.3	172.6	24.9	14.4	195.9	33.6	17.2
Unweighted Arithmetic Average	20.1	6.2	31.0	141.7	19.0	13.4	161.8	25.1	15.6

Source: Data derived from information supplied by the Economics and Statistics Division of the Department of Trade and Industry.

Notes: (i) Capital stake excluding investment in oil industry, insurance and banking.

(ii) Other investments refer to agriculture, mining, and distribution.

(iii) Amount of assets is net assets shown in the investing companies' books at year ends indicated.

(iv) Earnings are post-tax profits excluding capital appreciation, royalties, and management fees.

(v) The figures for 1963 and 1964 include investments and earnings in Singapore whose element cannot now be identified.

(vi) Small roundings in the raw data may account for fluctuation in the earnings rate.

accountants are employed in the Malaysian affiliates. Further, in almost all cases, British firms of international accountants are engaged as auditors of these manufacturing companies. The accounting standards in both the affiliates and the parent companies are the same, so that the accounts of the affiliates in Malaysia are not different from those of the U.K. parent companies.

Against the three factors mentioned above, two major points can be raised which may lead one to suppose that the reported profits of the Malaysian affiliates might be slightly inflated.

Firstly, the existence of tariff protection[24] and other government concessions may add to companies' profitability by way of sheltering the local market from the full force of world competition. Secondly, firms may be tempted to shift profits to Malaysia through the intra-firm pricing mechanism, since Malaysia is a low tax country in comparison to the U.K. The tax differential provides an incentive for U.K. firms in Malaysia to accumulate high profits in the country out of which more dividends can be declared or more reinvestment made. Given the current (1973/4) company tax structure in the U.K. there is a basis for companies preferring to have higher incomes in Malaysia than in the U.K., where more than 66 per cent of company income would go in paying taxes; whereas in Malaysia, only about 49 per cent of company income would be taxed. This point is better illustrated by Table 8.6.

Hence, assuming that the U.K. investing company wishes to maximize its after-tax earnings and has no altruistic or patriotic motive for paying company taxes in the U.K., it makes sense to have high profits in the company's Malaysian affiliates. Such profits can be distributed as dividends or reinvested, and evidence exists that Malaysian-originated funds had been reinvested by British firms in the neighbouring countries. Profits earned in Malaysian affiliates can be remitted anywhere the investing company chooses, since there is no strict exchange regulation limiting the outflow of funds from the country.[25] The use of Malaysia as a financial springboard by British companies moving into other countries in South-East Asia is a new development which merits an entirely separate study.

The level of British company profits in Malaysia is influenced by two other factors. Firstly, British companies are expected to finance their investments out of ploughed-back profits. Consequently chief executives resident in Malaysia are under pressure to make U.K. companies in the country profitable. It is possible that such pressure may tempt them to seek measures to exaggerate reported profits. Secondly, the strength of the Malaysian dollar pro-

TABLE 8.6

COMPARISON BETWEEN MALAYSIAN AND U.K. TAXES ON COMPANY INCOMES, 1973/1974

(as per cent of $100)

Country	*(1)* *Tax on Company Profit*	*(2)* *Withholding Tax*	*(3)* *Actual Amount available for Distribution*
U.K.	45.0	38.75	33.69
Malaysia	40.0	15.0	51.0

Column (*3*) is calculated thus:

		in U.K.	*in Malaysia*
	Say company profit	$100.00	$100.00
less	company tax (col. *1*)	45.00	40.00
–	amount available for distribution	55.00	60.00
less	withholding tax (col. *2*)	21.31	9.00
–	profit available for eventual distribution	33.69	51.00

Notes: (i) Under certain conditions stipulated by the amendments to the *Investment Incentives Act, 1968*, companies in receipt of dividends are exempted from payment of withholding tax. This would enhance the attractiveness of having high profits in Malaysia.

(ii) Double Taxation Agreement may alter the position represented in the Table.

(iii) Companies enjoying 'pioneer status' as defined in the *Investment Incentives Act* are exempted from both company and withholding taxes during their pioneer status period. In addition, losses (other than capital allowances) can be carried forward almost indefinitely, and can be offset against any other income a pioneer company may have in the country.

vides an inducement for companies to hold on to income denominated in Malaysian currency which has appreciated relative to the pound sterling between 1966 and 1973.[26] Moreover, the proximity of the country to the Asia-Dollar Market in Singapore and the linking of Malaysian banks dealing in the Asian Currency Unit with British companies through interlocking directorships may encourage profit growth, and also facilitate the movement of profits at will.

On the other hand, there is no evidence to show that U.K. affiliates in Malaysia are tampering with their reported profits. It is arguable that companies have little desire to exhibit profits in their Malaysian affiliates if such profits do not benefit them. There is also no special merit in inflating profits of overseas affiliates since it may court political criticism. On balance, the most likely tendency in overseas investments, particularly in wholly-owned subsidiaries, is to understate profits slightly. As most U.K. manufacturing concerns in Malaysia are either wholly-owned or parent-firm controlled, it is more likely that their reported profits are conservatively stated than exaggerated.

COMPARISONS BETWEEN FIRMS

To discover whether there were any differences in profits between U.K. firms and others in the same sectors, rates of return were calculated for comparable firms within the same industry. The greatest problem encountered in making such comparisons is the virtual absence of strictly comparable pairs of firms. Invariably the U.K. firms in Malaysian industries are overwhelmingly large in relation to the rest of the firms in the same industries. There is, for instance, no comparable non-U.K. firm the size of Malayan Tobacco Bhd. (British–American Tobacco) which, since 1968, has $45 million paid-up capital. There is also no company comparable to Fraser & Neave Ltd. with its $36 million issued capital in the beverage industry. In the food processing industry, Cold Storage Ltd. with its $39.8 million paid-up capital is in a class of its own. Similarly, Guinness Bhd., Dunlop Malaysian Industries, United Engineers, Metal Box, and others are firms dominant in their respective sub-sectors of Malaysian manufacturing.

The differences in dates of establishment of industrial firms render inter-firm comparisons more difficult, since firms may incur losses, or make very low rates of profit, in the early years of their existence. Any differences in accounting procedures among firms may also influence their profitabilities which in turn make it hazardous to attempt to make comparisons between firms.

Nevertheless, a comparison was made between five pairs of firms—a pair being a U.K. and a non-U.K. firm—of approximately comparable technology, competitive structures, and capital intensity. In this connexion, representatives of U.K. firms were asked to name their respective notable competitors. Care was taken to ensure that the firms chosen for comparison were as far as possible of similar characteristics except in nationality.

Since our interest was to determine the efficiency of capital employed in the firms, we concentrated attention on comparisons of the rate of return on capital. Since one would expect that firms selected were carrying on business as profitably as they could in their respective sub-sectors, differences in their rates of return could be taken as indicative of differing efficiency of capital usage.

TABLE 8.7

COMPARATIVE PROFITS OF SELECTED FIRMS IN SELECTED INDUSTRIES, 1968 AND 1971

Industry/Firm	*1968*				*1971*			
	(*1*) *Gross Earnings (as % of paid-up capital)*	(*2*) *Capital Employed* ($'000)	(*3*) *Profit Post-tax* ($'000)	(*4*) (3)/(2) (%)	(*1*) *Gross Earnings (as % of paid-up capital)*	(*2*) *Capital Employed* ($'000)	(*3*) *Profit Post-tax* ($'000)	(*4*) (3)/(2) (%)
I Food Manufacturing								
(a) U.K. firm	21.3	46,638	4,410	9.5	30.0	59,572	7,261	12.2
(b) non-U.K. firm	22.1	2,178	209	9.6	18.5	9,489	768	8.1
II Beverage Manufacturing								
(a) U.K. firm	51.7	16,371	4,131	25.2	57.1	20,998	5,350	25.5
(b) non-U.K. firm	39.4	81,165	9,999	12.3	52.8	96,475	11,993	12.4
III Electrical Engineering								
(a) U.K. firm*	8.3	1,400	108	7.7	60.0	2,309	780	33.7
(b) non-U.K. firm	15.5	998	79	7.9	2.2	4,583	65	1.4
IV Non-Metallic Mineral								
(a) U.K. firm	11.2	26,572	1,081	4.1	12.7	25,599	1,352	5.3
(b) non-U.K. firm	35.2	20,461	3,151	15.4	48.1	25,071	4,279	17.1
V Metal Manufacturing								
(a) U.K. firm	30.9	6,542	621	9.5	33.9	7,039	832	11.8
(b) non-U.K. firm*	13.6	4,071	207	5.1	26.5	5,701	743	13.0

*1969 data used instead of 1968

Source: Data calculated from The Stock Exchange of Malaysia and Singapore, *Company Reports*, Vol. VII, 1973.

Notes: (1) Gross Earnings is the percentage of earnings before taxation over paid-up capital.

(2) Capital Employed is the sum total of fixed and current assets less current liabilities and sundry provisions as shown in the company accounts at year end.

(3) Profit Post-tax is the net operating profit after deduction of company tax.

(4) Column *4* gives the rates of return on capital employed.

Table 8.7 shows the comparative profitability of selected firms in selected industries in 1968 and 1971.

Table 8.7 shows that in the food, electrical engineering, and non-metallic mineral industries U.K. firms were less profitable in 1968 compared to their competitors. Returns on capital employed in British food manufacturing and electrical engineering firms were marginally less than returns on capital employed by their competitors. In the case of non-metallic mineral industry, the profitability of the non-British firm was almost four times that of the British firm.

The later part of the 1960s represented the 'learning period' for many British firms, and as they assumed normal trading positions over the period they improved their profitability rapidly. Hence, the profitability of the firms improved remarkably in the period 1968–71. Except for the firms in the non-metallic mineral and metal manufacturing industries between 1968 and 1971, British firms achieved rates of return substantially higher than their respective competitors. There is also some evidence seeming to show that British manufacturing firms in general earn higher profits than similar non-British firms in the same industries. The evidence, afforded by many firms encountered in the study, supports the view that British firms rapidly gained efficiency, and earned more than their competitors once they assumed normal trading positions.

RETURNS ON CAPITAL AT HOME AND ABROAD

As Tables 8.3A and 8.3B, 8.4, and 8.5 had indicated average returns on U.K. capital in Malaysia during the periods 1955–64, 1960–5 and 1963–71 were respectively 19.8 per cent, 15.9 per cent, and 15.6 per cent. Table 8.3B shows that the average post-tax profitability rates of U.K. companies in various industrial groups in Malaysia were higher than those of U.K. companies in all other countries. Table 8.8 shows that the average returns of selected individual companies in the country in the period 1969–71 were also generally higher than those of the same companies in their world-wide operations as recorded in their consolidated accounts in the U.K. It was not strictly possible to make direct comparisons between returns to capital of these companies in their Malaysian and U.K. operations due to the unavailability of data; but from the information supplied by company representatives it can be said that on the whole, from 1969 to 1971, individual companies

TABLE 8.8

PRE-TAX PROFITS AS RETURNS ON CAPITAL EMPLOYED BY TEN SELECTED BRITISH INDUSTRIAL COMPANIES, 1969–1971

(per cent)

Name of Company	1969		1970		1971		Average 1969/71	
	U.K.	Malaysia	U.K.	Malaysia	U.K.	Malaysia	U.K.	Malaysia
British-American Tobacco	26.3	31.6	23.3	30.4	25.1	28.4	24.9	30.1
A. Guinness, Son & Co.	20.6	22.1	26.3	25.4	27.2	30.0	24.7	25.8
Dunlop Industries	14.5	17.9	13.4	26.4	12.9	29.3	13.6	24.5
Metal Box	16.8	20.9	17.2	28.4	17.1	22.6	17.0	24.0
Inchcape	11.0	18.6	15.0	30.0	14.0	19.6	13.3	22.7
General Electric Co.	19.2	7.7	11.8	21.1	13.2	38.1	14.7	22.3
Shell	19.7	20.7	18.9	22.3	18.2	18.8	18.9	20.6
B.I.C.C.	13.9	10.2	13.9	5.9	14.9	21.9	14.2	12.7
ICI	13.1	12.3	14.1	17.6	11.8	14.3	13.0	14.7
Assoc. Portland Cement	13.6	13.6	11.3	8.2	9.9	11.9	11.6	11.2
Arithmetic Average (unweighted)	16.9	17.6	16.5	21.6	16.4	23.5	16.6	20.9

Sources: U.K. figures derived from *The Times 1000 Leading Companies in Britain and Overseas*, 1970–1 and 1971–2; Malaysian figures derived from The Stock Exchange of Malaysia and Singapore, *Company Reports*, Vol. VII, 1973.

Notes: (i) 'Shell' refers to Shell Transport and Trading Co. in U.K. and Shell Refining Co. Bhd. in Malaysia.

(ii) Figures for ICI (U.K.) for 1968 and 1970 included those of Imperial Metal Industries.

(iii) Pre-tax profits refer to net operating profits before taxation. Capital employed is the sum total of fixed and current assets less current liabilities and sundry provisions.

(iv) Returns from U.K. operations refer to the global operations including all overseas affiliates—accounting for an estimated one-quarter of the reported incomes in the years selected.

(v) For full names of the selected companies, see sources.

achieved higher returns to capital in their Malaysian subsidiaries than in their U.K. operations.

In a comparison of average rates of return on U.K. capital[27] invested at home and abroad in the period 1960 to 1964, Dunning found that the ratio of net income after tax to net assets in overseas enterprises was 8 per cent while that in home enterprises was 7.5 per cent.[28] The average U.K. direct investments in overseas enterprises from 1960 to 1965 brought a return of 9 per cent in the developing and 7.1 per cent in the developed countries.[29] On this basis, the rate of return of U.K. capital in the developing countries was 20 per cent higher than that in the developed countries. Dunning's study clearly shows that British capital overseas earned more than capital at home.

In Table 8.8 ten firms from different industrial sectors and with widely differing products are compared. These firms were selected on the basis that they were operating under normal trading situations in the U.K. and in Malaysia for the period chosen. The years were selected with a view to eliminate, or at least minimize, the inflationary effects on reported profits of tax benefits and other government concessions. The result of the exercise (Table 8.8) shows that from 1969 to 1971 the average return on capital for the ten selected companies was 16.6 per cent in the U.K. and 20.9 per cent in Malaysia. The rates of return shown in the Table refer to pre-tax profits. Since company and withholding taxes are higher in Britain than in Malaysia (see Table 8.6), the returns on investors' funds are much higher in Malaysia than in the U.K. The evidence suggests that British companies enjoy higher rates of return in Malaysia than in the U.K.[30]

WHAT ACCOUNTS FOR HIGH PROFITS IN MALAYSIA?

None of the firms surveyed in the course of this study made any continuous losses during the 1960 to 1971 period. With very rare exceptions, newly established firms have been observed to make profits commencing from either the second or third year of commercial production. In many instances the losses recorded in the first or second year were not strictly operating losses but those occasioned by charging company formation expenses to the profit and loss accounts.

We have seen that most U.K. firms in Malaysia earn higher rates of profit compared either (Table 8.7) to their competitors in the country, or (Table 8.3A) to their parent companies in the U.K. The pertinent question to be raised is: what accounts for the high profitability of British firms in Malaysia? Without freer access to data on costs of inputs and prices of outputs one can do no more than indicate broadly the probable reasons for the relatively higher returns of British companies in Malaysia.

One explanation is that U.K. firms are generally favourably placed for obtaining credit and finance in Malaysia. As mentioned in Chapter 5, most U.K. manufacturing firms owe their origins to the long-established agency houses and/or the reputation of established and world-wide brands of products. Furthermore, having London-based parent companies means that many U.K. manufacturing firms possess tremendous commercial goodwill that ensures their credit-worthiness in Malaysia. The close associations of many directors of U.K. firms with local banks and with politically influential citizens means that U.K. firms are placed in advantageous positions when they need to raise funds.[31] Very few indigenous firms or other foreign firms enjoy the same privileges as U.K. firms in the country.[32]

U.K. firms have been known to obtain easy and cheap credit with a minimum offer of security and sometimes with none. As far as the banks in Malaysia are concerned, their best assurance of repayment of a loan lies in the borrower's proven ability 'to conduct his affairs profitably so that income is produced from which the interest and principal payments can be met'.[33] Companies of long standing, such as the established British concerns with a sustained record of good management and profitable operations, are usually able to obtain credit facilities 'without the posting of any tangible security'.[34]

In general, financial institutions in the country prefer to lend funds to the foreign companies who are generally thought to be better able than local concerns to repay their borrowings. The risk of default is believed to be greater in indigenous than foreign concerns. Consequently, domestic firms found it much more difficult to raise loans than the foreign firms.[35] Since the creation of the Asia-Dollar Market in Singapore in 1968, foreign firms in the country can raise additional funds from the market. Besides, the highly profitable nature of most British firms in the country meant that they are able to generate funds required for expansion internally.

Between mid-1961 and mid-1970 the average minimum bank lending rate to the manufacturing sector in Malaysia was 5.05 per cent,[36] as opposed to the average U.K. rate of 7.47 per cent between the end of 1960 and mid-1969.[37] It was certainly cheaper for the U.K. affiliates in Malaysia to raise funds there than for their parent companies to raise loans in the U.K. where, during the 1960s, the bank rate rose steadily as a result of attempts by the monetary authorities to support the pound and reduce the balance of payments deficit.[38]

The profits of firms are also influenced by their cost structures. While there are no comprehensive data on the cost structures of individual firms the aggregate data from the 1968 Census of Manufacturing Industries, as shown in Table 8.9 below, indicate that British firms had lower costs in relation to their sales.

The cost structures vary significantly between industries and between firms in the same industry. Nonetheless the aggregate census data show how the high profitability in British firms came about. Whereas the proportion of costs of materials and labour for Singaporean, Malaysian, and all firms covered by the census amounted to over 83 per cent of sales, they constituted only about 77.6 per cent for British firms. Consequently gross profits of British firms were higher in comparison to the gross profits of other firms in the manufacturing sector.

Costs of land and labour per unit of output in U.K. are higher relative to those in Malaysia. The estimated cost of land and industrial facilities for firms surveyed averaged between one-tenth and

TABLE 8.9

COSTS AND SALES IN BRITISH, SINGAPOREAN, AND MALAYSIAN MANUFACTURING FIRMS, 1968

	Costs		*Gross*	*Gross*
	Non-labour	*Labour*	*Profit*	*Sales*
British firms $'000	416,500	37,291	130,850	584,641
(%)	(71.2)	(6.4)	(22.4)	(100)
Singaporean firms $'000	329,648	37,379	70,758	437,785
(%)	(75.3)	(8.5)	(16.2)	(100)
Malaysian firms $'000	1,233,347	162,300	233,516	1,629,163
(%)	(75.7)	(10)	(14.3)	(100)
All firms covered by the census $'000	2,294,297	266,957	517,269	3,078,523
(%)	(74.5)	(8.7)	(16.8)	(100)

Source: Data derived from *Census of Manufacturing Industries, 1968*, p. 38.

Notes: (i) Gross profit is profit before taxation and depreciation charges.
(ii) 'All firms covered by the census' includes all foreign and indigenous firms.

one-eighth of what these would cost had the companies set up similar production facilities in the U.K. As for labour costs, the differentials for comparable grades of labour and per unit of output costs of labour in U.K. and Malaysia cannot be indicated precisely because comprehensive data are not available. What we can do is to compare approximately average hourly wages for manufacturing workers[39] in the two countries using information derived from interviews and published United Nations data. Our results, tabulated below in Table 8.10, indicate that industrial wage rates in Malaysia in 1960 and 1969 were respectively about one-third and one-quarter those of the U.K. An important point to note is that whereas wage rates grew at 1.2 per cent in Malaysia for the period under consideration, the growth rate for wages in the U.K. was 6.39 per cent.

Without more refined data, all that is suggested at this stage, using available information on cost structures, is that low production costs of British firms in Malaysia in relation to their gross sales have contributed to U.K. firms' profits being higher than those of other firms in the country.

It is possible that the high earnings of British manufacturing companies in Malaysia have been positively aided by benefits of tax exemption and protection offered by the government under its

TABLE 8.10

COMPARATIVE AVERAGE EARNINGS PER HOUR IN THE MANUFACTURING SECTOR IN MALAYSIA AND U.K., 1960 AND 1969

Country	*Amount in National Currency*		*Amount in US$ Equivalent*		*Average Increase (p.a.) 1960–9*
	1960	*1969*	*1960*	*1969*	(%)
Malaysia	$0.86	$0.96	0.281	0.331	1.2
U.K.	32p	55.36p	0.95	1.841	6.39
Earnings in Malaysia as percentage of those in the U.K.			29.6	24.7	

Source: International Labour Office, *Year Book of Labour Statistics*, 1970.

Notes: 1. Earnings relate to average earnings of wage earners in manufacturing industries. Earnings include bonuses, cost of living allowances, taxes, social insurance contributions payable by the employed person and, in some cases, payments in kind, but excluding social insurance contributions payable by the employers, family allowances and other social security benefits.

2. Amounts in US$ calculated at the average exchange rates prevailing for the respective years, adjusted for cost of living variations to render the figures, as far as possible, comparable.

3. Amounts calculated on the basis of an eight-hour day.

investment incentive scheme. There is evidence in some developing countries to show that high profits in industries were the result of high tariff protection which created monopoly positions for manufacturers in the domestic economy.[40] Little, *et al.*, argued that high monopoly profits resulting from protection against outside competition are usually detrimental to long-run efficiency[41] since they often lead to the establishment of too many firms, each with too small a capacity for low-cost operations and too small a share of the market to utilize even this capacity fully.

While we lack unquestionable evidence on the direct relationship of protection and the monopoly positions of British companies in Malaysia,[42] the industrial structure of British capital mentioned earlier[43] does show that British manufacturing concerns in the country occupy monopolistic positions, further reinforced by the tendency of these firms to advertise more widely than other firms,[44] while the capital intensity of British companies, noted in Chapter 5, constitutes a barrier to entry into the market by other firms. These factors, among others, have been looked to for an explanation of variations in industrial profits.[45]

Other factors accounting for high profits are the quality of managers employed in the U.K. subsidiaries and the absence of labour problems affecting production. Companies interviewed claimed that their executives were well qualified and experienced. It is common practice for senior personnel to be head-office appointments and trained in the U.K. by the parent companies. Since promotion and remuneration of these people are related to the subsidiary company earnings there is motivation to attain the highest standards of performance. While little is known about the quality and performance of the managers in the other manufacturing companies in Malaysia, managers in U.K. companies seem to be hired on the basis of their qualifications and competence in their jobs. Inconclusive evidence encountered also suggests that managers in U.K. companies are better paid than those in most non-British companies.

Since labour is not highly unionized, the firing and hiring of workers normally do not lead to disruptive stoppages of work. In view of the high level of unemployment in Malaysia the labour force is willing to work very hard with few complaints because they regard it as a privilege to work in British companies where the pay is slightly higher than in other companies. Besides, the payment of bonuses in many British firms also motivates labour to work effectively.

Compared to their competitors, British companies in Malaysia have longer experience in manufacturing and a bigger share of the market. Their established brand names obviously give them an advantage over new-comers with comparatively unknown and untested products. These factors may also have positively influenced profits. Besides, as suggested by the executives, companies expanding overseas were generally more dynamic than those which do not. It is expected that dynamic companies would be more profitable. Furthermore, U.K. firms claimed that in their Malaysian subsidiaries they used sophisticated management techniques, better technical knowledge, greater financial resources, and more established marketing channels than their competitors. The U.K. firms believed they were more efficient than their competitors in general. It is impossible to test these claims satisfactorily, but some indicators of the efficiency of the firms are briefly examined below.

THE PERFORMANCE AND EFFICIENCY OF BRITISH COMPANIES

There is no generally accepted definition of business performance. To the production engineer it can mean one thing, to the investment analyst, marketing director, or industrial economist, quite another; and in the last resort business performance is a relative concept which cannot be assessed except in the light of particular aims, needs, and potentials.[46] The use of the profit/net capital ratios (*P/NA*) in comparing earnings of overseas investments, does not accurately reflect the differences in the efficiency of resource usage of the companies in question. In fact, the employment of the *P/NA* ratio as a measure of business performance raises serious economic objections, since *inter alia* the *P/NA* ratio takes no account of the opportunity cost of capital, and insufficiently allows for differences in capital-output ratios and degrees of monopoly power. To the economist, the efficiency of a firm is best measured in terms of output per unit of input employed. Input employed represents the cost of using resources in one way rather than another, and must therefore be valued in opportunity cost terms.

Unfortunately no time series data are available on output/input ratios for British and other firms, although the *Census of Manufacturing Industries, 1968* provides some data on costs of inputs of some industries for a single year. Using the census data and the performance indicators discussed below, some idea may be formed about firms' productivity.

The following indicators have been used to describe the various aspects of industry performance.[47]

1. *Output Per Unit of Expenditure on Labour and Capital* (*O/LK*): Instead of measuring the productivity of each input separately, it is possible to use a 'total factor index' which measures the output per unit of expenditure on both capital and labour together. An index of this kind, suggested by Professor Dunning,[48] is $O/(WL + rk)$, where W is the average wage rate, r is the opportunity cost of capital, and the denominator $(WL + rk)$ is the total expenditure on labour and capital. The index suggested by Dunning measures the 'overall efficiency' of the industry, instead of relating it to only one scarce factor.

In the actual calculations, the results of which are presented in Table 8.11, output is taken to be the value added; WL is total expenditure on wages and salaries in industry; r is taken to be 8 per cent, the approximate cost of capital to the industrial sector.

2. *Output Per Unit of Labour* (*O/L*): This indicator (*2*) measures the contribution of labour to the production process, and is therefore a measure of labour productivity.

3. *Output Per Unit of Capital* (*O/K*): Finally indicator (*3*) indicates the productivity of the net assets of the companies in the various industry groups. It was not possible to use all these indicators on an individual company basis, owing to lack of necessary data. In calculating the performance indicators it is assumed that there was perfect mobility of labour and that capital was raised locally and was equally accessible to all firms.

The performance indicators tabulated in Table 8.11 allowed an analysis of the comparative performance of British and non-British firms in industry to be made in general terms. On the basis of indicator (*1*) shown in the Table, it can be said that British firms in Malaysia were more productive than non-British firms. When the aggregate output for all industry and unit expenditure on labour and capital were used to compare firms in industry, British firms seemed to be 86 per cent more productive than non-British firms. In certain industrial groups, e.g. in the manufacture of tobacco and rubber products, British companies appeared to be over 100 per cent more productive than other companies; but in the manufacture of beverages and machinery, the performance of British firms was only marginally better.

In terms of performances measured by output per unit of labour, i.e. indicator (*2*) in Table 8.11, British companies were generally better than other companies. This was expected since, as

TABLE 8.11

INDICATORS OF THE PERFORMANCE OF INDUSTRIAL COMPANIES IN MALAYSIA, 1968
(per cent)

Description of Industry Group	*Indicator (1): (O/LK)*		*Indicator (2): (O/L)*		*Indicator (3): (O/K)*	
	British	*Non-British*	*British*	*Non-British*	*British*	*Non-British*
Food manufacturing	191	100	278	100	98	100
Beverage manufacturing	109	100	209	100	64	100
Tobacco manufacturing	236	100	379	100	210	100
Rubber products	263	100	350	100	134	100
Chemical and chemical products	148	100	353	100	123	100
Machinery (non-electrical)	102	100	100	100	116	100
Electrical engineering	114	100	125	100	80	100
All manufacturing industry	186	100	274	100	97	100

Source: Calculated from data based on the *Census of Manufacturing Industries, 1968*, and information derived from interviews.

Notes: In (*O*/*LK*), *O* is Value Added, and *LK* is the 'total factor index'. As explained in the text, in the actual calculations the index suggested by Professor Dunning was used. Indicator (*1*) measures the output per unit of expenditure on labour and capital.

Indicator (*2*) measures output (*O*) per unit of labour (*L*), a unit of labour being the average income received by a full-time paid industrial employee according to the census.

Indicator (*3*) is a measure of output (*O*) per unit of net fixed assets (*K*), a unit of fixed assets being the average amount of fixed assets of the companies in each group of industry. Industrial fixed assets are defined as all goods that have a normal economic life of more than one year. The values shown refer to year-end values according to the books of accounts. Amounts include additions during the year, net of depreciations.

shown earlier, capital per employee was greater in the British concerns.

On the basis of indicators (*1*) and (*2*), British firms as a whole can be said to be more efficient than non-British firms. However, according to indicator (*3*) British industrial capital did not perform as well as industrial capital of non-British concerns. This tendency partly reflected the excess capacity in U.K. companies, and partly the fact that in 1968, the year the census data were collected, many capital-intensive British firms were newly established and had still to assume normal production and trading positions.

One has to be very cautious about reading too much into the performance indicators presented in the Table, given the issues surrounding the concept of performance and the imperfections inherent in the aggregate data used. There are a number of objections to the use of aggregate data and global ratios such as those used in Table 8.11 in interpreting company efficiency. The indicators do not tell anything about the performance of the individual firms. The performance of firms is affected by several other factors, such as the industrial mix, scale economies, and technical efficiency of resource usage. Without adequate data it is impossible to isolate the factors that affect the performance of British companies in Malaysia. One can only make general comments linking the productivity characteristics of U.K. firms and their distribution in the Malaysian economy.

It was seen in Chapters 6 and 7 that U.K. companies were concentrated in the group of firms that were research- and capital-intensive. The group distribution was such that the majority of U.K. firms were concentrated in those areas with high growth rates in the 1960s. It was suggested that many British firms were monopolistically positioned in the economy; in terms of sales and assets per industrial establishment, British firms were considerably larger than the average Malaysian firm.[49] It is possible to argue that the comparatively high performance of the British may be attributable to a combination of industrial distribution, technology, competitive structure, and capital intensity effects. No less significant was the ease with which they can acquire finance.[50] Equally important was the quality of the managers they employ.[51] In sum the British companies had great advantages *vis-à-vis* other firms in the country; advantages in terms of finance, production, and marketing. These advantages, among other factors, helped to account for the good performance of British industrial companies and their high profitability compared to other firms in the Malaysian industrial sector.

PROFIT APPROPRIATION AND INTERNAL FINANCE

Profits after payment of taxes provide companies with funds for dividends and reinvestment. How these funds are allocated between dividends and reinvestment depends on the policies of the companies concerning the use of their earnings. Two broad policies evident among the companies studies are (a) a dividend-oriented policy, and (b) an investment-oriented policy. In companies with a dividend-oriented policy, the payment of dividends takes precedence over the investment needs of the companies. In many cases this would imply a sustained policy of appropriating a certain portion of their earnings each year, and in the event of fluctuating earnings the payment of dividends is supplemented by payments out of reserves. Such a dividend-oriented policy entails large annual transfers of funds from Malaysia to the U.K.[52] since, as was noted in Chapter 6, the shareholders of these companies are residents of the U.K. (see Table 6.2).

Companies with investment-oriented policies consider the investment needs of their affiliates as demanding the first call on their earnings with the residual paid out as dividends. This policy seems to be widely adopted by companies when their affiliates experience normal trading conditions, usually after four years or so from the time they set up production facilities abroad. Wholly-owned subsidiaries regard reinvestment of their earnings as of paramount importance since the U.K. parent firms expect their overseas operations to be self-financing. The limited reinvestment opportunities due to market limitations meant that many companies reinvest their earnings in the country in activities that were unrelated to their original investment: i.e., the companies diversify their investments into other activities which the local management in Malaysia consider feasible. In several cases, as stated before, the larger companies have used their Malaysian-generated funds to set up affiliates of their Malaysian concerns in other parts of South-East Asia.[53]

In practice, most companies pursue both dividend- and investment-oriented policies. Part of their earnings would be paid as dividends to the parent companies and the various shareholders, with the remainder either retained for ploughing back into their businesses or invested in another field considered suitable. The evidence collected suggests that companies do not follow any rigid approach in their dividend and investment policies. The broad pattern seems to be that companies adopt a dividend policy in the earlier years of their operations, and a more investment-oriented policy when the need for capital for reinvestment is more strongly felt. This situation may be explained by the fact that companies associate greater risks with their overseas investments in the initial period—the 'learning period'—than when their affiliates are more established.

In the earlier periods of operation, dividend payments are looked upon as rewards that satisfy shareholders and reassure the parent firms of the viability of their investments. It was also evident that a number of parent companies wished to recoup their capital outlay as quickly as possible. In cases where the Malaysian affiliates were enjoying tax concessions it seemed sensible for them to recoup capital outlay through the dividend-oriented policy. Whenever there were minority Malaysian shareholders in the affiliates the policy was directed towards paying dividends designed to impress these shareholders.

Companies tended to move from a dividend-oriented policy towards a more investment-oriented policy when the initial capital outlays had been recouped. The pattern of dividend payments varied from company to company and from year to year within the same company. Between 1967 and 1971 four general patterns were noticeable. Firstly, some companies (e.g. Boustead, Rothmans, Shell, and Metal Box) paid out annually a constant proportion[54] of their profits as dividends. Secondly, some companies with fluctuating levels of profits in the period 1967 to 1971 (e.g. Jardine Waugh and Malayan Cables) seemed to have paid a decreasing proportion of their profits as dividends. Thirdly, a number of well-established firms (e.g. Dunlop, Guinness, Inchcape, and Malayan Tobacco) paid out an increasing proportion of their profits as dividends.[55] Finally, some companies had no consistent pattern of dividend payments.[56]

As indicated in Table 8.12, the dividends that British companies paid during the period 1967 to 1971 ranged from 6 per cent to more than 65 per cent on their issued and fully-paid share capital. Over one-half of the companies paid between 14 and 24 per cent annual dividends from 1967 to 1971. Occasionally, a number of companies paid over 40 per cent dividends, and there were instances when a company paid 70 per cent dividends on its paid-up ordinary share capital.

The pay-out ratio, i.e. the proportion of after-tax profit paid out as dividends, for most companies varied from year to year; and from 1967 to 1971 the dividends paid represented amounts ranging from 50 to 70 per cent of the after-tax profits of the

TABLE 8.12

PAYMENT OF DIVIDENDS BY THIRTY-FOUR SELECTED COMPANIES, 1967–1971

Dividends Paid (% of share capital issued and paid-up)	*1967*	*1968*	*1969*	*1970*	*1971*
Over 65%	1	0	0	0	1
45 – 64%	0	19	1	1	0
25 – 44%	5	6	6	9	10
14 – 24%	16	18	18	18	18
10 – 13%	8	6	5	3	3
Below 10%	4	3	4	3	2

Source: Company Reports and interviews.

companies surveyed. Clearly, dividend payments absorbed a large proportion of, and were sensitive to changes in, earnings of the companies. Although there were instances when firms supplemented the payment of dividends from reserves, the long-term plan of the majority of companies was to maintain a consistent pattern of dividends.

As noted earlier (see Chapter 5, p. 130) British companies provided considerable funds for their operations from internal finance. By internal finance is meant that reinvestment or ploughing back of company-generated funds or cash flow–i.e., net profit after tax and provisions for depreciation. In the period 1963 to 1970, cash flow accounted for between 30 and 90 per cent of the total sources of funds of the companies; and in the period 1967 to 1971 this source of funds provided companies with between one-half to two-thirds of all funds they used.

As indicated in Table 8.13, funds arising from provision for depreciation were substantially larger than retained earnings. This was a result of some companies enjoying the benefits of accelerated depreciation permitted under certain conditions provided by the *Investment Incentives Act, 1968.* In the five years preceding 1971 provisions for depreciation constituted almost 70 per cent of the internal finance of a selected thirty-four companies in a wide variety of industrial groups. Retained earnings of these companies, according to Table 8.13, made up a little over 30 per cent of total internal finance.

Internal finance made up 65 per cent of companies' net investment. If the internally-generated funds were to finance investment

TABLE 8.13

INTERNAL FINANCE ACCORDING TO THE ESTIMATES OF THIRTY-FOUR SELECTED COMPANIES, 1967–1971

	$'000	(%)
Internal Finance	684,868	(100)
of which		
Retained earnings	208,884	(30.5)
Provision for depreciation	475,984	(69.5)
Net Investment	1,053,643	(100)
of which		
Fixed assets	790,232	(75)
Net working capital	263,411	(25)
Internal Finance as percentage of Net Investment		(65)
Internal Finance as percentage of Investment in Fixed Assets		(87)

Source: Sources of data as in Table 8.12.

Notes: (i) Net Investment is the sum of net fixed assets and net working capital defined as current assets less current liabilities.

(ii) Fixed Assets include investments in unconsolidated subsidiaries and trade investments net of accumulated depreciation.

in fixed assets they would have paid for about 87 per cent of the fixed assets.

Taking reported profits at their face value, British firms in Malaysia have achieved impressive records. The ability of British industrial firms to generate substantial amounts of internal finance enhanced their credit ratings in the eyes of the financial institutions in the country. Their good credit ratings undoubtedly made it easy for them to raise additional funds from the financial sector when necessary. In terms of profitability the British manufacturing firms have succeeded in attaining their goals. In terms of their net contribution to the economy the private profitability is an inadequate measure. Subsequent chapters will examine the performance of the firms more fully within the wider context of the Malaysian economy.

1. In the Accountants International Study Group, *Reporting by Diversified Companies: Current Recommended Practice in Canada, The United Kingdom and the United States*, Birmingham, Hopkins and Bailey Limited, 1972, it was recommended that such financial statements should include information on the companies' separate business activities.

2. How stock valuation affects profitability considerably is illustrated by the famous Pergamon Press case where two large public accounting firms valued Pergamon

Press Ltd.'s stock and work-in-progress differently, resulting in turning the company's reported profits of about £2 million into a loss of about £2 million. This case was discussed in one of the papers presented at the Summer Course, Churchill College, Cambridge, 1970, of the Institute of Chartered Accountants in England and Wales. See *What is Profit? Six View Points* [*sic*], Institute of Chartered Accountants, 1970, pp. 47–51, and also the article of the Pergamon Press case in the *Sunday Times*, 30 August 1970.

3. The determination and implications of intra-firm pricing in the context of overseas investments are discussed fully in S. Lall, 'Transfer Pricing by Multinational Manufacturing Firms', *Bulletin of the Oxford University Institute of Economics and Statistics, Oxford*, Vol. 35, No. 3, August 1973, pp. 173–95.

4. See for instance C. L. Nelson, 'An Accountant's View of Profit Measurement', in H. W. Stevenson and J. R. Nelson, eds., *Profit in the Modern Economy: Selected Papers from a Conference on Understanding Profits*, Minneapolis, Minnesota University Press, 1967, pp. 73–81.

5. See M. J. Gordon, 'An Economist's View of Profit Measurement', in Stevenson and Nelson, eds., op. cit., pp. 63–72, and the reference quoted therein.

6. On the relative merits of economic and accounting concepts of profits see D. Solomons, 'Economic and Accounting Concepts of Income', *Accounting Review*, Vol. 36, No. 3, July 1961, pp. 374–83.

7. See the Institute of Chartered Accountants in England and Wales, Summer Course, 1970, *What is Profit? Six View Points* [*sic*], op. cit.

8. In the discussion that follows all dollar values used are taken from unadjusted company accounts, and no allowance has been made for differences in depreciation procedures, or capital revaluation in the calculation.

9. Many writers have argued that businessmen may sacrifice income for the sake of more leisure; may be more interested in their own salaries, bonuses, etc., than in the profits of the firms *per se*; or may be striving for security, status, power, prestige, and other values in a manner that is inconsistent with attainment of maximum profit.

Among writers who questioned the empirical correctness of the time-honoured profit maximization hypothesis are: R. M. Cyert and J. G. March, *A Behavioral Theory of the Firm*, Englewood Cliffs, Prentice-Hall, 1963; J. Williamson, 'Profit, Growth and Sales Maximisation', *Economica*, February 1966; F. Machlup, 'Theories of The Firm: Marginalist, Behavioral, Managerial', *American Economic Review*, March 1967; and W. J. Baumol, *Business Behaviour, Value and Growth*, New York, Harcourt Brace (rev. ed.), 1967. The profit maximization assumption is succinctly discussed in D. Needham, *Economic Analysis and Industrial Structure*, Holt, Rinehart and Winston Inc., 1969, pp. 2–12.

In defence of the assumption, see B. D. Mabry and D. L. Siders, 'An Empirical Test of the Sales Maximisation Hypothesis', *Southern Economic Journal*, January 1967, pp. 367–77.

10. Cyert and March, op. cit.

11. The information is based on the field work. Quotations are edited versions of conversation with interviewees; no alterations have been made to the sense of the spoken sentences.

12. The Malaysian government is suspicious of companies that try to recoup all their capital outlay in one year and expect an annual rate of return of 30 to 40 per cent as well. This point was commented upon by a special adviser to the Prime Minister in a special issue of ESSO, *Eastern Review*, July–August 1971.

13. Baumol, op. cit., pp. 45–6. See empirical test of Baumol's hypothesis by Mabry and Siders, op. cit., pp. 367–77.

14. J. W. McGuire, J. S. Y. Chin, and A. O. Elbing, 'Executive Incomes, Sales and Profits', *American Economic Review*, Vol. 111, September 1962.

15. In the long run, an increase in sales is a good proxy for an increase in profits. See Mabry and Siders, op. cit.

16. In the 1960s Malaysia did not have highly developed financial institutions outside the commercial banks which were the main source of finance for various economic activities in the country. Banks charge different rates on their loans and advances to the

various sectors of the economy. See details in Bank Negara, 'Interest Rates in the Malaysian Economy', *Quarterly Economic Bulletin*, Vol. 3 (3), September 1970.

17. ibid., p. 133.

18. W. B. Reddaway, *et al.*, *Effects of U.K. Direct Investment Overseas* (Final Report) (1968), p. 216.

19. J. H. Dunning, 'U.S. Subsidiaries in Britain and Other U.K. Competitors', *Business Ratios*, Dan and Bradstreet Ltd., Vol. 1, Autumn 1966, p. 6.

20. J. H. Dunning, *Studies in International Investment*, George Allen and Unwin Ltd., 1970, Chapter 2, Tables 2 and 4.

21. This is based on information gathered from the Economics and Statistics Division of the Department of Trade and Industry, confirmed by a number of informants during field work. Very few companies were willing to disclose the exact amount of management fees they derived from their operations in Malaysia.

22. The majority of U.K. manufacturing affiliates have technical agreements with the parent companies. In the research-intensive industries firms are known to have included research fees to the parent companies in their pre-production expenses in the year of establishment. In the words of a company executive, on balance, the affiliates of U.K. companies in Malaysia over the years have contributed their 'fair' share of the parents' costs of R & D, given the output and size of the establishments in Malaysia.

23. Information supplied by the Department of Trade and Industry, Economics and Statistics Division.

24. By standards prevailing in many underdeveloped countries tariff protection in Malaysia in the 1960s was modest, as will be seen in Chapter 9.

25. The Malaysian dollar is freely convertible to any world currency; see pp. 36 and 214, above.

26. In 1966, £1 was worth $8.50. In March 1973, £1 was only equivalent to $6.30, while in March 1974 the pound was exchangeable for only $5.40. The pound has fallen in value *vis-à-vis* the Malaysian dollar by 36.5 per cent in a period of eight years.

27. Excluding investments in oil, banking, and insurance.

28. J. H. Dunning, *Studies in International Investment*, p. 85.

29. Loc. cit., p. 57.

30. In terms of growth of output and sales, according to the companies consulted, the companies achieved higher rates in Malaysia than in the U.K. in the five years preceding 1972. According to the *Management Today's* 'City Growth League' three companies with substantial operations in Malaysia ranked among the top eight. See details in *Management Today*, August 1973, p. 85.

31. As indicated earlier, many companies are connected with financial institutions by virtue of the interlocking directorates of these institutions and the industrial companies in the country.

32. There is a certain degree of 'dualism' in the financial market in that British and local concerns are faced with different sets of market rates and opportunities for borrowing funds. For an elaborate discussion on this issue see H. Myint, 'Dualism and The Internal Integration of The Underdeveloped Economies', *Banca Nazionale de Lavoro*, June 1970.

33. Bank Negara Malaysia, *Quarterly Economic Bulletin*, September 1970, p. 121.

34. ibid.

35. This is based on information gathered from interviews with Malaysian businessmen. Large domestic firms which have interlocking directorates with financial institutions in the country tend to have the same borrowing advantage as the foreign firms with similar position, except that the foreign companies tend to have better management than the local firms in general: and that the foreign industrial companies are connected not only with foreign banks operating in the country but also with locally-owned banks. The small domestic industrial companies have borrowing disadvantages; not many of them have interlocking directorates with banks, and very few of them can provide tangible collateral securities for their borrowings. Consequently, they do not obtain any preferential treatment from the lending institutions, and cases have been known where the local small firms borrow funds at rates higher than those offered to the large foreign companies.

36. See details of the interest rate structure in Bank Negara, *Quarterly Economic Bulletin*, September 1970, pp. 124–42.

37. See Schweizerische Bankgesellschaft, *An International Survey of Interest Rates, Patterns and Differentials*, Zurich, 1970, pp. 20–3.

38. The economic and balance of payment problem of the U.K. prompted the Bank of England to institute frequent changes in its interest policy during the 1960s. From the beginning of 1960 to mid-1969 it repegged the discount rate no less than twenty-four times. The 1960s were characterized by a rising average interest rate of up to 7.89 per cent in 1969 thus making the U.K. rates by far the highest compared with those prevailing in Switzerland, Belgium, France, Germany, Italy, the Netherlands, Spain, the United States, and Japan in the same period. See details in *An International Survey of Interest Rates*, and also Schweizerische Bankgesellschaft, *Interest Rates and Interest Structure: An International Comparison of Interest Rates Based on Interest Indicators*, Zurich, January 1969.

39. Low wages *per se* do not necessarily mean low labour cost to industry; but on the basis of information provided by company executives, labour cost per unit of output in British industrial concerns in the 1960s was lower in Malaysia than in the U.K.

40. See I. Little, T. Scitovsky, and M. Scott, *Industry and Trade in Some Developing Countries: A Comparative Study* (OECD), Oxford University Press, 1970.

41. ibid., p. 98. High profits result from protection against outside competition, which creates a monopoly position for domestic manufacturers. While these high profits often encourage domestic competition, deliberately promoted also by government, this is usually not of a kind to favour efficiency. In the findings of Little, *et al.*, high profits in manufacturing secured by import restriction, whether or not they are curbed or eliminated by domestic competition, encourage high costs of production and the wasteful use of capital—one of whose most striking and most tangible manifestations is the under-utilization of productive capacity.

42. Protection cannot solely account for the monopolistic positions of British industry in Malaysia, considering that British industry started there during the period when protection was either low or non-existent. Throughout the period of the study (1963–71) as will be seen in Chapter 9, protection in Malaysia was low in comparison to the level of protection in other countries (Table 10.14).

43. See pp. 12–13, p. 92 et seq., and p. 135 et seq.; British companies were in control of one-third or more of the shares of their respective markets in the country in the 1960s.

44. Based on data in *Census of Manufacturing Industries, 1968*, and field work information.

45. In the developed countries, according to empirical investigations, profit rates increase with concentration of the market in few firms and barriers to entry into the market. See for example, P. Asch, *Economic Theory and the Antitrust Dilemma*, New York, Wiley, 1970; and S. E. Holtermann, 'Market Structure and Economic Performance in U.K. Manufacturing Industries', *Journal of Industrial Economics*, Vol. 22 (2), December 1973.

46. See Dunning, 'U.S. Subsidiaries in Britain and Other U.K. Competitors', and J. H. Dunning, 'Profitability, Productivity and Measures of Business Performance', *The Investment Analyst*, June 1969.

47. The indicators used here follow those of S. E. Holtermann, 'Market Structure and Economic Performance in U.K. Manufacturing Industries', *Journal of Industrial Economics*, December 1973, pp. 124–5.

48. See Dunning, 'Profitability, Productivity and Measures of Business Performance'.

49. According to data in the *Census of Manufacturing Industries, 1968*, each British industrial concern on average accounted for over $2 million assets and $6 million sales. On the other hand, the average assets and sales figures for each industrial concern covered by the census were respectively $99,000 and $342,000.

British firms dominated the respective sectors they were in; and in general the firms were set up mainly in order to preserve and promote their established market as described in Chapter 4.

50. According to information derived from interviews with bankers, even Malaysian-owned banks, given the choice, prefer to lend to British companies than to other com-

panies because British companies are regarded as having a good reputation and high credit rating.

51. This is not to suggest that there are no managers of good quality in the employment of other firms in Malaysia. What companies interviewed were emphasizing was that British firms on the whole secure efficient managers whom they can attract and retain by the attractive remuneration offered.

52. This will be examined fully in Chapter 9.

53. No exact information is available on the amount of funds going from Malaysia to finance newly-established Malaysian affiliates of British companies in the region. In 1972, for example, six executives estimated that their companies together financed nearly $6 million investment in affiliates in various countries in the region. Clearly this amount was small in comparison with what the same companies reinvested in Malaysia in that year; but what is important is that local Malaysian personnel were responsible for some of these South-East Asian investments.

54. That is dividend payments were kept in terms of what was paid before. This meant that over the period dividend payments were held to some ratio of current profits which each company would maintain. In part, the constant proportion of profits paid out as dividends reflected the steady performance of the firms with this pattern of dividend payment.

55. In 1967, for example, Dunlop, Guinness, and Inchcape respectively paid 10 per cent, 20 per cent and $11\frac{3}{4}$ per cent dividends. In 1969 these companies paid respectively 15 per cent, 30 per cent, and $12\frac{1}{2}$ per cent, while in 1971 the respective dividend payments were 25 per cent, 35 per cent and 25 per cent. The ability of these companies to pay large dividends was a reflection of their high profitability.

56. In addition to the fluctuating profit levels of these companies, the increasing funds needed to be retained in these companies in the 1967–71 period seemed to have affected the consistency in the pattern of their dividend payments.

9 Direct and Indirect Effects of British Investment on the Host Country

DIRECT EFFECTS

THE most obvious benefit derived from British investment is the additional capital it brings. However, one cannot accurately quantify this additional capital owing to a number of accounting problems. A considerable proportion of British capital coming into Malaysia from outside Britain[1] has neither been recorded in U.K. official transactions nor clearly distinguished in Malaysian official accounts. It was difficult for a company to estimate the value of its original investment in Malaysia[2] and where second-hand machinery from the parent companies had been used to establish their overseas subsidiaries there were problems in valuing the machinery.[3]

Where taxation and other government concessions are available on the basis of sums originally invested there is a temptation to exaggerate investment values.[4] In cases where the foreign subsidiary has local equity participation the costs of technological expertise and other corporate resources from the investing parent company can either be under-estimated or exaggerated.[5] In estimating the flow of capital into Malaysian manufacturing it may be necessary, because of the difficulties mentioned, to settle for approximate amounts, bearing in mind that the actual amounts may be a little more than the recorded figures. Table 9.1 roughly indicates the additions to real capital in Malaysia attributable to U.K. companies.

It can be seen that in 1967 and 1970 more than one-half of the recorded long-term capital inflows came from British investments. With the exception of 1968—the year after the devaluation of the pound—and 1969—the year when there was a race riot in Kuala Lumpur—the contribution to the available capital in Malaysia by British investors was quite significant.

Table 9.2 shows the estimated contribution of British industry to manufacturing output, export, and employment for the period 1960 to 1970. The important points highlighted are, firstly,

TABLE 9.1
WEST MALAYSIA, ESTIMATED TOTAL PRIVATE CAPITAL INFLOWS, 1963–1971
($ million)

Year	(*1*) *Net Long-term Capital by all Companies*	(*2*) *Amounts by U.K. Companies*	(*3*) (2) *as % of* (*1*)
1963	+235	+30.0	12.8
1964	+270	+53.2	19.7
1965	+165	+46.3	28.0
1966	+150	+26.6	17.7
1967	+170	+92.6	54.5
1968	+130	+ 5.1	3.9
1969	+ 93	−1.5	−1.6
1970	+140	+77.9	55.6
1971	+160	+24.3	15.2

Sources: Amounts for all companies derived from 'Balance of Payments' Table in *Economic Report, 1972–73*, The Treasury, Kuala Lumpur, 1972; amounts by U.K. companies derived from unpublished estimates of the Economics and Statistics Division, Department of Trade and Industry, privately communicated (1972).

Notes: (1) + denotes net inflow; − denotes net outflow.
(2) Amounts by U.K. companies do not include amounts belonging to U.K. nationals but not resident in the U.K.

that about one-quarter of the total manufacturing value added between 1966 and 1970 was accounted for by U.K. companies and, secondly, that about 30 per cent of the increase in the exports was attributable to British firms. Also the growth rate of manufacturing output of British firms (estimated to be around 12 per cent) was higher than the national average (10.4 per cent from 1966 to 1970). Company evidence[6] indicated that a number of British firms (e.g. firms under the control of Harper Gilfillan, Sime Darby, and William Jacks) increased output by more than 200 per cent during the same period. Several companies (e.g. Dunlop, Shell, Cold Storage, Malayan Tobacco, Malayan Cables, Metal Box, and Guinness) expanded output by 100 to 190 per cent, and many other companies increased output by 50 to 100 per cent. Clearly we can associate the increments in industrial output in Malaysia with the commencement of British manufacturing in the country. The variety of these manufacturing firms must have contributed

TABLE 9.2
WEST MALAYSIA, BRITISH CONTRIBUTION TO MANUFACTURING OUTPUT, EXPORTS, AND EMPLOYMENT, 1960–1970

	Value Added		*Exports*		*Employment*	
	(*1*) ($ *mil.*)	(2) (%)	(*1*) ($ *mil.*)	(2) (%)	(*1*) ('*000*)	(2) (%)
1960	425	33	136	25	. . .	5
1961	408	. . .	174	. . .	. . .	. . .
1963	515	30	189	25	. . .	6
1965	682	26	282	35	217	7
1966	733	. . .	314	. . .	. . .	. . .
1967	853	24*	317	35	261	7*
1968	941	21@	362	37	. . .	8@
1970	1,118	25	515	39	270	8
1966–70:						
Average growth rate (%)	10.4	12	12.8	. . .	4.5	1
Total increase ($ million)	436	25	233	30	53	10

Sources and *Notes*:

1. Columns (*1*) derived from *Second Malaysia Plan*, p. 148; and columns (*2*) derived, unless otherwise indicated, from information gathered during interviews.

2. * denotes information based on Department of Statistics, Kuala Lumpur, survey data; @ denotes information based on *Census of Manufacturing, 1968* data; . . . data not available.

3. Columns (*1*) data pertaining to all manufacturing industries in Malaysia; columns (*2*) represent proportions of data in (*1*) attributable to firms covered by this study. It is important to note that information in (*2*) are estimates presented in the Table.

4. It is also very important to note that the value added has not been adjusted for import content of manufacturing inputs, and possible price distortion resulting from tariff protection and price changes. Conceivably, manufacturing value added would be very much less than the amounts in the Table when they are adjusted to reflect the factors mentioned.

also to the product-mix of industrial production available both for domestic consumption and for export.

In the initial stages of manufacturing, most British companies sent experienced technical and managerial personnel from the U.K. to set up plants and train Malaysian successors; and this was a definite gain to the country which was, and still is, short of technical and managerial personnel.

The long-run benefit of having British personnel in the overseas subsidiaries consists of training local people to take over management, technical, and other business functions, thus diversifying employment opportunities and upgrading the jobs available for local citizens. Information about the composition of managerial and technical jobs in British firms in Malaysia suggests that where local people are available to take over the jobs, they replace the expatriates. By the time a company assumes normal production and trading position, the proportion of British expatriates in general is reduced to about 30 per cent of the total management personnel. In certain cases (e.g. Shell, Dunlop, Metal Box, Guinness, and Rothmans), competent local people have been promoted to chief executive positions in the companies.

Also available to the manufacturing companies in Malaysia are the parent-company technology and other corporate resources which are positive factors in raising industrial productivity. The subsidiary companies enjoy the benefits of the research and development of parent companies, without incurring large financial outlays. It may be considered a disadvantage not to have research facilities developed locally so that local people may benefit from the training of research personnel and added employment for technicians. This objection is less relevant for the country where research skills are scarce and there are other more pressing development needs, or where the products of research in the advanced countries are available relatively cheaply.

During the period of the First Plan, 1966 to 1970, the significance of the additional capital arising out of U.K. direct investment in Malaysia is seen in Table 9.3.

The cumulative capital inflows represented 3.4 per cent of gross total private investments, and nearly 9 per cent of new investments in manufacturing for 1966 to 1970. The increases in manufacturing output and exports of manufactures in the same period (Table 9.2) accounted for by British companies were respectively 25 per cent and 30 per cent of the total. The total contribution of U.K. manufacturing to the economy is highly important.

In producing locally those goods which were once imported one can also say that British firms have helped to achieve one of the host country's main industrial objectives, i.e. import-substitution.

EFFECTS ON INCOME

(i) Income Accruing to Employees

This represents the most obvious gain to the host country. The amounts depend on the number of employees and the level of wages and salaries paid. We can measure approximately the amounts if we know the relationship between sales or value added and cost of labour to the firms. The net benefit will depend on the opportunity costs of labour employed in the firms, and the distribution of labour earnings. In our estimate we will assume that there are two classes of labour employed by these firms, scarce

TABLE 9.3

WEST MALAYSIA, PRIVATE INVESTMENT, INVESTMENT IN MACHINERY AND EQUIPMENT, AND BRITISH DIRECT CAPITAL INFLOW, 1966–1970

($ million, current prices)

Year	(*1*) *Gross Private Investment*	(*2*) *Investment in Machinery and Equipment*	(*3*) *Inflow of U.K. Capital into Manufacturing*	(*5*) *(3) as % of (1)*	(*5*) *(3) as % of (2)*
1966	904	385	26.6	2.9	6.9
1967	1,003	343	92.6	9.2	27.0
1968	978	360	5.1	0.5	1.4
1969	930	367	–1.5	–0.1	–0.4
1970	1,236	494	77.9	6.3	15.8
Cumulative 1966–1970	5,051	1,949	174.1	3.4	8.9

Sources: Columns (*1*) and (*2*) derived from *Second Malaysia Plan*, p. 26; column (*3*) is based on Table 9.1.

Notes: (i) The bulk of private investment in machinery and equipment represented investment in manufacturing plants; similarly, the majority of the capital inflow from U.K. companies went into the manufacturing sector. This must be so because, as noted in the *Second Malaysia Plan* (paras. 89–90), private foreign investment in agriculture and mining diminished considerably by 1965. New investments in oil-palm development by the private sector were offset by an approximately parallel reduction in new investments in rubber.

(ii) – Denotes net outflow.

labour, i.e. those with skill and experience, and non-scarce labour, i.e. those who are not necessarily unskilled and inexperienced, but unable to be gainfully employed in other sectors of the economy.[7]

It is known from the *Census of Manufacturing Industries, 1978* that income accruing to labour in British-owned manufacturing firms constituted 20.6 per cent of value added.[8] In absolute terms the unadjusted labour income for 1968 was about $40 million. One does not know exactly how this amount was divided between scarce and non-scarce labour, but information gathered during field work suggests the ratio of scarce to non-scarce labour earnings in British manufacturing companies to be approximately 4 : 1. Using such a ratio, and on the basis of the 1968 census data, the estimated scarce labour earnings were $32 million, and non-scarce labour earnings $8 million in 1968.

It would appear that the net income gain to non-scarce labour employed in British manufacturing was $8 million, assuming that this category of labour had zero opportunity cost.[9] The income gain to scarce labour is a little more complex to determine because of the various opportunity costs this category of labour has. Moreover, allowance must be made for the fact that part of the scarce labour income in British manufacturing firms accrues to expatriate personnel.[10]

Some top executives are paid partly from the U.K., but this should not affect the exercise of estimating the scarce labour income effects. Although it is known that expatriates constitute about 30 per cent of the total scarce labour employed in British manufacturing firms, the proportion of their earnings is much higher,[11] as much as 60 per cent of the income accruing to labour in some companies. For most companies, the estimated income of expatriates constitutes approximately 40 per cent of the total amount of unadjusted income accruing to scarce labour.[12]

On the basis of the foregoing description, the estimated unadjusted income of scarce labour for 1968 is approximately $19.2 million. This suggests that the adjusted (total non-scarce and scarce) labour income was ($8 million + $19.2 million) $27.2 million. If labour had no opportunity costs, the net income effect arising out of British manufacturing in Malaysia in 1968 could be regarded as a gain of $27.2 million. However, scarce domestic labour has opportunity costs, and since the pay structure in British firms is slightly higher than that of the national average, it is necessary to adjust the earnings of labour to reflect these costs.

It is possible to treat the opportunity costs in a variety of sophisticated ways, but it does not seem worthwhile to devote too much effort to such calculations since we are interested only in a broad measure of what we know to be a definite gain to labour. As far as the bulk of labour employed in British manufacturing in Malaysia is concerned, the real alternative for them is a lower level of earnings which they would get in the next best alternative employment. This was certainly the case in the late 1960s when the avenues for alternative industrial employment were few. In 1971, although certain American, German, and Japanese firms offered high pay to the Malaysian labour they employed, British manufacturing concerns in the country generally offered a higher level of pay for local labour than could be earned elsewhere. In the same year, the levels of pay enjoyed by labour in British manufacturing concerns were approximately 10 to 20 per cent higher than those prevailing in the rest of the manufacturing sector.[13] Taking this factor into consideration it would appear that the estimated net labour income gain in 1968 was between $2.7 million and $5.4 million. Taking a round figure of $5 million, the net gain in respect of labour income would represent approximately 2.6 per cent of the value added of $194 million for 1968.[14]

There are strong arguments supporting the claim that the earnings of manufacturing employees in British firms constituted direct gains. According to the 1968 census of manufacturing,[15] value added per industrial employee was around $7,233 for the manufacturing sector as a whole. The value added per employee in indigenously-owned manufacturing concerns was around $5,418; and by way of contrast the value added per employee in British-owned manufacturing concerns was $19,688. The ratios of a unit of labour employed in manufacturing to value added in manufacturing for the whole manufacturing sector, for indigenously-owned concerns and for British-owned concerns were, respectively, 1 : 3.3, 1 : 2.8, and 1 : 4.9. These ratios suggest that manufacturing productivity has improved, since in 1958, when according to a United Nations expert,[16] the overall productivity ratio of a unit of labour to industrial value added was 1 : 2.3. From 1971 to 1973, manufacturing value added in real terms grew by about 15.4 per cent per annum.[17]

The estimated income accruing to labour employed in U.K. manufacturing industries from 1963 to 1970 is shown in Table 9.4. The Table shows that both value added in manufacturing and labour's share in the value added have increased by more than 80 per cent from 1963 to 1970. The increase in the share of domestic labour seemed to have slightly exceeded the increase in value added by about 1.9 per cent. The share of labour in the value added might be higher than this percentage when the yearly increase of the rate of pay to labour is taken into account.[18]

TABLE 9.4
ESTIMATED INCOME ACCRUING TO LABOUR EMPLOYED IN U.K. MANUFACTURING INDUSTRIES IN MALAYSIA, 1963–1970

	1963	*1965*	*1967*	*1968*	*1970*	*% Increase 1963–1970*
1. Value added of U.K. manufacturing ($ million)	155	177	204	194	280	80.6
2. Share of domestic labour in the value added ($ million)	4	4.6	5.3	5	7.3	82.5

Source and *Notes*:
Line (1) is derived from Table 9.2; the notes in Table 9.2 apply here also. Line (2) is arrived at by calculating the 2.6 per cent amounts (as estimated in the text) of the value added figures in line (1).

From the foregoing discussion (leaving aside the possible social effects (discussed later in this chapter) of the employment of labour in British firms), it can be said that employees recruited locally have directly benefited by an estimated 2.6 per cent of the total value added of the firms employing them.

(ii) Income Accruing to the Investing Firms and the Local Private Sector

Income in this category consists mainly of retained earnings, accumulated depreciation allowances, dividends earned by local equity participants, and income directly accruing to local factors other than labour employed in the firms.

The immediate interest here is in an approximate quantitative measure; hence an attempt is made to calculate the magnitude of the retained earnings assuming that on average the firms set aside 30 per cent of their earnings for retention in the firms. Expressed as a percentage of value added[19] retained earnings of the firms covered during field work were about 9 per cent in 1971. If this percentage were treated as representative for all U.K. manufacturing firms during the period 1963 to 1970, the magnitude of retained earnings is as shown in Table 9.5 below. The main point illustrated by the above estimates of retained earnings is that they constituted an additional direct benefit of considerable importance to the local manufacturing sector. As discussed in the earlier chapters, retained earnings constitute an important source of finance of the firms.

As for the accumulated depreciation allowances in the manufacturing companies, they may be regarded as a pure income gain to the economy since the cost of foreign capital is covered entirely by the remitted and remissible items of earnings, dividends, and

TABLE 9.5

ESTIMATED TOTAL RETAINED EARNINGS BY U.K. MANUFACTURING FIRMS IN MALAYSIA, 1963–1970

($ million)

	1963	*1965*	*1967*	*1968*	*1970*
1. Value added	155	177	204	194	280
2. Retained earnings	13.9	15.9	18.3	17.5	25.2

Source and *Notes*:

Line (1) is derived from Table 9.4. Amounts in line (2) are calculated on the basis of firms retaining the equivalent of about 9 per cent of their value added.

TABLE 9.6

ESTIMATED AMOUNTS OF ALLOWANCES FOR DEPRECIATION BY U.K. MANUFACTURING COMPANIES, 1963–1970
($ million)

	1963	*1965*	*1967*	*1968*	*1970*
(1) Depreciation allowance	19.6	22.4	25.9	24.6	35.6
(2) Capital inflows	30.0	46.3	92.6	5.1	77.9
(3) (1) as % of (2)	65.3	48.4	28.0	482	45.7

Source and *Notes*:
(i) Information gathered during field work suggests that the amounts set aside in depreciation allowances by companies as roughly equivalent to 12.7 per cent of the value added of these companies. The estimates in (1) were based on this.
(ii) Amounts in (2) were derived from Table 9.1.

interest. The depreciation allowances set aside by the foreign firms cannot be legally remitted overseas and must be used within the host economy. Allowing for the different rates and methods of depreciation widely practised in the manufacturing sector,[20] our empirical findings suggest that U.K. firms on average set aside an amount for depreciation which roughly equals 4 per cent of the value of sales. As in the case of the preceding calculation, we have to convert this percentage into a measure that will allow us to gauge the absolute amounts of the economic gains from the depreciation allowances. We have the various value added estimates for the years between 1963 and 1970: information gathered from companies allows us to estimate the depreciation allowances of these companies, with results shown in Table 9.6.

The noteworthy point arising from Table 9.6 is that the depreciation allowances have been large in comparison to the inflow of new capital. As noted in Chapter 8, allowance for depreciation constitutes a significant source of internal finance for the companies surveyed.

To determine the amount of dividends received by local shareholders we first have to determine the total dividends declared by the companies, and then apportion the amounts due to British and local shareholders. We know the companies' rates of declared dividends varied between 6 and 70 per cent of their issued and fully-paid share capital from 1967 to 1971, although during the same period the majority of companies paid between 14 and 24 per cent dividends. If we make a conservative assumption that they declared annually about 14 per cent dividends we can arrive at the

TABLE 9.7

ESTIMATE OF DIVIDENDS DECLARED BY U.K. MANUFACTURING COMPANIES, 1963–1970

	1963	1965	1967	1968	1970
(1) Share capital ($ million)	75	90	110	100	185
(2) Estimated dividend ($)	10.5	12.6	15.4	14.0	25.9
(3) Estimated dividend accruing to local interests ($ million)	1.6	1.9	2.3	2.1	3.9

Sources and *Notes*:

Line (1) derived from (a) *Fraser's Facts and Figures*, Stock, Share and Exchange Brokers, Singapore, 1964, Private Publication; (b) *Handbook of Malaysia and Singapore Stock Exchange, 1972*. The share capital refers only to those manufacturing companies that declare dividends. The amounts are estimates only as some of the companies which have minor manufacturing interests are excluded, even though they declared dividends. Companies not listed on the local stock exchange are not included.

Line (2) was calculated on the basis that the companies declared 14 per cent dividends.

Line (3) was calculated on the basis that local equity participants had 15 per cent share of the dividends. This is an arbitrary percentage because the local participation in British manufacturing companies varied from nil to 50 per cent as described in Chapter 6. Our 15 per cent is based on information gathered when interviewing companies.

estimates in Table 9.7. At least a small proportion of withholding tax on the dividends accruing to the shareholders of British companies would be paid tó the Malaysian government, but the subject of government receipts will be dealt with in the subsequent section.[21]

TABLE 9.8

ESTIMATED INCOME ACCRUING TO LOCAL FACTORS OTHER THAN LABOUR EMPLOYED IN U.K. MANUFACTURING, 1963–1970

($ million)

	1963	1965	1967	1968	1970
1. Interest and rent	5.0	5.7	6.6	6.3	9.1
2. Other services*	13.6	15.5	17.9	17.0	24.5
3. Total	18.6	21.2	24.5	23.3	33.6

Notes: *Mainly audit, legal, advertising, insurance, secretarial, and related professional services.

Line (3) was computed on the basis of 12 per cent of manufacturing value added accruing to local factors other than labour employed in the firms. Lines (2) and (1) were computed on the basis that they respectively made up 73 per cent of the total amounts in line (3).

Income directly accruing to local factors of production other than labour constitutes about 12 per cent of the value added of the manufacturing firms.[22] The estimated amounts are shown in Table 9.8.

To the extent that the income received represented amounts over and above what could be obtained in the next best alternative sources, a positive contribution may be said to have made by the manufacturing firms.

FISCAL ASPECTS OF THE INCOME EFFECTS

Broadly there are two issues involved in assessing the income accruing to the government from the foreign manufacturing sector. The first is the government income from taxes on profits, interest, and royalties, and from levies on the imports of factor inputs of the foreign firms. Some manufactures are also subjected to a nominal export tax; and there are other miscellaneous taxes imposed on the manufacturing sector, e.g. development tax (5 per cent of all commercial income); turnover tax[23] (2 per cent of turnover); payroll tax[24] (2 per cent of company payroll); sales tax[25] (5 per cent of sales imposed at the wholesale stage); penal tax for late payment of company tax (10 per cent over and above the normal assessment)[26] and, until 1971, a 10 per cent surcharge on company imports of goods or equipment of U.S. origin.[27] For the companies interviewed, the total effect of all these taxes between 1963 and 1970 added up to an annual payment to the Malaysian government of sums roughly equivalent to 42 per cent of profits.[28]

The second important issue in the assessment of the fiscal effects of government income from taxes on the manufacturing sector is the fiscal effects of protection. There are two sides to this question of protection. On one hand the government gains from levying customs duties on direct imports: on the other, the government and the community may suffer losses from the subsidization of industries, because protection affects resource allocations.[29] This can be complicated and is a separate subject which cannot be pursued in any detail here.

Converted into a proportion of value added, the 42 per cent tax on profits represented in 1968 about one-third of manufacturing value added.[30] If we use this proportion to estimate the tax received by the government we arrive at Table 9.9.

The important point to be drawn from the above is that the development of British manufacturing in Malaysia has resulted in

TABLE 9.9

ESTIMATED INCOME RECEIVED BY THE GOVERNMENT FROM U.K. MANUFACTURING ACTIVITIES, 1963–1970

($ million)

	1963	*1965*	*1967*	*1968*	*1970*
Gross income	51.6	59.0	68.0	64.7	93.3
Net income	46.5	53.1	61.2	58.2	84.0

Source: Estimated on the basis of one-third of the value added of manufacturing firms in each of the years; adjusted for government rebates estimated to be 10 per cent of gross income.

the creation of an important source of direct income to the government. The full impact of the taxes collected is probably substantially affected by the fiscal and other government incentives designed to stimulate industrialization. As a single source of income British manufacturing concerns provided about 3 per cent of the Malaysian government revenue in the period 1963 to 1970 as shown in Table 9.10. On average, receipts from these companies accounted for approximately 16 per cent of the taxes collected by the government during the years 1963 to 1970. Table 9.11 summarizes the direct income derived from British manufacturing concerns for the period surveyed.

TABLE 9.10

WEST MALAYSIA: CURRENT REVENUE, DIRECT INCOME TAXES, AND RECEIPTS FROM U.K. MANUFACTURING, 1963–1970

($ million)

	1963	*1965*	*1967*	*1968*	*1970*
1. Total current revenue	1,360	1,591	1,840	1,891	2,400
2. Income taxes*	245	302	426	452	657
3. Receipts from U.K. manufacturing	46.5	53.1	61.2	58.2	84.0
4. (3) as % of (2)	19	18	15	13	13
5. (3) as % of (1)	3	3	3	3	4

Source: Lines (1) and (2) derived from Bank Negara, *Quarterly Economic Bulletin*, March 1973. Line (3) taken from Table 9.9.

Notes: *Including tin profit tax and development tax. The percentages in lines (4) and (5) are rounded off to the nearest whole figure.

TABLE 9.11

SUMMARY OF DIRECT INCOME EFFECTS OF BRITISH MANUFACTURING ON THE ECONOMY OF WEST MALAYSIA, 1963–1970

($ million)

	1963	*1965*	*1967*	*1968*	*1970*
1. Income accruing to local labour	4.0	4.6	5.3	5.0	7.3
2. Income retained in the firms	13.9	15.9	18.3	17.5	25.2
3. Depreciation allowances	19.6	22.4	25.9	24.6	35.6
4. Dividends accruing to local equity	1.6	1.9	2.3	2.1	3.9
5. Income accruing to local factors*	18.6	21.2	24.5	23.3	33.6
6. Taxes received by the government	46.5	53.1	61.2	58.2	84.0
Estimated income effect on the economy	104.2	119.1	137.5	130.7	189.6
(per cent)	(67.3)	(67.3)	(67.3)	(67.3)	(67.3)
Estimated receipts by U.K. investors	50.8	57.9	66.5	63.3	90.4
(per cent)	(32.7)	(32.7)	(32.7)	(32.7)	(32.7)
Estimated value added	155.0	177.0	204.0	194.0	280.0
(per cent)	(100.0)	(100.0)	(100.0)	(100.0)	(100.0)

Sources: Tables 9.4–9.10.

Note: *Other than labour directly employed.

TABLE 9.12

VALUE ADDED OF BRITISH MANUFACTURING AND MALAYSIA'S GROSS NATIONAL PRODUCT, 1963–1970

	1963	*1965*	*1967*	*1968*	*1970*
1. GNP ($ million)	7,354	8,593	9,653	10,068	11,629
2. Value added of British manufacturing ($ million)	155	177	204	194	280
3. (2) as % of (1)	2.1	2.1	2.1	2.0	2.4

Sources: Bank Negara Malaysia, *Quarterly Economic Bulletin*, Vol. 6 (1), March 1973; and Table 9.11.

It is important to note that the amounts shown in Table 9.11 have not been adjusted for the import content of value added and the possible distortion effects of tariff protection and price changes. The opportunity cost of using resources to derive the incomes has not been fully discussed, but would no doubt affect the real magnitude of the income effects. Thus the income effects summarized in the Table cannot be definitely taken to be the real measure of net gains arising from British firms engaged in Malaysian manufacturing. Nonetheless, the Table provides crude evidence for suggesting that British manufacturing companies have conferred non-negligible direct benefits on the host country. Table 9.12 also shows that from 1963 to 1970 British manufacturing value added constituted about 2.1 per cent of Malaysia's gross national product. This is an approximate indication of the contribution of British investment in Malaysian industry to the domestic economy.

EMPLOYMENT CREATED IN BRITISH MANUFACTURING

Table 9.13 shows estimated employment in British manufacturing in the period 1963 to 1970.

The employment created by the firms is small relative to their contribution to other parts of the Malaysian economy. As a whole, manufacturing employees in British concerns constituted about 7 per cent of the country's local manufacturing employment. In terms of the total number of people employed in the country, employees in British industrial firms constituted less than 1 per cent, but as mentioned in Chapter 6, British manufacturing firms

TABLE 9.13

ESTIMATED EMPLOYMENT IN BRITISH MANUFACTURING, 1963–1970

	1963	*1965*	*1967*	*1968*	*1970*	*Per Cent Increase 1963–70*
1. Estimated total manufacturing employment ('000)	201	217	261	265	270	34.3
2. Number employed in British manufacturing firms ('000)	12.1	15.1	18.2	18.6	21.6	78.5
3. Number in (2) as % of (1)	6	7	7	7	8	–
4. Estimated total number of employment in all sectors ('000)	2,500	2,590	2,675	2,763	2,940	17.6
5. Number in (2) as % of (4)	0.5	0.6	0.7	0.7	0.7	–

Sources:

(i) Number of employees in British manufacturing based on information gathered at interviews.

(ii) Estimates for the number of employees in lines (1) and (4) are based on source in footnote 1, p. 260 above.

must have increased the variety of employment in the country in the 1960s.

IMPORT-SUBSTITUTION INDUSTRIALIZATION IN MALAYSIA

Import-substitution industries in Malaysia[31] seem to show characteristics different from those of the other underdeveloped countries.

Professor Power (1971)[32] who studied the structure of protection in the country, remarked that Malaysia has learnt from the experiences of the other underdeveloped countries that excessive protection encourages inefficiencies, and breeds a complacent attitude towards innovation and growth. It appeared that import-substitution industrialization in Malaysia depended more on the natural encouragement of growth of the domestic economy than on tariff protection. Because of the relatively low level of protection, the industries that developed were able to export their goods. The domestic market in which the industries have developed was not distorted by either protection or inflation, so that the changing pattern of comparative advantage played an important role in the growth of the industries.

TABLE 9.14
AVERAGE EFFECTIVE RATE OF PROTECTION FOR MANUFACTURING IN RELATION TO OFFICIAL EXCHANGE RATES IN SELECTED UNDERDEVELOPED COUNTRIES
(per cent)

Country	*Year*	*Consumption Goods*	*Intermediate Goods*	*Capital Goods*	*All Manufacturing*
India@	1961	n.a.	n.a.	n.a.	313
Pakistan	1963/4	883	88	155	271
Argentina	1958	164	167	133	162
Brazil	1966	230	68	31	118
Philippines*	1965	94	65	80	49
Mexico	1960	22	34	55	27
Taiwan+	1965	n.a.	n.a.	n.a.	33
Malaysia	1965	25	10	2	8

Sources: Sources and methods of computation (according to the Corden method) for all countries except Malaysia, see Little *et al.*, pp. 427 n.
Sources and method of computation for Malaysia (also using the Corden method), see B. Balassa *et al.*, *The Structure of Protection in Developing Countries*, Johns Hopkins University Press, 1971, p. 220n.

Notes: @ Denotes rate for one-sixth of large-scale manufacturing only. For all other industries, the rates were higher.
* Denotes for home market only.
\+ Denotes very approximate estimate.

The effective rate of protection for manufacturing industries in Malaysia had not been as high as the rates prevalent in many underdeveloped countries in the 1960s, as suggested by Table 9.14. There is therefore a basis for claiming that market prices had not been too distorted in Malaysian industries. What is even more significant is that during the period 1951 to 1967, inflation rates for the underdeveloped countries according to the estimate of Little, *et al.*,[33] varied between 2 per cent per annum and 36 per cent per annum. In contrast, the rate of inflation in Malaysia was below 1 per cent.[34] Consequently, the distortion of prices was greater for the other countries than was the case in Malaysia. The debate about inflation is still inconclusive as to whether it is favourable to, or inimical to, economic growth.[35] Professor Kaldor, among others, believes that inflation is a necessary adjunct to economic growth;[36] –a view that is not highly rated by businessmen interviewed in the course of the present study. This is hardly the place to join in the debate about inflation and economic growth,[37] but evidence in South-East Asia suggests that an inflation-free country tends to have higher real economic growth than a country that is suffering from inflation. As an illustration, Indonesia in the 1960s, with its 50–100 per cent inflation rates,[38] had economic stagnation and deterioration;[39] while in contrast Malaysia, with its relatively inflation-free economy, had sustained for many years a 6.7 per cent annual growth of the national product.[40] The important point is that the price mechanism is less distorted in Malaysia than in any of the countries listed in Table 9.14.

The relative lack of distortion of market prices in Malaysia enables Malaysian industries to compete in the world market. An examination of the export performance of Malaysian manufactured goods and the role of British firms is made next to assess the relative success of the import-substitution industrialization programme.

PATTERNS OF MANUFACTURED EXPORTS

Manufactured goods still represent a small fraction of total exports, though their relative importance increased between 1963 and 1971 and has since increased still further.[41] Table 9.15 shows the approximate pattern of manufactured exports from Malaysia from 1963 to 1971.

Some of the newly-established capital-intensive industries such as petroleum refining, cement, and iron and steel products are making a significant contribution to gross export receipt. Exports of plywood and veneers, clothing and textile products have shown very rapid rates of increase in recent years. As reflected in the more rapid increase in the exports of intermediate goods, the growth of the manufacture of electronic components has contributed significantly to the country's export of manufacture.[42]

Another significant development in the export of manufactured goods has been the gradual decrease in their import content: there has been a gradual shift by the manufacturing companies to the use of locally available factor inputs. This tendency is reflected in Table 9.16, which shows the proportion of imported (intermediate and direct primary) factor inputs in the total cost of production of the manufacturing firms.

The figures for import content shown in the Table should be interpreted cautiously since they refer to the average import content. The absolute import content in each industry (as well as in each firm within an industry) varies a great deal.

TABLE 9.15

EXPORT OF MANUFACTURED GOODS FROM WEST MALAYSIA, 1963–1971

	1963	*1966*	*1969*	*1971*	*Per Cent Increase 1963–1971*
	(*$ million, current prices*)				
1. Consumer goods	40.4	83.3	80.0	120.0	197
2. Intermediate goods	56.8	79.2	130.6	563.5	892
3. Capital goods	34.0	43.6	132.8	160.6	372
Total Manufactured Exports	131.2	206.1	343.4	845.9	715
Total Manufactured Exports as Percentage of all Exports	4.9	7.5	8.8	16.9	

Source: Data taken from *Monthly Statistics of External Trade*, various issues.

Notes: (i) Consumer goods mean manufactured beverages and tobacco, canned pineapples, dairy products, textiles, footwear, consumer durables, and animal feedstuffs; intermediate goods include plywood, veneer wood, petroleum, rubber products, cement and building materials, chemicals, fertilizers, paints, and electronic components; while capital goods mean manufactured iron and steel, machinery, and transport equipment.

(ii) The manufactured goods in the Table exclude processed primary commodities such as rubber, tin, palm oil, and timber.

(iii) The amounts in the Table do not include re-exports of manufactured goods, and exports to East Malaysia.

For many firms there was a marked shift in their use of local materials,[43] because, firstly, more and better quality materials (e.g. metals and industrial chemicals) were available, and, secondly, domestic prices of these materials did not rise as fast as prices of similar materials in the industrialized countries.[44] The net effect of the shift to using locally-obtainable materials was the relative lowering of the average import content in the manufacturing sector. Obviously, had domestic prices moved as rapidly as those in the developed countries there would be less incentive for (foreign) manufacturers to use local materials, and this would have resulted in uncompetitive exports of manufactures. For nearly half the number of firms interviewed, exporting part of their manufacturing output had contributed significantly to the diversification of the country's export of manufactures as well as to the widespread destinations of exported goods. The range of products can be seen from Tables 7.7 and 9.15 (note ii).

TABLE 9.16

ESTIMATED IMPORT CONTENT OF INTERMEDIATE AND DIRECT PRIMARY INPUT OF MANUFACTURING OUTPUT, 1960–1971

Industry Producing	*Average Import Content as Percentage of Total Cost of Production*			
	1960	*1965*	*1971*	*Change between 1960 and 1971*
1. Consumer goods	43.7	41.3	39.5	–4.2
2. Intermediate goods	19.3	19.0	18.0	–1.3
3. Capital goods	20.2	17.7	16.0	–4.2

Sources: Data for 1960 and 1965 based on computation of input coefficients in S. Y. Lo, *The Development Performance of West Malaysia*, Kuala Lumpur, Heinemann (Asia) Ltd., 1972, pp. 140–1. Estimate for 1971 based on interviews and Survey Data of Industry, Kuala Lumpur, Department of Statistics.

Notes: (i) Classification of industry into consumer, intermediate, and capital goods is as in Table 9.15.

(ii) Table excludes processing of primary commodities such as rubber, tin, palm oil, and timber.

IMPLICATIONS OF THE INDUSTRIALIZATION POLICY

It is too early to reach a firm conclusion about the extent of the industrialization and its full implication for the Malaysian economy, but a general comment seems appropriate. The discussion above revealed that British firms have helped the country to achieve some successes in exporting manufactured goods. The important point to note is that import-substitution in Malaysia, in contrast to that in most underdeveloped economies, is an export-creating activity: it is not merely directed towards the domestic economy. As indicated, the range of manufactured exports covers a variety of skill-content suggestive of the fact that the country's comparative advantage is changing. Most important of all is the fact that industries producing intermediate and capital goods using moderately skilled labour seem able to compete with other countries such as India, Pakistan, and the Philippines which were early starters in their industrial programmes. The ability of Malaysia to export to other countries in the world, at world prices, seems to suggest that an underdeveloped country need not remain solely a primary commodity exporter. Such evidence as there is also points to the suitability of Malaysia as a potentially extensive supplier of technologically sophisticated goods to the region. It may well be possible for the country to export these goods on an increasingly world-wide basis. If the country could follow the Japanese example of absorbing, adapting, and developing imported technology (as a basis for the development of local technical ability, rather than a substitute for it), it seems possible to think of the country as using manufacturing industry as a source of export-led growth, just as in the past the export of rubber and tin has been the source of growth for the country.[45]

To sustain growth of the manufacturing sector it is necessary for firms to re-invest their profits in the economy. Table 9.15 seems to suggest that growth in manufactured exports is a possibility. It would seem appropriate that the industrialization policy should be directed towards maintaining the competitiveness of the manufacturing sector, not by recourse to protection, but perhaps by paying more attention to improving labour skills, assisting research into productivity, and exploring new avenues of trade.

THE INDIRECT EFFECTS OF BRITISH MANUFACTURING

This section also covers the external benefits of the manufacturing sector to the rest of the economy, arising from the presence of British manufacturing firms in the country. As originally conceived in Marshall's *Principles of Economics*,[46] the concept of external economies originates from the joint and composite demand and supply of goods and services. However, in the current usage of the term, particularly in the context of externalities of investments, the concept has been stretched to embrace virtually all the indirect effects of investments that are felt by the economy.[47] The essential characteristics of the external effects are that they are not under the control of those experiencing the effects, and they are not the deliberate creation of the original investors.

In our examination of the external effects of British investments in Malaysian industry we came across effects which were induced by the foreign investors. To the extent that such effects may not have the characteristics of the original concept of external economies, the instances we cite may be regarded as responses of entrepreneurs to market opportunities triggered by the original investors. An obvious example is the inducement provided by specific companies for other companies to come into the country to set up production. We have seen this illustrated in the chapter on the agency houses where we have mentioned that such companies as Inchcape, Harper Gilfillan, and William Jacks induced between them more than one hundred other companies to come into the country. Many of the agency houses are the 'local' partners of many other manufacturing companies from the U.K., and from other industrialized countries as well. The other very important contribution of the agency houses is the provision of domestic and export marketing outlets. Marketing outlets are crucial to the continuous growth of the manufacturing sector. In a country where the marketing expertise and networks originating locally are not yet highly developed, the private foreign investor provides extremely useful assistance. In view of the vital marketing role of the foreign companies, the success of the sales of locally-made products can be largely attributable to them.

By providing their own entrepreneurship the foreign industrial investors take the risks involved in the manufacturing activities. They are responsible for the outcome of their ventures. Indigenous participants may of course be in a position to assume the role of entrepreneurship, but there seems little doubt that the British companies provided the initial entrepreneurship in the industrialization process, especially where organizing production on a large scale is concerned. The significance of entrepreneurship as a factor of production, and as a catalyst in industrial development, is generally well known.[48]

The other major contribution of the British firms is the provision of technical knowledge. It is significant to note that it was the British Standards Institution which was the model of the Standards Institution of Malaysia (SIM).[49] Standards of factory lay-out, safety, and related aspects of production processes in the U.K. are transplanted to Malaysia largely through the manufacturing companies. Technical knowledge is also transmitted through the introduction of new products, new methods of production, formal and informal training of employees, and contacts with the rest of the economy. Much of the technical knowledge that the firms bring into the economy depends on the relationship between the Malaysian subsidiaries and their U.K. parent companies. Since the subsidiaries are largely wholly-owned entities there is reason to believe that they have full access to the parent company's technological and other resources. The payment of technical fees, royalties, and related service fees is further evidence that the Malaysian subsidiaries are making use of their parent companies' technical knowledge.

Additional contributions of these foreign firms are the diffusion of technology throughout the local economy, the transfer of knowledge of employees who may leave the firms for other employment, the demonstration effects of their methods of business administration, and the stimulus they give to competition, as well as the linkages that they provide in the economy. Although we have no general measuring units for all the above indirect contributions we have encountered micro-economic evidence suggesting their occurrence.

ASSIMILATION OF KNOWLEDGE FROM AND LINKAGES OF BRITISH FIRMS IN THE MALAYSIAN ECONOMY

One authority on economic development, J. Schumpeter, considers 'development' as 'changes in economic life (of a country that) are not forced upon it from without but arise by (the country's) own initiative, from within. Should it turn out that there are no such changes arising in the economic sphere itself, and that the phenomenon that we call economic development is in practice simply founded upon the fact that the (economic) data change and that the economy continuously adapts itself to them, then we should say there is *no* economic development . . . but that the economy . . . is dragged along by the changes in the surrounding world. . . .'[50] Other writers[51] have also emphasized the need to assimilate knowledge about increasing production as a necessary concomitant factor of sustained economic development. It is the pre-occupation of many economists in the 1970s to study the issues involved in the assimilation of technology in the underdeveloped countries.[52] Some writers, when they discover that the assimilation process has either been slow or non-existent, have treated the problem as 'the problem of technological dependence'.[53]

The problem of technology transfer is aggravated by the fact that technological knowledge is the monopoly of firms in advanced countries. According to the 'product-cycle' theory,[54] the technology that many underdeveloped countries are exposed to is limited to the technology associated in producing components or parts of a finished item. Industries producing components have been called 'runaway industries',[55] implying that they have little or no linkage with the economy of the host country. The argument put forward by a critic of these industries is that the technology needed for the component manufactures is very specific, and is the private property of the MNEs.[56] Therefore, the assimilation of such technology is minimal or nil. More sweeping perhaps is the general charge by some writers[57] that foreign investors are not interested in the assimilation of knowledge by, and economic development of, the host countries, because foreign investment is part of the 'neo-colonialist' plot to subjugate the peoples of the underdeveloped countries. Needless to say, the present study cannot be viewed in terms of such popular generalities.

The assimilation of knowledge, in particular knowledge about production and management, and the linkage effects of manufacturing so important in the literature of development economics,[58] are important indirect contributions of British firms to the Malaysian economy. In fact, assimilation of knowledge and linkage of industries were clearly very important to the idea of industrialization in Malaysia when the authors of the *First Malaysia Plan* (p. 131) referred to the part foreign investors 'will play in helping to modernize industrial technology'.

The greatest manifestation of assimilation of (manufacturing) knowledge occurs when local people can do a complicated job by themselves, repair machines necessary in the production process, organize production on their own account, export their own products, conduct research into production and marketing techniques, and perhaps at a later stage design and build (and possibly sell) machines and other materials necessary for production. In other words, in the Schumpeterian sense, the imported knowledge must be absorbed by the local people and integrated into the whole process of production of goods and services. Obviously, the very presence of foreign firms in the country is a testimony to the limited extent of the assimilation of knowledge by local people. However, the very presence of the foreigners in the country is a source of ideas and knowledge. Historically, even Englishmen (in the sixteenth and seventeenth centuries), Germans (in the nineteenth century), and Japanese (in the later part of the nineteenth century) also learnt from foreigners,[59] and foreign firms.

Local people can gain experience and competence in organizing production in foreign firms, after which they can set up business on their own account. The evidence to be cited later refers to the incidence of local people who are either in charge of production in British firms, or those who are ex-employees of British firms and have gone into the business of manufacturing on their own.

The concept of linkages as used by Hirschman[60] distinguishes a backward linkage, which refers to investment in the production of inputs for the industry in question, from a forward linkage, which refers to investment in industries using the output of the industry as input. These linkages refer to the direct effect of one investment on another, and are distinguished from the type of investment behaviour as understood in macro-economics, where investment in one period is made a function of income generated by investment in previous periods. The essential difference between the investment induced by the linkage effect and that induced by the multiplier-accelerator effect lies in the nature and strength of the inducement to invest. The linkage effect induced a smaller range of industries either supplying or buying inputs to and from one another. The inducement to invest generated through the multiplier-accelerator effects has far-reaching effects throughout the entire economy.

The linkage effects in some respects merge with the concept of assimilation of knowledge outlined earlier, when the linkages are viewed in the terms of external economies suggested by Scitovsky.[61] According to Scitovsky, externalities can be separated into a pecuniary externality and a technological externality. A pecuniary externality is generated when the action of a firm affects the profitability of another through the price mechanism. For example, an investment by industry *A* might raise profits in industry *B* which uses output of *A*, or supplies inputs to *A*. In the case of a technological externality, the actions of one industry might affect the profitability of another through non-market interdependence. Thus, if industry *A* finances the training of skilled workers who subsequently take employment in *B* there is a technological externality generated between the industries, but not reflected directly in the price mechanism. In the sense elucidated by Scitovsky, the pecuniary externality is similar to the linkage effect described earlier; while the assimilation of knowledge outlined previously coincides with the technological externality. The rest of the description below attempts to outline the contributions of British firms to the Malaysian economy in terms of the externalities just mentioned.

Between 1963 and 1970 an estimated 1,000 skilled employees, excluding executives, left British manufacturing firms for other employment. This estimate, based on interviews, does not seem to suggest any massive assimilation of knowledge[62] since most of the workers concerned left for other (similar) foreign firms. Very few went into domestic enterprises, largely because domestic enterprises did not offer sufficient inducement in terms of better pay. There is, however, other evidence suggestive of the assimilation of knowledge by local employees of the British firms. For example, more than 60 per cent of the technical and scientific staff of the firms are local people educated either at the local colleges or abroad. In 1969 an observer noted that these people have been assimilating factory technology and management practices.[63] The proportion of Malaysians associated with technical aspects of production can be specified. Cold Storage, for example, employs about 80 per cent local people at the technical level. Their functions range from those of refrigeration engineers to food technologists. At Guthrie Berhad, Harper Gilfillan, United Engineers, and other light engineering firms, nearly all the technical personnel, apart from the production controllers, are local people. It is common practice for former engineering workers in these firms to set up engineering businesses on their own. It is also common practice for foreign firms to subcontract the design and building of milling, mining, and water treatment equipment to the local firms owned by the ex-employees of the British firms. It should be mentioned that Malaysian technologists have to a large extent been responsible for the design and construction of the Multi-Disc Magnetic Separators,[64] mining equipment widely in use at home and abroad.

In almost all firms manufacturing rubber products the majority of the rubber technologists are Malaysian. At Dunlop, for instance, research and product adaptation are largely carried out by local people. A substantial amount of research on the behaviour of tyres in tropical climatic conditions is conducted in the country. At present (1973) a big research programme at Dunlop Malaysian Industries is in progress to discover the technique of manufacturing truck, bulldozer, and tractor tyres that will give traction in jungle tracks and speed on the highways. Information is fed from the Malaysian subsidiary to the U.K. head office.

In rubber technology local people can claim modest successes in production as well as in end-use technology.[65] Almost all the research is conducted with the co-operation of British companies, the Rubber Research Institute (RRI), and the Rubber Technology Centre (RTC). Similarly in palm oil and wood technology local people are conducting research both in British companies and in government institutions.

In the area of management, many firms like Sime Darby, Harrisons & Crosfield, Guthrie, and Boustead recruit annually an increasing number of young local people to be trained as potential managers. Many of the local people already in their employment are being promoted to the top managerial level. The MNEs are also active in the area of promoting local people to management levels. In 1972 the chief executives of Shell, Metal Box, and Dunlop were local people. Other firms that have Malaysians as their chief executives were Rothmans of Pall Mall (M) Berhad and Fraser and Neave. It is reasonable to assume that these local people have assimilated considerable knowledge of various aspects of managerial work.

The latest development in the area of management is seen where local executives are used by the firms to set up, and initially manage, other subsidiaries in neighbouring countries, particularly in Thailand and Indonesia. Here is clear evidence that local people have accumulated the experience required for competence in business administration.

Perhaps the best illustrations of local people who have assimilated knowledge from British firms are provided by two cases. The first concerns an ex-welder who in 1967 started on a very modest scale a spare-part business. Within a year, the man in question managed to stimulate the interest of a couple of friends to start a footwear factory. Within two years they started a number of other manufacturing concerns, so that in 1970 they owned at least two dozen companies, half of which were engaged in manufacturing. In 1973 they managed to export their products not only to neighbouring countries but also to the industrialized countries of Japan, Western Europe, and North America.[66]

The second case is more interesting. The man who started business on his own was a middle-rank executive with a large British food manufacturing company. He went into the business of manufacturing bakers' and other types of food yeasts. By 1972, the food-yeast manufacturing company became the largest food-yeast supplier in the country, producing over 350 tons in that year. The company became the major supplier of yeasts to many food manufacturing concerns, including the British company which the man in question used to work for, and by 1973 had already established an export trade to neighbouring countries. This case is interesting because it shows that the local man mastered not only the manufacturing process, but also the general selling techniques required.

There are a number of other cases of successful ventures by ex-employees of British firms, but the pattern they show seems to conform to the two illustrations above. Without further investigation one does not know how successful these businesses were, but that would be more relevant to a study of entrepreneurship induced by the demonstration effect of foreign business in the country.

Other major examples of local people assimilating imported knowledge are in the area of drawing and design and in data processing. The drawing, design, and construction of air-conditioned buses suitable for tropical use are also carried out by local people. Recently, local people have also been involved in drawing, and building small ships and platforms for oil rigs. Local people are also the main employees of data processing firms which obtain contracts to punch data on cards and tapes for the MNEs, some of whom fly their data from the industrialized countries to be processed by local people.

The gist of this information is that there are signs of the acquisition of knowledge by local people employed in British firms, and that evidence can be found of technological externalities created by those firms.

However, the evidence encountered seems limited to knowledge that is elementary, in the sense that the knowledge apparently assimilated is that associated with the operations of enterprises. This knowledge can be acquired by other means, such as apprenticeship to a foreign firm overseas, or by hiring experts to come to the country to train local people. The assimilation of this operational knowledge has not prevented the problem of technological dependency on the advanced countries from arising. The situation clearly suggests that Malaysia has a long way to go before it has sufficient people capable of drawing, designing, and constructing machines that make other machines and equipment necessary for the sustained growth of the manufacturing sector.

To carry the discussion a step further one needs to know why the assimilation of knowledge has been limited. It is necessary to know what knowledge is available and what is not available in the country, or in the British firms. One also needs to know to what extent local people are given access to the knowledge available in British firms. The information gathered from executives indicated that to a large extent local people are exposed to most of the technical knowledge available in the British firms. Exceptions exist in areas of process technology. By process technology is meant the technical knowledge (as represented by, for example, formulae and 'secret ingredients') actually 'embodied' in the production process. For example, local people employed in a brewery are not aware of the formulae for brewing all the different types of beers; and in the metal manufacturing industry local people do not have access to information about the manufacture of specialized alloys. The reasons are twofold: firstly, the knowledge is kept in the heads of the technical personnel and secondly, some material inputs embodying the process technology are imported, so that local people, even if they are physically in contact with the materials, will never know how they are actually made.

Given that the local people are capable of assimilating knowledge, the main potential limitation to its assimilation is the availability of the knowledge itself. The availability of knowledge and the extent to which British firms in the country provide it are the themes of the following paragraphs.

According to the United Nations study on the 'Channels and Mechanisms for the Transfer of Technology from Developed to Developing Countries'[67] technical knowledge can be divided into several elements,[68] namely:

1. knowledge about feasibility studies and market surveys;
2. knowledge for determining the range of technology to manufacture the product in question, and for choosing the most appropriate techniques;
3. engineering knowledge for design of production plant and machines;
4. engineering knowledge for the actual construction and installation of equipment;
5. knowledge about process technology;
6. knowledge about management and operating production facilities;
7. marketing knowledge;
8. technical knowledge necessary for improving the efficiency of established processes by minor innovation.

Technical knowledge numbers (1) to (5) may be called the pre-investment or construction knowledge. Numbers (6) to (8) are technical knowledge needed for the operation of industries.

From the above list a Table can be constructed to show the extent to which knowledge is available in the country, the extent to which British firms can provide the knowledge, and the extent to which the local people have gained the knowledge from British firms. The information used was derived from interviews and suffers limitations in that some of it may have been heavily weighted by the interviewees to project a good image of their firms.

Table 9.17 shows the estimated extent to which technical and management knowledge has been absorbed by local people. It is noteworthy that where local people have been exposed to knowledge in the British firms the degree of assimilation of the knowledge is high. When the local people are partially exposed, as in items (a) (i), (ii), (iv), (v), and (b) (vii), the degree of their assimilation of the knowledge is limited. In the area of designing and constructing machines and plant, where there is no locally available source, the local people have no exposure to the knowledge at

TABLE 9.17
AVAILABILITY OF KNOWLEDGE AND ITS ESTIMATED ASSIMILATION FROM BRITISH FIRMS IN MALAYSIA, 1972

Knowledge Necessary in	I Availability From: Local Firms	British Firms	Other Firms	Must be Imported; i.e. Not Available	II Estimated Degree of Exposure of Local Employees in British Firms to the Knowledge	III Estimated Degree of Assimilation in II
	(in Malaysia)					
(a) *Construction of Industry*						
(i) feasibility studies and market surveys	A	A	A	S	(2)	(P)
(ii) determining the range of technology feasible and choice of technique	N	A	A	S	(3)	(P)
(iii) design and production of machine and plant	N	N	N	Y	(4)	(N)
(iv) construction and installation of equipment	N	A	A	S	(2)	(P)
(v) process technology	N	A	A	S	(3)	(N)
(b) *Operation of Industry*						
(vi) management and operation of facilities	A	A	A	S	(1)	(C)
(vii) marketing	A	A	A	S	(2)	(P)
(viii) improving efficiency of established processes by minor innovations	A	A	A	S	(1)	(C)

Source: Interviews.

Notes:
A = Knowledge available in the country from firms indicated.
S = Specialized knowledge not available in the country; source must be imported.
N = Nil, or negligible.
P = Knowledge partially assimilated because of limited exposure.
C = Knowledge is completely assimilated resulting from complete exposure.
Y = Must be imported as there is no locally available source.
(1) = Complete exposure of local employees; and there have been instances when employees who have gained the knowledge have gone into business on their own.
(2) = Exposure limited to personnel in present employment.
(3) = Partial exposure only.
(4) = Very little, or no exposure at all.

all. In this respect, the country is technologically very dependent on imported sources. This situation is likely to be perpetuated so long as the country lacks heavy machine-tool industries and skilled people to man them. As noted earlier, there is very limited exposure of local people to knowledge of process technology, even in firms where local people are employed at high technical levels. Process technology is often patented, and what is unpatented is still kept secret. Local people who have some access to this knowledge are bound by promises of confidentiality, so that even if they know about aspects of the technology they are not in a position to exploit the knowledge for private gain.

The implications are that it would seem necessary to induce the firms to increase the exposure of local employees to all aspects of production technology. Inducements can be in the form of financial incentives or other forms of concession designed to compensate for the costs incurred. It would seem necessary to review the *Investment Incentives Act* to take account of technological transfer and training of skills. The weakest point of the Act is the absence of provisions for the acquisition of skills by local people. Incentives are given under the provisions of the Act for the amounts of capital brought into the country, the extent of use of local labour, and other factor inputs, as well as the quantity of exports, but there is no mention of incentives to firms that raise the levels of skills of local labour.

The other area of policy implication is that it would seem necessary to initiate more local scientific work relevant to the activities of the industrial sector. Considering that most of the technological and scientific staff in British firms are local people, it should be within the capability of local people to develop and harness technical and scientific knowledge, as demonstrated in the rubber industry. If the industrial sector is to be as important as agriculture more research should be undertaken to promote the industrial sector.

One other noteworthy point suggested by Table 9.17 is that even at the operational level of industry the assimilation of knowledge of marketing by local people seems to be incomplete. This is a very important area because it does seem obvious that the paucity of marketing knowledge would set a limit to the expansion of production in industries. The chapter on the agency houses showed that local industrialists are dependent on British companies to market industrial products both at home and abroad. In this light, it seems clear that the dependence of local industries on British companies is extensive.

The conclusion from the foregoing evidence is that local employees have assimilated some knowledge of technology and management from the British firms. The knowledge that appears to have been completely assimilated is concerned with operating, rather than constructing an industrial enterprise.

INDUSTRIAL LINKAGES

An investigation by Thoburn (1973) has shown that Malaysian exports of primary products have given rise to a substantial light engineering industry which has linkages with other sectors of industry,[69] including locally-owned firms. British companies such as the McAlister Group (taken over by United Engineers in 1971), James Warren, and Hargill have been pioneers in the development of engineering production. United Engineers, incorporated in 1921, for instance has been a training place for many local proprietors of the present-day engineering firms. In the manufacture of machines and equipment for mining, rubber milling, and palm oil processing, the British firms often subcontract to these local firms. The degree of linkage between British engineering firms and the rest of the local economy is indicated by the proportion of the local content in the costs of manufacturing the machines and equipment.[70] In the manufacture of tin dredgers (costing approximately $10 million each) it was found that just over one-fifth of the costs involved in the construction related to local content; and in the manufacture of gravel pumps (each costing about $0.2 million), at least 39 per cent of the construction expenditure represented local content. The local content for the manufacture of oil palm mills (of 40 tons/hour milling capacity) and rubber-processing factories (of a capacity of 10 tons/day dry rubber content) are, respectively, 46 per cent and 62 per cent. The local content of replacement parts is generally higher than the proportion noted for the whole machine and plant.[71]

In the electrical engineering industry British companies also have linkages between themselves as well as with other companies. Malayan Cables (a subsidiary of BICC) supplies a large proportion of cables, insulated wires, flexible cords and other requirements of electrical conduction. In turn, the company makes use of locally-manufactured materials (e.g. PVC insulation material, rubber insulators, copper, and other metals as well as packaging materials) as its inputs. Local firms, in addition to being supplied by British firms with materials, also supply other British firms with material inputs such as moulded plastics, compressed bakelite, punched and turned metals, high quality wooden cabinets, and packaging materials. Similarly, other branches of engineering such as automative and civil engineering also create some form of linkages.

For example, the entry of Wearne Brothers Ltd. into the motor assembly business gave rise to the development of ancillary industries producing motor-vehicle components such as batteries, parts of engines, plastic and metal components, as well as rubber parts used in motor vehicles. The participation of companies like Taylor Woodrow in the construction industry together with the building boom of the late 1960s and early 1970s encouraged the growth of industries supplying building and construction materials. In general the engineering industry has developed entirely through market forces, in the 1960s at least.[72] In view of the extensive linkages the industry generates, and in view of the dominance of British interests in the industry, there is a basis for arguing that British firms have contributed to industrial growth through technological externalities and linkage effects.

One can cite other examples of linkages in the chemical and in some food-processing industries (e.g. flour milling), but one is not certain whether the linkages provided by some of these industries are 'good' linkages,[73] particularly when some of them developed behind tariff walls.

In the consumer goods industry the linkages were considerable, as indicated by the extent of their purchases of local materials. For example, in the case of a food manufacturing concern in 1971 the local purchases of material inputs accounted for nearly 60 per cent of the total value of inputs; in a tobacco manufacturing concern the proportion was nearly 50 per cent, and in a company processing rubber products the proportion of its locally-purchased inputs was almost 60 per cent of its total value of material inputs in the same year. Likewise, in the case of a number of firms in the producer and intermediate goods industries (e.g. in industries producing chemical and chemical products, non-metallic mineral products, basic metals and metal products, and transport equipment) their locally-purchased material inputs constituted from 30 to 60 per cent of the total value of their material inputs in 1971. Conceivably, the total linkage effects of these industries would be greater, since they also supply local concerns with their outputs which are part of the inputs of the local firms. What seems to be clear is that British firms have linkage effects on the industrial sector and that they generate external economies, thus helping to strengthen the manufacturing sector.

THE GROWTH OF ANCILLARY COMMERCIAL INSTITUTION

The presence of British manufacturing in the country induces the development of ancillary commercial institutions like banking, insurance, the stock exchange and, more recently, consultancy, merchant banking, and management services. Many British firms are well connected with the large British banks in the country through their common directorships. Similarly, the larger and better-known British insurance companies in the country are also connected with many of the manufacturing firms.

The development of the local stock exchange has undoubtedly been aided by the presence of British companies. The older companies such as Boustead, Fraser and Neave, Malayan Cement, Malayan Cables, Wearne Brothers, Malayan Tobacco, Metal Box, United Engineers, and Harper Gilfillan were among the earlier companies that were first quoted on the local stock exchange. British firms (e.g. Fraser's Stockbrokers, and Seagroatt and Cambell) were also among the early providers of stock and share broking services in the country. The local stock exchange provides a medium through which funds can be channelled from the investing public to provide for equity or loan participation in commerce and industry.

The increasing demand for short-term loans has led to the development of the local money market—which mobilizes savings for investment. The availability of locally-manufactured consumer durables has also led to the demand for credit facilities. In both cases the demands have been induced by the development of industry, and, in response to these demands, financial institutions like the Credit Corporation (M) Bhd., a subsidiary of The Chartered Bank, emerged in the late 1960s. At the same time, the industrial community needed the assistance of specialized services in corporate finance, international finance, and investment management. Hence in 1970 several merchant banking organizations (e.g. MIMB Bhd. and Chartered Merchant Bankers) came into being. These merchant bankers provide, either on a one-off or continuing basis, capital and management advice for companies in industry.

Technical and management consultancy firms such as Impac and Interconsult, also came into existence in response to demands for such services as feasibility studies, market surveys, stock market research, and specialized services in the area of company operations. The demand for data processing services stimulated the development of such hard-ware and soft-ware computer goods firms as On-Line (M) Sdn. Bhd., Database Bhd., and Dataprep (M) Sdn. Bhd. British manufacturing firms are by no means the sole users of these institutions, but they have been instrumental in the development of these service companies, many of which are subsidiaries of British concerns.

Three significant points arise from the presence of the commercial services in the country. Firstly, the services facilitate the monetization and the modernization of the manufacturing sector. Both foreign and local firms benefit from these facilities. Existing and potential investors are provided with services which match those available in the developed countries. Secondly, these services are also made available to countries in the region. Some of the management and consultancy firms, for example, service their clients in the neighbouring countries. This situation may lead to the country becoming an important centre for facilitating the arrival of foreign investors who may otherwise be hesitant to invest in the region. Thirdly, as local people gain competence in some of the modern techniques of servicing the needs of industries, the service companies may be able to secure some international business. This point is well illustrated by the data processing industry. The existence of low-paid but trained and skilled punch-card operators in the country has enabled some data processing companies in America and Europe to send their data to be partly processed by their subsidiaries in Malaysia.[74] Conceivably, the service may extend further into additional subcontracting in technical areas, such as drawing and design,[75] by companies in the developed countries where they are faced with rising labour costs and union problems. One could hypothesize that the presence of technically trained low-cost labour in the country would encourage the development of service industry capable of accepting work of precise quality and specification from the advanced countries. This would be a significant spill-over effect of British foreign investment. Briefly, one can state that as a result of British industrial investment in Malaysia the service sector has expanded owing to the development of British firms and in response to the needs of industry in general, as well as the result of the formation of British subsidiary companies to provide services to industry.

FOREIGN INVESTMENT AND THE DEVELOPMENT OF THE 'MIDDLE-CLASS'

There seems to be no objective definition of what a 'middle-class' person is.[76] In the context of a plural society such as Malaysia's the task of defining[77] the middle-class portion of society is specially difficult and there has been no systematic socio-economic investigation in this area. While it is not possible to make a conclusive observation on this subject it is possible to outline general pointers towards the contribution of British investments to the growth of the Malaysian middle-class—the middle-class being regarded, according to MacDougall's classification as constituting among others professional and technical personnel, merchants, traders, and clerical workers.

One cannot (indeed one should not) attribute the growth of the Malaysian middle-class solely to British investments. However, such evidence as there is seems suggestive of the significant role of British business in building the urban areas and the middle-class section of the population. McGee and McTaggart (1967), for example, observed that the growth of Petaling Jaya[78] was largely due to the large number of houses built by the Malaya Borneo Building Society Ltd. (MBBS), a company controlled by the Commonwealth Development Corporation, in the late 1950s. In 1957 there were about thirty factories in the Petaling Jaya industrial estate,[79] and most of them belonged to British concerns. Of all foreign companies (other than those companies controlled from Singapore) in Malaysia in 1968, British companies accounted for 78 per cent of their industrial workers at all levels of skills.[80] A significant proportion of the industrial employees in British concerns can be regarded as belonging to the middle-class group of the population.

Like the ancillary services discussed in the preceding section, the middle-class population in the country is both a manifestation of and an instrument for industrial development. As a group, the middle-class plays an important role in creating effective domestic demand for industrial products. The lack of such effective demand is a factor inhibiting industrialization in underdeveloped countries.[81] Attitudes, values and *mores* conducive to the growth of industrialization are presumably more widespread in an urban middle-class society than in a tradition-bound agrarian or peasant society.[82] In general the growth of the middle-class is conducive to the growth of industries. In view of the increasing number of people employed in British companies (see Table 9.13) it is possible to suggest that the number of people in British firms who can be regarded as belonging to the middle-class must have increased also in the 1963 to 1970 period. In this light it can be said that British firms have made an important social contribution.

EXPORT OF MANUFACTURED GOODS AND TERMS OF TRADE

As discussed on pp. 275–7 above, it is still possible for an outward-looking small country like Malaysia to export manufactured products to the advanced countries. As shown below, it is vital for the export of manufactured products to grow to pay for rising imports, and to offset falling prices of the primary products.

According to a calculation of the Malaysian Department of Statistics, Malaysia's terms of trade are deteriorating owing to falling export prices, as shown in Table 9.18. Import prices have been rising faster than export prices. From 1963 to 1970 import prices for Malaysia increased on average by about 1.5 per cent per annum, while at the same time export prices decreased by an average rate of 1.4 per cent per annum. It is apparent that had it not been for the growth in exports of manufactures (and to a lesser extent the export of palm oil), the country's terms of trade would have been worse than is shown in the Table. What is even more disconcerting is the fact that import prices increased by 5.7 per cent in 1970–1, while at the same time export prices declined by 8.1 per cent.

The rapid increase in the prices of imported manufactured products in the early 1970s, particularly in the prices of fuels, machinery, and other industrial goods, turned the terms of trade further against Malaysia. Effectively it has meant that the country has to export more of her products to pay for the same quantity of imports. Considering that the development needs of the country require more machinery and other manufactures she has to produce and export even larger quantities than in the past in order to pay for the import requirements. The scope for shifting sources of imports from high cost to low cost countries is now limited, since all the countries producing capital goods are experiencing domestic price inflation and rising production costs. The world-wide shortages of commodities, including foodstuffs, aggravate the situation. The danger of imported inflation into Malaysia, which was inflation-free in the 1960s, is real. Such inflation would lead to increasing costs of production and, hence, would affect the competitiveness of the exports from the country. Furthermore, the cost of shipping goods from Malaysia to the industrialized countries doubled between 1969 and 1972[83] and between 1972 and 1973 there was another 14 per cent increase.[84]

Considering the fact that Malaysia's exports of manufactured goods have the effect of moderating the deteriorating terms of

TABLE 9.18

MALAYSIA: EXPORT AND IMPORT PRICES, 1963–1971

Export Price Index, 1963 = 100

Year	*SITC* Total	*(0)* Food	*(2)* Crude Materials Inedible	*(4)* Oils and Fats	*(6)* Manufactured Goods by Materials	'Terms of Trade'
1962	102	101	103	101	100	102
1963	100	100	100	100	100	100
1964	102	104	93	109	132	101
1965	107	103	93	126	153	107
1966	103	104	90	110	142	101
1967	94	94	79	104	132	94
1968	89	94	75	81	125	86
1969	102	92	93	78	135	97
1970	99	91	83	113	144	94
1971	91	95	71	114	138	82
Change (%)						
1963–70	−1.4	−0.6	−4.8	+1.9	+4.7	−2.8
1970–1	−8.1	+4.4	−14.5	+0.9	−4.2	−13.1
Share of Exports:						
1971 (%)	100	7	45	10	29	

Import Price Index, 1963 = 100

Year	*SITC* Total	*(0)* Food	*(3)* Fuels	*(6)* Manufactures (by materials)	*(7)* Machinery	*(5–8)* Industrial Products
1962	100	100	99	102	107	104
1963	100	100	100	100	100	100
1964	101	101	102	101	99	100
1965	100	98	99	101	99	100
1966	102	104	97	100	101	102
1967	100	104	92	99	102	101
1968	104	112	91	102	102	103
1969	105	107	81	102	111	107
1970	105	96	86	111	115	113
1971	111	101	108	114	124	119
Change (%)						
1963–70	+1.5	+0.1	+1.1	+1.9	+3.1	+2.5
1970–1	+5.7	+5.2	+25.6	+2.7	+7.8	+5.9
Share in Imports:						
1971 (%)	100	18	7	20	31	65

Source and *Notes*:

Unpublished calculation of the Department of Statistics, Kuala Lumpur. Laspeyras index, based on unit values of Standard International Trade Classification.

trade, there seems to be a good reason for promoting more exports of manufactured goods from the country. To the extent that British firms with their world-wide marketing channels helped in promoting manufactured exports[85] they can be considered as making another positive contribution to the host economy.

THE BALANCE OF PAYMENTS EFFECTS

Interpreting and tracing commercial transactions in the balance of payments accounts raises a number of problems, particularly in the case of Malaysia where the balance of payments accounting system is rather rudimentary.[86] The analysis in this section must be interpreted with great caution because of basic problems encountered in the course of making this study. The first problem is associated with the question of the availability of accurate data. The main data are derived from unpublished sources gathered from the Economics and Statistics Division of the Department of Trade and Industry, companies interviewed, and Bank Negara, Malaysia's central bank. Some discrepancies are present in the data from the various sources, namely, the Department of Trade and Industry data are incomplete since they do not include remittances from British subsidiaries in Malaysia to countries other than Britain; for obvious reasons, data from the companies are incomplete since some companies do not give sufficient information on what they do with their money; the Bank Negara data do not distinguish between the outflows of capital from agriculture and mining, and outflows from manufacturing.

The second problem is associated with the construction of the country's balance of payments accounts, which may affect the accuracy of the exercise of tracing the effects of company transactions on these accounts. In the 'Transfers Account', for example, no distinction is made between 'current' and 'capital' transfers. In addition, there is a large category of transactions called 'Errors and Omissions' which includes a variety of statistical movements.[87] The existence of the unidentified capital movements complicates the attempt to trace as accurately as possible the net effect of foreign capital movements in the balance of payments. Empirical evidence suggests that the large foreign companies shift their temporarily unused funds into the Asia-Dollar Market, but this is not explicitly obvious from the Malaysian balance of payments accounts. Potentially, this situation can be very costly to the country, particularly in times of crisis. The lack of proper recording of the short-term capital movements weakens this attempt to compare the movements of funds by the companies studied.

In this study, the data used will be those obtained from the Department of Trade and Industry, supplemented by information gathered from the companies. The balance of payments data will be those of the Bank Negara Malaysia. The best that can be done in the circumstances is to trace the balance of payments effects step by step, bearing in mind that the results are only approximations of the actual amounts involved.

Contrary to the experience of many underdeveloped countries, Malaysia has not suffered from any balance of payments crisis, as indicated in Table 9.19. Deficits in the 'Balance on Goods, Services and Transfers' accounts came about largely as a result of the country's efforts at economic development, which led to significant increases in the imports of goods and services from abroad, including private transfer payments. The deficits have not given rise to any real cause for concern since there has been adequate foreign finance in the form of inflows of private capital and official loans. Thus, the balance in the long-term capital account has been in surplus, sufficient to finance whatever deficits arose in the current account. The most important aspect of the country's capital account is that official foreign long-term capital in the form of foreign loans has been small compared to private long-term capital inflows in the 1960s.[88]

There seems good reason to believe that the industrialization programme of the 1960s was not prompted by a balance of payments crisis. The adverse terms of trade outlined in Table 9.18, the rising demand for imports occasioned by the needs of the development programme, and the increasing income remittances from private investors who entered the economy in the early 1960s and earlier, inevitably would lead to balance of payments problems in later years and, in the absence of additional capital inflows, make it probable that official borrowing would be necessary.[89]

The remittances of foreign companies represent costs, in terms of foreign exchange, to the country. One is interested to quantify the amounts of these remittances and to trace their movements in the balance of payments accounts.

The Merchandise Balance

British companies, in particular the agency houses, handle a substantial portion of the country's external trade. Table 9.20 summarizes the amounts involved in the merchandise accounts.

It is estimated that the agency houses handle more than one-

TABLE 9.19

MALAYSIA: SUMMARY OF THE BALANCE OF PAYMENTS, 1963–1971
($ million)

Item	*1963*	*1964*	*1965*	*1966*	*1967*	*1968*	*1969*	*1970*	*1971*
1. Merchandise balance	+286	+275	+526	+559	+447	+643	+1,481	+983	+633
2. Balance on goods and services	–38	–54	+180	+146	+124	+237	+862	+349	–51
3. Balance on goods, services, and transfers	–219	–128	+122	+40	–18	+94	+683	+166	–218
4. Balance on long-term capital	+357	+192	+250	+192	+241	+156	+299	+150	+557
5. Errors and omissions	–207	–275	–351	–385	–296	–277	–454	–259	–214
6. Overall balance (surplus + deficit –)	–74	–140	+137	–164	–256	–27	+528	+57	+125
7. Special drawing rights								+64	+61
8. Net change in external reserves	–74	–140	+137	–164	–256*	–27	+528	+121	+186
External reserves	2,822	2,838	2,918	2,801	2,179@	2,299	2,817	2,893	3,147

Sources: Data derived from Bank Negara and The Treasury, Kuala Lumpur.

Notes: * Excluding loss from sterling devaluation in November 1967.

@ Including loss from sterling devaluation in November 1967.

(1) *Merchandise balance* means Exports less Imports.

(2) *Balance on goods and services* means merchandise balance including net balances on services, e.g. freight and insurance, travel, investment income, other transportation, and miscellaneous service transactions.

(3) *Balance on goods, services, and transfers* includes items (1), (2), and net balance on transfers accounts.

(4) *Balance on long-term capital* represents net movements of companies', government's and other official capital transactions.

(5) *Errors and omissions* is made up of net short-term capital movements of the private sector mainly. 'Balancing' item or statistical residual is also included in the amounts.

TABLE 9.20

SUMMARY OF THE MERCHANDISE BALANCE, 1963–1971

($ million)

	1963	*1964*	*1965*	*1966*	*1967*	*1968*	*1969*	*1970*	*1971*
xports (f.o.b.)	3,296	3,346	3,752	3,808	3,679	4,070	4,966	5,106	4,956
nports (f.o.b.)	2,892	3,010	3,071	3,226	3,202	3,427	3,505	4,123	4,323
erchandise alance	+286	+275	+526	+559	+477	+643	+1,481	+983	+633

Source: Source as in Table 9.19.
Notes: (i) Amounts adjusted for valuation and coverage to a balance of payments basis.
(ii) Imports include purchase of military goods, but excluding purchased aircraft for the Malaysia–Singapore Airlines.

half of imports and nearly 80 per cent of exports. The surplus of export earnings over import payments remains in London as a sterling balance of the agency houses.[90] This is so because the trade in commodities and other merchandise handled by the agency houses operates more or less on a consignment basis, i.e., the values of exports consigned from Malaysia are credited to the agency's London office accounts and the values of imports dispatched to Malaysia are debited to the same accounts. When credit and debit entries 'match' no cash settlement need take place. In this manner, the agency houses save on bank exchange commissions.

The sterling balances of these agency houses can at best be regarded as current or short-term external assets (or non-official foreign exchange reserves). Since these balances, in fact, partly represent gross profits of the companies held abroad the foreign owners will have exclusive rights of use of the funds. Even if the balances were to be remitted to Malaysia they would in due course be remitted to the foreign owners, in which case it is not clear whether the balances can be regarded as overseas assets of Malaysia. If the agency houses were domestically owned, then it would appear that the balances could be regarded as the country's external assets. It is reasonable to expect that domestic owners may be open to persuasion to allow the balances to earn an income for the monetary authorities, or to be used for domestic investment. It is on this aspect of the agency houses' overseas transactions that Puthucheary[91] and Wheelwright[92] based their attacks on the foreign firms in Malaysia.[93] Their solution is to restrict the overseas remittances of these foreign firms so that more domestic investible funds will be available.[94] It is by no means certain that this simple solution can lead to more funds being available for investment in industry, in view of the complex motivations to invest in Malaysian industries noted in Chapter 4. The experience of those countries with tight control over foreign remittances suggests that the foreign investor can devise ways and means of remitting funds abroad,[95] such that the net effect of restrictions is a whittling down of the host country's chances of attracting further foreign capital. It would seem that in the final analysis, whether or not the foreign entrepreneurs reinvest their funds would depend on their motivation to invest further, which in turn would be influenced by their expectations of the profitability of the investments and their ability to remit profits from the host to the home country.

Apart from the social costs, the dominant position of the agency houses in the external trade brings about an interesting phenomenon in economic development. This is to be seen in the fact that in spite of the unbroken sequence of favourable merchandise balances shown in Table 9.20, the private sector of the country has been a net exporter of capital, as suggested by the capital account which will be examined below. Hence there seems to be a situation where in terms of national accounting, national savings have exceeded gross fixed capital formation, and the excess has been lent abroad. The implication of the situation is that there is a limited domestic demand for the services of private capital kept abroad. That being the case, it seems obvious that the prerequisite for attracting this capital is the creation of demand, namely by improving opportunities for investment.

Balance on Goods and Services

It can be seen from Table 9.21 that the freight, insurance, and service charges for handling Malaysian international trade amounted to \$164 million in 1963 and in 1971 the charges amounted to \$265 million, thus showing a 62 per cent increase in the period. The item 'Travel' represents mainly the cost of using foreign transport by Malaysian residents which need not be dealt with here.

'Investment Income' represents mainly the outflow of profits from direct foreign investment. The figures need careful interpretation, because according to the convention of balance of payments accounting in Malaysia it is assumed that the entire profits from foreign-owned companies in the country are remitted overseas. Thus, the amounts shown in Table 9.21 are overstating the

TABLE 9.21
THE BALANCE OF GOODS AND SERVICES, 1963–1971
($ million)

Item	*1963*	*1964*	*1965*	*1966*	*1967*	*1968*	*1969*	*1970*	*1971*
Services (net)									
(a) *Freight and insurance*	–164	–169	–178	–179	–179	–198	–198	–247	–265
(b) Travel	–69	–74	–80	–78	–69	–73	–96	–105	–102
(c) *Investment income*	–195	–230	–255	–268	–144	–154	–308	–213	–227
(d) *Other services*	–43	–50	–53	–74	–91	–100	–96	–118	–115
(e) Government transactions	+150	+197	+225	+189	+132	+125	+97	+60	+44
Service balance	–321	–326	–341	–407	–351	–400	–601	–623	–665
Non-monetary gold	–3	–3	–5	–6	–2	–6	–18	–11	–19
Merchandise balance	+286	+275	+526	+559	+447	+643	+1481	+983	+633
Balance of goods and services	–38	–54	+180	+146	+124	+237	+862	+349	–51

Source: As for Table 9.19.

actual outflow by the amounts of profits reinvested by the foreign companies or paid as dividends to Malaysian nationals. In fact the reinvestments are lumped together (in the form of contra-entries) in the private long-term capital outflow accounts. Hence, reinvested profits are treated as new investments each year.

The item 'Other services' represents the cost of services resulting from the payments abroad of management fees, technical service fees, royalties on patents and copyrights, and other miscellaneous items like commissions, film rentals, and subscriptions. The item 'Government transactions' which is shown in the Table as representing net receipts denotes mainly goods and services received by the government sector for which it does not have to pay. In the early 1960s the main receipts were military goods and defence facilities provided by British, Australian, and New Zealand armed forces.[96] These receipts are dwindling fast since the British government adopted the policy of phased withdrawal from bases East of Suez. In 1972 such receipts were no longer significant in amount (about $25 million).[97]

The three crucial items in the service accounts are the investment income, freight and insurance, and service charges. Extracting the investment income and service charges from the accounts and using the information gathered in the field work, Table 9.23 can be constructed to show the magnitude of income remission in the balance of payments accounts arising from British manufacturing companies.

As shown in Table 9.22 yearly profit remittances by the U.K. manufacturing firms were erratic during the period 1963 to 1971, although there was an increase of approximately 67 per cent between the amounts at the beginning and end of the period. Royalties and service fees on the other hand showed a steady increase from $6 million in 1963 to $23 million in 1971. During the same period, profit remittances of U.K. manufacturing firms in Malaysia represented, on average, about 26 per cent of all remittances of the foreign firms in the country.[98] Clearly the amounts involved every year are important, particularly when compared to the inflows of capital from the companies to the manufacturing sector as shown in Table 9.23; the data contained therein provide a good reason for suggesting that these foreign remittances have been a contributory factor in aggravating the balance of payments position, particularly when it was shown (in Table 9.18) that the terms of trade are moving against the country. The rising amount of royalties and service fees (Table 9.22) is also indicative of the increasing cost of technological dependency of the country on

TABLE 9.22

REMITTED BRITISH INDUSTRIAL INVESTMENT INCOME AS PERCENTAGE OF TOTAL PRIVATE FOREIGN INVESTMENT REMITTANCES FROM MALAYSIA, 1963–1971
($ million)

Item	*1963*	*1964*	*1965*	*1966*	*1967*	*1968*	*1969*	*1970*	*1971*
All industrial investment incomes	–195	–230	–255	–268	–144	–154	–308	–213	–227
Services	–43	–50	–53	–74	–91	–100	–96	–118	–115
1. Total	–238	–280	–318	–342	–235	–254	–404	–331	–342
2. Manufacturing income of U.K. firms	–63	–51	–65	–65	–51	–61	–40	–88	–105
3. Royalties and service fees	–6	–7	–9	–12	–14	–14	–15	–20	–23
4. (2) + (3)	–69	–58	–74	–77	–65	–75	–55	–108	–128
(4) as percentage of (1)	29	21	23	23	28	30	14	33	37

Sources: Data derived from sources in Table 9.19, and interviews.

Notes: (i) Amounts referring to all industrial investment incomes include re-invested portions of all profits accruing to foreign companies. 'Services' are amounts referring to technical fees, royalties, and other services remitted by all manufacturing companies.

(ii) Items (2) and (3) are remitted profits and fees from U.K.-owned firms in Malaysia.

TABLE 9.23
INFLOW AND REMITTANCE OF FUNDS FROM BRITISH MANUFACTURING COMPANIES IN MALAYSIA, 1963–1971
($ million)

Year	*Remittances of Funds*	*Inflow of Funds*	*Net Outflow*
1963	–69.0	+30.0	–39.0
1964	–58.0	+53.2	–4.8
1965	–74.0	+46.3	–27.7
1966	–77.0	+26.6	–50.4
1967	–65.0	+92.6	+27.6
1968	–75.0	+5.1	–69.9
1969	–55.0	–1.5	–56.5
1970	–108.0	+77.9	–30.1
1971	–128.0	+24.3	–103.7
Cumulative Total 1963–71	–709.0	+354.5	–354.5

Sources: Data on remittances from Table 9.22; data on inflows from Table 9.1.

Notes: (i) Inflows are understated by the amounts of inflows from British-owned companies not resident in the U.K. (See note (ii) of Table 9.1.) Thus, the net outflows may be overstated. On the other hand, the remittances represent only those recorded as receipts in the U.K., excluding remittances to British nationals resident elsewhere in the world. So, on balance, it would seem that the net outflows shown can be taken to be the approximate measure of income of manufacturing companies operating in Malaysia received in the U.K., from 1963 to 1971.

(ii) –denotes outflow; + denotes inflow.

foreign sources. In making this statement one has to be very careful, since the effects of induced income changes in the economy have not been fully explored. The wider implication of the present situation is that the indirect benefits of the foreign investment will have to be a great deal larger to offset the obvious drain of funds from the country. All that can be said at this stage is that the nominal balance of payments cost of the foreign investment has been substantial.

Transfers Account

Before considering the movement of the capital account it will be illuminating to complete the examination of the current accounts by examining very briefly the 'Transfers Account' summarized in Table 9.24. The most important item in the Table is the net private transfers—the main constituent (about one-half)[99] being remittances of British personnel serving in the various companies. About one-half of the remittances attributable to those

TABLE 9.24

THE BALANCE ON GOODS, SERVICES, AND TRANSFERS ACCOUNTS, 1963–1971

($ million)

Item (Net)	*1963*	*1964*	*1965*	*1966*	*1967*	*1968*	*1969*	*1970*	*1971*
Balance on goods and services	–38	–54	+180	+146	+124	+237	+862	+349	–51
Net transfers:									
a. Private	–206	–201	–195	–196	–185	–180	–209	–199	–188
b. Government	+25	+127	+137	+90	+43	+37	+30	+16	+21
Balance on goods, services and transfers	–219	–128	+122	+40	–18	+94	+683	+166	–218

Sources: Data derived from sources in Table 9.19.

Note: (i) Transfers refer to international transactions without any *quid pro quo*. The most important item recorded in the *Private* transfers is the remittances of families and individuals. Of these remittances, the most significant is the remittances of British personnel in Malaysian industries. *Government* transfers in the Table constitute receipts in the form of inter-governmental grants, both in cash and in kind, other than military assistance.

personnel originate from remittances of personnel serving industrial companies; the other half belongs to those in other sectors of the economy.

As mentioned above, British personnel enjoy a higher level of pay than local personnel in the Malaysian subsidiaries. In fact, between 50 and 60 per cent of the remuneration attributable to scarce labour in the manufacturing companies is accounted for by remuneration of expatriate executives, other than directors. The numbers of these executives are being reduced as more local people are promoted to the top company jobs. Almost all the larger companies are rapidly reducing the number of their expatriate officers, both for reasons of economy and to conform to the government requests that top positions of foreign companies should be Malaysianized as quickly as feasible.

As a result of these policies, the aggregate private transfers of these expatriate executives have shown a slight decrease over the years, as indicated in Table 9.24. When the outflows of funds and the personnel remittances of the foreign employees are added together, the picture of the amounts of overseas remittances from the industrial companies is as outlined in Table 9.25.

TABLE 9.25

REMITTANCES OVERSEAS BY BRITISH COMPANIES AND PERSONNEL, 1963–1971

Year	*Amounts Remitted by Companies/by Personnel ($ million)*		*(1) Total*	*(2) (1) as % of GNP*	*(3) (1) as % of Exports Value f.o.b.*
			(at current prices)		
1963	69	52	121	1.6	3.7
1964	58	51	109	1.4	3.3
1965	74	49	123	1.4	3.3
1966	77	49	126	1.4	3.3
1967	65	46	111	1.2	3.0
1968	75	45	120	1.2	2.9
1969	55	52	107	1.0	2.2
1970	108	50	158	1.4	3.1
1971	128	47	175	1.4	3.5
Cumulative Total 1963–71	709	441	1,150	1.3	3.1

Sources and *Notes*:

(i) Data on company remittances based on Table 9.24.

(ii) Personnel remittances estimated from various issues of the *National Accounts of West Malaysia*, Department of Statistics, Kuala Lumpur, the various Transfers Accounts in the Balance of Payments as calculated by Bank Negara, and information gathered at interviews.

(iii) Calculations of columns (*2*) and (*3*) are made by expressing column (*1*) as percentages of GNP (at current prices) derived from Bank Negara, *Quarterly Economic Bulletin*, March 1973, p. 51; and Export values (f.o.b.) derived from Bank Negara, op. cit., pp. 71–2.

As can be seen from the Table, industrial companies remitted an estimated total of $709 million during the period 1963 to 1971, and in addition expatriate personnel in those companies personally remitted about $441 million in the period. In terms of the country's GNP, these remittances constituted, on average, approximately 1.3 per cent of each year's total, or in terms of exports approximately 3.1 per cent of the annual proceeds of the country's exports. It is important to note that these remittances are in respect of funds only; i.e. they exclude remittances on account of payment for purchases of material inputs or capital equipment. At best, these amounts can only be regarded as the nominal balance of payments effects. It is impossible to say whether an alternative set of investors in industries presently occupied by the British companies would have produced a substantially different picture of foreign remittances of funds. What one can say is that the remittances would have been a little less than they are at present, had the investment been made by local people, assuming local people would not remit their funds overseas.[100]

Short-term Capital and Unrecorded Transactions

The major item in 'Short-term Capital and Unrecorded Transactions' is the 'Errors and Omissions' which, as shown in Table 9.19, varied in amounts between 1963 and 1971 from $207 million to $454 million. Although the amounts are labelled 'short-term', the net effect is by no means felt only in the short term since the amounts have appeared consistently high throughout the 1963–71 period. In 1964, for example, 'the short-term' errors and omissions (which, for good reasons explained below, can be regarded as short-term capital outflows) exceeded even the long-term net inflow. The cause for concern is that such large amounts in the international accounts camouflaged as 'errors and omissions' will create difficulties in any effort by the authorities to monitor the capital shifting activities of the large transnational companies. It is not argued here that shifting of capital should be stopped, but rather it is felt that from the point of view of policy making it would be helpful if movements of capital were clearly recorded instead of concealed as 'errors and omissions'.

It was found that large companies in Malaysia shift any funds that are temporarily not needed into the Asia-Dollar Market, situated in Singapore, where they can earn an interest higher than that offered by the commercial banks.[101] Because of the undisclosed nature of transactions in the Asia-Dollar Market it is understandable that the Malaysian Department of Statistics has been unable to define the extent of capital movements into and out of the Asia-Dollar Market. A large proportion of such movements of capital is thus regarded as 'errors and omissions' in the international accounts.[102]

Prior to the existence of the Asia-Dollar Market in 1968, a great deal of the short-term capital of the foreign companies in Malaysia found its way to the money market in Singapore[103] where it was used in the financing of international trade, and from where it filtered through to London.[104]

Most British companies at first had their head offices in Singapore, firstly because Singapore was, until 1965, part of Malaysia, and secondly because Singapore was and still is the hub of international trade in South-East Asia. Since the Singapore dollar was freely interchangeable with the Malaysian dollar, and since the two countries shared a common stock exchange until May 1973, there was no compelling reason why the companies thought they should have two head offices in a very small geographical area. Temporary surplus funds were channelled to the head offices in Singapore, and from there to the rest of the outside world.[105] When funds were needed in the country, a reverse flow could easily be arranged. Hence, money could come from the outside world through the Singapore offices of these companies, and eventually to Malaysia. Technically, therefore, Malaysia could be deprived of the proceeds of her export earnings, and there could never be any effective means of monitoring the nature and direction of short-term capital movements, should the agency houses and foreign companies choose to remit their funds through the agency house system of direct (or consignment) dealings between their (Singapore) local offices and the home office in London, as described previously. Many Malaysian commercial banks also have their head offices in Singapore, so that the proceeds of Malaysia's exports can remain in the Singapore office without actually coming to Malaysia where the short-term capital and money market is not as sophisticated as in Singapore. Consequently, throughout the 1960s, much of the proceeds of Malaysia's exports were held up temporarily in Singapore before they found their way to the capital and financial markets of the world.[106] As in the case of trade, all other international transactions were also conducted through Singapore. The net effect was the backlog of proper recordings of international transactions in Kuala Lumpur. Such a backlog resulted in the large amounts of 'errors and omissions' in the balance of payments.

On the basis of information discussed so far it seems apparent that the country does not get the full benefit of the proceeds of its international trade and related transactions. The situation does not look so bad when first the institutional framework of the country is examined, and secondly when, as will be studied in the section below, the long-term capital movement into the country is examined.

The relatively underdeveloped nature of the money market in Malaysia compared to Singapore accounted for the reluctance of short-term capital to return to or remain in Malaysia. The modern development of Singapore as a major centre of international trade had its origin in the 1820s. By the 1950s the Singapore money market which developed around the international trade was very sophisticated compared to the money market in Kuala Lumpur, which had only one money broker at that time.[107] Even today, according to executives interviewed, one of the reasons why a large proportion of British company profits are remitted abroad annually is that the relatively underdeveloped local financial and capital market cannot offer a wide variety of opportunities for investment. The policy implication is that if more of the capital of the foreign companies were to be attracted into the country the development efforts in the country should be in the areas of improving the money and capital market.[108] This was partly the idea behind the termination of the currency interchangeability between Malaysia and Singapore in May 1973.[109]

The Long-term Capital Account

The long-term capital account covers the bulk of what is commonly known as the inflows and outflows of capital. For Malaysia the long-term capital account has fortunately been in surplus, sufficient to finance whatever deficits have arisen in the current account. This situation is illustrated in Table 9.26.

The significant points to note from Table 9.26 are, firstly, that private long-term capital inflows seem to be sluggish, and secondly, that government international borrowing is rapidly increasing, from $51 million in 1966 to $377 million in 1971.

On the basis of the foregoing discussion it is by no means clear whether foreign manufacturing investment can be regarded as making a net contribution to the country's foreign exchange. The evidence from the outflows of company incomes and services (Table 9.22) as well as the private transfers of foreigners in the economy (Table 9.24) and the comparatively small net long-term inflow of private foreign capital (Table 9.26) point to the conclusion that foreigners were responsible for substantial outflows of capital from Malaysia in the period 1963 to 1971. Had it not been for the surpluses on the merchandise balance (Table 9.20) and the ever-increasing government borrowings (Table 9.26), the outflows of funds from Malaysia, mainly on account of the private foreign investor, would have aggravated the balance of payments position.

From the evidence of Table 9.23 and Table 9.25, there is good reason to believe that British manufacturing companies took more funds out of Malaysia than they put in. In terms of aggregate amounts, between 1963 and 1971, British manufacturing companies remitted $354 million to the country (Table 9.23), and at the same time they took out $1,150 million (Table 9.25). It would be incorrect to infer from this that British manufacturing companies have definitely taken out more than they put into the economy as a whole. As noted in Table 9.12 the net contribution of the British manufacturing companies to GNP from 1963 to

TABLE 9.26

LONG-TERM CAPITAL MOVEMENTS, 1963–1971

($ million)

Item	*1963*	*1964*	*1965*	*1966*	*1967*	*1968*	*1969*	*1970*	*1971*
Net movements in companies	+270	+165	+150	+170	+130	+93	+140	+160	+160
Government and statutory bodies	+89	+20	+105	+51	+134	+113	+166	–2	+377
Other official capital	–2	+7	–5	–29	–23	–50	–7	–8	+20
Balance on long-term capital	+357	+192	+250	+192	+241	+156	+299	+250	+557
Balance on goods, services and transfers	–219	–128	+122	+40	–18	+94	+683	+166	–218
Short-term capital and unrecorded transactions	–212	–204	–235	–396	–479	–277	–454	–259	–214
Overall balance (Surplus +/Deficit –)	–74	–140	+137	–164	–256	–27	+528	+57	+125

Sources: Data derived from sources in Table 9.19.

Notes: (i) Net movements in the long-term capital of companies represent the net inflow of long-term private capital into Malaysia. Ploughed-back profits (i.e. the contra-entry to the item called 'Investment income' which is the outflows of funds from the private sector mentioned in Table 9.22), form a substantial portion of the net inflow of long-term private capital.

(ii) The net inflows on account of government and statutory bodies are the official long-term liabilities of the government. The inflows arise mainly from drawings on inter-governmental loans and loans from international institutions (e.g. the World Bank and the Asian Development Bank), as well as market loans raised in London, New York, and other European financial centres.

(iii) The item called 'Other official capital' refers to Malaysia's subscriptions to the International Tin Buffer Stock and other international institutions; and state governments' repayment on foreign loans.

1970 was about 2.1 per cent; while, as indicated in Table 9.25, the amounts remitted overseas by the British manufacturing companies constituted approximately 1.3 per cent of GNP. Considering that these companies also helped in the promotion of manufactured exports, and manufactured exports as suggested by Table 9.18 help to prevent the deterioration of the country's terms of trade, there are valid reasons for arguing that the companies contribute positively to the growth of the economy. Moreover, as discussed in the previous section, these manufacturing companies brought about indirect benefits in the forms of external economies. Access to expertise and external markets as well as the widening of the industrial base of the economy resulting from the British companies' presence have probably offset the balance of payments costs of servicing the investment.

THE LONG-TERM BALANCE OF PAYMENTS EFFECTS

In general, British manufacturing firms in Malaysia from 1963 to 1971 made valuable contributions to the country's economic development. These firms train and promote local people within their organizations to fill managerial and technical positions required to run the firms. In many cases the chief executives are themselves drawn from local people. The firms can claim that they have achieved some success in 'integrating' themselves into the economy by having local people in the higher ranks of their organizations.

The time will come when the British firms in Malaysia will be managed entirely by local people, so that the only foreign element that remains will be the ownership of capital. In the words of Professor Penrose:[110] 'after the foreign-owned firms have developed lives of their own . . . employing largely local managerial and technical staff and have become integral parts of the local economy' one is entitled to ask whether their continued expansion would be making any special contribution to the economy because of their being foreign-owned, other than the foreign exchange they would refrain from paying abroad. One would tend to agree with Professor Penrose that as the foreign firms develop, the intangible benefits they give to the underdeveloped economy might become less and less significant.[111] At the same time, the dividends paid on them can be greater and greater as the firms continue to grow.

The trend shown in Table 9.22 points to the increasing payments of dividends and other fees in connexion with British investment in Malaysian manufacturing. The long-term capital inflows on account of the private foreign firms indicated in Table 9.26 do not suggest that they are on the increase. As far as British investors are concerned, three factors can be cited to support the suggestion that future inflows of capital from Britain into Malaysia will be declining.[112] Firstly, investment in various types of industry in the manufacturing sector has already been made in the early 1960s. Inflows of capital to the agricultural and mining sectors are limited, since for obvious reasons the various state governments prefer to exploit these sectors on their own rather than alienate vast tracts of land to the foreign investor. Some foreign capital may flow into petroleum production, but the amounts are bound to be small since the larger British oil companies are already in the country, and since they are bound to raise most of their capital through borrowing locally rather than bringing in new capital. Some capital may flow into palm oil cultivation, but most likely it would come from the existing rubber-plantation owners.

The second factor that limits the flow of capital from the United Kingdom to Malaysia was the introduction in 1965 of the corporation tax in the U.K. on British-owned overseas trading companies. The net effect of the current British government tax treatment of companies investing overseas places such companies at a disadvantage as against companies investing at home in Britain.[113]

The third factor is the general reduction of British overseas investment, associated with the disequilibrium of the U.K. balance of payments position, which also affects the direct investment of British firms in the underdeveloped countries.[114] A substantial portion of new investment by British companies from 1963 to 1971 was from reinvestment of profits of existing companies,[115] which technically originated from the underdeveloped countries themselves.

In periods of serious balance of payments strain for Britain it is natural for overseas investment by Britain in other countries to be viewed with special doubts by policy-makers in Britain.[116] However likely it may be that the investment will in the long run bring benefits to Britain, the immediate effect will almost certainly be a curtailment of overseas long-term capital commitments.

One of the main features of the sterling area as it has evolved since 1939 has been the continued ability of private capital to flow from Britain to the rest of the area more freely than to other countries.[117] When the British government floated the pound sterling in June 1972 it also restricted the definition of the sterling area to comprise only Great Britain and Northern Ireland. In so doing every other country in the world is regarded as a foreign country to which the British flow of capital is subject to restrictions. This will mean that outflows of capital to Malaysia will be restricted, and financing of British investments there will have to be made to a greater extent from a combination of ploughing back of profits and raising loans locally.

According to a study made under the auspices of the Royal Institute of International Affairs,[118] British armed forces and British aid encouraged British overseas investment.[119] The British armed forces' withdrawal from Malaysia was completed by 1972. British aid to Malaysia, which has never been large[120] compared to British aid to the African countries (e.g. Nigeria, Kenya, Ghana, and Malawi), or the West Indies, or even India, Pakistan, and Ceylon (Sri Lanka), has been almost entirely directed towards education and training, which in the short term does not significantly affect capital outflows from Britain into the country.[121]

In the absence of substantial inflows of long-term private capital,[122] and with the persistent tendency to deterioration in the terms of trade (shown in Table 9.18), it is likely that the outflows of private funds (at the 1963–71 level as shown in Tables 9.22 and 9.25) may cause a balance of payments problem for the country in the years to come. The relatively high levels of government foreign borrowing in the early 1970s,[123] which in fact have been the main prop in preventing the occurrence of disequilibrium in the balance of payments, are suggestive of the long-term effects that the foreign investments may have on the country's balance of payments. It is certainly an unsatisfactory means of financing a deficit balance in the current account. The solution seems to be in the expansion of export earnings, since a high level of export earnings would help to reduce the need for government borrowings to prevent the deterioration in the balance of payments.

POLICY IMPLICATIONS

From the point of view of policy-making, a case can be made at the present stage of foreign industrial development in the country for the proposition that it is in the long-term interest of the country to limit the growth of foreign ownership in the existing companies.[124] Essentially it will mean that the expansion of existing companies has to be financed from local equity funds, or that local interests should purchase some of the existing equity in the foreign firms. The real problem seems to be that most local people may not be able to afford to purchase the equity in the open market; and in certain cases, only a small portion of the equity is freely traded on the local stock market. Nonetheless, the reduction of foreign equity in the existing companies would reduce the proportion of profits paid abroad, and would impose a smaller burden on the balance of payments.[125]

It is possible to argue, as Bank Negara has done,[126] that the running deficits in the current balance (i.e. balance on goods, services, and transfers account) have been the result of the country's massive efforts to accelerate development, and that the balance of payments will not be in any fundamental stage of disequilibrium provided deficits in the current account are made good by inflows of private and official capital. The evidence as examined in the various balances in the balance of payments accounts[127] seems to suggest that part of the official borrowing is necessary to prevent deficits in the balance of payments resulting from the sustained outflows of funds from the private sector. In other words, the surpluses on the merchandise balance and the inflows of capital on account of the private sector together have not been sufficient to cover the outflow of funds on account of foreign companies' remittances of dividends and fees, foreign individuals' remittances of earnings, and foreign companies' shifting of short-term capital outside the country. In brief, private outflows of funds from Malaysia have exceeded the private inflows during the period 1963 to 1971.

So long as the external reserves (Table 9.18) remain at relatively high levels[128] compared to most underdeveloped countries, and sufficient to maintain international confidence in the ability of the country to meet its international financial obligations, official borrowings may not be a problem. The evidence shown in the *Mid-Term Review of the Second Malaysia Plan, 1971–75* (p. 52), suggests that the external reserves are gradually being eroded, and presumably with this goes the erosion of the potential capability of the country to borrow internationally. The conclusion from this section is that the foreign investment in the manufacturing sector has been earning some, but not sufficient, foreign exchange for the country through the exports of manufactures.

It would seem appropriate that the government should ensure that private foreign investors earn their own foreign exchange and that the government should not borrow merely to finance capital outflows on account of the foreign investors.

1. Private communications with the Overseas Section of the Confederation of British Industry.

2. For the problems connected with quantifying British industrial capital, see Chapter 6, Sections 1 and 2.

3. See p. 145.

4. Private conversation with a FIDA officer.

5. Representatives of the multinational enterprises claimed that they have charged their Malaysian subsidiaries the proper amounts for R & D taking into consideration the size of operations there.

6. Based on company reports and publications of the Singapore Malaysia Stock Exchange.

7. In a country with a high (between 7 and 9 per cent) level of unemployment some of the labour can be assumed to be 'non-scarce' with no alternative employment, and zero opportunity cost. Most of such non-scarce labour is unskilled and probably illiterate; but a small part may be fairly well educated (e.g. ex-soldiers, police constables 'retired' at 40, and recent high-school leavers) but unable to get gainful employment. Because of the existence of these people it is preferable to use the terms 'scarce' and 'non-scarce', rather than 'skilled' and 'unskilled' to describe labour in Malaysia. For a more refined discussion on labour in Malaysia see S. H. Saw, 'The Structure of Labour Force in Malaya', *International Labour Review*, Vol. 98 (1), July 1968; and 'A Survey of Labour Utilisation in West Malaysia, 1971–75' (mimeo.), Kuala Lumpur, Economic Planning Unit, Prime Minister's Department, November 1970 (3 vols.).

8. See *Census of Manufacturing Industries, 1968* (hereafter referred to as the 1968 census), p. 38. One has to adjust the value added represented in the census because it covered only a sample of establishments rather than firms. A firm may comprise a number of establishments, such that when one compares total manufacturing value added reported in the *Second Malaysia Plan, 1971–75* (p. 148)–which represents value added of firms instead of establishments–one finds the census figures understated by about 7 per cent. Accordingly one adjusts the census figure of $181 million value added for British manufacturing to $194 million. From this amount, one estimates the unadjusted income accruing to labour as $40 million, i.e. 20.6 per cent of the value added. One may note that the 20.6 per cent labour share in manufacturing value added is low compared to the average share of about 50 per cent in the case of labour in manufacturing in developed countries. See details of this in P. J. Loftus, 'Labour's Share in Manufacture', *Lloyds Bank Review* (No. 92), April 1969, pp. 15–25.

9. This is a simplifying assumption. With adjustments taking into consideration the slightly higher wage rates in British firms compared to the national average wage rates, it would appear that the net gain to non-scarce labour would be less than the estimated $8 million.

10. Information from interviews with executives. Most expatriates live on their overseas allowances while they send home the bulk of their salaries. This will be considered in the analysis of the balance of payments effect later.

11. Expatriates are usually paid at a very much higher level than locally-recruited counterparts with the same qualifications, experience, and responsibilities.

12. From interviews it was found that incomes of expatriate executives constituted nearly 50 per cent of all incomes accruing to scarce labour. We estimated that a portion of the expatriate incomes was consumed locally; and adjusting for the fact that some expatriate executives do spend a large portion of their income in the country, it would seem reasonable to estimate that, in total 40 per cent of all income accruing to scarce labour was remitted overseas by the expatriate executives. We may regard the earnings remitted as having little or no direct income effect on the host country. We shall analyse the implications later when we deal with aspects of the balance of payments effects of British manufacturing on the Malaysian economy.

13. Based on information gathered at interviews.

14. Our estimate is slightly on the conservative side because in actual fact the percentage of value added attributable to labour gains may be higher than the 2.6 we calculated. This is explained thus: we noted earlier that the non-scarce labour income was $8 million. To the extent that the non-scarce labour was drawn from the pool of urban unemployed labour (which we know to be the case in a number of factories in

West Malaysia), where the earnings—and marginal productivity—were virtually nil, it would seem that the $8 million constituted a net income gained. Expressed as a percentage of manufacturing value added, of $194 million, the non-scarce labour earnings represent 4.1 per cent. Our conservative estimate is made in the light of our lack of precise knowledge about the possible repercussions on the economy of employing labour in British manufacturing.

15. All figures calculated from data in the *Census of Manufacturing Industries, 1968.*

16. See P. J. Loftus (Director of the Statistical Office of the U.N.), 'Labour's Share in Manufacturing', *Lloyds Bank Review,* No. 92, April 1969, p. 24.

17. *Mid-Term Review of the Second Malaysia Plan, 1971–75,* p. 141.

18. In the 1960s the annual increase in wages was very small, see p. 245. In fact as suggested in Chapter 8, one of the reasons why British subsidiaries in Malaysia were profitable was that labour costs remained fairly stable compared to labour costs in the U.K.

19. It is unusual to express retained earnings in terms of value added. It is so done here merely as a means of estimating the amounts of retained earnings in aggregate terms.

20. For simplicity, no account is taken of the accelerated depreciation allowances permitted in the *Investment Incentives Act, 1968.*

21. No attempt is made here to estimate dividends received net of tax. This is because the policy of the government regarding withholding tax is quite complicated. Some companies, under certain conditions stipulated in the *Investment Incentives Act* are allowed various types of concessions on the taxes they have to pay. See details in *Income Tax Act, 1967,* Section 109, Schedule 1(2); and also the *Investment Incentives Act, 1968,* Part II, Clause 21 et seq.

22. This is based on field work information. Data in the *Census of Manufacturing Industries, 1968* suggested that all industries incurred about 11.8 per cent of value added in expenses on services of factors other than labour directly employed.

23. This tax was repealed in 1971 and substituted by import surtax ranging from 2 to 4 per cent *ad valorem.*

24. Payroll tax abolished in January 1971.

25. Introduced after the introduction of *The Sales Tax Act,* February 1972.

26. None of the companies interviewed had to pay this tax since they were generally prompt in their tax payments.

27. This was the remnant of the days when Malaysia was in the sterling area and when it was thought necessary to protect sterling. This surcharge was abolished in December 1971.

28. Companies which acquired for part of their production activities certain tax exemptions on account of the provisions of the *Investment Incentives Act, 1968,* paid a lesser percentage than this. One or two of the older companies paid slightly more—about 45 per cent; but generally the 42 per cent seemed the normal rate for the majority of the companies between 1963 and 1970.

29. See full discussion in W. M. Corden, *The Theory of Protection,* Oxford University Press, 1971, and the 78 references therein.

30. Profits of British companies in the *Census of Manufacturing Industries, 1968* is estimated to be around $154 million, 42 per cent of this amounts to $64.7; which is approximately 1/3 of value added of $194 million.

31. We have shown in Chapter 2 (pp. 52–6) that the industries that have developed in Malaysia are a mixture of import-substitutes industries as well as those that produce both for the domestic and the export markets.

32. J. H. Power, 'The Structure of Protection in West Malaysia', in B. Balassa, *et al.*, *The Structure of Protection in Developing Countries,* Johns Hopkins University Press, 1971, pp. 203–22.

33. I. Little, T. Scitovsky and M. Scott, *Industry and Trade in Some Developing Countries: A Comparative Study* (OECD), Oxford University Press, 1970, p. 76n and *passim.*

34. I. Little and D. G. Tipping, *A Social Cost Benefit Analysis of the Kulai Oil Palm*

Estate, West Malaysia, OECD, Paris, 1972, p. 39; see also *U.N. Economic Survey for Asia and the Far East, 1972*, U.N., 1973, p. 73. As discussed in Chapter 3, the Malaysian economy is an open economy in which foreign trade forms a large proportion of the gross domestic product.

35. See among others, H. S. Ellis, 'The Conflict Between Growth and Control of Inflation', in K. Berrill, ed., *Economic Development with Special Reference to East Asia*, Macmillan, 1964.

36. N. Kaldor, 'Economic Growth and the Problem of Inflation', *Economica*, Parts I and II, August and November 1959, pp. 212–26, and pp. 287–98.

37. There are almost as many economists who believe that inflation can help economic growth of the underdeveloped countries as there are those who believe that it can retard growth; see discussion by Professor Ellis in K. Berrill, op. cit. An interesting discussion of inflation as a mechanism for promoting development is found in W. A. Lewis, *The Theory of Economic Growth*, George Allen and Unwin, 1965, Chapter V. Lewis does not suggest that inflation helps economic development; rather he argues that inflation may be used as a substitute for taxation and voluntary saving, i.e. 'forced saving' may be introduced through government initiated inflation (via extra credit creation). Lewis, however, warned that 'once the possibility of resorting to it (inflation) is admitted, governments cannot be trusted to know where to draw the line . . . (to stop inflation)', p. 406. If the experiences of the advanced countries like Britain and America are any guide to the underdeveloped countries, the real problem seems to be not initiating inflation, but controlling it. The experience of Indonesia in the late 1950s and throughout the 1960s, seems to confirm the view that the scope for inflation as a device to stimulate capital formation and economic growth is certainly limited. See Paauw, below, footnote 39.

38. See comment by Sadli, in K. Berrill, op. cit., p. 271.

39. See D. S. Paauw, 'Financing Economic Development in Indonesia', *Economic Development and Cultural Change*, January 1956, pp. 171–85; H. Myint, *Economic Theory and the Underdeveloped Countries*, Oxford University Press, 1971, p. 278, and *passim*; and Asian Development Bank, *South-east Asia's Economy in the 1970s*, Longman, 1971, p. 373.

40. Asian Development Bank, op. cit., p. 385; and *The Second Malaysia Plan, 1971–75, passim*. One reason for the lack of economic growth in Indonesia was that inflation was so severe that the main efforts of the authorities were mainly directed at rehabilitation and stabilization.

41. In 1972, net export of manufactures accounted for 20 per cent of all exports. The provisional trade figures for 1973 indicated that the export of manufactures had increased by 61.5 per cent over the 1972 figures. See details in *The Mid-Term Review of the Second Malaysia Plan, 1971–75*, p. 142, and Bank Negara, *Annual Report 1973*, p. 108.

42. The manufacture of electronic components and other electrical products has expanded very rapidly with the arrival of American, Japanese, and German firms since 1970. Over 90 per cent of the output of these firms is exported. In 1972 alone, over forty electronic component manufacturing companies came into the country. See details in *Malaysia Industrial Digest*, Vol. 6 (1), First Quarter, 1973.

43. Information gathered at the interviews. Manufacturers gain an incentive in the form of tax credits when they increase the local content of their manufacturing material inputs. (See *Investment Incentives Act, 1968*, Clause 26 (2) (c) and its subsequent amendments.) The offer of such an incentive *per se* did not affect the local content of many firms interviewed; but the rising world prices did influence firms interviewed to increase their local content of industrial inputs.

44. Using data from the International Monetary Fund and the Organisation for Economic Co-operation and Development, the Malaysian Treasury calculated that since 1963 prices in U.K., U.S.A., Japan, Australia, and Germany have increased in 1971 respectively by 57 per cent, 37 per cent, 67 per cent, 35 per cent, and 34 per cent. By contrast, during the same period, prices in Malaysia increased only by about 7 per cent. (See The Treasury, *Economic Report, 1972–3*, Kuala Lumpur, 1972, p. 41.) Here is further support for the claim that prices in Malaysia had generally been stable as referred to earlier above.

45. By far the best analysis of export as a source of growth to the Malaysian economy is to be found in J. T. Thoburn, 'Export and Economic Growth in West Malaysia', *Oxford Economic Papers*, Vol. 25 (1), March 1973, pp. 88–111.

46. Eighth edition, Macmillan, 1966, Chapter VI.

47. See discussions in E. J. Mishan, 'Reflections on Recent Development in the Concept of External Effects', *Canadian Journal of Political Economy*, February 1965, pp. 3–34; and 'Post-war Literature on Externalities; An Interpretative Essay', *Journal of Economic Literature*, March 1971, pp. 1–28.

48. See H. J. Habakkuk, 'The Entrepreneur and Economic Development', in I. Livingstone, ed., *Economic Policy for Development*, Penguin, 1971, pp. 37–52 and the reference therein. See also P. Kilby, ed., *Entrepreneurship and Economic Development*, Collier-Macmillan, 1971.

49. The SIM was being converted to the metric system in 1977.

50. *The Theory of Economic Development*, Harvard University Press, 1934, p. 63.

51. Among others see C. Furtado, *Development and Underdevelopment* (translation), University of California Press, 1964, and W. A. Lewis, *The Theory of Economic Growth*, George Allen and Unwin, 1965.

52. See contributions by various writers in *The Journal of Development Studies* (Special Issue on Science and Technology in Development), Vol. 9 (1), October 1972; and also various contributors in *Social and Economic Studies* (Special Number on Development and Underdevelopment), Vol. 22 (1), March 1973. Several studies by UNCTAD have also been devoted to the issue. A selective reference is to be found in United Nations, 'The Channels and Mechanisms for the Transfer of Technology from Developed to Developing Countries' (mimeo.), Geneva, UNCTAD, TD/B/AC.11/5, 1971.

53. *Journal of Development Studies*, Vol. 9 (1), October 1972, p. 2.

54. See pp. 187–8, above.

55. C. M. Cooper, 'Science, Technology and Production in the Underdeveloped Countries: An Introduction', *Journal of Development Studies*, Vol. 9 (1), October 1972, p. 6.

56. Cooper, op. cit., p. 6 and p. 9, *passim*.

57. Among others see J. Woodies, *Introduction to Neo-Colonialism*, New York, International Publishers, 1971; various contributors in R. I. Rhodes, ed., *Imperialism and Underdevelopment*, New York, Monthly Review Press, 1970; and S. Amin, *Neo-Colonialism in West Africa* (translated from the French), Penguin, 1973.

58. The concept of linkage effects in development economics is part of the theory of capital formation in underdeveloped countries. See the treatment of it in A. O. Hirschman, *The Strategy of Economic Development*, Yale University Press, 1958, pp. 98–119, *passim*.

59. See Lewis, op. cit., p. 197. It should be mentioned that even Communist countries like the USSR and China do make use of foreign technology, although they may be less dependent on foreign technical knowledge in the way that small underdeveloped countries are. Because of the different orientation of the respective economies of these countries, comparisons of this kind are quite useless.

60. See details in A. O. Hirschman, *The Strategy of Economic Development*, pp. 98–119. The concept of linkages has been criticized on grounds that some investment projects do not have widespread linkages, and that in poor countries interested parties may use the linkage effect concept spuriously to justify socially unprofitable projects. See arguments in 'bad' and 'good' linkages in I. M. D. Little and J. A. Mirrlees, *Manual of Industrial Project Appraisal in Developing Countries*, Vol. II, Paris, OECD, 1968, pp. 212–19; and 'A Reply to Some Criticisms of the OECD Manual', *Bulletin of the Oxford University Institute of Economics and Statistics*, Vol. 34 (1), 1972, pp. 164–5.

61. T. Scitovsky, 'Two Concepts of External Economies', *Journal of Political Economy*, Vol. 62 (1), 1954, p. 146. Profit calculations do not take full account of the externalities. According to Scitovsky, the market mechanism may be an inadequate transmission medium of technological externalities. Hence, private profits and social benefits do not coincide.

62. Some form of assimilation of knowledge and skills must have taken place among those who stayed with the firms.

63. See J. M. Gullick, *Malaysia*, Ernest Benn Ltd., 1969, pp. 240–1.

64. Marketed world-wide under the trade mark of McLean Separators and Hargill-Sheahan Separators, patented by Hargill Engineering Berhad.

65. A great deal of research is proceeding in Malaysia including research into the use of rubber in road construction which is done in association with the British Road Research Laboratory.

66. Information obtained from interviews. The companies in question are quite small with an average paid-up capital of $3.5 million (compared with the average capital of British companies in the country of over $20 million).

67. UNCTAD, *The Channels and Mechanisms for the Transfer of Technology from Developed to Developing Countries*, TD/B/AC.11/5, Geneva, 1971.

68. Loc. cit., pp. 6--7.

69. J. T. Thoburn, 'Exports and the Malaysian Engineering Industry: A Case Study of Backward Linkage', *Oxford Bulletin of Economics and Statistics*, Vol. 35 (2), May 1973, pp. 91–118.

70. See ibid., pp. 99–100, for details.

71. Loc. cit.

72. Capital goods industry in the 1960s was relatively unprotected, see Table 9.14.

73. For explanations of 'bad' and 'good' linkages of industries, see I. M. D. Little and J. A. Mirrlees, *Manual of Industrial Project Appraisal in Developing Countries* (II) OECD, pp. 212–19; see also *Bulletin of the Oxford University Institute of Economics and Statistics*, Vol. 34 (1), 1972, pp. 164–5, and *passim*. Basically the linkage effect may be said to be 'good' when the industries involved do not require high protection for their establishment.

74. This is a new development. Computer data are flown into the country for punching, either on tapes or cards, by low-wage punch operators; following which the punched tapes or cards are flown back to the advanced countries. Similar arrangements also occur in other countries in South-East Asia and the West Indies. See G. K. Helleiner, 'Manufactured Exports from Less-Developed Countries and Multinational Firms', *The Economic Journal*, March 1973, p. 29.

75. There are examples of British firms in Malaysia accepting contracts from foreign companies for technical drawing for oil rigs and sophisticated water-pumps. In some cases the fabrication of parts of the equipment (from locally available high-quality materials) is also done in the country. According to a company executive interviewed, most of the technical work has been done by locally-trained people, mainly graduates of the local National Institute of Technology and the Faculty of Engineering of the local university. This implies that there is scope for the local educational establishments to expand their output of technically-trained graduates and thereby contribute towards the supply of technicians.

76. An interesting attempt to define the middle class and to associate the group with the growth of industrialization is to be found in R. Lewis and A. Maude, *The English Middle Class*, Phoenix House, 1949.

77. See an early attempt at describing the growth of the middle class in Malaysia in F. G. Carnell, 'The Development of A Middle Class in Burma, Thailand, and Malaya', in Institute International des Civilisations Differentes, *Development of a Middle Class in Tropical and Sub-Tropical Countries*, Bruxelles, INCID, 1956, pp. 271–9.

According to a recent study (J. MacDougall, *Shared Burdens: A Study in Communal Discrimination by Political Parties in Malaysia and Singapore*, Harvard University Press, 1969) the social structure in Malaysia may be classified thus:
1. *Upper Class*—private industrialists, managers, financiers, estate owners, and high civil servants; 2. *Middle Class*—professional and technical personnel, merchants and traders, teachers, clerical workers, and religious leaders; and 3. *Lower Class*—peasants, craftsmen, factory workers, vendors, transport and commercial workers, the rank and file of the armed forces, and other labourers.

78. T. G. McGee and W. D. McTaggart, 'Petaling Jaya: A Socio-Economic Survey', Wellington, University of Victoria, *Pacific Viewpoint* Monograph, 1967.

79. Loc. cit., p. 5.

80. Total industrial employees of American, European, and Japanese firms in 1968 was about 48,000, of which 37,000 were employed by British firms. See *Census of Manufacturing Industries, 1968*, p. 38.

81. Among others see R. Nurkse, *Problems of Capital Formation in Underdeveloped Countries*, Oxford, Blackwell, 1953; and P. C. Packard, 'Paucity of Demand for Industrial Commodities as an Obstacle to Industrialization', *Development and Change*, Vol. 1(3), 1969/70, pp. 8–18.

82. See discussion on the role of subjective factors in industrial development in E. E. Hagen, *On the Theory of Social Change*, Homewood, Illinois, Dorsey Press, 1962; E. E. Hagen, *The Economics of Development*, Illinois, Richard Irwin, 1968; and also P. T. Bauer, *Dissent on Development*, Weidenfeld and Nicolson, 1971, *passim*. Occupational mobility and opportunities for better-paid jobs are certainly more widespread in urban societies in Malaysia. People with high incomes tend to come from the middle-class section of the population. See details of exposition in C. Hirschman, 'Ethnic Stratification in West Malaysia', unpublished Ph.D. thesis, University of Wisconsin, 1972.

83. The Treasury, *Economic Report, 1972–73*, Kuala Lumpur, 1972, p. 14.

84. *Mid-Term Review of the Second Malaysia Plan, 1971–75*, p. 112.

85. See p. 136, Chapter 4, *passim*.

86. In general, constructing and interpreting the balance of payments can be difficult even in countries with advanced national accounting systems. See R. N. Cooper, 'The Balance of Payments in Review', *Journal of Political Economy*, Vol. 74 (3), June 1966. An account of the construction of Malaysia's balance of payments accounts is to be found in Bank Negara, *Quarterly Economic Bulletin*, Vol. 2 (1), March 1969.

87. The magnitude of the 'Errors and Omissions' may be gauged from Table 9.19.

88. For example, in 1963 the total net long-term capital flow was $270 million, while the official long-term capital amounted to $87 million. The position changed in the early 1970s. In 1971 for instance, the government borrowing from external sources amounted to $376 million, while in the same year net private capital inflow was only $160 million.

89. In 1972, according to Bank Negara, official external borrowing amounted to $540 million while private long-term capital inflow for the year was only $180 million. The *Second Malaysia Plan, 1971–75* (p. 79) envisages that foreign borrowing would amount to $720 million by 1975.

90. The agency houses operate world-wide so that they have similar arrangements with their offices in other countries. The principle of operation is similar whether they operate using sterling, U.S. dollars, German marks, or Japanese yen. Eventually the final accounts will filter through to the London head office.

91. Puthucheary, *Ownership and Control of the Malaysian Economy*, pp. 150–61.

92. Wheelwright, *Industrialization in Malaysia*, p. 108 et seq.

93. Puthucheary and Wheelwright did not explain, as we did above, the international financial transactions of the foreign companies. They only suggested that the 'homing tendency' of profits of foreign companies should be arrested to provide funds for investment in Malaysia.

94. See Puthucheary, op. cit., p. 158, and *passim*, where the author talks of 'checking the "homing tendency" of foreign profits'. Wheelwright, op. cit., p. 107, and *passim* also argued along the same lines.

95. The foreign company can bypass the exchange restrictions of any country by raising prices of goods and services sold to the subsidiary in the country with the tight remittance policy. The experience of countries with an over-valued currency shows that foreign companies can effectively siphon away funds from their subsidiaries by 'over-invoicing' (i.e. inflating costs of) imports of material inputs and capital goods supplied to the subsidiaries; see G. C. Winston, 'Over-Invoicing, Under-utilisation and Distorted Industrial Growth', *Pakistan Development Review*, Vol. 10 (4), 1970, pp. 405–21. See also J. Bhagwati, 'Fiscal Policies, the Faking of Foreign Exchange Declarations and the Balance of Payments', *Bulletin of the Oxford University Institute of Economics and Statistics*, February 1967. For a discussion on the methods of withdrawing funds from their subsidiaries abroad by the large multinational or transnational firms see S. M. Robins and R. B. Stobaugh, *Money in the Multinational Enterprises*, Basic Books Inc.,

1973, Chapter V. In practice, therefore, restrictions on funds devised by many of the underdeveloped countries are unable to arrest capital outflows and thus they cannot be an effective way of increasing domestic capital formation as argued by Puthucheary and Wheelwright.

96. Other receipts were the expenditures of foreign diplomatic corps in the country (less expenditures of the country's diplomatic missions abroad). As far as British investments in Malaysia are concerned, the military defence arrangements arising out of them may be regarded as giving another set of benefits to the host country, firstly because the defence bases create local employment, provide a stabilizing force, and relieve the host government of the need to spend on external defence. Secondly, when the defence forces were withdrawn, important facilities were left behind for use by the government. These facilities (e.g. air bases, buildings, military installations like the defence radar network, and military hospitals and barracks) valued at £25 million were handed over to the Malaysian government at various dates between 1968 and 1971. See Cmnd. 3822; Cmnd. 3968; *Treasury Minute* Cmnd. 4319, and Cmnd. 4629.

97. Bank Negara, *Quarterly Economic Bulletin*, March 1973, p. 72.

98. Remitted incomes from British companies engaged in the rubber plantations, oil palm estates, and tin mining were, according to data from the DTI, as follows:

	1963	1964	1965	1966	1967	1968	1969	1970	1971
1. Amounts ($ mil.)	120	141	140	144	105	98	170	165	142
2. (1) as percentage of profit remittances of foreign companies	61	61	55	54	73	64	80	77	63

99. The proportion varies a little with the political situation of the country. During the years of the Indonesian 'confrontation' the personnel remittances were quite high, accounting for about 70 per cent of all private transfers.

100. But in all probability, as will be evident from this chapter, the GNP would have been smaller without the foreign investment.

101. See Table 7.11. The question of transfer of funds of the Asia-Dollar Market is discussed in Chapter 7, Section 15, above.

102. Bank Negara argues that it is incorrect to regard the 'Errors and Omissions' in the balance of payments as unreported outflow of private capital. Its explanation of the items is that they are 'unidentified short-term capital movements (essentially private in character) constituting the balancing item in the Malaysian balance of payments, where it appears annually as a debit (i.e. outflow)'. See Bank Negara, *Quarterly Economic Bulletin*, Vol. 2 (1), March 1969, p. 47.

In contrast, in the U.K. balance of payments, balancing items are recognized as 'timing errors in recording of transactions', and in part 'unrecorded capital flows'. See Central Statistical Office, *United Kingdom Balance of Payments*, 1972, HMSO, 1972, p. 83.

Whatever the official statistical explanation given of the 'Errors and Omissions', the fact that the item appears large, and persistently represents outflows during the period 1963–71 in the balance of payments, is indicative of the poor recording of capital movements in the international accounts.

103. A story on the development of the money market in Singapore and in Malaysia is to be found in P. J. Drake, *Financial Development in Malaysia and Singapore*, Australian National University Press, 1969, Chapter 12.

104. ibid., p. 201.

105. This is certainly the practice of the agency houses and the larger manufacturing companies.

106. The information on which the paragraph was based was supplied by three of the banks' representatives interviewed. The development of the Asia-Dollar Market in 1968 further affected the Malaysian money market badly in the sense that Malaysia again continued to be a net lender of short-term capital to the rest of the world.

107. Drake, op. cit., p. 202.

108. There are indications that the underdeveloped money market in Malaysia was

due to the lack of government foresight in promoting the local money market. In the 1950s and early 1960s domestic savings built up in the Employees Provident Fund (EPF) and the Post Office Savings Banks were transferred abroad (mainly to London), very much in line with the practices of the foreign commercial companies. What the government can do to influence the development of the local money market is discussed in Drake, op. cit., Chapter 13.

109. The two main objectives behind the termination of the currency interchangeability between Malaysia and Singapore were firstly, to ensure that foreign exchange receipts from the country's exports would be remitted to commercial banks in Malaysia, and secondly, to institute an effective system of monitoring the nature and direction of foreign exchange transactions in the country.

Following termination of the interchangeability arrangement, the authorities in Kuala Lumpur are also setting up a separate Malaysian stock exchange, and are trying to establish Kuala Lumpur as an international marketing centre for rubber, tin, palm oil, pepper, and tropical hardwoods. See details in Bank Negara, *Quarterly Economic Bulletin*, Vol. 6, June/September 1973, pp. 95–8.

110. E. T. Penrose, 'Some Problems of Policy Toward Direct Private Foreign Investment in Developing Countries', *Middle Eastern Economic Review, Economic Bulletin*, A.U.B., 1962, p. 135.

111. ibid., p. 136.

112. The three factors discussed here were drawn from executives interviewed. For a different view, see story about Jim Slater (British 'Zaibatsu') moving into Asia in the *Far Eastern Economic Review*, 25 March 1972, pp. 65–8.

113. An elaborate treatment of this theme is found in the Confederation of British Industry, *Overseas Investment—Why and How*, CBI, 1967, pp. 26–7.

114. According to the calculation of Professor Coppock the position of the long-term private U.K. investment overseas from 1952 to 1971 is thus:

	1952–5	*1956–60*	*1961–4*	*1965–8*	*1969–71*
Net Private Investment Abroad (£ million)	−120	−133	−79	−106	+69

It can be seen that the increase in the net outflow was small for 1965–8, and negative for 1969–71. Substantial parts of these overseas investments were financed from sources abroad. See details in D. J. Coppock, 'Foreign Trade and the Balance of Payments', in A. R. Prest and D. J. Coppock, eds., *The U.K. Economy, A Manual of Applied Economics*, Weidenfeld and Nicolson (4th ed.), 1972, p. 140.

115. Central Statistical Office, *United Kingdom Balance of Payments*, 1972, HMSO, 1972, p. 29. In the case of British companies in Malaysia, the bulk of the new investments in the period originated in local borrowings, the shifting of capital from agriculture and trading into manufacturing.

116. See details in J. O. N. Perkins, *Sterling Area. The Commonwealth and World Economic Growth*, Cambridge University Press, 1967, Chapter 8.

117. ibid., p. 102.

118. S. Strange, *Sterling and British Policy*, Oxford University Press, 1971.

119. ibid., p. 180.

120. Information based on *An Account of British Aid Programme*, HMSO, 1969; *British Aid Statistics*, 1965–9 and 1966–71, HMSO, 1970; *Overseas Aid: A Brief Study*, Central Office of Information, 1972 and reports of the Select Committee on Overseas Aid, HMSO, 1970 and 1971.

121. Not as much as when aid is used to finance imports from Britain by the aid recipients.

122. Table 9.26 shows that the long-term inflow of private capital has not been high enough even to offset the private transfers shown in Table 9.24.

123. According to the *Mid-Term Review of the Second Malaysia Plan, 1971–75*, government long-term foreign borrowing was $1,185, and private long-term capital inflow was $547 million during the period 1971–3. By 1975, it is expected that government long-term foreign borrowings would total $1,743 million compared to private long-term capital inflow of $947 million. See details in the *Mid-Term Review of the Second Malaysia Plan, 1971–75*, p. 52.

124. Conceivably this may not be necessary if local companies can grow at a faster rate than the foreign companies; or if the foreign companies earn sufficiently large foreign exchange to finance their overseas remittances.

125. Alternatively foreigners may be persuaded to remit annually small amounts of the incomes they earn in Malaysia such that the annual remittances do not aggravate the balance of payments position.

126. Bank Negara, *Quarterly Economic Bulletin*, March 1969, p. 48.

127. See Tables 9.19–9.26, and the analysis in the text.

128. Next to Thailand, Malaysia among the countries in the ECAFE (now ESCAP) region, had high levels of international liquidity between the years 1968 and 1971. See details in *U.N. Economic Survey of Asia and the Far East, 1972*, Bangkok, ECAFE, 1973, p. 82.

10 Summary and Conclusions

THIS study has examined empirically the role of British industrial enterprises in Malaysia in the 1960s, the period when the country embarked on an industrialization programme based on free enterprise.

Prior to the intensified development of manufacturing in the country, Malaysia had relied upon primary exports of rubber and tin for its growth. British capital and entrepreneurship had played a dominant role in the development of the country's primary industry since the early 1900s. In the mid-1960s, British industrial capital began to assume an important role in the economy which had always been orientated to a private enterprise system, wherein, private foreign enterprises had been encouraged to modernize the economy. Foreign capital began participating in the industrial sector which had not been excessively protected by tariffs and import controls in the period examined. The government limited its role to the maintenance of internal stability and to the provision of industrial investment incentives in the nature of site development and tax concessions.

A variety of British firms was represented in those sectors of industry that catered for the domestic and, later, export markets. Most of these firms were motivated by their desire to protect their share of the local market which they previously supplied largely with the assistance of the 'agency houses'. Through the diversification of their activities, the agencies also began manufacturing locally, either on their own account or in partnership with their principals, the British manufacturers. A number of British MNEs also began manufacturing in Malaysia in the 1960s.

As a group, from 1963 to 1971, the British industrial companies were distributed in the research and capital-intensive sector of Malaysian manufacturing. They were among the largest industrial firms in the country, in terms of their share of output and sales; although in terms of employment created and total British overseas industrial investments they were very small. They were very profitable, and they generally provided their own funds from their own cash flows or from local sources.

Unlike import-substitute industries in many less developed countries the British firms in import-substitution industries in Malaysia in the 1960s were efficient, as evident from their ability to contribute to industrial output and to compete in the international market. They also generated technological and pecuniary externalities to the host economy.

Evidently, as seen in the foregoing chapters, British industrial capital became an increasingly important part of total British investment in Malaysia from the early 1960s.

A number of companies with industrial investments in the country were the subject of inquiry in the course of research for the present study which suggests a number of conclusions. In the first place company representatives considered the investment climate in Malaysia congenial to private foreign investments. They regarded the government's role in the economy, on the whole, as consistent with the free enterprise orientation of the country's economic policy, which provided many attractive features compared to many less developed or other countries of the region.

Secondly, it was established that British industrial firms dominated the country's manufacturing sector in the period 1963 to 1971. They assumed a commanding role in the domestic market for manufactured goods. They were in monopolistic positions and were able to generate considerable funds internally. They were also able to raise funds from local sources easily and often without security or collateral offered. Much of the capital they employed did not come from Britain. This was reflected in the trickle of capital flows from Britain to Malaysia in the official accounts for the period under study.

Thirdly, it was found that British firms were not so much motivated to invest in Malaysia by the offer of government incentives as by the desire of the firms to take advantage of markets already established, to consolidate their position in those markets, to take advantage of the growth of the Malaysian market and to overcome the expected rise in tariffs which would have excluded them from it.

Fourthly, many British firms began manufacturing in the country before tariff protection was an important instrument of industrial promotion. The firms were profitable and efficient. Their profitability was higher than their competitors' and also higher than that of their total world-wide operations.

Fifthly and probably most important, contrary to the suppositions of Puthucheary (1960) and Wheelwright (1965), the agency firms had been instrumental in assisting the initial industrialization of Malaysia. These firms provided assistance to British manufacturers coming to Malaysia, to manufacturers wishing to export from the country and to those who wished to take advantage of the services of the auxiliary industrial service institutions belonging to the agency firms. It is a misnomer to call them 'agency firms' now, because as a result of their diversification they have assumed the aspect of conglomerates.

Sixthly, as argued by Penrose (1959), in the absence of markedly unfavourable environmental conditions, there is a strong tendency for a business enterprise to grow, and diversification is one of the means of achieving growth. British affiliates in Malaysia from 1963 to 1971 have expanded their enterprises by diversification, which supports Penrose's thesis. By branching into different activities British affiliates have managed to maintain their growth. The limitation imposed on the firms by the domestic market was compensated by their diversification and export trade.

Seventhly, British MNEs in Malaysia from 1963 to 1971 did not act in any way detrimental to the national interest of the host country, contrary to the hypotheses of Streeten (1971) and others. On the contrary, based on their contributions to industrial output and exports, the MNEs contributed to various facets of the host country's national objectives in addition to that of creating employment. As a group, the MNEs have been increasingly promoting local people to high levels within their organizations.

From the empirical evidence, one can say that British industrial output on average accounted for about 2.1 per cent of Malaysia's GNP per annum from 1963 to 1971; and at the same time their overseas remittances amounted to about 1.3 per cent of GNP. Considering that the firms also generated external economies, helped in the promotion of manufactured exports, and in general helped to enlarge the manufacturing sector, they have on the whole made a useful net contribution to the Malaysian economy in the period investigated.

The significant results of this examination reveals that contrary to the experience of many of the underdeveloped countries that have adopted import-substitution industrialization, the industrialization policy of Malaysia based on an outward-looking strategy has nurtured the development of efficient industries that have increased net national output.

The case of British industrial investment in Malaysia shows that private direct foreign investment can benefit the underdeveloped host country. On balance, the empirical investigation suggests that

British industrial investments did confer positive benefits on a developing country like Malaysia. However, as the flow of additional British capital slows down or ceases, while outflows in terms of foreign remittances continue it would be essential for the fund-remitting firms to earn sufficient foreign exchange in order not to aggravate the country's balance of payments position.

Bibliography

1. OFFICIAL PUBLICATIONS

(a) **Malaysian**
(all published by The Government Press, Kuala Lumpur)
Bank Negara Malaysia
Annual Reports, various issues.
Quarterly Economic Bulletin, March 1973; March 1969; May 1973; September 1973.
Department of Statistics
Annual Bulletin of Statistics, various issues.
Annual Statistics of External Trade, various issues.
Census of Manufacturing Industries, 1963, and *1968*.
Survey of Manufacturing Industries, 1969.
Socio-Economic Sample Survey of Household, Employment and Unemployment in West Malaysia, 1967–68.
Report of The Financial Survey of Limited Companies in Malaysia, 1967.
Economic Planning Unit, Prime Minister's Department
First Malaysia Plan, 1966–70 (1965).
Second Malaysia Plan, 1971–75 (1971).
Mid-Term Review of The First Malaysia Plan, 1966–70 (1969).
Mid-Term Review of The Second Malaysia Plan, 1971–75 (1973).
FIDA, Federal Industrial Development Authority
Malaysia, Industrial Digest, Published Quarterly.
All About Investment Incentives (1971).
Incorporating a Manufacturing Company (1971).
Labour and Wage Rates (1971).
Power, Water and Telephone Rates for Industry (1971).
Getting Approvals for Industrial Projects (1971).
(1969), *Malaysia, A New Industrial Development Strategy.*
(1970), *Malaysia: Your Profit Centre in Asia.*
Ministry of Commerce and Industry
(1968), *Investment Incentives Act.*
(1971), *Investment Incentives Act* (Amendment).

(1972), *Investment Incentives Act* (Amendment).

OECD Document

(1973), *Flow of Resources to Developing Countries*, Paris.

Annual Reports, various years.

The Treasury (1972), *Economic Report*, 1972/73.

Minister of Finance (1971), *Budget Speech.*

World Bank Reports (International Bank for Reconstruction and Development)

(1955), *The Economic Development of Malaya*, Baltimore, Johns Hopkins Press, 1955 (IBRD 1955 Report).

(1963), *Report of the Economic Aspects of Malaysia* (Rueff Report).

(b) **Others**

Beale, L. B. (1929), *A Review of the Trade of British Malaya*, HMSO, 1929.

Board of Trade Journal, 6.11.1961; 9.9.1962; 15.11.1963; 7.8.1964; 17.6.1966; 21.6.1968; 25.3.1970; 4.3.1970; 23.9.1970.

(23.3.1972, Trade and Industry.)

(15.11.1973, Trade and Industry.)

Central Office of Information

(1950), *An Economic Review of Malaya*, 1945–49, HMSO.

(1971), *Britain's International Investment Position*, HMSO.

(1972), *British Aid Statistics*, 1965–69; 1966–71, HMSO.

HMSO, *Overseas Economic Survey, 1952.*

Department of Trade and Industry (DTI)

(1971), *British Private Investment in Developing Countries*, HMSO.

(1972), *Hints to Businessmen, Malaysia and Brunei.*

(1972), *Business Monitor M 4, Overseas Transactions.*

The Stock Exchange of Malaysia/Singapore

Listing Manual.

Company Reports Vol. I–II.

United Nations

(1970), *Yearbook of Labour Statistics*, Geneva.

(1971), *Industrial Development Asia and The Far East: Report on the Second Asian Conference on Industrialization at Tokyo*, U.N. E/CN. II/945.

(1971), *U.N., Economic Survey of Asia and The Far East*, Bangkok.

(1973), *U.N., Economic Survey of Asia and The Far East*, Bangkok.

UNCTAD Reports

1. *Balance of Payments Effects of Private Foreign Investment Case Studies of Jamaica and Kenya*, TD/B/C-3/79 Add 2, July 1970.
2. *The Channels and Mechanisms for the Transfer of Technology from Developed to Developing Countries*, TD/B/AC.II/5, April 1971.
3. *Balance of Payments and Income Effects of Private Foreign Investment in Manufacturing, Case Studies of India and Iran*, TD/B/C-3(V)/Misc. 1, December 1971.
4. *Balance of Payments and Income Effects of Private Foreign Investment in Manufacturing, Case Studies of Columbia and Malaysia*, TD/B/C/3(VI)/Misc. 1, June 1973.

Dept. of Economic and Social Affairs, 1973, *Multinational Corporations in World Development*, New York, ST/ECA/190.

Various Annual Reports and Statements of Accounts of Companies Interviewed.

2. BOOKS

Accountants International Study Group (1972), *Reporting by Diversified Companies, Current Recommended Practices in Canada, the U.K. and the U.S.A.*, Birmingham, Hopkins and Bailey.

Ady, P. H., ed. (1971), *Private Foreign Investment and the Developing World*, Praeger.

Aharoni, Y. (1966), *The Foreign Investment Decision Process*, Boston, Harvard University Press.

Allen, G. C., and Donnithorne, A. G. (1954, 1962), *Western Enterprise in Indonesia and Malaya*, George Allen and Unwin.

Amin, S. (1973), *Neo-Colonialism in West Africa* (translated from the French), Penguin.

Asch, P. (1970), *Economic Theory and the Antitrust Dilemma*, New York, Wiley.

Asian Development Bank (1971), *Southeast Asia's Economy in the 1970s*, Longman.

Balassa, B., *et al.* (1971), *The Structure of Protection in Developing Countries*, Baltimore, Johns Hopkins University Press.

Baranson, J. (1969), *Industrial Technologies for Developing Economics*, Praeger.

Barr, R. J., ed. (1959), *American Trade with Asia and the Far East*, Wisconsin, Marquette University Press.

Basu, S. K. (1958), *The Managing Agency System, In prospect and retrospect*, Calcutta, The World Press Pte.

Bauer, P. T. (1971), *Dissent on Development. Studies and Debate in Development Economics*, Weidenfeld and Nicolson.

Baumol, W. J. (1967), *Business Behaviour, Value and Growth*, New York, Barcourt Brace and World Inc. (rev. ed.).

Beckerman, W. (1974), *In Defence of Economic Growth*, Jonathan Cape.

Berrill, K., ed. (1964), *Economic Development with Special Reference to East Asia*, Macmillan.

Bhagwati, J., and Eckaus, R., eds. (1972), *Development and Planning: Essays in Honour of Paul Rosentein-Rodan*, George Allen and Unwin.

Brash, D. T. (1966), *American Investment in Australian Industry*, Canberra, Australian National University Press.

Brooke, M. E., and Remmers, H. L. (1970), *The Strategy of Multinational Enterprise: Organisation and Finance*, Longman.

_____ eds. (1972), *The Multinational Company in Europe: Some Key Problems*, Longman.

Cairncross, A. K. (1973), *Foreign Investment 1870–1913*, Cambridge University Press.

Callis, H. G. (1942), *Foreign Capital in Southeast Asia* (mimeo.), Institute of Pacific Relations, New York.

Cameron, J. (1865), *Our Tropical Possessions: Malayan India, Singapore, Penang, Province Wellesley and Malacca*, London.

Campbell, Lord, *et al.* (1971), *Britain, the EEC and The Third World*, The Overseas Development Institute.

Chartered Bank, The (1971), *Malaysia, A Business Guide*, The Chartered Bank, Kuala Lumpur.

Confederation of British Industry (CBI) (1961), *A Trade in Transition, Report of the Southeast Asian Trade Delegation.*

_____ (1967), *Overseas Investment: Why and How?*

Cowan, C. D. (1961, reprinted 1967), *Nineteenth Century Malaya*, Oxford University Press.

Crosson, P. R. (1966), *Economic Growth in Malaysia*, Washington, D.C., National Planning Association.

Cunyngham-Brown, S. (1971), *The Traders*, Guthrie and Co. (U.K.) Ltd.

Cyert, R. M., and March, J. G. (1963), *A Behavioral Theory of The Firm*, Englewood Cliffs, Prentice-Hall.

Drake, P. J. (1969), *Financial Development in Malaya and Singapore*, Canberra, Australian National University Press.

Dunning, J. H. (1958), *American Investment in British Manufac-*

turing Industry, George Allen and Unwin.

——— (1970), *Studies in International Investment*, George Allen and Unwin.

——— ed. (1971), *The Multinational Enterprise*, George Allen and Unwin.

——— ed. (1972), *International Investment: Selected Readings*, Penguin.

——— (1973), *United States Industry in Britain*, Economic Advisory Group, Business Research Study, *The Financial Times*.

Economist Intelligence Unit (1971), *The Growth and Spread of Multinational Companies, Quarterly Econ. Report*, Special Issue, No. 5.

Edwards, C. T. (1970), *Public Finance in Malaya and Singapore*, Canberra, Australian National University Press.

Einzig, P. (1973), *The Euro-Dollar System*, Macmillan (5th ed.).

Fei, H. (1954), *Europe: The World's Banker 1870–1914*, Yale University Press.

Freeman, R. A. (1968), *Socialism and Private Enterprise in Equatorial Asia—The case of Malaya and Indonesia*, Stanford, Stanford University Press.

Gabriel, P. P. (1967), *The International Transfer of Corporate Skills*, Harvard University Press.

Galbraith, J. K. (1963), *American Capitalism*, Penguin.

George, T. J. S. (1973), *Lee Kuan Yew's Singapore*, Andre Deutsch.

Girvan, N. (1971), *Foreign Capital and Economic Underdevelopment in Jamaica*, Jamaican Institute of Social and Economic Research, University of the West Indies Press.

Goh, K. S. (1972), *The Economics of Modernisation*, Singapore, Asia Pacific Press.

Gordon, L., and Grommers, E. L. (1962), *United States Manufacturing Investment in Brazil*, Boston.

Gray, H. P. (1972), *The Economics of Business Investment Abroad*, Macmillan.

Grubel, H. G., and Morgan, T., eds. (1973), *Exchange Rate Policies in Southeast Asia*, Lexington Books.

Gull, E. M. (1943), *British Economic Interests in the Far East*, Institute of Pacific Relations, Oxford University Press.

Gullick, J. M. (1969), *Malaysia*, Ernest Benn.

Gurtov, M. (1970), *Southeast Asia, Tomorrow, Problems and Prospects For U.S. Policy*, Johns Hopkins University Press.

Hahlo, H. R., Smith, J. C., and Wright, R. W., eds. (1973), *Multinationalism and the Multinational Enterprise: Legal, Economic and Managerial Aspects*, New York, Oceana Publications Inc.

Helleiner, G. K. (1972), *International Trade and Economic Development*, Penguin.

Hiner, O. S. (1972), *Business Administration: An Introductory Study*, Longman.

Hirschman, A. O. (1959), *The Strategy of Economic Development*, Yale University Press.

Hobson, C. K. (1914, reissued in 1963 with a preface by Sir Roy Harrod), *The Export of Capital*, Constable.

Hughes, H., and You, P. S., eds. (1969), *Foreign Investment and Industrialization in Singapore*, Canberra, Australian National University Press.

Imlah, A. H. (1958), *Economic Elements in the Pax Britannica*, Harvard University Press.

Industrial Policy Group (1970), *The Case For Direct Investment*, No. 4.

——— (1972), *Economic Growth, Profits and Investments*, No. 10.

Institute of Chartered Accountants in England and Wales (1970), *What is Profit? Six View Points* [*sic*], Papers presented at a Summer Course at Churchill College, University of Cambridge.

Institute of Southeast Asian Studies (1973), *New Directions in the International Relations of Southeast Asia* (ed. T. S. Lau), University of Singapore.

——— (1973), *Multinational Corporations and Their Implications For Southeast Asia* (ed. by E. P. T. Lim).

International Chamber of Commerce (ICC) (1968), *Joint Ventures In Developing Countries*, Report of the Committee on International Investments and Economic Development approved by the Executive Committee of ICC, Geneva.

Ismail, A. H. (1971), *A Study of Total Expenditure Elasticities for West Malaysia*, Paper No. 1, Kuala Lumpur, The National University.

Johnson, H. G. (1967), *Economic Policies Towards Less Developed Countries*, George Allen and Unwin.

Kapoor, A., and Cotten, J. E., eds. (1973), *Foreign Investments in Asia*, New Jersey, The Darwin Press.

Kapoor, A., and Grub, P. D., eds. (1972), *The Multinational Enterprise In Transition: Selected Readings and Essays*, Princeton, The Darwin Press.

Kenen, P. E., and Lawrence, R., eds. (1968), *The Open Economy: Essays on International Trade and Finance*, Columbia University Press.

Kidron, M. (1965), *Foreign Investments in India*, Oxford University Press.

Kilby, P. (1969), *Industrialization in an Open Economy, 1945–66*, Cambridge University Press.

Kindleberger, C. P. (1963), *International Economics*, Illinois, Irwin (3rd ed.).

——— ed. (1971), *The International Corporation: A Symposium*, The M.I.T. Press.

Kirby, E. S. (1967), *Economic Development in East Asia*, George Allen and Unwin.

Levitt, K. (1971), *Silent Surrender, The American Empire in Canada*, New York, Liveright.

Lewis, W. A. (1965), *Theory of Economic Growth*, George Allen and Unwin.

Li, D. J. (1955), *British Malaya: An Economic Analysis*, New York, American Press.

Lilienthal, D. E. (1953), *Big Business: A New Era*, New York, Harper.

Lim, C. Y. (1967), *Economic Development of Modern Malaya*, Oxford University Press.

Lim, D. (1973), *Economic Growth and Development in West Malaysia, 1947–1970*, Oxford University Press.

Lim, L. L. (1971), *Some Aspects of Income Differentials in West Malaysia*, Kuala Lumpur, University of Malaya.

Little, I. M. D., and Mirrlees, J. A. (1968), *Manual of Industrial Project Appraisal in Developing Countries*, Vol. II, OECD, Paris.

Little, I. M. D., Scitovsky, T., and Scott, M. (1970), *Industry and Trade in Some Developing Countries: A Comparative Study*, OECD, Oxford University Press.

Little, I., and Tipping, D. G. (1972), *A Social Cost Benefit Analysis of the Kulai Oil Palm Estate, West Malaysia*, OECD, Paris.

Litvak, I. A., and Maule, C. J., eds. (1970), *Foreign Investments: The Experience of Host Countries*, Praeger.

Lo, S. Y. (1972), *The Development Performance of West Malaysia, 1955–67*, Kuala Lumpur, Heinemann Books.

Lockwood, W. W. (1954), *The Economic Development of Japan*, Princeton University Press.

Ma, R., and You, P. S., eds. (1965), *The Malayan Economy in Transition*, Singapore Institute of Management.

——— (1968), *The Economy of Malaysia and Singapore*, Singapore, University Handbook Series.

MacDougall, J. (1969), *Shared Burdens: A Study in Communal Discrimination by Political Parties in Malaysia and Singapore*, Harvard University Press.

Mahathir bin Mohamed (1970), *The Malay Dilemma*, Singapore, Donald Moore.

Maizels, A. (1963), *Industrial Growth and World Trade*, Cambridge University Press.

Manser, W. A. P. (1973), *The Financial Role of Multinational Enterprises*, Cassell/Associated Business Programmes Ltd.

Marzouk, G. A. (1972), *A Case Study of Thailand: Economic Development and Policies*, Rotterdam University Press.

McHale, T. R. (1967), *Rubber and The Malaysian Economy*, Singapore, MPH Printers.

Meadows, D. H., *et al.* (1972), *The Limits to Growth*, Pan Books Ltd.

Muscat, R. J. (1966), *Development Strategy in Thailand, A Survey of Economic Growth,* Praeger.

Myint, H. (1969), *The Economics of the Developing Countries*, Hutchinson University Library Series (3rd ed.).

_____(1971), *Economic Theory and the Underdeveloped Countries*, Oxford University Press.

_____(1972), *Southeast Asia's Economy: Development Policies in the 1970s*, Penguin.

Myrdal, G. (1967), *Asian Drama, An Inquiry Into the Poverty of Nations* (3 vols.), Penguin.

Needham, D. (1969), *Economic Analysis and Industrial Structure*, Holt, Rinehart, and Winston Inc.

Newbould, G. D., and Jackson, A. S. (1972), *The Receding Ideal*, Liverpool, Guthstead.

Nurkse, R. (1953), *Problems of Capital Formation in Underdeveloped Countries*, Oxford, Blackwell.

Parker, R. H. (1972), *Understanding Company Financial Statements*, Pelican.

Peacock, A. T., and Hanser, G., eds. (1965), *Government Finance and Economic Development*, OECD, Paris.

Penrose, E. T. (1959), *The Theory of the Growth of the Firm*, Oxford, Blackwell (5th impression).

_____(1968), *The Large International Firm in Developing Countries*, George Allen and Unwin.

Perkins, J. O. N. (1967), *Sterling Area: The Commonwealth and World Economic Growth*, Cambridge University Press.

Pratten, C. F. (1971), *Economies of Scale in Manufacturing Industry*, Cambridge University Press, 1971.

Prest, A. R., and Coppock, D. J. (1972), *The U.K. Economy, A Manual of Applied Economics*, Weidenfeld and Nicolson (4th ed.).

Purvis, M. J. (1965), *Research Report on the Food Economy of Malaysia and Brunei*, Cornell University, Department of Agricultural Economics.

Puthucheary, J. J. (1960), *Ownership and Control in the Malayan Economy*, Singapore, Donald Moore.

Reddaway, W. E., Potter, S. I., and Taylor, C. T. (1967 (Interim), 1968 (Final)), *Effects of U.K. Direct Investment Overseas* (Reddaway Report), Cambridge University Press.

Reuber, G. L. (1973), *Private Foreign Investment in Development*, Oxford, Clarendon Press.

Rhodes, R. I., ed. (1970), *Imperialism and Underdevelopment*, New York, Monthly Review Press.

Robins, S. M., and Stobaugh, R. B. Jr. (1973), *Money in Multinational Enterprises*, Boston, Harvard Business School.

Robinson, E. A. G. (1972), *Fifty Years of Commonwealth Economic Development*, Cambridge University Press.

Robinson, H. J. (1961), *The Motivation and Flow of Private Foreign Investment*, Menlo Park, California, Stanford Research Institute.

Rolfe, S. E., ed. (1969), *Report of the XXII Congress of the International Chamber of Commerce*, Istanbul.

Rolfe, S. E., and Damm, W., eds. (1970), *The Multinational Corporation in the World Economy*, Praeger Special Studies Series.

Rook, A. (1971), *Transfer Pricing, A Measure of Management Performance in Multi-Divisional Companies*, British Institute of Management Survey Report, No. 8.

Rowan, Sir Leslie, *et al.* (1965), *Investment and Development, The Role of Private Investment in Developing Countries*, Overseas Development Institute.

Rowthorn, R., *International Big Business 1957–67*, Cambridge University Press, 1971.

Royal Institute of International Affairs (1937, repr. 1965), *The Problem of International Investment*, Frank Cass.

Schweizerische Bankgesellschaft (1969), *Interest Rate and Interest Structure, An International Comparison of Interest Rates Based on Interest Indicators*, Zurich.

——— (1970), *An International Survey of Interest Rates, Patterns and Differentials*, Zurich.

Shawcross, Sir Hartley, Caine, Sir Sidney, and Duncan, Val (1967), *Overseas Investment or Economic Nationalism?*, Institute of Economic Affairs.

Silcock, T. H. (1954), *The Economy of Malaya*, Singapore, Eastern Universities Press.

Silcock, T. H., and Fisk, E. K., eds. (1963), *The Political Economy of Independent Malaya*, Canberra, Australian National University Press.

Steuer, M. D., *et al.* (1973), *The Impact of Foreign Direct Investment on the United Kingdom*, HMSO.

Stevenson, H. W., and Nelson, J. R., eds. (1967), *Profits in the Modern Economy, Selected Papers from a Conference on Understanding Profits*, Minneapolis, Minnesota University Press.

Stopford, J. M., and Wells, L. T. (1972), *Managing the Multinational Enterprise*, Longman.

Strange, S. (1971), *Sterling and British Policy* (Royal Institute of International Affairs), Oxford University Press.

Streeten, P. (1972), *The Frontiers of Development Studies*, Macmillan.

_____ (1973), *Trade Strategies for Development*, Papers of the Ninth Cambridge Conference on Development Problems 1972, Macmillan.

Streeten, P. P. and Lall, S., *et al.* (1973), *Balance of Payments and Income Effects of Private Foreign Investment in Manufacturing: Case Studies of Columbia and Malaysia* (mimeo.), UNCTAD Secretariat, July.

Tregonning, K. G. (1964), *A History of Modern Malaya*, Singapore, Eastern Universities Press.

_____ (1965), *The British in Malaysia*, Tucson, University of Arizona Press.

_____ (1966), *Singapore Cold Storage, 1903–66*, Singapore.

Turner, I. (1974), *Multinational Companies and The Third World*, Allen Lane.

U.S. Department of Commerce (1963), *Factors Limiting U.S. Investments Abroad*, Vol. II.

_____ (1971), *Overseas Business Report, 71–00044*.

_____ (1972), *The Multinational Corporation, Studies on U.S. Foreign Investment*, Washington, D.C.

Vernon, R. (1971), *Sovereignty at Bay*, Longman.

_____ (1972), *The Economic Environment of International Business*, New Jersey, Prentice-Hall.

_____ (1972), *The Economic and Political Consequences of Multinational Enterprise: An Anthology*, Harvard University Press.

Wallace, D. Jr., and Ruoff-Koch, H., eds. (1973), *International Control of Investment*, The Dusseldorf Conference on Multinational Corporations, Praeger.

Ward, B., *et al.* (1971), *The Widening Gap: Development in the 1970s*, Columbia University Press.

Watkins Report (Watkins, M. W., *et al.*) (1968), *Foreign Ownership and the Structure of Canadian Industry*, Report of the Task Force on Canadian Industry, Privy Council Office, Ottawa.

Wheelwright, E. L. (1965), *Industrialisation in Malaysia*, Melbourne, Melbourne University Press.

——(1972), *UNIDO Industrial Mission to Malaysia*, Kuala Lumpur.

White, L. J. (1974), *Industrial Concentration and Power in Pakistan*, New Jersey, Princeton University Press.

Who Owns Whom (1968), London, Roskill.

Wilkins, M. (1970), *The Emergence of Multinational Enterprise*, Boston, Harvard University Press.

Wilson, J. S. G., and Scheffer, L. F., eds. (1974), *Multinational Enterprises: Financial and Monetary Aspects*, Leiden, A. W. Sitjhoff.

Woodies, J. (1971), *Introduction to Neo-Colonialism*, New York, International Publishers.

Yip, Y. H. (1969), *The Development of the Tin Mining Industry*, Kuala Lumpur, University of Malaya Press.

3. ARTICLES

Abdul Rahman, Tengku (1965), 'Malaysia: Key Area in Southeast Asia', *Foreign Affairs*, No. 4, July.

Adler, J. H. (1972), 'The World Bank's Concept of Development—An In-House *Dogmeneschihte*', in Bhagwati and Eckaus, eds., *Development and Planning: Essays in Honour of Paul Rosentein-Rodan*, George Allen and Unwin.

Aliber, R. Z. (1971), 'A Theory of Direct Foreign Investment', in Kindleberger, C. P., ed., *The International Corporation: A Symposium*, The M.I.T. Press.

Arndt, H. W. (1954), 'A Suggestion For Simplifying The Theory of International Capital Movements', *Economia Internazionale*, Vol. VII, pp. 467–79.

Bell, H. F. (1960), 'Attitudes to Overseas Investments', *Australian Quarterly*, Vol. 32(3), September, pp. 49–57.

Bhagwati, J. (1967), 'Fiscal Policies, the Faking of Foreign Exchange Declarations and the Balance of Payments', *Bulletin of The Oxford Institute of Economics and Statistics*, Vol. 29(1), February.

Blake, D. J. (1974), 'Inflation in Malaysia: Its Nature and Extent', *United Malayan Banking Corporation Economic Review*, Vol. X(1), pp. 43–55.

Bogaars, G. (1955), 'The Effect of the Opening of the Suez Canal on The Trade and Development of Singapore', *Journal of the Royal Asiatic Society Malayan Branch*, Vol. 28.

Bradley, G. E., and Bursk, E. C. (1972), 'Multinationalism and the 29th Day', *Harvard Business Review*, January/February, pp. 37–47.

Breton, A. (1964), 'The Economics of Nationalism', *Journal of Political Economy*, Vol. 72(4), August, pp. 376–86.

Bruton, H. J. (1970), 'The Import Substitution Strategy of Economic Development: A Survey', *Pakistan Development Review*, Vol. 10(2), pp. 123–46.

Carnell, F. G. (1956), 'The Development of a Middle Class In Burma, Thailand and Malaya', in *The Development of A Middle Class in Tropical and Sub-Tropical Countries*, Bruxelles, pp. 271–9.

Caulkin, S. (1973), 'British Cars—What's Wrong?', *Management Today*, December, p. 74, et seq.

Caves, R. E. (1971), 'International Corporations: The Industrial Economics of Foreign Investment', *Economica* (*New Series*), Vol. 38(149), February, pp. 1–27.

Chenery, H. B., and Taylor, L. (1968), 'Development Pattern Among Countries and Over Time', *Review of Economics and Statistics*, Vol. 50(4).

Cooper, C. M. (1972), 'Science, Technology and Production in the Underdeveloped Countries: An Introduction', *Journal of Development Studies*, Special Issue on Science Technology and Production.

Cooper, R. N. (1966), 'The Balance of Payments In Review', *Journal of Political Economy*, Vol. 74(3), June.

_____(1972), 'European Economic Community's System of Generalised Tariff Preference: A Critique', *Journal of Development Studies*, Vol. 8(4), July.

Cowan, C. D. (1936), 'Early Penang and the Rise of Singapore', *Journal of the Royal Asiatic Society Malayan Branch*, Vol. 14, Part III.

De la Torre, J. (1971), 'Exports of Manufactured Goods From Developing Countries: Marketing Factors and the Role of Foreign Enterprise', *Journal of International Business Studies*, Spring, pp. 26–39.

Desai, M. J. (*c.* 1966), 'Cost and Returns of Overseas Investment from the Point of View of the Host Country' (mimeo.), Institute of Development Studies, Sussex Communication Series 25.

Dooley, P. C. (1969), 'The Interlocking Directorate', *American*

Economic Review, Vol. 59, June, p. 314, et seq.

Drake, P. J. (1970), 'The New-Issue Boom In Malaya and Singapore, 1961–1964', *Economic Development and Cultural Change*, Vol. 18, pp. 73–91.

——(1972), 'Natural Resources versus Foreign Borrowing in Economic Development', *Economic Journal*, September, pp. 951–62.

Dunning, J. H. (1964), 'Does Foreign Investment Pay?', *Moorgate and Wall Street*, Autumn, pp. 5–36.

——(1966), 'Further Thoughts on Foreign Investment', *Moorgate and Wall Street*, Autumn.

——(1966), 'U.S. Subsidiaries in Britain and Other U.K. Competitors', *Business Ratios* (1), Dan and Bradstreet Ltd., Autumn.

——(1969), 'The Reddaway and Hufbauer/Aller Reports', *Bankers Magazine*, May, June, and July.

——(1969), 'Profitability, Productivity and Measures of Business Performance', *The Investment Analyst*, June.

——(1973), 'Multinational Enterprises and Nation States', in Kapoor and Grub, eds., *The Multinational Enterprise in Transition*, Princeton, The Darwin Press, 1972.

——(1974), 'Multinational Enterprises and Domestic Capital Formation', in J. S. G. Wilson and C. F. Scheffer, eds., *Multinational Enterprises—Financial and Monetary Aspects*, Leiden, Sijthoff.

Ewing, D. W. (1972), 'MNC on Trial', *Harvard Business Review*, May/June, pp. 130–43.

Fogelberg, G., and Laurent, C. R. (1973), 'Interlocking Directorates: A Study of Large Companies in New Zealand', *Journal of Business Policy*, Vol. 3(2), 1972, pp. 16–21.

Foster, G., 'Complicated Chemistry of I.C.I.', *Management Today*, May 1973.

Friedman, M. (1969), 'The Euro-Dollar Market: Some First Principles', *The Morgan Guaranty Survey*, October, pp. 4–14.

Girvan, N. (1970), 'Multinational Corporations and Dependent Under-development in Mineral Export Economies', *Social and Economic Studies*, Vol. 19(4), December.

Greenberg, M. (1941), 'Malaya: Britain's Dollar Arsenal', *Amerasia*, Vol. 5, June, pp. 144–51.

Grubel, G., and Morgan, T., eds. (1972), *Exchange Rate Policy in Southeast Asia*, Lexington Books.

Habakkuk, H. J. (1971), 'The Entrepreneur and Economic Development', in I. Livingstone, ed., *Economic Policy For Development: Readings*, Penguin.

Hakam, A. N. (1966), 'The Motivation To Investment and the Locational Pattern of Foreign Private Industrial Investments in Nigeria', *Nigerian Journal of Economics and Social Studies*, Vol. VIII(1), March, pp. 49–65.

Helleiner, G. K. (1973), 'Manufactured Exports From Less Developed Countries and Multinational Firms', *The Economic Journal*, March, pp. 21–47.

Hirschman, A. O. (1969), 'How to Divest in Latin America and Why', in B. Ward, *et al.*, eds., *The Widening Gap, Development in the 1970s*, Columbia University Press, 1971.

Hirschman, C. (1971), 'Ownership and Control in the Manufacturing Sector of West Malaysia', *United Malayan Banking Corporation Economic Review*, Vol. VII(1), pp. 21–30.

Holtermann, S. E. (1973), 'Market Structure and Economic Performance in U.K. Manufacturing Industries', *Journal of Industrial Economics*, Vol. 22(2), December, pp. 119–39.

Hymer, S. (1960), 'The International Operations of National Firms, A Study of Direct Investment', quoted in C. P. Kindleberger, ed., *The International Corporation*, p. 18.

——— (1972), 'The Multinational Corporation and Uneven Development', in Kapoor and Grub, *The Multinational Enterprise In Transition*, pp. 438–44.

Industrial Policy Group (1970), *The Case For Overseas Investment*, I.P.G. Research Publication Service.

Johns, B. L. (1967), 'Private Overseas Investment in Australia: Profitability and Motivation', *Economic Record*, June.

Johnson, H. G. (1970), 'The Efficiency and Welfare Implications of the International Corporation', in C. P. Kindleberger, ed., *The International Corporation*, p. 35, et seq.

——— (1973), 'Economic Benefits of the Multinational Enterprise', in Hahlo, *et al.*, eds., *Multinationalism and The Multinational Enterprise*, Chapter 7.

Kaldor, N. (1959), 'Economic Growth and the Problem of Inflation', *Economica*, Parts I and II, August and November.

Kanapathy, V. (1970), 'Foreign Investment in Malaysia, Experience and Prospects', *United Malayan Banking Corporation Economic Review*, Vol. 6(2), pp. 1–22.

Klopstock, F. H. (1970), 'Money Creation in the Euro-Dollar Market, a Note on Prof. M. Friedman's Views', Reserve Bank of New York, *Monthly Review*, Vol. 52(1), January.

Knopper, A. T. (1970), 'A Multinational Corporation in the Third World', *Columbia Journal of Business*, July/August.

Kraar, L. (1974), 'Singapore, The Country Runs like a Corporation', *Fortune*, Vol. XC(1), July, p. 85, et seq.

Lall, S. (1973), 'Transfer Pricing by Multinational Manufacturing Firms', *Bulletin of the Oxford University Institute of Economics and Statistics*, Oxford, Vol. 35(3), August.

Lee, S. A. (1974), 'Fiscal Policy and Political Transitions: The Case of Malaya 1948–60', *Journal of Southeast Asian Studies*, Vol. 5(1), March.

Lee, S. Y. (1971), 'The Asia Dollar Market in Singapore', *The Malayan Economic Review*, Vol. XVI(1), April, pp. 46–56.

Little, I. M. D., and Mirrlees, J. A. (1972), 'A Reply to Some Criticisms of the OECD Manual', *Oxford University Bulletin of the Institute of Economics and Statistics*, Vol. 34(1).

Loftus, P. J. (1969), 'Labour's Share in Manufacturing', *Lloyds Bank Review*, No. 92, April.

Mabry, B. D., and Siders, D. L. (1967), 'An Empirical Test of the Sales Maximisation Hypothesis', *Southern Economic Journal*, January.

Machlup, R. (1967), 'Theories of the Firm: Marginalist, Behavioral, Managerial', *American Economic Review*, Vol. LVII, March, pp. 1–31.

______(1970), 'Euro-Dollar Creation: A Mystery Story', *Banca Nazionale Del Lavoro Quarterly Review*, No. 94, September.

Marcrae, N. (1972), 'The Future of International Business: A Survey', *The Economist*, 22 January (Supplement).

Mathai, M. K. (1969), 'Incentives for Investment in Malaysia', *Bulletin for International Fiscal Documentation*, Vol. 23(11), November, pp. 503–15.

May, R. S. (1965), 'Direct Overseas Investment in Nigeria 1953–63. Some Aspects of Its Constitution and Contribution to Nigerian Economic Development', *Scottish Journal of Political Economy*, Vol. 12, pp. 243–66.

______(1967), 'Earnings of U.K. and U.S. Direct Investments in the Less Developed Countries, 1959–64', *Scottish Journal of Political Economy*, Vol. 14, November, pp. 195–225.

______(1968), 'Direct Investment in Less Developed Countries: British Investments 1958–65', *Journal of Development Studies*, April, pp. 386–423.

McGee, T. G., and McTaggart, W. D. (1967), 'Petaling Jaya: A Socio-Economic Survey', *Pacific Viewpoint*, Wellington, University of Victoria.

McGuire, J. W., Chin, J. S. Y., and Elbing, A. O. (1962), 'Executive Incomes, Sales and Profits', *American Economic Review*, September.

Merican, M. A. (1972), 'Exchange Rate Experience and Policy in Malaysia Since World War II', in Grubel and Morgan, eds., *Exchange Rate Policy in Southeast Asia*, Lexington Books.

Moffatt, G. G. (1967), 'The Foreign Ownership and Balance of Payments Effects of Direct Investment from Abroad', *Australian Economic Papers*, June, pp. 1–24.

Morley, S. A., and Smith, G. W. (1972), 'Import Substitution and Foreign Investment', *Oxford Economic Papers*, March 1971, pp. 120–35.

Myint, H. (1967), 'Inward and Outward-Looking Countries of Southeast Asia', *The Malayan Economic Review*, Vol. 12(1), pp. 1–13.

——(1970), 'Dualism and the Internal Integration of the Underdeveloped Economics', *Banca Nazionale Del Lavoro Quarterly Review*, No. 93, June, pp. 128–56.

Paauw, D. S. (1956), 'Financing Economic Development in Indonesia', *Economic Development and Cultural Change*, January.

Packard, P. C. (1970), 'Paucity of Demand for Industrial Commodities as an Obstacle to Industrialization', *Development and Change*, Vol. 1(3), pp. 8–18.

Paish, Sir George (1909), 'Great Britain's Capital Investment in Other Lands', *Journal of the Royal Statistical Society*, Vol. 72.

Pelmutter, H. V. (1969), 'The Tortuous Evolution of the Multinational Corporation', *Columbia Journal of World Business*, January/February.

——(1969), 'The Emerging East-West Ventures: The Transideological Enterprise', *Columbia Journal of World Business*, September/October, pp. 39–50.

Penrose, E. T. (1956), 'Foreign Investment and The Growth of the Firm', *Economic Journal*, Vol. 66, pp. 220–35.

——(1962), 'Some Problems of Policy Toward Direct Private Foreign Investment in Developing Countries', *Middle Eastern Economic Review*, *Economic Bulletin* (A.U.B.), pp. 121–39.

——(1971), 'The State and Multinational Enterprises in Less Developed Countries', in J. H. Dunning, ed., *The Multinational Enterprise*, George Allen and Unwin, Chapter 8.

Piper, J. R., Jr. (1971), 'How U.S. Firms Evaluate Foreign Investment Opportunities', *Business Topics*, Vol. 19(3), Summer, pp. 11–21.

Power, J. H. (1971), 'The Structure of Protection in West Malaysia', in B. Balassa, *et al.*, eds., *The Structure of Protection in*

Developing Countries, Baltimore, Johns Hopkins Press, 1971.

Rapp, W. V. (1967), 'A Theory of Changing Pattern Under Economic Growth: Tested for Japan', *Yale Economic Essays*, Fall.

Ray, G. R. (1972), 'On Defining "Diffusion" of New Technology', *Business Economics*, Vol. 4, Pt. II, pp. 82–8.

Robinson, R. D. (1972), 'The Future of International Management', *International Labour Review*, Vol. 98(1), July 1968, pp. 55–72.

Scitovsky, T. (1954), 'Two Concepts of External Economics', *Journal of Political Economy*, LXII, pp. 143–51.

Shell International Petroleum Co. (1972), 'Multinational Enterprise' (mimeo.), Shell Centre, 1972.

Silcock, T. H. (1961), 'The Economy of Malaya: The Relevance of the Competitive Laissez-Faire Model', in C. B. Hoover, ed., *The Economic Systems of The Commonwealth*, Duke University Press, Durham, U.S.A.

Simmonds, K., and Connell, R. (1974), 'Breaking The Boardroom Barriers: The Importance of Being British', *Journal of Management Studies*, Vol. II(2), May.

Soemitro, R. (1968), 'Investment of Foreign Capital in Indonesia', *Bulletin of International Fiscal Documentation*, Vol. 22(11), pp. 496–510.

Solomons, D. (1961), 'Economic and Accounting Concepts of Income', *Accounting Review*, Vol. 36(3), July.

Stobaugh, R. B., Jr. (1969), 'Where In the World Should We Put That Plant?', *Harvard Business Review*, January/February, p. 129, et seq.

——— (1969), 'How to Analyse Foreign Investment Climate', *Harvard Business Review*, September/October, p. 100, et seq.

Streeten, P. P., and Lall, S. (1971), 'Costs and Benefits of Multinational Enterprises in Less Developed Countries', in Dunning, ed., *The Multinational Enterprise*, George Allen and Unwin.

——— (1974), 'Evaluation of Methods and Main Findings of UNCTAD Study of Private Overseas Investment in Selected Less Developed Countries' (mimeo.), Queen Elizabeth House.

Sunkel, O. (1969), 'National Development Policy and External Dependence in Latin America', *Journal of Development Studies*, Vol. 6(1), October.

Thoburn, J. T. (1973), 'Export and Economic Growth in West Malaysia', *Oxford Economics Papers*, Vol. 25(1), March, pp. 88–111.

——— (1973), 'Exports and the Malaysian Engineering Industry: A Case Study of Backward Linkage', *Oxford University Bulle-*

tin of the Institute of Economics and Statistics, May, pp. 99–118.

Todaro, M. P. (1970), 'Some Thoughts on the Transfer of Technology from Developed to less Developed Nations', *East African Economic Review*, Vol. 2(1), June, pp. 53–65.

Vernon, R. (1966), 'International Investment and International Trade in The Product Cycle', *Quarterly Journal of Economics*, Vol. 89, pp. 190–207.

Vogel, J. O. (1972), 'The Real Culprit in International Monetary Crisis: The Impact of the Multinational Corporation', *Business Horizons*, Vol. 15(2).

Wallenberg, M. (1973), 'The Impact of Multinational Corporations on Development and International Relations', *Skandinaviska Enskilda Banken, Quarterly Review*, Vol. 4, pp. 126–35.

Wheelwright, E. L. (1963), 'Overseas Investment in Australia', in A. Hunter, ed., *The Economics of Australian Industry*, Melbourne, Melbourne University Press.

Williams, S. (1969), 'Negotiating Investment in Emerging Countries', *Harvard Business Review*, September/October, pp. 100–8.

Williamson, J. (1966), 'Profit, Growth and Sales Maximisation', *Economica*, February, pp. 1–16.

Zinkin, M. (1968), 'Multinational Companies', *Moorgate and Wall Street*, Autumn, pp. 6–19.

4. UNPUBLISHED MATERIAL

Boustead & Co. (n.d.), 'East India Merchants Established 1828' (Private).

Duri, N. (1972), 'Foreign Capital in the Economic Development of Ethiopia', Ph.D. thesis, University of Reading.

Fernando, L. E. N. (1971), 'Some Aspects of Private Foreign Enterprise in Ceylon', Ph.D. thesis, University of Hull.

Hirschman, C. (1972), 'Ethnic Stratification in West Malaysia', Ph.D. thesis, University of Wisconsin.

Isarangkun, Chiru (1970), 'Manufacturing Industries in Thailand', Ph.D. thesis, Australian National University, Canberra.

Khera, H. S. (1973), 'Some Aspects of the Economics of the Oil Palm Industry in Malaysia', Ph.D. thesis, The University of Hull.

Razaleigh Hamzah, Tengku (1972), 'Joint Ventures in Malaysia', Paper presented at the Conference on Business Opportunities in South-east Asia, organized by *The Financial Times* in association with BOAC.

Ridzuan bin Akil (1972), 'Growth, Structural Change and Employment Creation in Malayan Manufacturing Industries Since Independence', Ph.D. thesis, University of Hull.

Saham, J. B. A. (1966), 'Some Aspects of Economic Development and Planning in Malaya, 1955–65', M.A. thesis, University of Canterbury, N.Z.

Silcock, J. P. (1972), 'Doing Business in South-east Asia: The View of a Merchant Banker', Paper presented at the Conference on Business Opportunities in South-east Asia.

Willey, S. (1972), 'Doing Business in Malaysia, The View of a British Industrialist', Paper presented at the Conference on Business Opportunities in South-east Asia.

Wilson, D. (1972), 'South-east Asia: A Political and Economic Approach', Paper presented at the Conference on Business Opportunities in South-east Asia.

Wilson, J. (1972), 'Doing Business in Malaysia, Singapore and Indonesia', Paper presented at the Conference on Business Opportunities in South-east Asia.

Wong, Pakshong M. (1972), 'Singapore as A Financial Centre', Paper presented at the Conference on Business Opportunities in South-east Asia.

5. MISCELLANEOUS SOURCES

The Economist, various issues.

Asia Research Bulletin (monthly publication), Singapore, various issues, 1972–3.

Far Eastern Economic Review Yearbook, various issues.

Far Eastern Economic Review (weekly magazine), Hong Kong, 7.6.1962; 29.11.1967; 25.3.1972; 1.4.1972; 9.7.1973.

Fortune, New York, May 1973; September 1973; July–August 1966; May 1974.

Fraser's Facts and Figures, Singapore, Fraser & Co. Stock Brokers, 1966.

Malaysian Business (monthly), various issues.

The Straits Times Directory, annual publication of the *Straits Times* newspaper, Kuala Lumpur.

The Straits Times (daily newspaper), 22.3.1972; 21.6.1972; 11.8.1972; 23.11.1972; 27.11.1972; 12.1.1973; 9.8.1973; 28.2.1974; and 22.3.1974.

The New Straits Times (daily newspaper), 18.9.1974.

The Times 1000 Leading Companies in Britain, 1970–71.

The Times, 22.9.1973; 2.11.1973.

The Financial Times, 2.11.1973.

Sunday Telegraph, 20.6.1974.

Index